For my family—my husband John, daughters
Martha, Sarah, and Olivia; my friend and mentor,
Raymond Simon, a pioneer in public relations
case studies; and special thanks to my case studies
students who pretested many of these cases.

Introduction

Depending on your nature or the circumstance, just about everything can be seen as a problem or an opportunity. In the public relations world, practitioners gain value within organizations based on their ability to turn problems or opportunities into positive outcomes.

Most problems can be avoided with good planning and good management. Sometimes, however, no amount of preparation or good decisions can prevent things from going wrong. After all, you can't control everything or everybody. And unlike the ordered classroom world where tactics and campaigns can be examined one element at a time, the real world is much more messy and chaotic. Practitioners must balance client needs with the resources of time, expertise, and money. Tough decisions have to be made, sometimes in a hurry, and with mixed results.

Case studies try to present the big picture as well as the inside perspective of what is happening within an organization. While it was tempting to feature successful, prize-winning campaigns recognized by the public relations industry, this book took a different approach. It sought cases that didn't always win an award with outcomes that weren't always successful. All the cases have a problem or opportunity. They are all designed to challenge you to think analytically, strategically, and practically.

You may even disagree with the strategies and tactics used. The idea was not to deconstruct only exemplary cases but to challenge you to assess the situations based on what you know about communication theory, ethics, the public relations process (research, planning, communication tactics, and evaluation), and management practices. Many cases end with an open scenario challenge that asks you to solve the problem or take advantage of an opportunity. You'll discover a lot of different opinions from your peers and there will be plenty of topics for great discussions!

All the cases in this textbook actually happened, and some were widely reported in the news media. Whenever possible, practitioners involved were interviewed to provide the fullest picture. Some cases, particularly the internship and early career cases, were based on real situations, but names and other information were changed to protect the participants' and organizations' identities; a few are composites based on the experiences of several practitioners and students.

The idea behind this book is that we learn best from experience. I hope you will share your experiences with your classmates and listen to others. Hopefully, this book is the next best thing to being there. I think you will agree that public relations is fun and challenging—and definitely never dull.

I am interested in your comments or suggestions. Please e-mail me at pswann@ utica.edu and let me know what you think.

Patricia Swann
Utica College
pswann@utica.edu

Table of Contents

Chapter 14
Internships and Early Career   323

Chapter One

The Purpose of Public Relations

HAVE AN ORGANIZATIONAL PURPOSE

What is "public relations"? If you asked a hundred people, you would probably get a hundred different replies—and several confused looks!

Whether you're a student getting ready to enter the public relations field or a practitioner already on the job, the answer to this question will provide focus, direction, and purpose for your career. A clear understanding of what public relations is and how it contributes to organizational effectiveness is necessary to making a difference in your organization.

Often, practitioners fall into the trap of being defined by the most visible and technical aspects of their job. "I write news releases." "I write and edit the company newsletter and other publications." "I get the media to cover our events." "I handle our company's communication." These are examples of practitioner products or "outputs."

What these responses do not convey is the strategy: *why* practitioners do all these communication-related activities. For example, a news release published or broadcast in the mass media about an organization's open house can help meet some obvious needs, such as increasing awareness of the event and the organization, and possibly getting people to attend the event. But why does the organization want people to attend an open house in the first place? How does the event, and publicizing it, tie in with the mission and goals of the organization? Who does the organization want to attract to the event? Specific groups? Men, women, kids, senior citizens, parents, singles, working professionals, job seekers—what the news release says, and how and when it says it, could make a big difference in the published/broadcast appeal to members of different groups. The result could be a well-attended open house or a public relations problem.

Defining What We Do

A good definition of public relations helps define the practitioner's organizational role. One early definition of public relations was created at the World Assembly of Public Relations in Mexico City in 1978:

> Public relations practice is the art and social science of analyzing trends, predicting their consequences, counseling organizational leaders, and implementing planned programs of action which serve both the organization's and the public's interest.

Scott M. Cutlip, Allen H. Center, and Glen M. Broom, authors of *Effective Public Relations,* wrote one of the best-known definitions:

> Public relations is the management function that establishes and maintains mutually beneficial relationships between an organization and the publics on whom its success and failure depends.

Interestingly, these definitions do not contain the word *communication.* What they emphasize instead is building relationships with specific groups of people because organizations and entities cannot exist on their own. They are not really able to do whatever they want because organizations are created to meet a need—almost always to provide goods and/or services for consumption. They rely on outside people or other organizations to buy those products and services or to support in some way their mission.

Inherent in the concept of building relationships is trust. Solid relationships require trust, which is often achieved over time by our words and deeds. Public relations practitioners are experts in managing the communication programs for an organization that promote mutual understanding and trust. Practitioners also counsel management to consider the consequences of organizational actions on its publics.

The Value of Public Relations

Public relations should have a purpose within the organization. And this purpose should provide value for an organization. What would happen if the public relations function was eliminated from your organization? Would anyone notice?

When public relations programs are not linked to the mission of an organization, public relations practitioners are often caught up in the production of meaningless work. An effective public relations office knows its organization's mission and supports it. For example, businesses that produce a product in a competitive environment may focus on product quality as a way to distinguish themselves from competitors. Public relations programs can help develop employee relations programs that promote a healthy and friendly working environment resulting in high morale, pride in workmanship, and—ultimately—a better product.

While many public relations practitioners are doing good work, sometimes their efforts are ignored because they fail to demonstrate the value of public relations in ways that management can appreciate.

One public relations legend, Patrick Jackson, once summed up the contributions of public relations for organizations. These nine contributions were featured in *Public Relations Strategies and Tactics.*[1]

1. *Awareness and information.* Public relations provides publicity and promotion to raise awareness and aid sales and fundraising efforts.
2. *Organizational motivation.* Public relations builds internal relationships to foster positive morale, teamwork, productivity, and corporate culture.
3. *Issue anticipation.* Public relations through environmental monitoring, research, and connections with its publics can provide an early warning system of potential problems.
4. *Opportunity identification.* Public relations through environmental monitoring, research, and connections with its publics can identify new markets, products, methods, allies, and positive issues.
5. *Crisis management.* Public relations can manage an appropriate response to crisis situations that will minimize the harm to an organization's reputation and allow it to continue functioning.
6. *Overcoming executive isolation.* Public relations through research and counseling keeps management in touch with what is happening so that appropriate decisions are made.
7. *Change agentry.* Public relations can assist with organizational changes through communication and other activities to ease resistance to change and promote a smooth transition for those affected by the changes.
8. *Social responsibility.* Public relations can take the lead in helping organizations act responsibly in such areas as the environment, workplace issues, and philanthropy. These actions can lead to greater public trust and positive feelings for the organization, which can increase mutual

understanding and translate into increased sales and use of services.

9. *Influencing public policy.* Public relations can use its connections to government officials and other influential individuals or groups to gain acceptance for its activities, products, or services and also remove political barriers.

Management Support

If a CEO understands the value of public relations to the company, all is well. If, on the other hand, a public relations department is known in the company for producing "fluff" and "bells and whistles," watch out! In bad times, companies find they can do without the bells, whistles, and fluff because they have no real value. Strategic public relations can build this internal understanding by demonstrating its value to an organization, especially the positive outcomes generated by the building of relationships with the organization's key stakeholders.

The commitment to establishing lasting and mutually beneficial relationships with key publics has to come from the organization's leadership ranks, where organizational policies and management strategies are determined. Public relations, in order to be effective, should have a seat at the management table to guide the organization's public relations and communication strategy. Organizations that "talk the talk" but aren't committed to "walk the talk" have often strayed from their missions. They may have made a series of decisions based on short-term gain, without considering their publics—and the effects on long-term relationships. Public relations plays an important organizational role in helping management understand the consequences of its actions and its responsibility to do the right thing.

Management will support things that make a positive and measurable difference for an organization, especially communication and relationship building activities that build stakeholders' awareness and understanding of organizational initiatives. But simply "getting the word out" has been complicated by the explosive growth of communication outlets and the fragmentation of audiences. Managing the communication function today involves many strategic decisions such as selecting the most appropriate and effective delivery vehicles, creating and producing effective messages for those delivery vehicles, and evaluating the effectiveness of the communication.

The complexity of communication strategy today is underscored in democratic societies that encourage open and liberal debate of virtually any topic. The First Amendment protects the right of organizations and individuals to freely express themselves in most situations. Citizens, especially, are free to criticize organizations, their products or services, and their leaders. Public relations helps organizations participate strategically in the "marketplace of ideas," so that viewpoints important to the organization are present in public debates that could affect the organization—including debates that aid the promotion of products and services.

Some of these public debates take place at the legislative level. Newly proposed legislation that could have positive or negative consequences for an organization may involve public relations practitioners who influence the debate and the legislative outcome by providing information; this strategy is often accomplished through government affairs and lobbying activities.

While organizations cannot participate in every conversation and debate taking place, public relations can identify and prioritize the communication needs most important to an organization and then create an effective communication plan. Management understands and wants communication with a defined purpose that protects and enhances the organization.

Business Sense

One factor preventing some practitioners from entering the ranks of management is a lack of understanding of basic business principles, management strategies, and number-crunching. Most executives have business management backgrounds and are driven by business goals and strategies that help organizations achieve their missions.

Public relations practitioners pride themselves on their communication skills, but some are unprepared or unable to read a balance sheet or explain a campaign's return on investment. Executives are not enthusiastic about departments that spend large sums of money; they want to see how such spending changes customer attitudes, boosts the consumption of the company's products or services, and increases profits. Public relations should not merely make a difference to an organization's bottom line; it should communicate that difference to top executives.

To be a part of management, a public relations practitioner should understand the language of business, how the organization operates, how it makes money, and how its strategic plan meets current and future challenges.

This textbook will introduce basic business terms, concepts, and management skills to begin building a business management foundation. Students and working practitioners can also read the business sections of their daily newspaper, watch cable and broadcast TV business shows, or take introductory college business courses to learn more about the business world.

Case study, in fact, has its roots in business education. It started at the Harvard Business School (HBS) when Arch Wilkinson Shaw began teaching a course using real examples of business problems. In 1921, HBS's first case study, "The General Shoe Company," was created to prepare business majors for the realities of the business world.[2]

The 1999 report of the commission on public relations education "Public Relations Education for the 21st Century: A Port of Entry" recommended a minor or double major in either business or the behavioral sciences.

THE PUBLIC RELATIONS PROCESS

Public relations helps build strategic relationships with stakeholders to solve problems and take advantage of opportunities, whether the client is an individual, a small organization, or a large entity. How an organization goes about solving its public relations problem or turning an opportunity into a windfall is determined by its public relations strategy—its overall game plan.

Public relations success rarely results from such one-shot activities as issuing a news release or brochure. Many practitioners, especially those just entering the field, find themselves tackling many writing tasks, planning special events, and working with the news media. Important as they are, these tasks are just part of what effective public relations practitioners do; they are, in effect, all examples of steps in a process. Most introductory public relations textbooks mention such public relations process models as research, action planning, communication, and evaluation (RACE), or research, objectives, programming, and evaluation (ROPE). The models RACE and ROPE are helpful because both easy-to-remember acronyms contain the four major aspects of the public relations process.

An organization begins the process by first recognizing that it has an opportunity or a problem important enough to the mission (or, in drastic cases, the survival) of the organization for some kind of action. This opportunity or problem starts the public relations process. Public relations practitioners at the management level follow these basic steps:

1. Research the issue that prompts the organization's concern (i.e., the opportunity or problem).
2. Develop goals and objectives that address the opportunity or problem.
3. Develop a public relations strategy that addresses goals and objectives.
4. Select and implement the communication tactics that would best achieve the strategy's goals and objectives.
5. Evaluate the effectiveness of the public relations program in reaching its goals and objectives.

Practitioners must complete the public relations process and evaluate the results of their efforts so that management can clearly see a return on its investment in money, staffing, and time. That requires research and evidence.

For example, a practitioner issues 300 news releases in a year and tracks the number of impressions (printed appearances or hits) generated in the media. The chief executive is unimpressed; he or she wants to know how the news releases helped increase demand for the company's products and services. Were the stories counted in the media positive about the organization, and did customer or other key publics' attitudes positively change after the public relations effort? If the practitioner can demonstrate those results, the CEO will see the value of public relations.

Although the words *management level* are used to describe the practitioner who carries out the public relations process, any practitioner with knowledge of this four-step process can use it—whether the practitioner's title carries the manager designation or not.

Student interns and practitioners who are just beginning their careers may be assigned to "technical" communication roles within a public relations department or firm. These entry-level positions are mostly concerned with message creation—the third step of the public relations process. While communication technician positions are excellent gateways into the professional world of public relations and important to the overall effectiveness of public relations work, practitioners assigned to such positions must keep in mind their work is just one step of the process. Writing news releases, features, and speeches, producing publications, creating audiovisuals, taking photographs, and coordinating press conferences or arranging media coverage are important activities; but if they are not connected with research, planning, and evaluation, they can easily miss their objectives.

To be effective, public relations needs all four steps; usually, only upper-level management can make sure all four steps happen. Author David M. Dozier[3] said that practitioners at the management level have strategic and operational management knowledge that includes developing goals, objectives, and strategies to solve problems or take advantage of opportunities, managing communication programs, and managing people and budgets.[4] He also said managers have the ability to carry out research, including environmental scanning, counsel management (negotiation knowledge) on its options when dealing with its publics, and understand the use of persuasion to achieve organizational goals.

Stakeholders = Publics

Each organization has many groups of people who take an interest in what the organization is up to. They include customers, investors, volunteers, employees, neighbors, and people who, for any number of reasons, may not like the company's product, service, policies, or some specific activity. Organizations have no control over who their publics are; publics choose the organization.

Companies tend to think of these groups of people, each with a stake in something the company does, as *stakeholders*. In public relations, these groups of stakeholders are also called *publics*. The members of each public have some common interest in what an organization says or does.

According to the definition you read earlier, public relations is "identifying, establishing, and maintaining mutually beneficial relationships" with these publics. An easy way to remember this concept is to think of "public relationships." Or you can reverse the term public relations and say "relationships with publics." This is what it's all about: building relationships and understanding with specific groups of people.

Building Strategic Relationships

Relationships don't simply happen. In our daily lives we seek relationships with people because they fulfill some personal need: They are fun to be around, they share our interests in music or sports, or maybe they come from a similar background.

Organizations also seek relationships with certain groups of people because they are important to achieving the organization's mission, enhancing its reputation, or protecting its long-term survival. But not all publics are supportive of the organization. Ronald D. Smith said in *Strategic Planning for Public Relations,* "A public is like your family. You don't pick them; they just are. . . . Publics may be helpful or annoying, friendly or not, but an organization must deal with them regardless."[5]

According to situational theory, organizations create publics when their actions positively or negatively impact others. Researchers James Grunig and Todd Hunt[6] segmented publics as *nonpublics,* those who are not affected by the organization's actions and do not interact with the organization; *latent publics,* those who are affected by the organization's actions but are not yet aware of it; *aware publics,* those who are aware that the organization is affecting them but have not taken any action; and *active publics,* those who do something about the organization's impact on them. Active publics can emerge at any time; often their appearance is anticipated but sometimes it is not. Public relations can facilitate the process of creating positive relationships.

Strategic relationships are often built over time through actions and words. Consider that good relationships, such as those between roommates in college or spouses in marriage, do not just happen. Strong relationships are developed as each participant observes and learns about others through experience—what they do, as well as what they say. Dialogue, in which both parties exchange information, is an effective means for two parties to work out problems. Trust, the ability to rely on the other party, builds as evidence accumulates that the person or organization is sincere, that it can deliver on its promises, and that it can and does follow through.

Good relationships should offer something of value to each participant. When a person or organization creates a relationship solely for its own gains; the relationship won't last long. Not many people are interested in being taken advantage of or being used without receiving something in return, even if it is just a sincere thank-you. Mutually beneficial relationships have a great advantage over the one-way kind too. They are much stronger over time, and can stand up to occasional mishaps and larger difficulties—both of which are bound to happen in any long-term relationship.

An Effective Early Warning System

Public relations can help organizations anticipate problems or see opportunities by identifying issues and trends. This function is called *environmental scanning* and, in fact, is an early warning system for organizations. Practitioners who scan the environment pay attention to what's happening to similar organizations or industries and apply the knowledge and lessons occurring to their own particular environment.

While organizations may have good environmental monitoring systems in place to gauge trends and anticipate issues, problems will still emerge. Human error and natural disasters are a part of life and are, therefore, inevitable. Since organizations cannot anticipate every problem, some day a crisis will come. It is then—in a time of crisis—when public relations can be especially valuable. Answering the "what if" with a strategic plan involves *issues management.*

The goal of the public relations practitioner should be to anticipate, identify, and plan for problems, but when a crisis strikes, public relations should be ready to respond with appropriate strategies. One goal of this book is to help you develop strategic thinking skills so you can anticipate and solve problems as they emerge.

In a 24/7 news environment, a rapid and expert response with the news media is required to prevent nearly instant and significant damage to an organization's carefully constructed reputation. Case studies, in particular, have provided new insights for practitioners managing crisis situations. Public relations practitioners play an important role in not only managing chaotic communication in a crisis environment but—more importantly—in counseling senior management to do the right thing, be truthful, accept responsibility if the organization made a mistake, and take immediate action to repair any damage.

Counseling Senior Management

If an organization is out of sync with public expectations and norms, or its survivability is threatened, public relations can counsel management on communication strategies or policy changes, which might help remedy or lessen the problem. This works best when the counsel is given directly to the chief executive officer. Sometimes senior management loses touch with how the rest of the world operates due to executive isolation or too much focus on short-term goals. To be effective in an advisory role, public relations practitioners need to maintain their management independence, not simply report up the chain of command. Direct access to senior management and involvement in management decision making are ultimately where practitioners can be most effective.

Leaders who think only they can see the problem clearly and only they have the solution to their problems tend to surround themselves with "yes people," subordinates who do not dare question the wisdom of their boss. Practitioners are seldom effective in such situations and are unlikely to be part of the organization's decision making. Public relations practitioners must choose their battles wisely. When problems are serious, involving long-term negative consequences or legal and public safety issues, public relations practitioners must take a stand for what is right—despite potential personal consequences.

In severe situations, such as the Enron business scandal, any employee may become the moral compass of an organization. These whistle-blowers have insider knowledge that may be unknown to others in the organization, including the public relations practitioner. Once a whistle-blower goes public with accusations of illegal activity or safety violations, the organization will face increasing pressure to mend its ways. Unfortunately, whistle-blowing can also mean damage to the organization's reputation: hardly the most strategic way to solve problems and move forward.

Do the Right Thing

What prevents people from doing the right thing? Most of us know people who have done bad things—often because they do not think they will be caught or the right thing may not be that obvious. Sometimes the dynamics of a situation—peer pressure, fear, rapidly unfolding events—makes people act in a way that they would not normally do if they had more time to think carefully and consider the consequences.

As managers of communication programs for organizations, most public relations problems stem from problems with what an organization communicates or doesn't communicate, and whether those words match the organization's deeds. Just about every veteran public relations person will say that the best practice is simply to always tell the truth. But this is not as easy as it sounds. During a crisis, for example, a practitioner may be prevented from communicating certain information due to legal issues involved. Sometimes practitioners are not fully informed of the details of a situation. Inexperience and not thinking through the consequences of one's actions often lead to mistakes.

Codes of conduct can be helpful, and the college classroom is one of the best times to study these guidelines; there is no pressure from the work world to distract you. You do not want to be digging through your desk files looking for a copy of your code of conduct during a crisis! Just as a student learns the skills of research, writing, and planning in public relations, the study of ethics is a valuable tool for achieving personal excellence in effective public relations.

Ethical behavior comes from the shared values held by a group or community. These core values are what individuals in the group or community decide are important. One core value in the Public Relations Society of America's code of conduct is honesty. This value relates to communicating accurate and truthful information. Core values help establish the ground rules for what is considered right and wrong within that group.

The Public Relations Society of America Member Code of Ethics

This book will use the Public Relations Society of America's Member Code of Ethics (see page 41) to examine the ethical dimensions of the cases. Many organizations also have their own codes of conduct that not only reveal their rules for conduct but also something about their culture, the way they do things, and what they value.

The Public Relations Society of America (PRSA) code covers six core values: advocacy, honesty, expertise, independence, loyalty, and fairness. *Advocacy* recognizes that public relations practitioners play an essential role in bringing another voice to the marketplace of ideas within a democratic society. *Honesty* (truthfulness) is necessary to maintain credibility and trust with publics. Objective counsel to others (*independence*) keeps organizations in touch with their environment.

Practitioners with *expertise* can build mutual understanding between organizations and their publics. Practitioners are not only *loyal* to their organizations or clients; they are also obligated to protect the public interest. *Fairness* means that organizations do not take unfair advantage of people and groups that they deal with, even when the organizations have more resources and power. People's opinions and their right to express them are also respected.

Public relations plays an important role in organizations and, by extension, in our society. Future practitioners who understand their ethical role will contribute positively to their employer and society by increasing understanding between organizations and their publics.

The PRSA Code of Ethics and its core provisions are provided in Chapter 4.

HOW PUBLIC RELATIONS RELATES TO OTHER DISCIPLINES

Public relations, as a communication and business discipline, shares many common characteristics with advertising, marketing, marketing communication, and journalism. Practitioners should be aware of these commonalities and how public relations practice may differ in its approach.

Advertising

Advertising is space or time purchased within the mass media for the purpose of persuading people to do something, such as buy a product, attend an event, or support a cause. Advertising is considered a controlled medium because the organization pays to control the appearance, content, and timing of the advertisement's placement in a mass medium, such as newspapers, radio, television, or the Internet. A newspaper, for example, cannot change the wording of a print ad or its size. It must be printed exactly as it is provided by the organization.

Marketing professionals mostly use advertising, but sometimes public relations practitioners will use ads to promote a public relations activity or support an image campaign to enhance an organization's reputation. This is true especially in the nonprofit world, where marketing is frequently incorporated into the public relations role. A college may create newspaper ads to announce new graduate programs or announce upcoming admission days. In corporate or agency settings, the role of advertising is often relegated to marketing.

When the message contains sensitive wording and any slight change could affect its intended meaning, especially during a crisis or other momentous situation, paid advertising is often used. For example, when a company must recall a product, it will want a carefully crafted message for its publics that explains what the organization has done and is doing to protect its product's users. When oil companies are trying to explain why corporate profits are at all-time highs, they will want to develop carefully worded messages to explain the situation. Often these advertisements or commercials are created when an organization thinks its messages are not getting through or are inaccurately portrayed in the news media.

Marketing

Marketing focuses on increasing customers and sales for an organization's product or service. Marketing is also concerned with ensuring the product or service is designed to meet customer needs, is attractively packaged, is distributed efficiently, and satisfies customers. Marketing professionals conduct research to find out what type of products consumers want and at what cost. The public relations profession has learned a great deal from marketing's strong reliance on research and planning to make decisions tied to the bottom line—making money by selling products or services. Public relations has steadily incorporated research and planning with goals, objectives, and strategies as part of its work.

Marketing's use of communication to raise awareness and create effective messages is another area that overlaps with public relations. Marketing's messages can be informative and persuasive—to build excitement and desire for a product or service. Advertising created for a public relations campaign may also have specific tasks, such as introducing new college degree programs or inviting people to an open house.

Marketing also values understanding its key publics. Market research helps segment its publics so that messages are created in the form of advertisements or commercials and delivered with precision to the right people through the right communication channels such as newspapers, radio, television, Internet, special events, and clothing. Besides advertising communication, marketing also uses celebrity endorsers and sponsorships, just as public relations does to communicate with its publics.

However, public relations messages often try to reach several key publics, beyond customers or potential customers. Employees, for example, are a key public that public relations traditionally seeks to build a strong relationship with, while marketing is more outwardly focused. Non-customers, such as activists and legislators proposing regulations, can potentially have great impact on an organization, and therefore demand the attention of public relations.

Public relations seeks to enhance the organization's reputation—not just its bottom line. It is typically a long process to build the necessary positive relationships that result in good reputations. Sometimes it requires organizations to change and adapt to new ways.

Integrated Marketing Communication

The fact that marketing and public relations use many of the same communication tactics has led many organizations to blend the two functions into what is commonly called *integrated marketing communication (IMC)*. This approach coordinates the communication activities of the marketing and public relations departments that, in the past, often operated independently. For some organizations, a lack of coordination between these departments has sometimes led to embarrassing mixed messages to key publics.

The concept of coordinating all organizational communication is a good idea. However, some researchers and educators are uncertain if complete merging of marketing and public relations is always in the best long-term interests of an organization. The driving need to produce profit and the potential for executive isolation can create an environment in which clear, unbiased thinking about long-term consequences of organizational actions is not always present. As a result, the hard sell might come first, and relationship-building activities second—or not at all.

Public relations should maintain its independence within the organization, allowing practitioners to counsel management about the long-term consequences of proposed actions—before decisions are made. For example, although a product campaign might be wildly successful in the short term, a questionable ad campaign or product can produce serious long-term consequences for an organization if all key publics are not considered.

Journalism

Journalists, such as Ivy Lee, were at the forefront of the development of modern day public relations. Early on, corporations realized the need to recruit journalists to develop their media relations programs so that they could capture their share of the public discussion in newspapers, magazines, and radio. After all, who could better understand the needs of journalists and package information the way they wanted it than a former journalist?

To this day, many public relations professionals have previous journalism experience. The common background and the traditional emphasis on media relations have created strong ties to the journalism profession.

Journalists and public relation practitioners package information for public consumption, and the two can often develop a close, dependent relationship. Journalists often rely on public relations professionals to provide ideas and information for their stories; public relations relies on journalists for access to a credible mass media vehicle that can distribute organizational messages to a wide audience at little expense.

Journalists are in the business of gathering and synthesizing information and converting that information into products that people want to read, hear, or view. The product—news content—can be informative, entertaining, or useful in some way to consumers' daily lives. Journalists judge whether or not information is newsworthy based on any of the following characteristics: timeliness, prominence, proximity, significance, unusualness, human interest, conflict, and newness. Journalists gather and package news content that is truthful and represents, to the best of the journalist's ability, a balanced account of what happened. If information supplied by the organization is considered newsworthy, the journalist will start his or her work. A journalist might speak to representatives of the organization that issued a news release but will probably also interview someone independent of the organization, such as competitors, consumers, or industry experts. Public relations practitioners have no control over the final version of a journalist's story. However, sometimes they can help shape the content by providing information from the organization or by suggesting "third-party endorsers," independent experts who have in-depth knowledge of specific issues. Journalists like using such sources because they can lend credibility to a news story; public relations practitioners may benefit because the experts may support or be sympathetic to the organization's perspective.

Public Relations' Advocacy Role

Public relations practitioners, unlike journalists, are hired by organizations to advocate their interests and to promote their views in public discourse. Notions of balance and objectivity, very important to journalists, do not apply to public relations in the same way. Still, truthfulness in all communication is the foundation that establishes the integrity of organizational public relations. But providing balance—both sides of the story—is not a common tactic in public relations. For example, when a new product is launched by an organization, a public relations practitioner probably won't focus on information in its news release or other promotional material about other products that compete for the customer's pocketbook. The practitioner likely will focus exclusively on its product's attributes, gathering accurate and positive information from product engineers, users, and outside experts.

Public relations practitioners' advocacy role takes them beyond writing for the mass news media. They produce many other types of communication products, including newsletters, direct mailers, and Web content. Their function within an organization is also much broader than writing. Public relations practitioners develop opportunities for interpersonal communication including special events and information exchanges such as product demonstrations. Public relations skills should also include counseling management, research, and planning.

Journalists, in comparison, have a more focused function; they gather and synthesize information in a growing variety of multimedia formats.

Journalists representing mass media are writing for a broad, general audience. Public relations practitioners segment the general public into key publics with messages created to address their interests and concerns in communication styles appropriate to each particular public. The key is to make sure that each message, no matter the target audience, is both easily understood and engaging.

COMMUNICATION THEORIES

How do organizations create effective communication programs? Successful practitioners know that program goals and communication strategies must be grounded in communication theory. Every case in this textbook can be analyzed through the lens of one or more communication theories. A short summary of some of these theories is provided below.

Theories about the Media, Relationships, and Behavior

- **Indirect effects theory.** The media can have an effect on people, but that effect is usually indirect because it is often "filtered" through other people, such as friends and social groups.[7]
- **Limited-effects theory.** The media have little effect on people because many factors intervene or mitigate the message.[8]
- **Cognitive dissonance.** Leon Festinger found people usually seek out and pay attention to media messages that do not threaten their established values and beliefs. Messages challenging a person's deeply held values and beliefs make a person uncomfortable (dissonance) and are often avoided.[9]
- **Selective processes.** Leon Festinger found that because people are uncomfortable with information that challenges their values and beliefs, they generally seek information that is more attuned to their own values and beliefs.[10]

- **Framing theory.** Journalists and editors make many critical decisions in their work ranging from whom to interview to what questions to ask and what specific words to use when writing a story. These decisions can be affected by public relations "frame strategists."[11]

- **Media uses and gratification theory.** People actively select and use the media to fulfill their own needs, such as finding information to make purchasing decisions or to be entertained.[12]

- **Hierarchy of needs theory.** People pay attention to messages based on their personal needs. These needs have been arranged in a pyramid form according to the most basic physiological needs for survival to the most complex ones dealing with self-fulfillment.[13]

- **Agenda setting theory.** While the media can't tell people what to think, the media can be effective in establishing what topics are talked about, according to Bernard Cohen's theory. An organization or issue can suddenly gain a national stage if the media decide it's worth a look.[14]

- **Two-step flow theory.** Some individuals actively take the time to seek and understand information on certain topics, making them, in effect, subject experts. These individuals are called *opinion leaders* and can have an effect on their followers. Later research has indicated that the most effective opinion leaders are those who share the same social status as their adherents.[15]

- **Diffusion theory.** This theory by Everett Rogers claims people make decisions or accept ideas following ordered steps: awareness, interest, trial, evaluation, and adoption.[16]

- **Systems theory.** Organizations cannot survive alone. They are interdependent on others and must interact to some degree with various constituencies in the political, economic, and social realms to survive and thrive. Every organization has stakeholders, such as employees, customers, and government regulators, who must be dealt with. Public relations helps to identify, build, and monitor these crucial relationships.[17]

- **Situational theory of publics.** Building strategic relationships for an organization involves understanding publics. Situational theory describes the factors that contribute to creating active publics based on their situation (problem recognition, constraint recognition, and level of involvement).[18]

Questions for Discussion

1. How do you define public relations?
2. How does public relations add value to an organization?
3. What is strategic public relations?
4. Identify your values as a student; as a classroom.
5. Create a code of conduct for your classroom.
6. How can a communication theory described in this chapter apply to communication situations on your campus?

Chapter Two

Proactive Public Relations

MONITOR YOUR ENVIRONMENT

People who wait for life to happen to them instead of making life happen may be caught off guard when things go wrong. In public relations, as in life, you have to prepare for potential problems before they occur. Being proactive is more than just common sense though; it makes the work a practitioner does more valuable to an organization.

Proactive public relations implies action that supports something: a project, a mission, a cause. In public relations, the cause is both the survival of the organization and the fulfillment of its mission.

Many things can keep organizations from fulfilling their mission. The quality of the product or service may be poor, governmental regulations may limit activities, activists may believe an organization is harming the environment or taking advantage of minorities, or workers can feel unappreciated. Even global issues have an effect: the changing marketplace caused by increasing foreign competition, for example. Plants close and jobs may be sent overseas.

Public relations practitioners should watch for issues likely to concern an organization's key publics. There are always individuals who will have specific problems with an organization. But when a growing number of people share a problem and want to do something about it, the problem becomes an issue. And while organizations traditionally pay more attention to groups than individuals, the Internet has become a powerful tool for determined individuals who can now single-handedly attract attention, share information, and grow a problem into an issue shared by many.

Issues management can be as simple as monitoring and responding appropriately when people or groups are negatively affected by an organization's actions. Once an issue of concern is identified and prioritized, public relations should monitor the situation and work to develop an equitable solution—one that benefits the organization and the public that has been negatively affected.

Seek Feedback and Encourage Dialog

While it would be nice if problems did not develop at all, that is unlikely; conflict is a fact of life. However, organizations that constantly monitor their environment, engage their key publics through active listening and dialog, and are transparent in their actions, can avoid or reduce conflict—and nip problems in the bud.

Transparency does not mean giving away the secret formula for Classic Coke, but it does mean making sure day-to-day operations meet regulations and are in line with generally accepted business practices. Organizations operating in a closed system often create an atmosphere of secrecy and isolation. What appears to be a controlled system actually becomes uncontrolled because employees are not sharing information with each other and are not paying attention to their environment.

Associated with the concept of transparency is feedback. While communicating what it does, an organization should also seek feedback from stakeholders. Beyond active listening, organizations can solicit opinions in a number of ways, including 1-800 numbers, e-mail, forums, and surveys.

Organizations that sincerely seek feedback and listen carefully can often establish a constructive dialog between the organization and its publics. This two-way communication model keeps the lines of communication open, helps develop mutual respect and understanding, and can lead to long-lasting solutions.

SWOT Analysis

Practitioners who are proactive are *doing something*. Activity for activity's sake, however, is not strategic. Just because a practitioner writes and sends out 300 news releases and creates 20 special events each year does not automatically address issues, fulfill an organization's mission, or meet its goals. Management must see a positive, quantifiable, bottom-line difference as a result of public relations activities.

Strategic public relations practitioners are *always thinking*. They have the ability, aided by specialized knowledge, to anticipate problems and opportunities. One way to start thinking strategically is by conducting a strengths, weaknesses, opportunities, and threats (SWOT) analysis. SWOT has been used by business professionals for many years to analyze products, services, and future markets. It is a good planning exercise for public relations professionals who need to assess where an organization stands.

By examining an organization, its environment, and publics based on strengths, weaknesses, opportunities, and threats, a public relations practitioner will be able to develop goals and objectives that really matter.

Get to Know the Organization

When evaluating an organization, think about the quality of the product or service. Look at sales and other indicators to measure the performance of the organization. How do this year's numbers compare to those of past years? What about assets? Everything from cash in the bank to equipment to the building can be looked at, measured, and compared to data from a year ago or 5 or 10 years ago.

Find out how the product is made or the service is accomplished. Shadow the employees directly involved in the organization's product or service; learn as much as you can. Read the company's product or service literature, research reports, and everything else you can get your hands on.

To understand the present, you need to know the past. Public relations practitioners should be familiar with their organization's history. Often, that history can explain a lot about an organization's current culture. How did the organization begin? Who founded it? How has the company changed since its inception? Has it grown or diversified? Does the executive officer have family ties to the organization's founder? Is the company publicly or privately owned? Annual reports, brochures, and other literature from archives can explain why things are the way they are.

Employees can also reveal the character and strength of an organization in its current state. Employees, after all, are an organization's greatest asset. Public relations practitioners should get out of the office and talk with employees. Take the time to make personal contact, instead of relying on letters and e-mails. Find out how long people have worked for the organization; senior employees carry the "institutional memory" that can be helpful in assessing the organization's strengths and weaknesses. Find out what employees like and don't like about working in their jobs. If employees are unionized, to what degree have union disputes created hard feelings between management and workers?

Get to Know the Environment

An organization's "environment" is more than the local community where the company is physically located. It also includes those places where publics can get the product or service the organization provides. That can extend across the state, the nation, or around the world.

In spite of our global and virtual connections, it is still good business for an organization to invest resources in the local community where its employees live. Organizations that have taken the time to get involved in a community by supporting positive causes will enhance their local reputation. Organizations with strong local reputations often can attract quality workers which, in turn, helps ensure quality products and services. Committed workers also spread the news about products and services to family members, neighbors, and the news media.

An organization's presence in a community, especially that of a large employer, creates expectations of involvement in community issues and causes. Failure to be a good corporate neighbor can make it more difficult to accomplish future projects, such as expansion or the easing of regulatory restrictions.

The environment also includes competitors. If you don't know the competitors as well as your own organization, you can't really prepare for future challenges and opportunities.

Depending on the nature of the organization, competitors may be down the street or a dozen time zones away. Even the local movie house has to keep an eye on competitors that can offer the same old product with new twists: comfortable seating, surround-sound audio systems, and digital formats.

Keeping track of competitors, and the industry as a whole, allows practitioners to see industry trends and plan for the future. Observing how other organizations deal with new obstacles and challenges can make it easier for your organization to learn quickly from the mistakes and successes of others.

Get to Know Your Publics

When looking at the organization and environment, the publics themselves are an inherent part of the analysis. Knowing what publics pay attention to is key to practicing strategic public relations.

As defined in Chapter 1, publics are groups whose members have a common interest that involves the organization. These publics contribute in some way to the organization's success or survival.

Each organization will have different publics. Some previously mentioned examples of publics include customers, employees, government officials, community residents, and activists. Public relations practitioners seek to build mutual understanding and, ultimately, support through relationships with these publics.

Segmenting the general public into key publics allows communication programs to effectively create and target messages that are likely to be of interest to a particular group. If you were trying to reach the attention of college-age students for a homecoming event, for example, the language and presentation of the material would be very different from the message for parents or alumni. Not only would the wording and presentation of the message be different—so would the way the message is sent; instead of a printed invitation it could be a cell phone text message for the college student.

Know your key publics! Just as it's easier to talk to someone you know than to a complete stranger, knowing more about your publics will help improve communication—and make it easier for a practitioner to establish a positive relationship. Practitioners need a deep understanding of their publics. What do customers, employees, the news media, and financial analysts know and say about your organization? Also, who are your publics' "influencers"—those formal and informal opinion leaders or trendsetters who can affect public opinion? They can be elected officials, community leaders, field and industry experts, or respected private citizens.

Beyond determining who your publics are and learning something about them, it's helpful to understand that not all publics are interacting with the organization. Researchers James Grunig and Todd Hunt[1] identified four stages of development for publics: *nonpublic, latent, aware,* and *active.* Grunig and Hunt noted that a public can remain in one stage indefinitely or develop from nonpublic to a latent, aware, or active public.

Nonpublics are not interested in what the organization is doing and therefore are not an immediate concern for the public relations practitioner. Limited resources of time, staffing, and money make communication with all groups impossible, so awareness of the nonpublics helps practitioners identify and focus resources on the groups that need attention.

Latent publics share common interests with the organization but are not aware of what the organization is doing. They need information that speaks to their needs and motivations.

Aware publics share common interests with an organization and have paid attention to organizational messages. But they need to be motivated to act on their information. *PR Reporter* suggested that a "triggering event," an event such as a sale or open house, provides the opportunity and motivation for publics to act on the information.

Finally, there is the *active* public. This group does not need a triggering event to be motivated into action, although they will probably take advantage of it anyway. They are interested and actively seeking information on their own. Active publics present opportunities for development beyond basic interaction with the organization.

Author Ronald D. Smith[2] identified one other stage of public development worth noting: the *apathetic* public. This group shares a common interest with an organization, and is aware of what the organization is doing, but chooses to do nothing. Members of this group may not be joiners—or they may not be interested enough to make the effort.

Knowledge of an organization's publics as well as their stage of development can aid the public relations practitioner in developing the right strategies to build strong relationships with mutual benefits for the organization and its stakeholders.

DEVELOP A PUBLIC RELATIONS STRATEGY

Once the organization, environment, and key publics are understood, it is easier to address a problem or opportunity with a public relations strategy based on goals and objectives that support the organizational mission.

In public relations, advanced and thorough planning means resources will be used wisely, and specific objectives will be achieved. Success isn't guaranteed—but it's more likely if you research and plan in advance and have goals and objectives.

A public relations goal is the overall plan, stated in general terms, that recognizes the issue and generally how it will be addressed. Ronald D. Smith's book *Strategic Planning for Public Relations* describes three types of campaign goals: reputation management goals, which deal with the identity and perception of the organization by its publics; relationship management goals, which focus on how the organization positively connects with its publics; and task management goals, which are concerned with getting certain things done.

Wal-Mart, for example, wants to win loyal customers. It uses a high-quality and low-price reputation management goal to win and keep loyal customers. A college that wants more freshman student applicants from area high schools might use a relationship management goal to better connect with high school counselors. A hospital may use a task management goal to increase knowledge among obstetricians about a new neonatal critical care service.

Objectives are clearly worded, time-oriented, and measurable. Their job is to increase awareness, acceptance, or action.[3] However, an objective itself does not provide step-by-step instructions on how it is to be achieved. Those details are described in "action steps" or tactics.

Let's say South College's relationship management goal has the objective of strengthening the college's relationship with local high school career counselors. The specific action objective is to get 10 percent more high school career counselors from area high schools to participate in the college faculty's summer career workshops. These workshops are designed to develop positive personal connections between high school counselors and the college's faculty and admission staff. The objective might sound like this: to have an effect on the actions of South College's six area high school counseling staffs, specifically to increase the number of area high school career counselors attending the college's summer 2007 career workshops by 10 percent.

The strategy of emphasizing closer connections with high school counselors would be carried out with additional tactics. When implemented, these tactics would hopefully achieve the goal of stronger college high school relationships, which might ultimately lead to more freshman applications. Some additional tactics might include sending out a mini-compact disk stressing the college's career center initiatives, faculty visits to area high schools, and hosting regular breakfast meetings to discuss career-related majors with high school career counselors.

A hospital that wants to increase obstetricians' knowledge about its hospital facilities could accomplish that goal with a task management goal. The hospital's strategy is to promote the maternity ward's new neonatal intensive care unit, which offers obstetricians the most modern maternity facility in the region. The hospital's objective is to increase awareness among area obstetricians about this new unit. The objective might sound like this: to have an effect on the awareness of area obstetricians, specifically to inform 32 affiliated and non-affiliated South Hospital obstetricians in South County about the new neonatal intensive care unit by March 1, 2007.

With the hospital's strategy there will be a list of activities or tactics that describe how to achieve the objective.

Tactics might include an open house, baby dolls with the hospital's name imprinted on their dresses that could be sent with a brochure about the neonatal intensive care unit to area obstetricians, and a hospital-sponsored conference on new neonatal research and practices by a nationally known obstetrician.

Once the activities are underway or completed, a review of their effectiveness would be the final step in a strategic public relations plan. Because the objectives and tactics are descriptive, containing agreed-upon measures of success, evaluation is easy to include in the campaign plan. For the college seeking to strengthen its relationships with area high school career counselors, a simple way to evaluate the overall effectiveness of the campaign would be to track the number of counselors who attend the college-sponsored events or the number of invitations that college professors receive from counselors to attend career fairs or classrooms. A survey could gauge the strength of the relationship between career counselors and the college.

The hospital promoting its neonatal intensive care unit could survey obstetricians' offices by phone to measure their level of awareness. A head count of obstetricians at the open house is another way the campaign's effectiveness could be measured.

Proactive public relations practitioners are constantly scanning their environment, listening to their publics, identifying issues of public concern, analyzing their organization's actions, and seeking mutually beneficial solutions to problems. With a full understanding of "what's going on and with whom," the practitioner is better prepared to address opportunities and problems. At the same time, careful research and planning are absolutely essential to creating a strategy in sync with the organization's mission.

Questions for Discussion

1. Define SWOT. Why is it important to the planning process?
2. How can a public relations practitioner monitor the environment?
3. What is issues management?
4. What are the stages of development for a public?
5. Why is transparency helpful to an organization?
6. What is a goal, objective, strategy, and tactic? Provide your own examples.

Chapter Three

The Case Method

THE NEXT BEST THING TO BEING THERE

We often hear that experience is the best teacher.

It's true that experience is the best way to learn many of life's lessons. That's why students do internships and go on field trips and professionals go to conferences and read professional literature. Techniques that have been proved over time to be effective are called *best practices*. They provide a window into how effective public relations really works.

But students can't always get experience on a trial basis or be sure what it is they need to experience or observe before graduation. And, of course, some real-life situations are better to read about than experience firsthand—especially threatening and dangerous ones.

When firsthand observation and experience aren't possible, we can do the next best thing: Talk to people who have been there, read about their experience, and imagine what they went through to overcome a difficult situation. It isn't the same as being there, perhaps, but this method does have certain advantages.

Case-based instruction describes real-world scenarios faced by early career and seasoned public relations professionals. Many cases in this book are based on news media accounts that present the basic facts of a situation addressing some public relations issue. The organization's internal strategy may not always be evident in these instances, but students can discuss the public actions of the organization and theorize what led to these actions.

Some cases are in-depth examples, carefully reconstructed for analysis of their practical lessons. In some instances, the case stops at a critical point and asks you to decide what should be done.

Students can and should apply their knowledge from prior classes and their own personal experiences to analyze and discuss the organization's and practitioner's actions, plus provide their own alternate solutions to the problems or opportunities identified in the case.

Sound easy? Reading a case and discussing what you read sounds simple until you start discussing the issues, concepts, and tactics in depth; often many factors are involved in decision making and sometimes it's a messy affair. But don't worry. The challenges are well worth the effort and result in a rich learning experience that's a lot of fun.

Case-Based Instructional Goals

So what will you gain from this course? It's a chance to apply all you have learned from previous classes and internship/work experiences and begin the transition from student to professional. You will:

- Apply your knowledge of public relations concepts, theories, and best practices to cases in different career settings.
- Develop your strategic thinking skills by using the public relations process that includes research, planning, action/communication, and evaluation.
- Develop problem-solving skills.
- Develop interpersonal, counseling, and management skills.
- Practice orally and in writing what you would say or do in certain situations.
- Learn new public relations tactics and strategies.

Since this class is probably quite different from any class you've had before, the following guidelines will help you get the most out of case-based instruction.

FIVE RULES FOR CASE STUDY
Rule 1: Read and Reread the Case *before* Class

Case-based instruction is not the typical lecture-style class in which students sit and quietly take notes. In fact, the teacher does not usually have a central role in the classroom. Instead, the spotlight is on you, the student. Learning happens through student-led discussion of cases and group activities. The teacher guides the learning process by assisting discussion to ensure that key concepts and principles are discussed and to create alternative scenarios.

In order to make this an exciting learning environment, you must come prepared and have a thorough knowledge of the assigned cases. Know the characters names, what happened, and in what order. It generally takes two readings, with note taking as you go along, to prepare each case.

There are opportunities to do your own research in a topic area or trace the case from its origins to its conclusion. Databases, such as the newspaper database Lexis-Nexis, and organizational Web sites offer virtual gold mines for background material. Web sites often include mission statements, archived news releases, annual reports, historical information, and more. Activist sites can offer different views and their own evidence about certain issues and events.

Some of the greatest resources are your textbooks from prior public relations and business management classes. If you do not own these, your library will most likely have copies.

Other public relations resources include *PR Week, Public Relations Tactics, The Public Relations Strategist* electronic and print newsletters ("Bulldog Reporter," "Jack O'Dwyer's Newsletter," etc.), and many Web sites.

Don't be afraid to go beyond the obvious public relations issues. Each case has unique attributes. Some deal with human interaction, business management, and personal dilemmas. Be curious and ask questions. Case analysis worksheets are provided at the end of this chapter to help you prepare for each case.

Rule 2: Make Connections

Next, begin to tie in the public relations issues. You can start with a SWOT (strengths, weaknesses, opportunities, and threats) analysis (see Chapter 2, "Proactive Public Relations"). When possible, analyze the organization's strategy, response, communication techniques, and other tactics. What were the organization's options? What would you have done differently?

You may be surprised to learn that your assessment of a case strategy can be very different from that of others in the classroom. What seems obvious to you may escape the notice of a classmate—and vice versa. Particularly in the choice of public relations tactics, there are many options. While many good communication theories and core principles have emerged from a growing body of knowledge, there is still plenty of room for debate about which strategies and tactics are "right"—and often, there may be more than one right answer!

Examine each case for elements of the public relations process (research, planning, communication, and evaluation). What's missing and how would you, as a practitioner, have added or changed these elements?

To help you organize and prepare for the case study method, this textbook offers four worksheets to deconstruct and analyze the cases:

- Preparing the Case
- Organizational Response
- Effective Communication
- Communication Tactics

Rule 3: Participate in the Discussion

Participating in the discussion is the most important element of the class. Your active involvement will deepen your understanding of the public relations practice. Beyond the public relations principles, theories, and strategies, this class can also help you develop counseling, strategic thinking, and rhetorical skills.

The counselor role in public relations is an important function in organizations that can be learned in case based instruction through role playing exercises. Advising management to see the big picture, carefully examining the potential consequences of its actions, and suggesting sound alternatives can be a tricky proposition even for experienced practitioners. While big egos, traditional ways of doing things, and management isolation sometimes prevent practitioners from providing this valuable service, you'll find that class discussions and role playing can help you develop counseling skills and build your credibility with managers.

That's because in public relations today, knowledge, experience, and strategy expertise aren't enough. Successful practitioners know how to present ideas to their peers and leaders in a convincing manner. While the business memo and proposal are alive and well, more often the ability to present your ideas orally when the golden opportunity arises is essential. Speaking up at the appropriate time and constructing logical and persuasive arguments are vastly underrated skills for new practitioners.

When you have to respond to direct questions from your classmates or teacher, you'll get valuable practice articulating your ideas—and you'll learn how to think on your feet, under pressure. When the boss asks for your opinion in a meeting or he/she gives you a minute in the hallway to present your case, can you do it logically, concisely, and persuasively? This is just one more good reason to be prepared: Have the facts, and a strategy at your fingertips. If you tell the boss you're not prepared to offer your ideas—or, worse, you don't remember all the facts—you will have missed an opportunity. And the boss won't be impressed.

Beyond dealing with the boss, being articulate is helpful in other instances: How would you deal with persistent reporters during a crisis? How do you establish authority within your department without crushing teamwork and creativity? By creating a scenario based on a scene from a case, students can begin practicing their strategic thinking and speaking skills.

You may also be asked to lead class discussion on a case. This will give you practice at organizing your thoughts, participating in active listening, and encouraging others to speak up.

A randomly selected student usually starts the case by presenting the key points concerning the case. Everyone should be prepared because it may be "your turn" to answer the next question or present your views or solutions to a problem posed. Anyone can be called on at any time to offer his or her reasoning and timing of certain actions. Students may also be subject to query, argument, and discussion from anyone in the classroom. Adding to the challenge, your professor may change an element in the case that will have to be factored into your problem solution.

Some case scenarios can expand into role-playing activities. Students in your class may be asked to dramatize a particular scene within the case. Not only do students practice their rhetorical skills, but dramatizing gives students a chance to observe how everything has the potential to send messages: body language, tone of voice, eye contact, active listening, and nervous habits. New twists can be added to the dramatization to see how good you are at thinking on your feet. You may be a little self-conscious at first, but most students find role playing enjoyable and an effective way to learn.

Remember, whenever you speak in a role playing scenario, you may be quoted. Especially in times of crisis, when events are moving quickly, the chance for error is great. Could your words be taken out of context? Did you talk beyond the known facts and speculate? This class will help you learn how to choose your words carefully, stay focused, and communicate effectively.

Teamwork and other kinds of collaborative efforts are common practice in public relations today. Most cases can incorporate in-class group activities, such as group discussions, debates, research, and analysis assignments—all good ways to practice working in a group or as part of a team. Your professor may select teams prior to a class or during a class.

The idea is to provide a variety of ways for you to practice and sharpen your rhetorical, counseling, and leadership skills in different situations.

Rule 4: Share Your Experiences

Some of the best class discussions and learning occur when students share personal experiences related to the case topic. If you have completed an internship, for example, you might share your observations on how public relations is practiced in a corporate, agency, or nonprofit setting.

You may want to relate experiences a family member has encountered as an employee or customer. Even a job at the local mall can provide fodder for discussion, especially in employee relations, management practices, and interpersonal relationships. There's no substitute for real-life experience; you'll often find that incidents, which you, family members, and other students have encountered in the workplace or elsewhere, can illustrate some of the concepts in this textbook.

Rule 5: Respect Others

Respect for all opinions is key to a successful discussion-based class. Everyone should have the chance to participate, and some students need more encouragement than others.

No one likes negative criticism or public embarrassment. While polite disagreement is encouraged, verbal attacks and dominating the discussion are not. Make your point and let others make theirs; be careful not to dominate the class discussion. Active listening should be as much a part of the class as forceful speaking.

- *Read and reread the case before class.* Come prepared!
- *Connect the dots.* Relate the material to public relations concepts and experiences.
- *Speak up.* Contribute to the class discussion.
- *Use your words.* Be logical, concise, and persuasive.
- And one final rule: *Have fun!*

Worksheet 1 looks at the organization/entity involved, the main characters involved, and the issue(s). Worksheet 2 looks at the organizational response to the problem or opportunity, Worksheet 3 looks at the communication/messages, and Worksheet 4 examines the ways organizations get their messages out to audiences.

Preparing for the Case 1

Not all the elements below will be present in all the cases. You may seek additional information about an organization, communication/public relations theories, and public relations concepts and tactics from suggested Web sites, including the Web site of the organization featured in the case study. Beyond examining the organization's Web site, look for activist sites or blogs that discuss the organization or issue relevant to the case study.

This worksheet will help you organize your thoughts for class discussion.

ORGANIZATION

Based on the information provided, describe what you know about the organization.

- Basic facts of the organization/entity
- Type of business/service (size, profit or nonprofit, new or old, etc.)
- Organizational culture: formal, informal?
- Organizational system: opened, closed? (transparency, interaction with outsiders)
- Environment: internal (managers, staff employees) and external (competitors and stakeholders such as customers and activists)
- SWOT: organizational strengths, weaknesses, opportunities, threats analysis
- Mission statement (if available)
- Annual reports (if available)
- Archival news releases or other communication (if available)
- Other

PROBLEM OR OPPORTUNITY

What's the public relations issue that causes the concern?

- Explain the problem
- Explain the opportunity

TIMELINE

Often it is helpful to develop a timeline of events. Knowing when and in what order events occur can provide important insights.

KEY PUBLICS

Who are the characters in this case? What did they do?

Who's directly affected by the actions of the organization?

- Internal (employees, management)
- External (competitors, investors, community, government officials, activists, etc.)
- Other

HUMAN FACTORS

Interactions with others in and outside the organization are important factors to consider.

- In particular, what did the public relations practitioner(s) do?
- Interpersonal relationships
- Organizational role, access to management
- Seniority
- Working with outside public relations firm employees
- Other _____

PRACTITIONER FACTORS

- Experience, expertise of practitioner
- What special skills or knowledge are necessary for success in this public relations setting?

- Media relations
- Investor relations
- Crisis communication management
- Public relations counseling
- Other _____

ETHICAL AND LEGAL CONSIDERATIONS

Following are some basic ethical questions:

- Is the action right or wrong according to what? Your own principles, your professional code, the law?
- Can someone be harmed by your decision (including your inaction)?
- Can you personally live with your decision?
- Can you justify your decision publicly for good reasons?

PUBLIC RELATIONS SOCIETY OF AMERICA MEMBER CODE OF ETHICS: CORE VALUES AND PROVISIONS

VALUES

- Advocacy
- Honesty
- Expertise
- Independence
- Loyalty
- Fairness

CODE PROVISIONS

- Free flow of information
- Competition
- Disclosure of information
- Safeguarding confidences
- Conflicts of interest
- Enhancing the profession

Organizational Response 2

A TYPOLOGY OF PROACTIVE ORGANIZATIONAL RESPONSES

There are many ways for organizations to act proactively so that activities are strategic and support the mission of an organization. Ronald D. Smith's *Strategic Planning for Public Relations*[1] textbook mentions the following action strategies: organizational performance, audience participation, special events, alliances and coalitions, sponsorships, strategic philanthropy, and activism. Communication strategies, he notes, include publicity, newsworthy information, and transparent communication. For case study, consider the following areas:

ENVIRONMENTAL SCANNING

- Mass media monitoring (Internet, newspapers, television, radio, etc.)
- Industry trend watching through professional conferences and trade publications
- Internal monitoring (employee suggestion box, casual conversations or checking with departments, customer service trends)
- Issue identification and prioritization

RESEARCH

- Informal research (discussions with key communicators, department heads, etc.)

Continued

Continued

- Secondary research (database research or Internet searches to help identify new trends or issues)
- Formal research (questionnaires, focus groups, content analysis, observations, and in-depth interviewing)

OUTREACH

- Management opportunities to interact informally with employees
- Management involvement with key community and industry organizations, including the formation of alliances and coalitions
- Organizational opportunities to interact face-to-face with the public through annual meetings, open houses, facility tours, key communicator group meetings, general meetings, speakers' bureau
- Formal media relations program to develop good working relationships between the organization and journalists
- Organizational communication programs, such as newsletters, brochures, Web sites, informational videos, news releases
- Community relations (sponsorships, philanthropy, and volunteerism)

A TYPOLOGY OF REACTIVE PUBLIC RELATIONS RESPONSES

There are many response options, especially when a problem or crisis emerges. They can range from the all-out attack, especially in instances of known hoaxes, to strategic silence, when an organization purposely chooses no comment or other responsive action in a situation. Author Ronald D. Smith examined the range of behavioral and verbal responses available to organizations when they are faced with accusations or other criticisms.[2]

PREEMPTIVE ACTION STRATEGY

- Preemptive action

OFFENSIVE RESPONSE STRATEGIES

- Attack
- Embarrassment
- Threat

DEFENSIVE RESPONSE STRATEGIES

- Denial
- Excuse
- Justification

DIVERSIONARY RESPONSE STRATEGIES

- Concession
- Ingratiation
- Disassociation
- Relabeling

VOCAL COMMISERATION STRATEGIES

- Concern
- Condolence
- Regret
- Apology

RECTIFYING BEHAVIOR STRATEGIES

- Investigation
- Corrective action
- Restitution
- Repentance

STRATEGIC INACTION

- Silence

YOUR ANALYSIS OF THE ORGANIZATIONAL RESPONSE

- What are the pros and cons of each response used in the cases?
- What might have been a better response strategy? Tactic? Why?

Effective Communication   3

Public relations practitioners are responsible for the organization's communication programs. Many cases in this textbook provide examples of the communication efforts in statements, news releases, advertising, and other collateral material. An analysis of key messages is helpful in reviewing many cases.

ANALYZING THE COMMUNICATION TIMING

- Create a chronology or timeline of events in the case.
- How much time elapsed between the pivotal information discovery, public communication of the information, and the organization's response to the information?
- If silence was used as a response to public information, was it effective in your opinion?

ANALYZING THE KEY MESSAGES
USE OF LANGUAGE

- Factual? Use of facts, statistics, examples, documents, other forms of evidence?
- Persuasive? There are many types of emotional appeal strategies including fear appeals, guilt appeals, patriotic appeals. What type of persuasive appeal was made?

WRITTEN ELEMENTS

- Are certain word choices more powerful than others?
- Are words chosen to appeal directly to a certain key audience?
- Are the messages easy to understand?
- Are the words humorous, shocking, or offensive? In what way?

SPOKEN ELEMENTS

- Who was the organizational spokesperson? Do you feel he or she was an appropriate spokesperson? Why?
- What kind of credibility does the spokesperson possess?
- Analyze the quotes by organizational spokespersons in news media accounts. Are they effective? Why?

VISUAL ELEMENTS

- What are the visual elements present in the message? Photographic, illustrative, iconic?
- In what way are the images used to attract attention? Communicate a message?
- Does the image provoke a feeling? Does it have a connection to a cultural past?
- Is the type of font communicating a message as well?

Ways Organizations Communicate   4

Strategic Planning for Public Relations provides an excellent guide to how organizations communicate.[3]

FACE-TO-FACE COMMUNICATION TACTICS

Public relations professionals generally agree the most effective way to communicate is face-to-face. However, it is often the most expensive way to reach audiences too. The expense is usually justified when the publics targeted by the communication event are crucial to the organization's function. For colleges, that would be prospective students and their parents (open houses); for publicly held corporations, that would include stockholders (annual meetings); and for the local Red Cross, a key public is its volunteers.

TYPES OF FACE-TO-FACE COMMUNICATION TACTICS

- Special events: Annual meetings, groundbreakings, open houses, grand openings, anniversary celebrations, awards/recognition events, sporting events, fund-raisers
- Group meetings: Question-and-answer sessions, civic club presentations
- Product exhibits
- Demonstrations
- Other _____

ORGANIZATIONAL MEDIA TACTICS

Organizations often create their own communication for employees and the outside world. The design and content of these communication products are controlled by the organization, which ensures that every element of message is presented the way the organization intended.

TYPES OF ORGANIZATIONAL MEDIA TACTICS

- Newsletters
- Brochures
- Posters
- Web sites
- Intranet
- E-mail
- E-bulletin boards
- E-chat rooms
- Blogs
- Cell phone text messages
- Letters
- Payroll stuffers
- Videos
- Photographs
- Slide shows (PowerPoint)
- Annual reports
- Bulletin boards
- Logos
- Buttons
- T-shirts
- Other _____

NEWS MEDIA TACTICS

The news media is a powerful vehicle for getting organizational messages to large audiences at no cost except in the production and dissemination of the information provided to the news media. The trade-off is the loss of control that comes with providing information to the media. There are no guarantees the information will be used or how it will be used.

TYPES OF NEWS MEDIA TACTICS

- News releases
- Video and audio news releases
- Media alerts
- News conferences
- Fact sheets (biographies, organizational histories, frequently asked questions, product specifications)
- Feature stories
- Press kits, print or electronic
- Satellite media tours: radio and television:
- op-ed guest columns, letters to the editor
- Conference calls
- Other _____

ADVERTISING/PROMOTIONAL MEDIA TACTICS

Mass media channels provide opportunities for placing messages within news, entertainment, or any setting where you think your key audiences are likely to view your messages. The message content, look, and placement are controlled by the organization, but for a price. Unlike news media tactics, which only cost the amount to produce and disseminate them, advertising and promotional media tactics also entail the cost of placement, which in mass media channels such as television and newspapers or magazines can become expensive.

TYPES OF ADVERTISING/PROMOTIONAL MEDIA TACTICS

- Display print ads (newspaper, magazines, programs)
- Television commercials
- Radio commercials
- Internet ads
- Billboards
- Promotional gift items (key chains, etc.)
- Clothing items (T-shirts, hats, etc.)
- Software items (interactive games, virtual tours, etc.)
- Other _____

Chapter Four

Ethics and the Public Interest

In recent years, public relations has been front-page news, but not always for altruistic reasons. Negative incidents brought to light by the national media have dealt largely with the ethics of organizations covertly influencing public opinion through public relations programs. And, in one case, the focus of news coverage was simply truthful business dealings.

Ethics provides the framework for deciding what behavior is right and what is wrong. On the surface, it seems so simple. After all, who doesn't know to tell the truth, play fairly, and avoid injuring others? In the business world, however, the black-and-white differences often turn gray when decisions are made in a hurry or management directs others to carry out questionable practices. For young and inexperienced practitioners, relying on superiors to do the right thing—a common assumption—may be naive. Textbook authors Lattimore et al. noted some of the troubling questions a practitioner may confront. Will he or she:[1]

- Lie for a client or employer?
- Engage in deception to collect information about another practitioner's clients?
- Help conceal a hazardous condition or illegal act?
- Present information that presents only part of the truth?
- Offer something (gift, travel, or information) to reporters or legislators that may compromise their reporting or decision making?
- Present true but misleading information in an interview or news conference that corrupts the channels of government?

Ethical decision making is best learned before one enters the workforce, away from the pressures of the job. Preventing ethical problems requires a system for determining what's right and wrong. Most professions provide a code of conduct to guide people in their decision making. The Public Relations Society of America (PRSA) has a code of ethics that embodies "professional values . . . vital to the integrity of the profession as a whole." A thorough understanding of this code of ethics will help a young practitioner make the right decisions even when that might mean confronting a client or boss who possesses more power, authority, and experience. The International Association of Business Communicators (IABC) also has an excellent code of ethics that is available at its Web site www.iabc.com.

A common theme that runs through many of PRSA's core values is protecting the public interest. This includes providing honest and accurate information so that customers can make the correct purchasing decisions. At its extreme, it includes protecting the public health if a product or service is found to be harmful.

The PRSA code has six core values: advocacy, honesty, expertise, independence, loyalty, and fairness. It also has six code provisions: free flow of information, competition, disclosure of information, safeguarding confidences, conflicts of interest, and enhancing the profession.[2]

The PRSA's "Ethical Decision-Making Guide Helps Resolve Ethical Dilemmas," by Kathy R. Fitzpatrick, offers the following process:[3]

Define the specific ethical issue/conflict.

1. Identify internal/external factors (e.g., legal, political, social, economic) that may influence the decision.
2. Identify key values.
3. Identify the parties who will be affected by the decision and define the public relations professional's obligation to each.
4. Select ethical principles to guide the decision-making process.
5. Make a decision and justify it.

PRSA MEMBER CODE OF ETHICS

PRSA Member Statement of Professional Values

This statement presents the core values of PRSA members and, more broadly, of the public relations profession. These values provide the foundation for the Member Code of Ethics and set the industry standard for the professional practice of public relations. These values are the fundamental beliefs that guide our behaviors and decision-making process. We believe our professional values are vital to the integrity of the profession as a whole.

Values

Advocacy

- We serve the public interest by acting as responsible advocates for those we represent.
- We provide a voice in the marketplace of ideas, facts, and viewpoints to aid informed public debate.

Honesty

- We adhere to the highest standards of accuracy and truth in advancing the interests of those we represent and in communicating with the public.

Expertise

- We acquire and responsibly use specialized knowledge and experience.
- We advance the profession through continued professional development, research, and education.
- We build mutual understanding, credibility, and relationships among a wide array of institutions and audiences.

Independence

- We provide objective counsel for those we represent.
- We are accountable for our actions.

Loyalty

- We are faithful to those we represent, while honoring our obligation to serve the public interest.

Fairness

- We deal fairly with clients, employers, competitors, peers, vendors, the media, and the general public.
- We respect all opinions and support the right of free expression.

PRSA CODE PROVISIONS
Free Flow of Information

Core Principle

Protecting and advancing the free flow of accurate and truthful information is essential to serving the public interest and contributing to informed decision making in a democratic society.

Intent

- To maintain the integrity of relationships with the media, government officials, and the public.
- To aid informed decision making.

Guidelines

A member shall:

- Preserve the integrity of the process of communication.
- Be honest and accurate in all communications.
- Act promptly to correct erroneous communications for which the practitioner is responsible.
- Preserve the free flow of unprejudiced information when giving or receiving gifts by ensuring that gifts are nominal, legal, and infrequent.

Examples of Improper Conduct under this Provision:

- A member representing a ski manufacturer gives a pair of expensive racing skis to a sports magazine columnist, to influence the columnist to write favorable articles about the product.
- A member entertains a government official beyond legal limits and/or in violation of government reporting requirements.

Competition

Core Principle

Promoting healthy and fair competition among professionals preserves an ethical climate while fostering a robust business environment.

Intent

- To promote respect and fair competition among public relations professionals.
- To serve the public interest by providing the widest choice of practitioner options.

Guidelines

A member shall:

- Follow ethical hiring practices designed to respect free and open competition without deliberately undermining a competitor.
- Preserve intellectual property rights in the marketplace.

Examples of Improper Conduct under this Provision:

- A member employed by a "client organization" shares helpful information with a counseling firm that is competing with others for the organization's business.
- A member spreads malicious and unfounded rumors about a competitor in order to alienate the competitor's clients and employees in a ploy to recruit people and business.

Disclosure of Information

Core Principle

Open communication fosters informed decision making in a democratic society.

Intent

To build trust with the public by revealing all information needed for responsible decision making.

Guidelines

A member shall:

- Be honest and accurate in all communications.
- Act promptly to correct erroneous communications for which the member is responsible.
- Investigate the truthfulness and accuracy of information released on behalf of those represented.
- Reveal the sponsors for causes and interests represented.
- Disclose financial interest (such as stock ownership) in a client's organization.
- Avoid deceptive practices.

Examples of Improper Conduct under this Provision:

- Front groups: A member implements "grass roots" campaigns or letter-writing campaigns to legislators on behalf of undisclosed interest groups.

- Lying by omission: A practitioner for a corporation knowingly fails to release financial information, giving a misleading impression of the corporation's performance.
- A member discovers inaccurate information disseminated via a Web site or media kit and does not correct the information.
- A member deceives the public by employing people to pose as volunteers to speak at public hearings and participate in "grass roots" campaigns.

Safeguarding Confidences

Core Principle

Client trust requires appropriate protection of confidential and private information.

Intent

To protect the privacy rights of clients, organizations, and individuals by safeguarding confidential information.

Guidelines

A member shall:

- Safeguard the confidences and privacy rights of present, former, and prospective clients and employees.
- Protect privileged, confidential, or insider information gained from a client or organization.
- Immediately advise an appropriate authority if a member discovers that confidential information is being divulged by an employee of a client company or organization.

Examples of Improper Conduct under this Provision:

- A member changes jobs, takes confidential information, and uses that information in the new position to the detriment of the former employer.
- A member intentionally leaks proprietary information to the detriment of some other party.

Conflicts of Interest

Core Principle

Avoiding real, potential, or perceived conflicts of interest builds the trust of clients, employers, and the publics.

Intent

- To earn trust and mutual respect with clients or employers.
- To build trust with the public by avoiding or ending situations that put one's personal or professional interests in conflict with society's interests.

Guidelines

A member shall:

- Act in the best interests of the client or employer, even subordinating the member's personal interests.
- Avoid actions and circumstances that may appear to compromise good business judgment or create a conflict between personal and professional interests.
- Disclose promptly any existing or potential conflict of interest to affected clients or organizations.
- Encourage clients and customers to determine if a conflict exists after notifying all affected parties.

Examples of Improper Conduct under this Provision

- The member fails to disclose that he or she has a strong financial interest in a client's chief competitor.
- The member represents a "competitor company" or a "conflicting interest" without informing a prospective client.

Enhancing the Profession

Core Principle

Public relations professionals work constantly to strengthen the public's trust in the profession.

Intent

- To build respect and credibility with the public for the profession of public relations.
- To improve, adapt, and expand professional practices.

Guidelines

A member shall:

- Acknowledge that there is an obligation to protect and enhance the profession.
- Keep informed and educated about practices in the profession to ensure ethical conduct.

- Actively pursue personal professional development.
- Decline representation of clients or organizations that urge or require actions contrary to this Code.
- Accurately define what public relations activities can accomplish.
- Counsel subordinates in proper ethical decision making.
- Require that subordinates adhere to the ethical requirements of the Code.
- Report ethical violations, whether committed by PRSA members or not, to the appropriate authority.

Examples of Improper Conduct under this Provision:

- A PRSA member declares publicly that a product the client sells is safe, without disclosing evidence to the contrary.
- A member initially assigns some questionable client work to a non-member practitioner to avoid the ethical obligation of PRSA membership.

What Would You Do?
Case Scenarios

POTENTIAL CELL PHONE PROBLEM
You are the public relations manager for a Fortune 500 telecommunications company that manufactures cell phones, among other products. You have just come from a two-hour management meeting in which several reports were given, including one from the customer service manager.

The customer service manager mentioned that a few complaints had been received recently from angry users of its hot-selling new series 80 phone models. Apparently, when the mobile phone was about to lose battery power, a very loud melody would play. The manager said he didn't know much more about the situation because another manager was handling it.

After the meeting, you check with the vice president of communication to see if you should put out a news release about the potential problem. She said the problem wasn't confirmed yet and "no action was needed."

However, in your research on another product, you read the customer relations internal reports and discover that the problem has actually been identified as a software flaw. You also read that the melody noise was described by several customers as "piercing" and "painful."

When you showed the vice president of communication these reports, she said that a "couple of complaints" does not warrant action. "Besides," she tells you, "they're one of the fastest-growing product lines."

What is the ethical situation or conflict? What would you do?

A LITTLE SOMETHING IN YOUR PRESS KIT

You are the media relations manager representing a pharmaceutical company whose new anti-inflammatory drug promises to be a blockbuster product. The Food and Drug Administration tentatively plans to approve it next month.

The company's marketing director wants you to make the rounds of all the major media outlets in New York City in person, to educate the media about the new product and get media coverage. You have an elaborate media kit containing background information about the product to drop off to all the medical editors. Tucked inside each press kit is a large envelope with gift certificates worth $200 for two meals at a new upscale restaurant. As you prepare to leave at the conclusion of each presentation, you give the editor the press kit and say, "I've enclosed a small thank-you inside."

What is the ethical situation or conflict?

WHEN IS A CITIZENS' GROUP A GRASSROOTS GROUP?

You are an account executive for a mid-sized public relations firm. You have been assigned to send out occasional news releases and create a Web site critical of a proposed new and very large commercial strip mall outside the city. The sponsor of this informational campaign is a group called "Concerned Citizens Against the XYZ Mall." They fear the negative impact that the new mall will create, including increased traffic, noise, crime, and suburban sprawl in an unspoiled natural environment.

The contact for Concerned Citizens Against the XYZ Mall who has provided all the information for the site is the wife of a downtown businessman, but you assume she represents many homeowners near the planned mall. One day, a newspaper reporter calls to ask for names of the group's leaders and who funds the organization.

Your contact person says that the group leaders would rather not talk to the media because they are afraid the mall developers will harass them. When pressed further, she tells you that the organizers and supporters of the group are all city business owners.

The account is a lucrative one, and you are concerned that you might lose it if you do not follow the organizers' wishes.

What is the ethical situation or conflict? What should you do?

NOT IN MY BACKYARD!

You are an assistant account executive at a public relations firm, which is working with the Fulton Solid Waste Authority. For the past two years, the Solid Waste Authority has been researching and testing 25 potential locations in the county to determine the top three sites for a new landfill. Residents near the potential sites are understandably nervous.

You have been assigned to help develop the information strategy for the announcement, including planning the venues for several public meetings and educational materials featuring a PowerPoint show that discusses the selection process.

The entire site evaluation process has been secret to ensure an orderly and equitable testing of all sites.

Trying to impress a new girlfriend, the assistant account executive talks about his job and lets slip that although all the testing was not complete, one site located in the Avondale area is really the most promising based on the initial test results. The girl just so happens to have relatives in Avondale and later tells them the news.

The next day, your firm's CEO gets a panicked call from the Fulton Solid Waste Authority executive director. A local newspaper reporter called, saying he's heard rumors that the Avondale site is a top contender for the new landfill. The Solid Waste Authority executive director does not want to talk to the reporter since testing is still ongoing.

Later that day the leak is traced back to the young assistant account executive.

What is the ethical situation or conflict? What can be done about the situation?

ROCKIN' PUBLIC RELATIONS

Your public relations firm specializes in fashion and brand repositioning. One of your clients is a mall-based chain of retail stores specializing in apparel and accessories influenced by rock music. Its band and concert T-shirts are a major source of revenue for the company. The public relations firm has worked with this fashion company for six years and has produced good results.

In recent months, the public relations firm has lost two other medium-sized clients. As a result, billings are down and the firm is eager to gain new contracts.

One day, a T-shirt company that sells its product though a Web site contacts the firm's CEO. It sells irreverent topical T-shirts, as well as a large number of rock music T-shirts. The CEO asks you to develop a proposal for this new client.

When you research the prospective client's Web site, you notice that one of the client's T-shirts (among many) carries controversial band lyrics that had purportedly inspired some teens to attack Muslims. Other T-shirts were demeaning to women: "Who needs brains when you have these?"

What is the ethical situation or conflict? What should you do?

City Utility or Cash Cow?
Top Agency Accused of Overbilling City

When the Los Angeles Department of Water and Power (LADWP) board requested an 18 percent water rate increase over two years for infrastructure repairs, federally mandated quality improvements, and security measures, it raised concerns. Still, more than a decade had passed since the last rate increase; most water users understood both the need for system repairs and increased post-9/11 protection of public drinking water.

LADWP, the largest municipal utility in the nation, provided its nearly 4 million residential and commercial users electricity and safe drinking water at rates lower than most California communities.[4] Apart from its low rates, LADWP was a success story because it provided the LA city government with much-needed revenue: 7 percent of LADWP's annual estimated electric revenues and 5 percent of its water revenues went to the city's general fund.[5] Also, LADWP required no tax support since its operations were financed by the sale of water and electric services.[6]

With all those facts and figures on its side, no doubt LADWP officials hoped for easy city council approval of the proposed rate hike. But neighborhood council members and some city council members questioned the increase and requested more information.

Three months after LADWP requested an 18 percent rate increase, LA City Comptroller Laura Chick's review of invoices from an outside public relations firm for LADWP-related work sparked concern; payment was denied until more information and clarification of the bills were provided by Fleishman-Hillard.

Two weeks later, April 1, 2004, Chick announced an audit of the city's multi-million dollar contract with Fleishman-Hillard for questionable expenses and the LADWP's oversight of the contract.

According to Chick's office, Fleishman-Hillard had been paid more than $24 million by LADWP from 1999–2004.[7]

The *Los Angeles Times* and the *Daily News of Los Angeles* reported that Fleishman-Hillard officials "could not be reached for comment."[8] The *Los Angeles Times* reporter's 7 p.m. call did not include further attempts to reach Fleishman-Hillard executives by cell phone or other means. Fleishman-Hillard, with an international reputation for crisis management and high ethical standards, was suddenly putting its reputation to the test.

As readers of the *Los Angeles Times* and other local news sources began to learn about the inner workings of LADWP, it became clear that the rate proposal and Fleishman-Hillard contract were in trouble. In a series of news articles, editorials, and columns, the *Los Angeles Times* and other local news media questioned LADWP's dealings with the nationally respected public relations firm Fleishman-Hillard:

• Why was a $3 million annual contract necessary for public relations services provided by Fleishman-Hillard when LADWP was a monopoly? As LA councilman Jack Weiss put it, "I've always wondered why a public utility needs an outside public relations firm to convince people to flick on their light switch and turn on their water faucet."[9]

• Why did LADWP's corporate communications budget increase by $1 million, to $13.3 million in 2003–2004, when it also had its $3 million Fleishman-Hillard contract? According to news accounts, 23 LADWP communication employees were paid from $41,154 to $108,242 a year.[10]

• Wasn't the $425-an-hour fee charged by Fleishman-Hillard's LA office top executive excessive? A January 3, 2003, bill for 2½ hours of "strategic counsel" cost customers $1,062 and never stated who got the strategic counseling; that month alone, nearly

$20,000 was charged by that one executive for strategic counsel.[11] Why was there a $1,275 bill for three hours so that a Fleishman-Hillard executive could attend "a lunch and a traveling exhibit on the DWP"?[12]

• Why, questioned LA city comptroller Chick, was the LADWP paying $50 to $100 for quarter-hour periods in which Fleishman-Hillard employees were just leaving telephone messages or sending e-mails?[13]

• Why was $175,000 paid for a LADWP parade float in the shape of a boombox or $1.2 million spent on a sponsorship pact with the Los Angeles Dodgers?[14]

A week after the city comptroller announced her audit, investigations were launched by the Los Angeles County District Attorney's office and the U.S. Attorney's Office in the Central District of California to determine if Mayor James K. Hahn sought contributions in return for city contracts. (No allegations were raised by investigators that Fleishman-Hillard received any direct benefit as a result of its contributions or other support.)

Expanded scrutiny of LADWP's professional relationship with Fleishman-Hillard revealed that $137,000 in political contributions were made to Mayor Hahn and other city politicians by the firm and its executives. The firm also provided pro bono services to Hahn and held fundraising events for him. The contributions and pro bono work had been reported the previous May by local news organizations.[15]

The *Los Angeles Times* reported July 15, 2004, that Fleishman-Hillard routinely inflated billing to LADWP, according to two former firm employees.[16] Two days later seven former Fleishman-Hillard employees told the *Los Angeles Times* that they "were encouraged or directed to inflate bills" to DWP.[17] One of those former employees was Diana Greenwood, daughter of *Los Angeles* Times editor Noel Greenwood, who worked on the DPW account in 1999.

She told the *Los Angeles Times* that practices like submitting false time sheets were "wrong, unethical and done on a regular basis" at Fleishman-Hillard.[18]

The day the initial allegations by former employees appeared in the *Los Angeles Times,* John Graham, chairman and chief executive officer of Fleishman-Hillard, sent an e-mail to employees stating:[19]

Today, the Los Angeles Times *ran a major article alleging that, over a period of years, some employees in our Los Angeles office intentionally billed a client, the Los Angeles Department of Water and Power, for work that was never performed. The article included allegations of other billing irregularities, as well as claims of preferential treatment given to individuals connected to this client.*

After 38 years at our firm, I cannot tell you how much this situation personally hurts me. In the nearly 60 years that Fleishman-Hillard has been serving thousands of clients, never before have such allegations been leveled against the people at our firm.

There are two things I want you to know. First, we are conducting a detailed review of the process and procedures related to our work on Los Angeles municipal projects. If we confirm any wrongdoing— including anything related to the allegations in the Times—we will take appropriate steps. Second, we are proud of the work our people have done and the results they have produced for the Los Angeles Department of Water and Power.

You have my full assurance that Fleishman-Hillard remains committed to its fundamental values of the exceptional work, quality client service, and the highest standards of ethics and integrity. . . .

Los Angeles City Attorney Rocky Delgadillo filed a lawsuit July 16, 2004, against Fleishman-Hillard for alleged overbilling based on his office's investigation and the *Los Angeles Times* report. In a news release announcing the lawsuit, Delgadillo said, "This is a case of outright fraud. The ratepayers of this city were ripped off— intentionally and maliciously."[20] The lawsuit claimed "Fleishman-Hillard knowingly and consistently falsified invoices for inflated hours and claimed to provide work that was not performed."

Fleishman-Hillard's own investigation was conducted by independent attorneys and its results were turned over to public investigating authorities. The agency also fully cooperated with the public investigation.

Graham sent another internal e-mail July 16, 2004, to Fleishman-Hillard employees:[21]

Recent allegations about past events in our Los Angeles office are very disturbing because, if they are true, then a small group of people has violated what we stand for as an agency and put our most valuable asset—our reputation—at risk.

We are investigating and we will discover what happened. If we confirm any wrongdoing, we will share that information with the appropriate authorities and take the necessary corrective actions, up to and including termination.

We have expanded the scope of our internal review to ensure it includes all aspects of the recent allegations in the Los Angeles Times and we have added dedicated and independent legal experts to conduct that review. The legal investigators will share their findings promptly with appropriate authorities.

Also, today we are placing Doug Dowie on administrative leave of absence. We believe that is best for Doug and the firm.

I deeply regret any pain this has caused you and the uncertainty it has raised for our clients. I promise you that we will take every necessary step to resolve these issues as soon as possible. Please distribute this to your staff as appropriate, and contact me if you have questions or concerns.

Meanwhile, Richard Kline, a Los Angeles Fleishman-Hillard executive, told the *Los Angeles Times* July 17, 2004, that "the firm has not concluded on the basis of published reports that Dowie did anything wrong. We are intensifying our investigation. We absolutely have not reached any conclusion."[22]

The same news article quoted portions of the July 16, 2004, internal memo to senior managers from Graham.

Fleishman-Hillard announced publicly three days later on April 20, 2004, it would not renew its contracts with LADWP or harbor departments and would terminate its contract with the airport department.[23] The firm also named Kline as the office's new general manager.

A public statement issued by Fleishman-Hillard's Kline explained the company's actions:[24]

We are in the business of client service. Unfortunately, our representation of the Department of Water and Power has become part of a larger public debate that has diverted attention from the department's important work to the provider of its communication services. That does not serve our client's best interests. Ideally, public attention would be on the department's work, rather than on the provider of its communications services. As a result, we believe the best course for DWP and our firm is to end the relationship.

Although our representation of the Port and the Airport is not *being debated today, we want to take this voluntary step so it does not become an issue for our clients.*

We believe we have accomplished much and performed properly in our work for these agencies.

Our work for the LADWP began by helping it prepare for energy deregulation. Today, the challenges are more numerous, including encouraging the wise use of scarce water supplies, environmental threats, state and federal legislation that could have detrimental impacts on the LADWP and the city, as well as the issues of diversity and economic development.

For the Port, our work has included helping promote initiatives to clean the air, including the AMP program to allow ships to use cleaner shore-side power. Although we have a contract with the airport, we have not done any work there for some time.

We value the opportunities we had with these agencies to help them achieve their communications goals. We will work with each of them, as needed, to ensure an orderly transition.

Los Angeles Times writer David Stratified noted that Fleishman-Hillard had made an amateur's mistake of "becoming the story."[25] He raised the question of how a top public relations firm could not see the signs of trouble when nearly a year before the alleged overbilling scandal broke, the media had begun to explore the relationship between Fleishman-Hillard and Mayor Hahn, focusing on political contributions.

An internal memo from Graham to Fleishman-Hillard employees July 29, 2004, outlined new steps the firm would implement to prevent future ethical problems. Graham said:[26]

> For nearly six decades, one of the cornerstones of our corporate philosophy has been our commitment to the highest ethical standards. That is why the recent allegations of billing irregularities in our Los Angeles office are so disturbing; they run counter to everything that this agency has stood for in 58 years. . . . Once all the facts are known, we will move swiftly to address any shortcomings. In addition, if the results of our investigation uncover any improper billings, we will reimburse clients.

The actions outlined in the memo included:[27]

> *Office Meetings*—I have directed each of our regional presidents to work with their general managers to conduct staff meetings over the next two weeks, to reinforce the firm's commitment to operating with the highest standards of client service, integrity, and business conduct and to reinforce that we would never accept or condone any misrepresentation of client billing. In addition, I will schedule conference calls with each of our U.S. offices and our partner companies, and I will meet with our California staff in person.
>
> *Ongoing Time Certification*—As you know, we recently began a new time entry and billing certification process. With each time entry on a client account, every staff member now must certify that they have reviewed and understand the firm's time entry policy, and that the time being entered is an accurate account of time worked. Further, each manager who is responsible for

approving invoices will sign a statement certifying that they understand the firm's billing policy, and that all time being charged to a client is accurate.

> *Public Service Sector Training*—To address the increasingly sophisticated compliance requirements of our public service accounts, all employees working on local or state government contracts will complete the same training process the firm uses for employees working on federal contracts. This enhanced training, conducted by our experienced contract managers working in Washington, D.C., and by outside experts as needed, will ensure that every team member working on a public service client is fully aware of the key operating provisions and expectations of relevant client contracts.
>
> *Client Reassurance*—Our nearly 100 Client Relationship Managers (CRMs), along with our regional presidents and general managers, are in ongoing communication with our clients around the globe. In discussing this matter, our CRMs and regional leaders have the authority to take any necessary steps to ensure that our clients have absolute confidence in our billing practices. In addition, going forward, we will conduct regular audits of our work performed on behalf of any regulated or public service sector clients.
>
> *Enhanced Ethics Program*—I understand and appreciate that we are an organization of highly ethical individuals. However, when our ethics are called into question, even in just one isolated area, it is appropriate to take steps to ensure we have the benefit of the best and freshest thinking. Therefore, we

have engaged a respected, independent ethics expert to assess the ethical commitment of the firm. This individual, who is on the faculty of a major U.S. university and is an active ethics leader in the United States and Europe, has finished the first phase of his review and will work with a subcommittee of the firm to put in place a curriculum of "case-based" ethics training for all staff. This approach will complement our operating policies and allow everyone to even further engage in living this core value. By year's end, every FH employee will be introduced to this approach to ethics training.

Hotline—*Within the next 10 days, we will announce a hotline giving every employee and anyone associated with our firm, from clients to suppliers, the ability to anonymously report any questionable or unethical behavior 24-hours a day, seven days a week. Every call to the hotline will result in a notification to me; Agnes Gioconda, our Chief Talent Officer; and the appropriate regional president.*

New Approach to Political Contributions—*We have revised our policies on political contributions to eliminate all contributions of corporate funds to candidates or ballot issues. In addition, we now require a three-part approval process at the local, regional, and corporate levels for any solicitation of political contributions from employees on FH premises, or on FH time, or using our name.*

Exit Interviews—*We are revamping our existing process. Going forward, talent development liaisons in St. Louis will conduct all exit interviews, which will be*

reviewed by our Chief Talent Officer, and the appropriate regional president.

Client Satisfaction Survey—*As always, we will thoroughly examine the results of this fall's annual client satisfaction survey and conduct follow-through one-on-one discussions with our clients on all matters such as account billing, administration of their business, and the results we generate. . . .*

Graham sent an e-mail to all Fleishman-Hillard employees worldwide on Aug. 9, 2004, explaining the new ethics hotline. He noted: "Let me emphasize that incidents of questionable or unethical behavior reported on the hotline—anything you feel runs contradictory to our core values or is a potential violation of the law or our operating policies—will be taken very seriously."[28]

Graham assured employees the hotline would protect the identity of the caller, that senior management would be engaged, and that there would be an investigation "to address any shortcomings we identify."

Throughout the controversy, Richard Kline, Fleishman-Hillard's regional president and LA general manager, participated in hundreds of interviews with the news and trade media, including a Q&A with *PR Week* and an opinion piece for the *Los Angeles Daily News.*

The Public Relations Society of America responded to the controversy by e-mailing a professional standards advisory to its membership. The advisory reminded its nearly 20,000 members that it is wrong to claim "compensation or credit for work that was never performed." Such practice is "unethical and weakens the public's trust in the public relations profession" and may be illegal.[29]

In announcing the city comptroller's audit results in November 2004, Chick said, "What my audit finds are millions of dollars of bills that boggle the mind and defy common sense. Fleishman-Hillard treated the ratepayers of Los Angeles like a cash cow, milking them for millions."[30]

The following year, Fleishman-Hillard agreed to a $5.7 million settlement of a civil suit with Los Angeles on April 19, 2005. The settlement included a $4.5 million cash payment and the forgiveness of approximately $1.2 million in outstanding bills.[31]

The announcement was accompanied by a Fleishman-Hillard news release that carried statements from Kline, Fleishman-Hillard's Los Angeles general manager and regional president:[32]

We sincerely apologize to the citizens of Los Angeles and to City officials. Other than these recent problems in our Los Angeles office, we have never had an issue of this type in the almost 60-year history of our firm. We take full responsibility for any billing issues, and we have taken steps to ensure the integrity of our billing process.

We have a strong and entirely new management team in Los Angeles, and we have moved forward with numerous new policies and procedures to highlight the importance of adhering to the highest ethical standards. With the proposed payment under this civil settlement, we believe we have taken a significant step in setting this matter right.

We have offered this substantial payment for several reasons. First out of basic respect for the citizens of Los Angeles, because we failed to meet our standards or those of the City with regard to this billing; second, because we know the ongoing costs of litigation in this matter would be significant; and finally, because resolving this dispute will help us focus on restoring our repu-

tation in Los Angeles and serving our clients.

According to City Attorney Delgadillo's news release announcing the nearly $6 million settlement: "A review of the evidence by a forensic accounting team in support of the City Attorney's litigation efforts found the city stood a high likelihood of recovering $850,000 if the case went to trial." Delgadillo said in the release, "Those who attempt to defraud the city will find that my office will continue to be a watchdog, unafraid to take on those who seek to cheat our residents—no matter how well-connected."[33]

POSTSCRIPT

The 18 percent water rate request was reduced to 11 percent and passed.[34] The acting head of LADWP, Frank Salas, was demoted to his former post as LADWP's chief administrative officer.[35] Los Angeles Mayor James Hahn banned all city agencies from contracting with public relations firms.[36] The *Los Angeles Times* reported that the nine-campus Los Angeles Community College District decided to review its invoices from a $395,000 annual contract with Fleishman-Hillard. The college's review turned up no irregularities; Fleishman-Hillard did not submit a proposal to renew its contract with the college.[37]

The *Los Angeles Times* reported August 31, 2004, that Los Angeles city comptroller Chick denied payment to Lee Andrews Group, a consulting firm, for June and July invoices totaling $74,000 for the LADWP because the invoices did not provide enough information. Chick requested that Lee Andrews Group resubmit its bills "in a format that specifies the services, products or deliverables that were provided." The article went on to explain the problem: "The rejected invoices include 23 hours of work billed by company President Donna Andrews at $218 per hour in May for 'strategic planning' and 'administration.' Other workers at the firm billed for the same services at rates ranging from $56 to $200 per hour. And the invoices included $45,000 for 'planning and coordination of business breakfasts.'"[38]

Two former Los Angeles Fleishman-Hillard executives, which included Fleishman-Hillard's former Los Angeles general manager Doug Dowie, were convicted May 16, 2006, by a federal court jury on conspiracy and wire fraud charges for their involvement in overbilling the LADWP; the two executives were also terminated by Fleishman-Hillard. A third former executive pled guilty to three counts of wire fraud.[39]

Mayor Hahn lost reelection in May 2005 to Antonio Villaraigosa, the city's first elected Latino mayor.[40] The new mayor a few months later appointed a new five-member Board of Commissioners for the LADWP.[41]

BACKGROUND ON THE LADWP CORPORATE COMMUNICATIONS

According to its Web site and news media reports, the LADWP employed 8,450 people with an annual budget of $3.27 billion in 2003–2004. LADWP is financed by sales of water and electrical services. No tax support is received. It is the largest power and water utility in the United States with 7,226 miles of pipe and 58,882 fire hydrants. Its total electrical generating capacity is 7,050 megawatts.

LADWP has an internal corporate communication staff of 23, including a media relations team that responds to media inquiries (arranging interview and media tours), and disseminates information about the LADWP through news releases, media advisories, fact sheets, and news conferences. It also keeps the news media informed during emergencies, such as power outages and water main breaks. In addition to the media team, there are photographers, graphic artists, and Web content editors.

Beyond media relations, the corporate communication staff work on educational materials for water and power conservation efforts, power safety, water quality issues, water supply and infrastructure issues, power supply, power content, power loads,

historical information, employee relations materials, and business and consumer materials.

Questions for Discussion

1. Why does a public utility and monopoly need private public relations services—or even internal public relations staff?

2. What could the Los Angeles Department of Water and Power have done to prevent this overbilling situation? What policies or procedures would you recommend for the utility's corporate communication office?

3. Do you think that Fleishman-Hillard responded appropriately to this crisis? What were its response options?

4. Examine the ethical guidelines implemented by Fleishman-Hillard during the crisis. Do you think the response was adequate, or would other actions or guidelines have been helpful?

5. What are the implications of this case for the public relations field?

Do Some Research

1. Examine the bills submitted by Fleishman-Hillard to the LADWP (examples are available on this textbook's resources Web site). What is your impression of the tasks and amounts in the billing? Do they seem reasonable? Why or why not? Describe other billing options beyond hourly billing.

2. Research the Los Angeles Department of Water and Power and Fleishman-Hillard's Web sites. Write a request for proposal (RFP) based on what you perceive are the public relations needs for the department. Your proposal should include background facts or a situation analysis about the LADWP.

3. Debate the following statements:

   Jack O'Dwyer wrote an editorial in his public relations industry newsletter on July 21, 2004, criticizing the pressure firms are under from their parent companies to maximize the number of billable hours to clients. He wrote, "F-H execs have got to 'make their numbers' or face severe consequences."

PR Week editor Julia Hood weighed in on the subject in an Aug. 2, 2004, editorial:[42] "Common in all discussions about the Fleishman-Hillard controversy is the question of whether agencies have been—particularly during the tough times—more focused on performance than on ethics and accountability. The question of the efficacy of hourly billing has emerged, as it does periodically—it's a tricky question to resolve. Junior staff members, in particular, need clear guidelines about what constitutes an accurate timesheet.

"Holding companies (Fleishman-Hillard is owned by Omnicom) can be accused of exerting unfair pressure, a charge Kline also dismisses. 'All of us have obligations to our companies who pay us every month to be credible financial fiscal managers,' he says. 'We have that obligation whether we are public or private. And it's all too easy for someone in a subsidiary company to fall back on the excuse that corporate or parent demanded or commanded, when in fact it is simply our fiduciary duty.'"

4. Below are Fleishman-Hillard's guiding principles for handling a crisis. Based on what you know about this case study and what you already know about crisis management, how well did the company follow its own principles for a crisis situation?

Make a realistic assessment of the situation—assemble all the facts. What is the ultimate goal for the company? How is the company perceived by employees, customers, donors, government officials, and the news media? Moreover, crises typically are fast-moving, complex, always-changing, and tough. Establishing and validating the facts on which public relations decisions are made can require extraordinary time and resources—a problem that is frequently unanticipated and usually underestimated.

Understand that the company must communicate. Silence is not an option. Choosing to sit on the communications sidelines, given this environment, is not an option. It is more important to use key messages consistently and persistently. Keeping lines of communication open between the company and employees and customers is especially important.

Organize for a crisis. Quickly identify extra resources that may be needed to deal with extraordinary events. Current staffing may not be enough. Assemble a team comprising operations, legal, sales and marketing, human resources, and PR. Centralize the flow of information through this team, and shorten lines of approval so the team can communicate quickly. Reduce the possibility of a crisis distracting the company from its ongoing business and clients by adding staff or other resources.

Take a realistic position with the media. Always be honest. Understand how to meet the media's information needs within their deadlines, but do so in a way that accurately portrays your situation. There are limits to the depth with which journalists can cover complex issues, one of them being time.

Don't overreact. Understand and remember the company's core values, especially if they are codified in some manner. (Example, the FH Philosophy posted on our Web site). Avoid getting dragged into irrelevant arguments. Exercise restraint and patience. It's as important to know when to be silent as when to speak. Seeking counsel from many sources inside and outside the company to get the best thinking is critical.

Terminology
- comptroller
- public utility
- forensic audit
- pro bono services

Web Resources
- **Public Relations Society of America** www.prsa.org (under "About PRSA" and click on Code of Ethics)

- **Fleishman-Hillard** www.fleishman.com
- **Los Angeles Department of Water and Power** www.ladwp.com/ladwp/homepage.jsp
- **City of Los Angeles Office of the Controller** www.lacity.org/ctr/
- **City of Los Angeles Office of the City Attorney** www.ci.la.ca.us/atty/

"In Washington, I'm Karen Ryan Reporting."
When Is a "Reporter" Not a Reporter?

Can one word make a difference?

When combined with election year politics and journalistic ethics, the answer is yes!

The ethical debate, some of it over the word *reporting,* began with a front-page story in the *New York Times.*[43] This article detailed a federal investigation by the General Accounting Office into new Medicare materials issued by the Health and Human Services Department.

Some of the informational materials were packaged as a video news release (VNR), the video equivalent of a print news release, and explained the benefits of a new Medicare drug benefit. Some versions of the VNRs, according to the *New York Times,* showed video clips of President George Bush receiving a standing ovation at a December 2003 bill-signing ceremony.[44] The Medicare legislation had been hotly debated in Congress; opponents of the administration plan said the $400 billion program (which later was revised to $534 billion)[45] was too costly

and didn't provide better benefits for recipients.

Produced by Home Front Communications, a Washington, D.C., video production company, two of the Medicare VNRs ended with a woman's voice saying, "I'm Karen Ryan reporting." A Spanish-language version of the VNR featured a man who identified himself as a reporter named Alberto Garcia interviewing a Bush administration official.[46]

VNRs are broadcast-quality story packages that can be used in their entirety or partially in local television broadcasts. In addition to the complete "story," most VNRs include additional video ("B-roll" video) and suggested scripts, so that local TV news staff can construct their own video report.

One VNR script suggested this introduction:[47]

In December, President Bush signed into law the first-ever prescription drug benefit for people with

Medicare. Since then, there have been a lot of questions about how the law will help older Americans and people with disabilities. Reporter Karen Ryan helps sort through the details.

The 90-second prepackaged VNR script follows:[48]

Voice-over: When President Bush signed the Medicare Prescription Drug Improvement and Modernization Act into law last month, millions of people who are covered by Medicare began asking how it will help them.

Tommy Thompson (Secretary DHHS): This is going to be the same Medicare system only with new benefits, more choices, more opportunities for enhanced benefits.

Voice-over: Most of the attention has focused on the new prescription drug benefit that takes effect in 2006. In the meantime, Medicare will offer some immediate help through a discount card. There will be more than one to choose from.

Leslie Norwalk (DHHS Acting Deputy Administrator): In June of this year, seniors will have access to a drug discount card that Medicare endorses, giving them discounts on their prescription drugs.

Voice-over: And some lower-income seniors get additional help: a $600 credit. Starting in 2005, the law provides new preventive services, such as a physical exam for all beneficiaries within the first six months of enrollment in Medicare.

Leslie Norwalk: This preventative benefit, along with others, including

cholesterol screening, diabetes screening, and heart disease screening, should help seniors stay healthy and have a better quality of life.

Voice-over: Medicare officials emphasize that no one will be forced to sign up for any of the new benefits.

Tommy Thompson: It's completely voluntary. Seniors will be able to partake in the new Medicare system or the old Medicare system.

Voice-over: Officials urged people to call 1-800-MEDICARE for more information about the new law.

Voice-over: In Washington, I'm Karen Ryan reporting.

Ryan was not a news reporter, although she had been a television journalist at one point in her career.[49] She was a public relations consultant and the operator of Karen Ryan Group Communications. For the Medicare VNRs, she had been hired to read the Medicare script provided by Home Front Communications, a company subcontracted for the project by the public relations firm Ketchum.[50] Production cost for the VNRs was $43,000.[51]

Critics said that the use of the word *reporting* or *reporter* in the VNRs was misleading because viewers had no way of knowing that the report they were seeing was paid for by its subject—the federal government—and was not the work of an objective journalist.

Three days after the *New York Times* article, the American Society of Newspaper Editors, the largest organization of supervising newspaper editors, joined several other journalism groups in protesting the use of people posing as journalists by sending a letter to Tommy Thompson, secretary of the Department of Health and Human Services (HHS). The society's president, Peter Bhatia, wrote, "It is fair, of course, for the government to communicate with citizens via press releases on video as well as print. It is not ethical or appropriate, however, to employ people to pose as journalists, either on or off camera."[52]

In addition to ethical considerations, critics pointed to legal concerns. Use of federal money for "publicity or propaganda purposes" without congressional authorization, the *New York Times* pointed out, is illegal according to the Government Accountability Office. The article detailed the scope of the publicity campaign: "$12.6 million for advertising this winter; $18.5 million to publicize drug discount cards this spring, about $18.5 million this summer, $30 million for a year of beneficiary education starting this fall, and $44 million starting in the fall of 2005."[53]

The Medicare VNRs were part of the HHS's $12.6 million educational campaign funds to promote the drug benefit program.[54] Bill Pierce, a spokesperson for HHS, said 40 stations in 33 markets had aired all or part of the video news release. Defending the distribution to the media, he said, "That's their choice. They know who sent it to them. They know this came from somebody with a viewpoint."[55]

Ryan, stung by critics who called her an "actor," "hooker," and "phony," agreed with Pierce. The VNRs were clearly labeled as coming from HHS. Ryan responded:[56]

> It's not about playing a reporter; I never pretended to do that. In just about every VNR a voice-over will say, "I'm so-and-so reporting." You're not telling a newsroom this is the way the story goes. You're telling them this is what a cut spot looks and sounds like with your information. Some of the coverage made it sound like HHS had a casting call and I was the best actor for the job.

HHS and Ryan said the ultimate responsibility for the use of the video belonged to the local television stations. The VNRs "were clearly marked as originating from the government."[57]

Ryan noted that deceiving the news media runs contrary to good media relations; it's a cooperative and respectful relationship built on trust. "PR people and news people have worked together for quite awhile," she said. "It's not a deceitful, terrible relationship. A TV producer would never know to cover certain things if a PR person never called."[58]

Kevin Foley, president of KEF Media Associates in Atlanta, said, "The media are the filter here and they have to pass judgment on what airs. They are not unwitting victims. If we can provide quality news content, why wouldn't they consider airing it?"[59]

The symbiotic relationship that exists between journalists and public relations professionals is often viewed as a necessary evil by journalists, who may need assistance with background information, interviews with employees, or access to facilities. Journalists may not have the resources of expertise, time, or personnel to cover stories without the help of public relations. Because public relations practitioners are advocates for their organization, their efforts are often viewed with a healthy dose of caution.

Public relations practitioners have always provided journalists with "information subsidies," usually in the form of print news releases, but also increasingly in VNR formats. As long as the information coming from the organization is clearly labeled for the journalists, it should be treated equally. Public Relations Society of America president Judith Turner Phair testified at a Senate Committee hearing on prepackaged news stories:[60]

> Just as "print" news releases follow the style of print journalism, VNRs utilize a format that is most adaptable to electronic media. Both print and video news releases present

information in a way that is preferred by these respective media and that meets public information needs and interests.

But we also believe that VNRs should be produced and disseminated with the highest levels of transparency, candor, and honesty. To provide open communication that fosters informed decision, we must do more than simply funnel information through the media to the public. We must reveal the sponsors for causes and interests represented and disclose all financial interests related to the VNR.

Another criticism of the Medicare VNRs concerned their dissemination. The VNRs were distributed through CNN Newsource, a service that allows television stations to download news footage produced by CNN or other affiliates as well as video news releases. Some news managers misread the label or thought the package was an actual news report. A month after the controversy began, CNN Newsource changed how it transmitted video news releases. The producer of the VNR is identified, the footage is labeled as a VNR, and it is transmitted separately from real-journalist-produced news footage under its own heading. News stations can also bar news releases from being sent or just receive B-roll footage of VNRs.[61]

POSTSCRIPT
What the General Accounting Office Said

A 16-page decision issued May 19, 2004, by federal investigators of the General Accounting Office found the Health and Human Services Medicare VNRs crossed the legal line and violated the government's publicity and propaganda prohibition because the packages were not attributed to the Center for Medicare Services (CMS).[62] Even though the stations received VNRs clearly labeled

as such, viewers did not know they were watching material packaged by the federal government—not journalists:[63]

Nothing in the story packages permit the viewer to know that Karen Ryan and Alberto Garcia were paid with federal funds through a contractor to report the message in the story package. The entire story package was developed with appropriated funds but appears to be an independent news story. The failure to identify HHS or CMS as the source within the story package is not remedied by the fact that the other materials in the VNR package identify HHS and CMS as the source of the materials or that the content of the story package did not attempt to attribute the agency's position to an individual outside the agency.

A second GAO opinion issued in January 2005 found similar problems with video news releases disseminated by the Office of National Drug Control Policy as part of its National Youth Anti-drug Media Campaign.

In congressional testimony, a GAO representative noted that federal agencies "have a right to inform the public about their activities and to defend the administration's point of view on policy matters," but there are statutory limitations on an agency's information dissemination.[64] In particular, the publicity and propaganda prohibition enacted in 1951 states: "No part of any appropriation contained in this or any other Act shall be used for publicity or propaganda purposes within the United Stated not heretofore authorized by Congress."[65]

Under this regulation, GAO has identified several specific activities as illegal: "One of the main targets of this prohibition is agency-produced material that is covert as to source. Our opinions have emphasized that the critical element of covert propaganda is concealment of the government's role in producing the materials."[66]

A subsequent investigation of seven federal departments by the GAO in 2005 found that during 2003, 2004, and the first two quarters of 2005, $1.6 billion in contracts was spent with public relations firms, advertising agencies, media organizations, and individual members of the media.[67]

What the U.S. Department of Justice Said

The U.S. Department of Justice disagreed with the GAO's opinion. A separate July 30, 2004, opinion issued by the General Counsel Office of Health and Human Services stated:[68]

> But we believe a line must be drawn to distinguish legitimate governmental information from improper governmental advocacy. The VNRs at issue here did not advocate a particular policy or position of HHS and CMS, but rather provide accurate (even if not comprehensive) information about the benefits provided under a recent Act of Congress: The MMA. Informing the public of the facts about a federal program is not the type of evil with which Congress was concerned in enacting the "publicity or propaganda" riders.

What the Federal Communication Commission Said

The Federal Communication Commission issued a public notice April 13, 2005, reminding all broadcast stations and cable systems of their legal obligations to "clearly disclose" to listeners and viewers "the nature, source, and sponsorship of the material they are viewing," especially when dealing with political material or controversial issues.[69] The sponsorship identification rules are part of the Communications Act of 1934. Violations could result in fines up to $10,000, license revocation, or imprisonment of up to a year.

What Other Investigations Said

A 2005 report by minority leaders in Congress entitled "Federal Public Relations Spending" noted:[70]

- In 2004, the Bush administration spent over $88 million on contracts with public relations agencies.

- The value of federal contracts with public relations agencies has increased significantly over the last four years. In 2000, the last year of the Clinton administration, the federal government spent $39 million on contracts with major public relations agencies. By 2004, the value of these public relations contracts had grown by almost $50 million, an increase of 128 percent.

- The center for Medicare and Medicaid Services spent over $94 million on contracts with public relations agencies over the last four years, the most of any federal agency.

Questions for Discussion

1. Using the Public Relations Society of America's Code of Conduct as your guide, what values and code provisions could you point to that involve this case?

2. What are the elements of a video news release? What is "B-roll"? Do video news releases present both sides of a story?

3. What steps could Health and Human Services have taken to prevent this controversy?

4. If printed news releases are accepted by the journalism world, why are video news releases different? How could a reader tell if a newspaper published a news release without changing its contents or identifying the source?

5. Is it acceptable for the federal government to spend millions of dollars informing taxpayers of a new program?

Do Some Research

1. Examine the U.S. Department of Justice and the U.S. Government Accountability Office legal opinions located on the textbook's Web site or at the www.usdoj.gov/olc and www.gao.gov sites. In writing, explain the rationale for each position and what evidence each group uses.

2. Examine the Radio-Television News Directors Association's guide and guidelines on the use of video news releases available from its Web site (http://www.rtnda.org/foi/compvnr.shtml). Do you think these guidelines will prevent future VNR problems?

3. Read the Center for Media and Democracy's report entitled "Fake TV News: Widespread and Undisclosed" at http://www.prwatch.org/fakenews/execsummary. Be ready to discuss the conclusions of this report in class.

Class Activities

1. Split the class into two groups to debate the U.S. Department of Justice and the U.S. Government Accountability Office legal opinions and other news media resources that take a pro-con stand on disclosure and informational versus propaganda issues.

2. Informational or propaganda? You decide. Read the Medicare script and discuss in class what parts, if any, might be considered propaganda.

Terminology

- propaganda
- publicity
- video news release (VNR)
- VNR package
- B-roll footage
- slates

Web Resources

- **U.S. Department of Justice** www.usdoj.gov/olc
- **U.S. Government Accountability Office** www.gao.gov
- **U.S. Federal Communications Commission** www.fcc.gov
- **Radio-Television News Directors Association** www.rtnda.org
- **Public Relations Society of America** www.prsa.org

Armstrong Williams
Disclosure Guidelines Snag Media Pundit and PR Firm

During the explosion in media over the past two decades, audiences have been subjected to an increasing amount of "infotainment": Many network, cable, radio, print, and online news outlets have tried to attract and keep an audience—at least in part—by blurring the line between news and entertainment.

With countless news and information programs fed by the 24/7 news cycle offering more choices for consumers, content providers have turned to a widening array of journalists, former government officials, public relations practitioners, and other pundits. Many of these commentators have programs that offer a mix of news and opinion.

One such commentator is Armstrong Williams. His work connections placed him with the country's power elite. He was a former aide to the late U.S. Senator Strom Thurmond and Clarence Thomas (now a Supreme Court justice), then chairman of the U.S. Equal Employment Opportunity Commission.[71] Williams worked in public relations as a vice president for governmental and international affairs with B&C Associates before starting the Graham Williams Group in 1990.[72]

Williams built a multimedia career as a conservative radio, cable television, and newspaper commentator. He hosted the radio and television show *The Right Side*,[73] and in 2004 he was host of a monthly prime time cable television special called *On Point with Armstrong Williams*.[74] He wrote a book entitled *Beyond Blame* and a nationally syndicated newspaper column. Williams's analysis of issues had been seen and heard on CNN, CNBC, and National Public Radio, among others.[75] In short, he had become one of the country's most prominent conservative African-American commentators. Another lesser known activity of Williams's was his Capitol Hill public relations firm, Graham Williams Group.

On January 7, 2005, a front-page *USA Today* article began a process that turned Williams from commentator into a subject of comment—and criticism. Williams was under contract to the U.S. Department of Education (DE) for $240,000 to promote the federal education reform program called No Child Left Behind (NCLB) Act.[76] Soon after the story broke, Williams's syndicated column carried by Tribune Media Services (TMS) was terminated when it was reported that he had written about NCLB at least four times during the time he was under contract with the DE.[77] Williams said he had disclosed the NCLB advertising campaign on his television show but not to other audiences.[78]

Fueled by a polarized political environment, the initial story led to others prompting a wide-ranging and much publicized discussion of the ethical issues involved.

The No Child Left Behind program, initiated by President George W. Bush and approved by Congress during his first term, required states to design accountability plans that ensured academic proficiency for every child. In May 2003, the DE contracted with Ketchum, a well-known public relations firm, to develop No Child Left Behind communication strategies.[79] In December 2003, the DE issued a work request under the contract aimed at reaching the African-American community.

In particular, DE was interested in using Williams's *The Right Side,* a cable TV and radio show, to reach viewers and listeners in such major markets as Washington, D.C., Los Angeles, Chicago, Dallas, Houston, and Philadelphia. As described in this excerpt from the Ketchum contract, Williams and his programs were particularly appealing and potentially effective messengers:[80]

Whereas others just report the news, "The Right Side" goes one step further, providing compelling insights into the political and social issues that Americans care about most, with a strong emphasis placed on moral striving and rededication to the family . . . "The Right Side" affords the opportunity to communicate with one of the most unique and diverse audiences in the industry: 30% American black, 21% Latino, 40% white.

At DE's request, Ketchum hired Williams to produce and place advertising. Specifically, the Ketchum contract required Williams to interview Secretary of Education Rod Paige for TV and radio spots that aired during Williams's show. The contract also stipulated that Williams would "regularly comment on NCLB during the course of his broadcasts"[81] and invite Paige along with other department officials to appear from "time to time as studio guests to discuss NCLB and other important education reform matters" on Williams's 'The Right Side.'"[82]

The contract also directed Williams to use "his long working relationship with *America's Black Forum*, where he appears as a guest commentator, to encourage the producers to periodically address the No Child Left Behind Act (Black Forum, according to Williams, had 67 million viewers; its reach included 87 percent of the urban market.)."[83] *America's Black Forum*, a news and public affairs show hosted by a group of respected black broadcast journalists, was seen on 112 television stations across the country, according to its Web site.[84]

The day the *USA Today* story broke, six Democratic members of Congress asked the Government Accountability Office (GAO) "to launch an investigation into the use of covert propaganda by the *entire* federal government." They were joined by Citizens for Responsibility and Ethics in Washington, a legal advocacy group, which "filed a series of Freedom of Information Act (FOIA) requests with 23 government

agencies, including all cabinet agencies" requesting copies of all contracts with public relations firms.[85]

The GAO has defined *propaganda* as that which self-aggrandizes a government agency, is used for "purely partisan purposes," or is "covert propaganda." *Covert propaganda* is defined as a government agency concealing its role in sponsoring the material. The salient question to help determine if information is "covert propaganda" is, Was the target audience misled or could they ascertain the information source?[86]

Williams admitted that advocating for No Child Left Behind in his syndicated column, even though he publicly supported the legislation prior to his contract with Ketchum, was a conflict of interest and should have been disclosed. In a letter posted on his Web site two days after the initial news reports, he said he had "exercised bad judgment in running paid advertising for an issue that I frequently write about in my column. People need to know that my column is uncorrupted by any outside influences. I would like to take this opportunity to apologize for my bad judgment."[87]

In a statement released January 13, 2005, DE Secretary Rod Paige said, "The funds for the Graham Williams Group's services went exclusively toward the production and airtime of advertisements in which I described the law and encouraged viewers and listeners to call the department's toll-free information line. Those funds covered those costs alone and nothing more."[88]

Rep. George Miller of California, the ranking minority leader on the House Committee on Education, responded the same day:[89]

The Bush Administration paid a journalist to covertly promote its agenda and it got caught. The deal was illegal and unethical. But Secretary Paige and President Bush cannot even bring themselves to admit they were wrong, apologize

*to the taxpayers, and pledge that
no such efforts will be conducted
again. The secretary's statement
today further indicates the Administration fails to appreciate the seriousness of this issue.*

Ketchum CEO Raymond Kotcher responded to the controversy in an op-ed column
entitled "Williams Scandal Is a 'Transformational Event in PR,'" published in the
January 13, 2005, issue of *PR Week.*
Kotcher said Williams should have
disclosed his relationship with the Department of Education, "particularly because
with government contracts (i.e., taxpayer-
funded initiatives), the public has a right
to know about the relationship that
spokespeople may have to the issues or
government agency they represent."[90]
Kotcher also said the firm was reviewing
all its federal contracts and that an outside review would examine Ketchum's
operating procedures for "recommendations to improve transparency as it relates
to government contracts."[91]

In the same issue of *PR Week,* a front-
page article on the Armstrong situation
started this way: "Ketchum bore no responsibility for disclosing columnist and pundit
Armstrong Williams's status as a paid advocate for the Department of Education (DoE),
said Lorraine Thelian, senior partner in
charge of North American operations for
the Omnicom agency [Ketchum's corporate
parent]."[92] The same article noted that
Williams told *PR Week,* "I made the decision. No one can blame Ketchum for my
lapse in ethical judgment." Additionally, a
sidebar story discussed the ethical dimensions of the case, using the Public Relations
Society of America and the Council of PR
Firms' codes of ethics. President Tom Martin
from the Arthur W. Page Society, described
the heart of the ethical debate this way:
"We can be passionate advocates for a particular position . . . but we have to make
clear the source of that advocacy."[93]

PR Week's Editor-in-Chief Julia Hood,
writing in an editorial in the same issue,
said, "[Williams's] selection as a legitimate
and credible spokesperson should have been
fully vetted as a function of Ketchum's relationship with the DoE . . . Ketchum has a
responsibility to its clients to make sure that
sub-contractors are playing by the rules."[94]

Three days later on January 19, 2005,
Ketchum CEO Kotcher released a new
statement to the media, which included
the following information:[95]

*Ketchum is committed to adhering
to industry guidelines and to high
ethical standards in every aspect of
its business practices. Ketchum has
its own Code of Business Ethics,
which includes a commitment to
present our clients' products, services, or positions truthfully and
accurately. Every new Ketchum colleague is asked to sign this code
upon joining the firm.*

*In working with the Department
of Education to create advertising
for its No Child Left Behind Act,
Ketchum contracted with the Graham Williams Group. Long before
he entered a contract with us, Mr.
Armstrong Williams, principal of
this advertising/public relations
agency and also a commentator,
was an advocate for the No Child
Left Behind program, which he
strongly supported during a number of television appearances.*

*We should have recognized the
potential issues in working with a
communications firm operated
by a commentator. Mr. Williams
repeatedly has acknowledged that
he should have disclosed the
nature of his relationship with the
Department of Education. We
agree. As a result this work did not
comply with the guidelines of our
agency and our industry. Under*

those guidelines, it is clear that we should have encouraged greater disclosure. There was a lapse of judgment in this situation. We regret that this has occurred.

We are taking this matter very seriously and have the following steps underway to make sure that we always meet the existing guidelines of both the agency and the industry.

We are putting in place a new policy for the signing and authorization of contracts with spokespeople.

In agency-wide communications, we have underscored our guidelines about how our people should represent our client work to the media. We have established a central number for our people to call if they have any questions.

We are developing a new process by which we deal with subcontracts. In short, all subcontractors will be expected to abide by the agency's ethical standards.

Over the past ten days we have worked with external legal counsel to investigate the facts associated with our contract with the Department and the Graham Williams Group.

While our review of the situation is still underway, we wanted to let you know where it stands at the moment and reiterate that we would never encourage this type of behavior. We certainly are not pleased by this turn of events and are committed to working with the government and our industry in addressing this situation.

Ketchum has been in existence for more than 80 years. We are proud of our heritage and more importantly we are proud of our values. We have always acted with

the highest integrity and are committed to ensuring our colleagues understand and abide by the guidelines under which we operate.

On April 4, 2005, a Q&A appeared in *PR Week* with Ketchum CEO Ray Kotcher. Kotcher noted, "While we had no legal obligations to ensure Mr. Williams disclosed on his show his financial relationship with the Department of Education, under the guidelines of our agency and our industry, it is clear that we should have encouraged him to do so. It has been determined that it was an unintentional error and certainly not typical of our standard practices. We regret this occurred and will continue to work with the government and our industry in addressing the situation."[96]

He also discussed the tailoring of the agency's policies in light of the new media environment:[97]

Historically, our policies have been designed to ensure that all Ketchum colleagues adhere to the highest standards and practices while providing outstanding service to our clients. Those policies always have emphasized truth, accuracy and respect. And we always strive to improve.

After revisiting our practices, specifically those relating to spokespeople and third parties, we modified some to ensure they provide crystal clear guidelines within which our colleagues can make decisions in their everyday work.

We revised the standard contract we used with subcontractors on government work. We also revised the contracts guiding the work with spokespeople and media tours. All of these contracts clearly spell out the disclosure responsibilities of all parties involved.

We also are introducing two new training courses for all colleagues in North America. The first educates on the new contracts and disclosure policies. The second is a workshop that instructs how to put the agency's new policies, procedures, and contracts into practice on an everyday basis.

Finally, we will be launching a specialized training program for those employees who handle public-sector accounts.

Four months after the controversy erupted, the Office of Inspector General for the DE issued a report of its investigation on April 15, 2005, that was critical of DE's management of the NCLB communication effort, particularly in regard to its handling of Graham Williams Group (GWG):[98]

While the Department did not explicitly violate any significant laws or regulations relevant to the formation of the Ketchum contract or Graham Williams Group work requests, they did make a series of bad management decisions, including the failure to share critical information with decision makers, and exercised poor judgment and oversight. As a result, the Department paid for work that most likely did not reach its intended audience and paid for deliverables that were never received. The ads that were received appear to be of poor quality, and the Department has no assurance the ads received the airtime for which it paid. The documentation we reviewed appears to indicate payment was attributed solely to the production of ads and airtime. However, because other activities relating to commentary were included in the Statement of Works and activity reports, and because the invoices

received and paid by the Department were vague, the appearance is that the Department may have been paying for more than just the advertising.

The inspector general's report found serious lapses of judgment and lack of management oversight on the part of DE in the selection of Williams's agency as a subcontractor. The report noted that DE did not "gain assurance that the GWG offered the best value to the government prior to directing Ketchum to use the GWG for the minority outreach campaign." The report also acknowledged, "one purpose of the overall Ketchum contract was to obtain '. . . expert advice on the development of multimedia communications plans that shall ensure [Department] materials and messages reach their intended audiences.' By directing Ketchum to utilize a particular subcontractor, the Department lost the opportunity to obtain 'expert advice' on how to best conduct this campaign."

The report went on to state:[99]

In the absence of an effective screening process, neither the Department nor Ketchum identified indicators that the demographic makeup of the GWG audience was not consistent with the audience targeted by the Department. The television ad produced and aired under this program indicates it seeks to convey information to economically disadvantaged parents. The ad states: "Parents in economically disadvantaged school districts can get information about how well their school district is performing, about their teachers' qualifications, and about whether their school is safe."

For example, GWG's proposal submitted to Ketchum included the following information:[100]

Studies by Paul Kagan Associates based on our affiliate shares and programming, reveal that Right Side Production's primary audience consists of sophisticated and affluent people who surround themselves with the finer things in life. Quality automotives, packaged goods, luxury travel and fine clothing and accessories are among the products that are advertised in this sophisticated program. Right Side Production's audience represents a market of uncompromising taste and spending power.

Beyond spending money that didn't reach the right demographic, another problem cited by the inspector general's report was that GWG's proposal indicated it could provide or attempt "to arrange favorable NCLB commentary through various media outlets."

A GWG proposal stated in part:[101]

GWG can help win the battle for media space by drawing upon our long-standing relationships with The Russ Par radio show, Stevie Wonder's KJLH (CA), and Sinclair broadcasting (which owns 63 network affiliates) and America's Black Forum (which has been carried by network affiliates for over 25 years), to promote the [NCLB]. We will utilize that platform to further educate the public on the benefits of this important reform. These favorable commentaries will amount to passive endorsements from the media outlets that carry them—media outlets that speak most directly and potentially to the African American and broader community.

Oversight of GWG's work was also cited as a problem. The inspector general's report noted: "There was no methodology in place

to validate that the GWG aired ads as reported in activity reports. Neither the Department nor Ketchum had a process to spot check that any of the ads were run as claimed by GWG. Representatives from both noted they were not spot checking the ads."[102] Ketchum's offer to pay for an independent third party to verify the airtime was turned down by the DE due to lack of funds. Neither the DE nor Ketchum was aware that Williams stopped airing his radio show in May 2004 even though radio ads were part of the contract at that time.

Another management issue, measurement of the overall effectiveness of GWG's work, was not completed. The inspector general's report stated: "There was no methodology to measure the effectiveness of the work performed by GWG. There was no measurement system to determine if the ads were effective in meeting the goals and target audience of the minority outreach campaign."[103] The only measurement of success cited by DE was increased hits to the NCLB Web site.[104]

A subsequent study by the U.S. Government Accountability Office concluded:

The Department of Education violated the fiscal year 2004 publicity or propaganda prohibition by contracting with Ketchum for the services of GWG to obtain commentary by Armstrong Williams on the NCLB Act without requiring Ketchum to ensure that Mr. Williams disclosed to his audiences the Department's role. The commentary obtained as a result of these contracts violated the publicity or propaganda prohibition because it was "covert," in that it did not disclose to the targeted audiences that it was sponsored by the Department and was paid for using appropriated funds.

OPEN SCENARIO
You are the Ketchum account executive assigned to the No Child Left Behind

educational campaign for the U.S. Department of Education. The contract was awarded to Ketchum after a competitive proposal process involving four other agencies. Today you received a call from the department of public affairs at the DE asking that you attend a meeting to discuss a minority outreach program relating to NCLB. During the meeting, the director of public affairs tells you that DE Secretary Rod Paige would like to use the services of radio and television talk show host and commentator Armstrong Williams through his public relations firm Graham Williams Group.

You are only familiar with Armstrong Williams by name and not much else. Usually, the agency would conduct its own research and then recommend a subcontractor based on the agency that could provide the best service for the lowest price. But this situation was different since it came from the senior administrator of the Department of Education, and it was, after all, the client's choice.

When you get back to your office, you decide to take the following steps to ensure effective management of the subcontract with GWG.

Questions for Discussion

1. What Public Relations Society of America values and ethics code provisions does this case address?
2. Why was Armstrong Williams criticized for not disclosing his contract with Ketchum and the Department of Education?
3. What is the difference between a commentator (TV host or syndicated newspaper columnist) and a journalist?
4. Explain the issue of "blurring the lines" of traditional media reporting with the influence of converged media technologies (cable, Web, satellite) and infotainment.
5. Is it ever OK for a journalist to also be a paid spokesperson?

6. Define propaganda. Are there any propaganda issues in this case?
7. Why is this an important case for the public relations industry?
8. Why was Armstrong Williams sought out for the No Child Left Behind minority outreach? What are some other strategies to reach minorities about NCLB issues?
9. What is your opinion of Secretary Rod Paige's response to the Armstrong Williams controversy?
10. How does the political environment fuel situations such as the one described here?

Do Some Research

1. Research the issue of disclosure by expert commentators and professional spokespersons of payments or financial interests. What are the recommended practice standards?
2. Examine the news release, issued April 15, 2005, by Citizens for Responsibility and Ethics in Washington (CREW), entitled "CREW Statement on the Inspector General's Report on the Department of Education Contract with Ketchum Public Relations" (at www.citizensforethics.org/press/news release.php?view=48). What are the main concerns raised by this organization?

Terminology
- commentator
- journalist
- subcontractor
- No Child Left Behind
- statement of work
- propaganda

Web Resources
- **Ketchum** www.ketchum.com
- **Public Relations Society of America** Member Code of Ethics: www.prsa.org

- **U.S. Department of Education Office of Inspector General** "Review of Formation Issues Regarding the Department of Education's Fiscal Year 2003 Contract with Ketchum, Inc., for Media Relations Services," April 2005: www.ed.gov/about/offices/list/oig/aireports.html
- **"Department of Education—Contract to Obtain Services of Armstrong Williams,"** file: B-305368 United States Government Accountability Office, September 30, 2005, accessed May 31, 2006: www.gao.gov/decisions/appro/305368.pdf
- **Citizens for Responsibility and Ethics in Washington (CREW)** www.citizensforethics.org

Letter from Kirkuk . . .
Make That 500 Letters!

A well-written letter to the editor appeared in the op-ed section of the weekly New Mexico *Mountain View Telegraph* around the time of the second anniversary of 9/11, approximately 18 months after the invasion of Iraq.[105]

The letter was from a soldier named Jason Marshall, a community resident currently serving in an Army airborne infantry regiment station in Iraq. He described the regiment's successful attack of enemy insurgents in the oil-rich Iraqi city of Kirkuk, the subsequent occupation of the city, and the regiment's successful efforts to rebuild the strategic Iraqi city. The letter noted the positive reactions of Kirkuk citizens:

> *The majority of the city has welcomed our presence with open arms. After nearly five months here, the people still come running from their homes, in the 110-degree heat, waving to us as our troops drive by on daily patrols of the city. Children smile and run up to shake hands, in their broken English shouting "Thank you, mister."*

The soldier's letter noted that the regiment had rebuilt the police force into an ethically "fair representation of the community," its fire department had been improved, new water treatment and sewage plants were being constructed and oil and gas distribution was improving. The letter also said that a newly elected government and court system were beginning to operate under democratic principles. In short, "the quality of life and security for the citizens has been largely restored and we are a large part of why that has happened."

Three days later a nearly identical letter appeared in the *Boston Globe's* letters to the editor section from a different soldier—Pfc. Adam C. Connell.[106] Soon, the same letter began appearing in newspapers across the country, each time signed by or attributed to a different soldier.

At that time, Americans had begun seeing signs that the war effort was bogging down. Private First Class Marshall's and Connell's letters were just the thing for hometown readers who wanted the inside story about what was going on in Iraq. Who better to tell the story than Private First Class Marshall or Connell?

They were soldiers in a unit called "The Rock," from the 2nd Battalion of the 503rd Airborne Infantry Regiment. Unfortunately, neither Marshall nor Connell wrote a letter, and Marshall didn't even sign his.[107] Yet their letters and hundreds of other identical letters were sent to soldiers' hometown newspapers explaining the positive rebuilding efforts underway in Kirkuk.

At the time, the Bush administration had requested an additional $87 billion to cover U.S. military operations in Iraq and Afghanistan. Opinion polls in September 2003 revealed rapidly declining support for the war effort. A *USA Today*/CNN/ Gallup Poll revealed only 50 percent of Americans felt the situation in Iraq was worth going to war over, down from 73 percent in April.[108]

A month later, *USA Today* published an article entitled "Newspapers Print Same Letter Signed by Different Soldiers."[109] The Gannett News Service (GNS) had found that 11 newspapers had printed the same letter that was signed by different soldiers from the same regiment that Marshall belonged to. Soldiers contacted by GNS either through their families or directly said they did not write the letter but "agreed with the letter's thrust."

Some commentators called the form letter "Astroturf," a fake grassroots effort, to build public support for the war effort.[110]

The letter's origin was traced to the battalion commander Lt. Col. Dominic Caraccilo, who said he wanted to publicize the soldiers' work and "share the pride with people back home."[111] Caraccilo was in charge of the 503rd Airborne Infantry Regiment, a paratroop unit with 800 soldiers. According to the *USA Today* article, Caraccilo said in

an e-mail to the 4th Infantry Division public affairs office:[112]

The letter was purely an effort . . . to afford our soldiers an opportunity to let their respective hometowns know what they are accomplishing here in Kirkuk. As you might expect, they are working at an extremely fast pace, and getting the good news back home is not always easy. We thought it would be a good idea to encapsulate what we as a battalion have accomplished since arriving in Iraq and share the pride with people back home.

Newspaper editors who had been duped were not amused. As one newspaper editorial said: "It creates the illusion of a groundswell of public sentiment where in fact none may exist."[113] Another editorial wondered why the Army did not take advantage of "the biggest R&R program for troops since the Vietnam War" (going on when the controversy occurred) to encourage soldiers to reach out to their hometown media about the positive work being done in Iraq by U.S. soldiers.[114]

Connell's mother told one paper she knew her 20-year-old son had not written the letter, which she sent to her local weekly paper the *Sharon Advocate* as well as the *Boston Globe*. "That didn't bother me. It was still getting a positive point across."[115]

Jason Marshall's mother Keli Marshall told the *Mountain View Telegraph:* "Everything that was in the letter sounded just like what he had been telling us. . . . In various conversations over the summer, he told us these things they were doing, so everything that was in it I'd already heard from his own mouth."[116] She said her son had not written the letter or signed it. "But he said he had read the letter and it was true. The only thing he said that was sort of misrepresented was that the letter made it sound like it was safe there, and it's not—it's a very dangerous place."

Open Scenario Challenge
Getting Positive Hometown Coverage Editors Appreciate

As the new military public affairs officer for the Rock, you are charged with preparing positive material about the battalion's activities that can be submitted to local newspapers. You have access to the Army and Air Force Public Affairs offices' hometown news service (see Web Resources below) to supplement your efforts. Using the sites in Web Resources as background information, develop a strategic communication plan that includes your ideas for generating positive coverage about the regiment's battalion's work in United States news media.

Questions for Discussion

1. What are the ethical problems of this case? Use the PRSA code of conduct to guide your answer.

2. What was the communication purpose of the Kirkuk soldiers' letters?

3. What could the Lt. Col. Dominic Caraccilo have done differently to communicate the soldiers' experiences to newspaper readers back home?

4. If a letter sender agrees completely with the contents of a form letter, why are newspapers still opposed to printing them?

5. Organized letter-writing campaigns have been around for years. Why are news media outlets concerned about them now more than ever?

6. What does the term *Astroturf* mean in relation to this case?

7. Many elected officials, public figures, and CEOs of companies and organizations are asked to submit guest columns for news publications. It is safe to say that many of those are ghostwritten by public relations practitioners. Why do the news outlets accept those?

Do Some Research

1. What are the requirements for a local and national newspaper's letters to the editor and guest columns found on an op-ed page? How can a public relations practitioner take advantage of these communication opportunities?

2. Find an organization on the Internet that provides form letters for supporters to send to their local news outlet. What recommendations or directions, if any, does the organization provide to the letter sender? Do you think the form letter was persuasive? Why?

3. How are news organizations identifying form letters to the editor? The National Conference of Editorial Writers has taken action on this subject. What is it doing?

Terminology

* Astroturf
* form letter
* letter-writing campaign

Web Resources

* **2nd Battalion of the 503rd Airborne Infantry Regiment backgrounder by U.S. military** www.military.com/
* **2nd Battalion of the 503rd Airborne Infantry Regiment backgrounder by Global Security** www.globalsecurity.org/
* **National Conference of Editorial Writers** www.ncew.org/
* **Public Relations Society of America, Member Code of Ethics** www.prsa.org/
* **Army and Air Force Offices of Public Affairs, Hometown News Service** hn.afnews.af.mil/webpages/about.htm

Corporate Social Responsibility
South African Wine Industry Promotes Ethical Practices

More consumers are increasingly aware that their inexpensive products come at a cost to those who produce them. For years, many third-world countries have produced cheap goods for customers in developed nations, but now more end users are demanding proof of better working conditions for those who make such products.

More Brits are drinking South African wines with a clear conscience because of an ethical accreditation program that began in 2002 as an outgrowth of an ethical trading initiative spearheaded by several large grocery chains in Britain. South Africa produces about 10 percent of the imported wine consumed in the United Kingdom and accounts for nearly half of South Africa's wine exports.[117] According to some research, sales would increase if consumers knew both producers and workers in South Africa were treated fairly; many consumers still associate South Africa with apartheid, the brutal policy of racial separation that officially ended in 1994.

According to the Web site of Wines of South Africa, the wine industry's trade association, South Africa ranks ninth in volume production of wine globally, producing 3.1 percent of the world's wine.[118] Some 257,000 people are employed both directly and indirectly in the South African wine industry, including farm laborers and those involved in packaging, retailing, and wine tourism.[119]

The Wine Industry Ethical Trade Association (WIETA) monitors its membership; WIETA members include vineyards and other businesses related to growing grapes for winemaking purposes. In 2003, WIETA Executive Director Nicky Taylor visited Western Cape wine lands to introduce and distribute the association's code of socially responsible and ethical labor practices.

WIETA's mission is to improve working conditions for employees in the wine industry by encouraging fair prices for grapes, decent living wages, the right to bargain, safe working conditions, and the elimination of child labor, discrimination, and excessive work hours.

According to WIETA's Web site, its code includes these specific principles:[120]

- Child labour shall not be utilized
- Employment shall be freely chosen
- The right to a healthy and safe working environment
- The right to freedom of association
- The right to a living wage
- Working hours shall not be excessive
- Harsh or inhumane treatment is prohibited
- Unfair discrimination is prohibited
- Regular employment shall be provided
- Workers' housing and tenure security rights will be respected

"One of the most widespread problems is the paternalist labor relations that exist between vineyard owners and their workers," Taylor said, "often exacerbated by the fact that most winery owners speak English or Afrikaans, but many workers tend to speak Xhosa—meaning communication and relations can be difficult."

WIETA has a long-term aim of empowering workers, to allow them to have a say in their working conditions, said Taylor. It has created informational materials, including a photocomic book, that educate workers of limited reading skills about WIETA's audits and its code.[121]

Membership in WIETA is voluntary and includes cellars, cooperatives, and corporate businesses involved in South African winemaking. Its members must permit regular auditing of their businesses as outlined in the code. Companies audited by WIETA are assessed on their compliance with 105 individual items by means of visual inspection, interviews of a ±10 percent

Courtesy of WIETA

representative sample of workers, interviews with key management staff, and inspection of documents held by the company.

WIETA's social audit that examined "young workers" issues, for example, included these items:[122]

- The TES employer has a photocopy of all its employees' ID book, including seasonal and contract workers.
- There are no children under the age of 15 working on the farm.
- Where work is given to young workers (between the ages of 15 and 18), the employer has:
  - Obtained the consent of the parents concerned.
  - Made inquiries at the young person's school (if any) in order to ensure that it does not interfere with his/her schooling activities.
- Work given to young workers does not involve
  - Work with pesticides or any agro chemicals.
- Work with dangerous cutting or other machinery.
- Young workers work no more than 35 hours per week.
- Young workers are paid at least the current hourly minimum wage prescribed by law (Sectoral Determina-

tion for Agriculture under the BCEA) (current amount R4.87 per hour).

WIETA monitors code compliance with independent social auditors trained by WIETA. Those who meet the code's criteria are accredited, and WIETA accreditation can be used as part of the business's marketing strategy.

The first round of audits held in 2004 at 30 wine-related businesses resulted in four accreditations. While not a large number, it represented significant progress considering that only a decade had passed since the initial introduction of labor legislation for South African farms. The following year, another 12 audits were conducted. By the end of the 2006 accreditation cycle, 20 wine-producing operations had achieved the rigorous accreditation.[123]

Early audits, according to WIETA's Web site, revealed that[124]

many workplaces have been found not to comply with health and safety regulations, often through a lack of understanding of the risks of certain winery practices. In this respect WIETA has served to educate the wineries and limit the dangers that workers are exposed to.

As in most wine producing regions, many workers in South African vineyards are temporary, and labor brokers who contract this seasonal labor force have been found to commit the most rights infringements by not always paying a decent wage or formally contracting their workers. WIETA is working to ensure that labor rights are respected throughout the supply chain.

"WIETA's greatest achievement has been to make winery owners aware of conditions that can be detrimental to the health, safety and comfort of their workers," Taylor said. She added:

> *Many winery owners did not know that using certain filtration media can cause silicosis and were inadvertently putting their cellar workers at risk. Now that WIETA has educated them on the problem, preventative measures can be taken. Housing for temporary cellar workers has also been improved and since the WIETA inspections, members have taken steps to rectify problems experienced by seasonal workers engaged through employment services, as many of the latter are not complying with their legal obligations. WIETA is considering carrying out further inspections during season time to ensure that standards are being maintained throughout the year.*

To provide more recognition for accredited members, WIETA is negotiating with the Fairtrade Labelling Organization, which certifies international free trade standards for companies worldwide, to accept WIETA accreditation as compliance with generic fair trade standards. A Fairtrade certification logo means the product has met stringent standards of socially responsible production and trade practices. Meanwhile, the two organizations are collaborating on auditing activities where the producer concerned is both a member of WIETA and a Fairtrade Labelling Organization (FLO) certified producer.

A marketing communication program in collaboration with Wines of South Africa (WOSA), a marketing body for South African wines abroad, is helping WIETA gain increased media attention.

Open Scenario Challenge

You are the public relations coordinator for WIETA. You are asked to develop a strategic marketing communication plan to educate the American market about this social responsibility program, which includes consumers and retailers. Your research and planning steps would involve . . .

Role Play Activity

You are the newly appointed public relations manager for a small but growing technology company. You are convinced that a corporate social responsibility program would benefit the company reputation in the long run and you personally think it's the right thing to do. You have an opportunity to explain the concept of CSR to the vice president of communication during a lunch. You begin by saying . . .

Questions for Discussion

1. What are the ethical issues that motivated the creation of the Wine Industry Ethical Trade Association?

2. What are the elements of a social audit? The Wine Industry Ethical Trade Association's Web site has a downloadable report that contains their social audit items (http://www.wieta.org.za/auditing.html) What aspects of the audit would resonate most with American and European consumers?

3. How is this type of accreditation good for business?

4. What are some of the social and environmental issues that Americans are interested in?

5. Full disclosure efforts, especially when it entails airing a company's "dirty laundry," can be viewed as a risky business practice. What would you say as a public relations person about discussing your company's mistakes publicly?

6. If you were the public relations manager for the Wine Industry Ethical Trade Association, how would you promote the organization's goals to the news media? How would you increase awareness of WIETA among consumers?

7. What is corporate citizenship or corporate social responsibility? How do cause-related marketing or corporate

philanthropy fit in with corporate social responsibility? What role do these concepts play in corporate reputation?

Do Some Research

1. Examine the Web sites of Dole and Chiquita for their corporate practices related to child labor laws and other workers' rights issues. Determine if either corporation has admitted to workers' rights violations and if the site proposes any remedies. What is the benefit to full transparency in corporate actions?

2. Examine Starbucks Coffee Company's corporate social responsibility (CSR) annual report detailing its programs on its Web site. Why do you think Starbucks has such a significant CSR program? What are the pros and cons of its CSR program? Would you have any suggestions to improve its reputation with CSR strategies?

3. Explain how social audits are a form of research. What other types of audits are used by organizations and public relations practitioners?

Terminology

- Apartheid
- Wine Industry Ethical Trade Association (WIETA)
- Fairtrade Labelling Organization
- trade industry group
- corporate social responsibility (CSR)
- paternalist labor relations
- social auditors

- full disclosure
- silicosis

Web Resources

- **Wine and Agricultural Industry Ethical Trade Association (WIETA)** www.wieta.org.za
- **Preparing for the WIETA Audit, Principal Employers, Wine and Agricultural Industry Ethical Trade Association (WIETA)** www.wieta.org.za/auditing.html
- **Wines of South Africa (WOSA)** www.wosa.co.za
- **Ethical Trade Initiative, South African Trade Project** www.ethicaltrade.org/Z/actvts/exproj/sawine/index.shtml
- **The Center for Corporate Citizenship at Boston College.** (This site contains reports and numerous links to other CRS sites) www.bcccc.net/
- **CSRwire** (CSRwire is a source of corporate social responsibility and sustainability, press releases, reports and information) http://www.csrwire.com/
- **Corporate Watch** www.corpwatch.org/
- **Fairtrade** www.fairtrade.net/index.html
- **South African Wine** www.wine.co.za/News/
- **Grape** www.grape.org.za/wine_links.htm
- **Starbucks** www.starbucks.com
- **Dole** www.dole.com
- **Chiquita** www.chiquita.com

Chapter Five

Media Relations

Media relations is often one of the first tasks a new public relations practitioner is assigned, and it is a high-visibility activity for any public relations professional. The results are viewed by the masses, and that can both raise awareness and help shape public opinion about the organization and its mission.

Media relations is described as the practitioner's *relationship* with the editors and reporters of the mass media that function as communication channels directly to the organization's stakeholders. These placements in the news media are prized for two reasons.

First, these types of news media placements (news stories, features, editorials, etc.) are viewed as more trusted information sources by readers, viewers, and listeners. The audience assumes a trusted and credible journalist has done his or her independent research. The resulting story that may include an organization's name and other positive information about the organization sounds more credible because it has been filtered and deemed newsworthy by a journalist and editor. This outside recognition is called *third-party endorsement.*

Second, unlike advertising, the information placement is free when included in a news story. Depending on the publication's circulation or audience reach, this could produce significant return on investment.

The emphasis on relationship building with journalists is important because the practitioner often works hard to create a positive rapport with the key beat reporters and editors likely to make decisions on editorial content. Editors function as gatekeepers, sifting through hundreds of news releases and calls weekly from organizations eager for media coverage.

Public relations practitioners who understand the challenges faced by journalists today, can package newsworthy material in the accepted news format, are accessible to journalists on deadline, and are professional in their interactions, will likely experience more success in their news media efforts.

To break through the clutter of competing news items, practitioners and news editors have shared many dos and don'ts that will go a long way toward building solid relationships with the media. Following are some key factors to keep in mind.

DO THE RESEARCH

Know the News Outlet

Editors often ignore story requests, or "pitches," because the practitioner is obviously not familiar with the type of editorial content sought by a particular news outlet. Read, watch, or listen to the news outlet to determine if a particular story fits the organization's editorial focus.

Often the news organization's Internet site provides past issues or articles that will serve as a guide for editorial content. Practitioners also use media directories, such as Bacon's and BurrellesLuce, that provide editorial information as well as contact and deadline information and circulation figures. Magazines often have editorial calendars in which these publications seek specific types of editorial material months in advance. Newspapers, television, radio, and Internet news outlets often have many special sections or segments, such as styles, health, or viewpoints that a practitioner can cater its organizational news toward.

A practitioner can also research specific reporters and their specialized areas of interest. If a reporter has written on a particular topic before, he or she may be interested in story pitches that present a new development or unique twist.

RESPECT DEADLINES

Many news operations are working under stressful deadlines often compounded by small staffs. One of the best ways to earn a good reputation with editors and reporters is to respect their deadlines. When a reporter calls, return that call immediately—not in two hours or the next day.

Practitioners should be accessible. Provide an e-mail address as well as office, home, and cell phone numbers to reporters. Many news operations collect news past regular business hours, especially for morning newspapers or evening or late news shows.

If a reporter asks a question and you don't know the answer, tell the reporter that you don't know but will call back with an answer. Always ask how much time you have before a reporter's deadline.

Because news organizations often have companion Internet sites, speed is essential in an increasingly competitive news environment. No longer are local television stations putting together a few daily newscasts. They are posting their stories throughout the day on the Internet and reporting updated versions on newscasts and podcasts, a downloadable digital rebroadcast. The same is true for newspapers and radio news organizations.

A practitioner's respect for deadlines will be appreciated by reporters. Over time, they remember who is a reliable source of information and will turn to that practitioner for future stories.

THINK AND WRITE LIKE A REPORTER

A common refrain of editors is "don't bury the lead." As stated earlier, editors and reporters receive hundreds of news releases and phone calls requesting coverage of events. It's their job to find the most interesting and newsworthy items for their mass audience.

The news release is the standard document that makes the case for news coverage. Unfortunately, many news releases end up in the trash because they do not meet the basic requirements of news or the writer "buried" the most important story element too far down in the text to effectively capture an editor's attention. Editors suggest getting to the point fast, within the first paragraph of the news release. Busy editors and reporters do not have the time to read two pages of background information to find out if your news release has anything important. News organizations are looking for news. While news can be defined in many ways, the following elements are often cited as meeting news criteria: timeliness, prominence, proximity, significance, unusualness, human interest, conflict, and newness.[1]

Timeliness refers to when the event occurred; old news usually does not appeal to news operations. A news item can also be timely if it is relevant to holidays, observances, or other national or international events in the news.

Prominence refers to the type of people involved in the news item. Well-known people, such as celebrities, professional athletes, or elected officials, are often of interest to news audiences.

Proximity refers to where the news is happening. A train wreck, murder, or a new factory opening may be big news in one community but not in another. People generally have a natural curiosity about what's happening in their community. The "news hole," the space not occupied by advertising, is only so big each day, so some newsworthy stories don't make the cut if they occur too far outside the media's audience reach.

Significance can be defined by its impact on people and things, such as the environment or an industry. A story can be judged newsworthy if it affects a significant number of people. Significance also refers to who the affected people are and where they live.

Unusualness is something that turns your head when you see it. Everyday occurrences do not normally make news. It is the unusual, out-of-the-ordinary event that attracts the audience's attention. A new twist on a common occurrence, such as a giant birthday cake in celebration of an organization's 100th anniversary, might attract the media.

Human interest relates to a good story told well about a person or people; it has interesting story elements that hold the audience's attention. The story can be about anything including the first female firefighter in a community or the postal worker who climbed Mount Everest. Usually every organization has interesting human interest stories to tell. Colleges often seek a graduate each spring who has overcome overwhelming obstacles to gain a college education.

Conflict occurs when people or organizations disagree. When these disagreements are made public, they often make news in the form of boycotts, strikes, rallies, and other public demonstrations.

Newness is a common news peg for pitches. Organizations always have new products or services to introduce or a new version of an existing product that is somehow different.

Beyond what makes news, reporters and editors appreciate information that is written in journalistic style. Releases written concisely with no jargon or technical terms stand a better chance of being read. State the newsworthy aspect of the news release early with all the necessary information to cover the event including the who, what, where, when, and why of the story. Suggest organizational leaders or experts who are available to talk to a reporter.

Offer *exclusives.* Sometimes, there will be stories, such as human interest stories, that are not major announcements and could be offered to a single news organization. Or, sometimes, a major story may have many different angles that you can tailor to different news outlets.

BUILD A LASTING RELATIONSHIP

Take the time to know the reporter as a person. Over time, find out something about the reporter. Read the reporter's stories and mention the ones you enjoyed reading. If a reporter does a good job on a story involving your organization, take the time to thank the reporter with a note or e-mail.

If a reporter makes an error, remain calm and ask the reporter how the erroneous information got into the story. If the error is big, ask for a correction. Always think long term. Crucial to building a relationship is trust. Always tell the truth and provide accurate information. Never ask for favors, such as a request for story placement. Offering gifts to reporters, even those of nominal value, can be problematic because journalists must remain neutral and independent in their reporting. Gifts can be interpreted as bribes to garner positive coverage or to minimize negative stories. If the public thought that journalists could be bought, their credibility as an independent news source would be damaged.

Pitching to *Brandweek*
Understand the Medium You Are Pitching To

Brandweek, a national trade newsweekly with offices in New York, Chicago, and Los Angeles, covers brand marketing news and America's top marketing professionals.

Managing Editor Chuck Stogel said, in addition to basic industry news, *Brandweek* seeks reports of new spending on advertising, promotions, and local, national, and global consumer marketing services. The publication is listed in major electronic media directories, such as Bacon's and BurrellesLuce, which explain the type of information the publication is looking for as well as contact information that can include staff names, titles, phone numbers, e-mail addresses, and mailing addresses.

Its media directory profile includes circulation, its circulation auditor, frequency of publication, type of subscription, ownership, coverage, formats (online/print), readership, and language availability.

Brandweek accepts news releases, photographs, and story ideas 11 days prior to publication. It receives numerous e-mailed, faxed, and phoned pitches every week. Media directory listings about *Brandweek* mention ways that news release submissions can be incorporated in *Brandweek's* editorial content: "Uses: Calendar, Industry, Letters, Personnel, Product, B/W Photos; Accepts publicity material."[2]

In addition to what media directories can provide, more detailed information is available on its Web site for free. Its month-by-month editorial calendar alerts content providers that *Brandweek* will include special January coverage in its auto report from the North American International Auto Show, the national Consumer Electronics Association show, a report on the agency of the year, and special reports on sports licensing and the Super Bowl preview. In February, the weekly gives special brand news coverage to the American International Toy Fair, including toy licensing and merchandising issues and consumer magazines' hot list of products. Often, special reports mirror major industry events, such as significant national consumer conferences, that are also reported on its Web site.

Its list for editorial contacts is as thorough as media directories and includes contact name, title, e-mail address, and coverage "beat." Stogel's, for example, is the golf industry as it relates to promotion and branding.

Stogel, with years of experience at *Brandweek*, offers public relations practitioners some advice about pitching effectively to any news media outlet:

- **Get news media experience.** Public relations practitioners who have some news media experience generally understand what news publications want. If possible, work for a news organization to gain experience.
- **The five Ws and H of journalism apply to public relations.** News organizations must have the essential facts: who, what, when, where, why, and how. Don't

issue information without answering those first. "All too often, we will get public relations releases, invitations, or press conference notices that actually leave out the date something is taking place, or the time, or the location," said Stogel. "Or key names, contacts, product prices, and more. This should be there from the first. We shouldn't have to be calling to find out this sort of information. Really. I've had press conference notices that did not have the time, or the location."

- **Again, no missing information; it wastes time.** One particular pet peeve of Stogel's is agency written news releases on behalf of a client that include the agency address but not the client company's address. "Well, from the journalism perspective, we want to know where the company is located," he said. "This often necessitates an e-mail exchange back to the agency to find out where the company client is located." Stogel once received a news release about a new product with no manufacturer suggested retail price included. He had to e-mail the contact to find out.

- **Know your media.** "I find that a lot of e-mailed releases or phone calls from public relations practitioners have no idea what my particular magazine is all about," Stogel said. "If they did know, they wouldn't be contacting us." *Brandweek*, for example, is available to business marketing executives and agency personnel by subscription only. "Our focus is on news-breaking stories about upcoming national consumer marketing initiatives by all the various business product and service industries in the U.S.," he said. "Yet, I get calls and e-mails to tell me about business-to-business initiatives, which we don't cover. To me, it's a waste of time and a nuisance."

- **Seriously, really *know* your media.** "Now, I know there are a lot of 'press release' trade books that just take press releases and run them. We don't. We have a staff of reporters that has built contacts in various industries and works at 'breaking' news before it's published elsewhere." Stogel said that the frequency of misguided news releases and pitches happens at small and large firms alike.

- **Respect an editor's time.** Misguided news releases waste an editor's time and if you do it often enough, he or she won't even look at your pitch. "Somewhere, from a media directory or other source, I am listed, and our magazine, as a business publication," Stogel explained. "And somebody has simply put us on the bulk e-mail list for all releases and such notices, and unfortunately phone calls. Yet, when you get 200 or more e-mails a day, like I do, you want to keep them to as few as necessary."

- **Really *respect* an editor's time.** Practitioners who e-mail editors with a news release or a conference invitation should not follow it up with a phone call to verify the editor received the e-mail. "Sometimes, the call comes even before I've read the e-mail," Stogel said. "In this techno age, with the overwhelming amount of e-mails and phone calls, it is infuriating to get both. Just send the e-mail. If we want more information, we will reply via e-mail or call."

- **Keep your news timely.** "I also get tons of 'after the fact' public relations news releases, to tell me that a company launched a certain product a month ago, or launched an advertising campaign several weeks ago," Stogel said. "It's vexing, but I do my best to explain that if these people knew my magazine, they would know our focus

is on upcoming initiatives before they happen, not after."

Open Scenario Challenge

You are the assistant account executive of a major public relations firm representing a national toy company. The company has developed a new digital media player for the preteen set. Its design includes a well-known cartoon character that's hugely popular with children. It has special safety features to protect children from dangerous decibel levels. You are asked to pitch this product to the appropriate news media. Using a media directory or by researching publications through the Internet, develop a targeted media placement plan that includes five national media outlets that will give your client the best coverage and reach the consumer. Your plan should include:

- Relevant facts about the news outlet
- A rationale for selecting the news media based on the organization's editorial requirements
- A written pitch that you will give to editors either in an e-mail (including subject line) or a brief phone conversation (you can create your own facts about the product).

You should prepare to voice your pitch orally to your supervisor since she often asks to hear it from you first. Also, be ready to explain your media selection.

Questions for Discussion

1. What are the challenges of getting a news release or other organizational information accepted by an editorial gatekeeper?

2. How can a public relations person gain a better understanding of the media he or she wants to pitch to?

3. Why does the managing editor of *Brandweek* recommend that public

relations students work at a news media outlet?

4. How can an editorial calendar help focus a pitch?

5. What else can *Brandweek*'s Web site tell a public relations practitioner?

6. Editors are busy people. What can a public relations practitioner do to respect an editor's time while still conducting an effective pitch?

Do Some Research

1. Research a company that specializes in news media contacts, such as Burrelles-Luce or Bacon's. Their services go well beyond targeting news media outlets appropriate for an organization's news. Explain the importance of their other services such as their media monitoring, management, and analysis services.

2. Examine a company that monitors the Internet, such as CyberAlert. What is the advantage to using this type of monitoring service?

3. Beyond counting press clippings, how can a practitioner evaluate the effectiveness of his or her media relations efforts?

Terminology

- brand marketing
- business-to-business conferences
- contact information
- editorial calendar
- editorial beat
- media directories
- pitching

Web Resources

- ***Brandweek's* home page** Its editorial calendar is under "contact us" at www.*Brandweek*.com

- **Bulldog Reporter** This company's Web site contains free pitching advice from professional journalists in its Journalists Speak Out column at www.bulldogreporter.com/products/reports/

- **Bacon's** Bacon's is one of several companies that provides media placement databases as well as media tracking and monitoring services at www.bacons.com/

- **BurrellesLuce** This is another media placement and tracking/monitoring service similar to Bacon's: www.burrellesluce.com/

Do the Research
An Editor's Response to a Misguided Story Pitch

Back from lunch, Jennifer Pullman noticed an e-mail reply from an editor at a national newspaper she had electronically pitched just before lunch. It was a mass-distributed message to hundreds of news editors that she had inherited from the previous account manager at her firm. The message read:

I suppose this is a form letter mass-emailed to lots of reporters and editors, but it's still insulting and reflects poorly on your firm. We already have a story on this on the front page of our newspaper today, and it's currently headlined prominently on our Web site. We don't need to go to the New York Times *to find out about this.*

Pullman was momentarily stung by the message, but after rereading it, she knew she had blundered. The pitch that this editor was blasting was a follow up to a news release that had been sent out the day before by another employee announcing a major hotel tourism initiative for Florida.

That morning, Pullman's quick Internet scanning of major news coverage had spotted a front-page *New York Times* article sparked by her agency's news release. Thrilled by the top-tier media placement, she decided to attach the *Times* article to her follow-up e-mail pitch; unfortunately, her attempt to share background with all recipients annoyed the editor at the competing national newspaper, which had run the story too.

While the offended newspaper had run the story in its print and online versions, Pullman knew she had to apologize to this editor if she hoped to ever get another story idea considered by him.

She decided to send another e-mail to the annoyed editor. The approach, she decided, would be the one she always followed when a mistake was made: Be honest and seek amends.

Doug,

Thank you for your quick reply. I can only say that your assessment is correct, and I want to offer a sincere apology to you for wasting your valuable time and not doing my job more thoroughly. I inadvertently missed your publication's coverage in my media scan this morning. It won't happen again. Our firm respects your publication and hopes to continue working with you in the future.
Sincerely,

Stephanie Pullman

Account Manager

XYZ Public Relations

Not long after she sent her e-mail, she received another response from the editor. It was short but only a little reassuring:

Apology accepted. If you want to do your job correctly, I'd like to point out one more thing about your pitch that was a problem. You sent it to the wrong person. Our newspaper has an editor that deals specifically with travel and tourism story ideas. More research next time will reduce your mistakes.

Pullman was grateful for the response and the frank exchange. She was determined to learn from her mistakes. A recent college graduate, she was quickly realizing there was more to media relations than just blanketing the news world with news releases and aimless pitches. She had made two major mistakes and decided to make some changes.

Open Scenario Challenge

Identify the two mistakes Pullman made with her e-mail follow-up pitch for the hotel industry in Florida. Determine how Pullman can take a more customized and effective approach to media relations. If your options require additional funding resources, develop a plan to present to your organization's president.

Questions for Discussion

1. What are the challenges of effective story pitching?
2. How would you develop an effective story pitch? What steps would you take?
3. Do you think that apologizing to the editor was appropriate? Why?

Do Some Research

1. The Internet and textbooks offer tips on effective pitching strategies. Make your own list based on your story idea.

2. Contact a local reporter and ask him or her what makes an effective story pitch and what tactics should be avoided.

Class Activities

1. Invite the college media relations person to the class to discuss how he or she pitches story ideas to the local and national media.

2. Invite a local editor or news director to class to discuss effective and ineffective story pitches.

3. Role-play a story pitch scenario over the phone between a news editor and a media relations person. You can use a recent news release from your college's Web site. Discuss as a class what was effective and what could be done differently.

Web Resources

- **BurrellsLuce** http://www.burrellesluce.com/
- **Bacon's** http://www.bacons.com/
- **Cyberalert** http://www.cyberalert.com/
- **Multivision Inc.** http://www.multivisioninc.com/index.php
- **MediaWorks** http://www.mediaworksgroup.com/articles/sound-bite.html and http://www.mediaworksgroup.com/index.html
- **Media Relations Maven** http://www.mediarelationsmaven.com/index.html

Can I Get That in Teal?
Car Colors Critical to Consumer Choice

In the heyday of the Model T, Henry Ford was said to have remarked that auto buyers could have any color car they wanted—as long as it was black. But over the last century, color has become more than a choice: It is now a critical factor in car-buying decisions.

Research shows that consumers consider color when making their buying decisions 91 percent of the time, and consumers will even switch to a different car brand to get the desired color 40 percent of the time, according to a DuPont-sponsored Yankelovich poll.[3]

DuPont Automotive Systems in Troy, Michigan, is the leading manufacturer of car paint worldwide. Its coatings business is part of a nearly $6 billion a year DuPont Automotive business that includes about a hundred products, including a variety of materials for every vehicle system.[4] But a premier product, sold directly to auto manufacturers, is car paint: more than 50 million gallons in nearly 200 colors and shades annually. DuPont Automotive's coatings were featured on 8 of the top 10 selling vehicles in North America in 2005 and are sold to virtually all of the world's major automakers.

To retain its supremacy in this industry, the unit must promote its paint innovations to automotive companies' design engineers who decide which paint will grace their new models.

DuPont Automotive actively promotes the technology involved in creating exciting, durable, low-cost, and environmentally safe paints. For example, an innovation that allows solids in paint to be sprayed as if they were a liquid reduced harmful solvent emissions and resulted in DuPont receiving the U.S. Environmental Protection Agency's Clear Air Excellence Award in 2003.[5] Carmakers are also interested in new coating methods and finish effect choices to boost differentiation yet lower paint application costs.

Other innovations involve the properties of its paint. DuPont Automotive has introduced new pigment combinations, including those that create a hue-shift based on the viewing angle. Auto safety is always a priority, and DuPont's glow-in-the-dark coating is another example of innovation.

DuPont Automotive's marketing communication plan focuses on business-to-business communication, including its annual design show for car designers, and media relations to heighten awareness among its key car manufacturing clients about its quality and innovative products. Terrence Cressy, director of communications and government affairs at DuPont Automotive, said its three-pronged strategy includes positioning the company as the worldwide leader of:

- Top coat paints and protective layers that can command a price premium at retail
- Advanced, environmentally compatible technology in producing durable and exciting colors
- Trend forecasting of customer tastes in color

Cressy said his company tests 100 new color concepts each year for its automotive clients, which include General Motors, Ford, DaimlerChrysler, Honda, and Toyota. The company tries to predict future color trends by monitoring home and clothing fashions and consumer electronics. It also participates in professional design organizations.

"We're basically in the business of color and the technology behind it that will make a finish appealing for the life of the vehicle," Cressy said. Unlike promoting cars themselves, however, attracting attention from the general consumer and news media for a single component of a vehicle—its paint—is, to say the least, a challenge. Located close to the "Motor City," DuPont Automotive has ready access to the automotive bureaus of every major news organization that either has an automotive beat reporter or covers the industry exclusively. While interest abounds for DuPont's latest innovations in industry trade publications, *Good Morning America* is not beating down Cressy's door . . . or is it?

Cressy said DuPont has generated significant consumer media interest by tapping into buyers' interest in car colors. Its annual DuPont Automotive Global Color Popularity Survey reports on yearly consumer color preferences and forecasts the hottest color trends for the next several years. The survey, which began in 1952, is issued right after Thanksgiving, when news is traditionally in a holiday lull and media are looking for year-end wrap-ups and forecasts of coming year trends. Its survey results have been carried in the *New York Times*, *Chicago Sun-Times*, *Toronto Sun*, *Seattle Times*, *USA Today* and on CNN, to name a few. The survey generates about 45 million media impressions annually.

Its 2005 survey, for example, found that silver maintained its six-year supremacy, edging out white, as the most popular vehicle color in the United States. And new grays in complex formulations that show an infusion of a variety of colors are up-and-coming contenders. Silver, according to the survey, is so popular because it conveys opulence and modernity in this age when technology sells.

The survey also found that a younger, more daring new generation of car buyers is not afraid to show its true colors. A growing appetite for more personalized automotive hues is driving the industry. This is evidenced by the presence of bright yellow in the top 10 colors of 2004 and 2005 and by the changing preference for true color in such electronics as cell phones, MP3 players, PDAs, and game boxes.

Open Scenario Challenge

Terrence Cressy, director of communication and government affairs at DuPont Automotive, has asked you to develop a new marketing communication plan that uses the annual DuPont Automotive Global Color Popularity Survey as its media relations motor. He needs a list of the top automotive publications and broadcast outlets that might be interested in using the results. He also wants you to develop a pitch on how to interest these editors in the survey in fresh but relevant ways. He says to keep the pitch to less than one minute.

Because of the trend toward "mass personalization" of color choice, he also wants to try something new: Promote the survey results to youth savvy publications interested in color innovations. He has asked you to develop a media plan that will significantly increase the youth appeal of DuPont's innovations in car coatings.

He also wants new ideas for its major special event to automotive designers—the Momentum Design Show. This event showcases DuPont's latest innovations in a variety of DuPont materials, including coatings for color, form, and function. An opening stunt to capture people's attentions and imaginations is needed.

News releases about DuPont's annual color survey and its design show are available from DuPont's Web site on its automotive section "News and Events."

Questions for Discussion

1. What are the main challenges of DuPont Automotive in gaining news media and mass media attention?

2. What media relations tactics does DuPont Automotive use to attract media attention?

3. What is business-to-business communication? Why is it important to DuPont Automotive?

4. What is trend forecasting? How is that used as a media relations tactic?

5. How does DuPont Automotive use social responsibility as a public relations strategy? What specific tactics does it use for this purpose?

Do Some Research

1. Research additional examples of how an organization's creation or sponsorship of opinion surveys results in positive publicity for the organization.

2. Research how organizations' creation of white papers or research reports results in positive publicity for an organization.

Terminology

- beat reporter
- business-to-business (B2B) communication
- impressions
- news bureau
- trend forecasting

Web sites

- **Dupont's home page** www2.dupont .com/DuPont_Home/en_US/
- **Dupont's Automotive section** www2 .dupont.com/Automotive/en_US/

Break the Silence—Make the Call
Private and Public Communication Strategies for Domestic Violence

The first time Kimberly's high school sweetheart hit her was two weeks before their wedding. She convinced herself that the punch in the arm was due to "wedding stress." Married at 18, she didn't know it marked the beginning of a life of violence that would hurt her for years to come.

For the next nine years, Kimberly's husband convinced her: His violent behavior was her fault. She never told anyone—family, friends, coworkers—when he hit her and threw things. Kimberly never filed a police report or showed her injuries to a doctor. Despite the beatings and death threats, she had a public image to maintain. Kimberly and her husband were active in their church; her husband was an ordained deacon. People looked up to them, Kimberly said, and often told her, "I wish we were like y'all."

At first, her husband's violent behavior happened only when they were alone. But when he began to show increasing signs of irritation with their two children, she made plans to escape. Breaking away wasn't easy; for years he had told her she was useless, stupid, and couldn't do anything on her own. With no significant work experience and no education beyond a high school diploma, Kimberly knew it would be hard. But to protect her children, she packed a few possessions and made the hardest decision of her life: a move to a family violence shelter where she and the children began a new life together.[6]

Despite its troubled start, Kimberly's story had a happy ending. For many women trapped in abusive relationships, the outcome is often grim. The federal government estimates between 1 and 3 million incidents of violence against a current or former spouse, boyfriend, or girlfriend occur each year. On average, husbands or boyfriends in

Break the Silence—Make the Call ad.
(Courtesy of Texas Council on Family Violence)

this country murder more than three women every day; in 2000, intimate partners were responsible for killing 1,247 women.[7]

In Texas, family violence had reached nearly epidemic proportions, according to the Texas Department of Human Services. It estimated there were more than 800,000 victims of family violence annually across the state.[8] In 2003, 153 Texas women were killed by their intimate partners, representing more than 10 percent (2 women per week) of the national rate. More disturbing was that just 5 percent of the victims received assistance from Texas domestic violence programs.[9]

Through a $2.75 million grant from the state Attorney General's Office, the Texas Council on Family Violence (TCFV) developed two public awareness campaigns, There is Help, There is Hope and Family and Friends, to publicize domestic violence programs and services and to provide information to the general public on ways they could assist friends and family living with domestic violence.

RESEARCH

"Domestic violence is often swept under the rug," said Kathy Miller, a former TCFV communications director. Because of its hidden nature, the scope of the problem is often difficult to grasp. Detailed information on domestic violence is often anecdotal, when it exists at all; basic statistics often underreport the problem. For example, police departments in Texas track the number of women killed as a result of domestic violence—but the data do not include women killed by ex-boyfriends. To understand the issues of domestic violence required to build an effective campaign, TCFV conducted extensive research.

Early research efforts included a statewide community audit, to determine critical needs, and 34 survivor focus groups. Both efforts pointed to a need for public awareness. In 2002, Saurage Research, of Houston, Texas, conducted telephone interviews with 1,200 Texans. To ensure understanding of the Hispanic population, the survey oversampled this minority population and used bilingual callers to investigate unique barriers Latino Texans face when they seek to escape domestic violence.

Six minority-only focus groups also were conducted from a total of 34 focus groups. Two focus groups consisted of African American, Anglo, and Hispanic Texans. Members of the six groups were drawn from both rural and urban areas of the state.

The research's key findings were:[10]

- **74 percent said they or someone they know had experienced domestic violence.**

- **31 percent had suffered "severe abuse."**
- **Victims first turned to friends, family, or coworkers.**
- **84 percent believed they could personally make a difference on the issue.**
- **Many never seek help; often friends and family didn't know where to seek help. This was particularly true of Latinas.**

Other important findings were:

- **Victims rarely knew how to leave safely or that abuse was not normal, never deserved.**
- **Victims were often unaware of the impact that abuse had on their children's behavior.**
- **Victims needed answers before they acted.**
- **Leaving an abusive relationship required tremendous courage.**
- **There were crucial cultural differences.**

The research indicated that 31 percent of all Texans reported that they had been severely abused at some point in their lifetime. Severe abuse is defined as physical abuse, sexual abuse, or being threatened by a spouse or dating partner. The study also revealed that more than one in four Texans (26 percent) had been physically abused—hit, pushed, or choked—by their spouse or partner.[11]

The research found several misperceptions contributing to the "barriers that domestic violence survivors face in finding pathways to safety," said Sheryl Cates, TCFV chief executive officer, in a news release announcing the survey's results. Seventy-one percent of survey respondents incorrectly blamed domestic violence survivors for their plight in response to the statement: "Victims who do not leave an abusive relationship share some of the blame for their abuse." The survey found Texans demonstrated "a willingness to blame domestic violence on circumstances beyond an abuser's control, rather than acknowledging the abuser's culpability. More than 86 percent of Texans were willing to blame sudden financial problems or job loss for the abuse; and more than 98 percent were willing to blame alcohol or other forms of substance abuse as the cause of the domestic abuse. While these problems can exacerbate an already abusive relationship, or increase the severity of abuse, they are not the factors responsible for that behavior," according to a TCFV news release.

"More than 96 percent of Texans failed to identify forcing your partner to have sex against their will as an act of domestic violence, and even fewer identified threatening one's partner or family, stalking or intentionally isolating one's partner from friends and family as forms of domestic violence," according to a TCFV news release.

Focus groups with Hispanic victims of domestic violence, similar to the experiences of all victims of domestic violence, revealed four barriers that inhibit them from seeking the help they need:

- *Isolation:* It is a common tactic used by batterers, but for Hispanic victims the feeling of isolation was often intensified by a language barrier, lack of support network, and/or the lack of legal immigration status.
- *Fear and threats:* Most often cited were threats that the abuser would report the victim to immigration services (INS) and that she would then be separated from her children or even lose them. In addition, Hispanic victims cited threats such as being told that no matter where they go, the abuser would find them.
- *Shame:* Family plays a central and important role in Hispanic culture and, traditionally, Hispanic women are taught the value of keeping the family together at all costs. Participants cited intense shame associated with breaking up the family unit as a significant barrier to action. The shame felt by victims was often enhanced by harsh criticism

from friends and families for taking such action. The intense fear of rejection from those people whose opinions they valued most often contributed to the decision not to seek assistance and to remain in an abusive relationship.

- *Lack of awareness:* Often cited by victims was the lack of awareness about available domestic violence services. Other barriers such as fear of being discovered by legal authorities and language or cultural isolation often kept Hispanic victims in the dark about the confidential support services available to them in their communities.[12]

CAMPAIGN STRATEGY

Based on the research, TCFV targeted survivors, their family members, friends and coworkers, community and civic leaders, business community, and the media for its awareness campaign, said Helen Vollmer, president of Vollmer Public Relations. Campaign goals included:

- Achieve 20 percent increase in Texas-based calls to the national family violence hotline during paid media flights.
- Mix paid and public service announcements to ensure a 2-to-1 minimum of free versus paid spots.
- Identify at least 10 grassroots partners.
- Distribute 1 million educational campaign materials.

An integrated, multilingual and culturally relevant campaign was created, said Vollmer, using existing materials, polling and research results, advertising and public service announcements, community events, media relations, business partnerships, and grassroots outreach. Communication materials emphasized the following messages:[13]

- Legitimize victims' situation.
- Recognize they are not alone.

- Recognize abuse is not normal.
- Ensure confidentiality.
- Enable them to call for assistance.
- Reinforce public awareness with "private" awareness.

Print materials featured print ads, outdoor ads, posters and flyers, a four-page brochure, "discreet" hotline cards and envelope inserts, and media kits. A Web site maintained by TCFV also hosted much of the campaign's information.

Break the Silence spokespersons included survivors of family violence, friends and family touched by family violence, and local female television anchors from Belo television and cable and Univision radio and television stations. Other high-profile spokespersons included Texas First Lady Anita Perry, a former intensive care nurse who had seen firsthand the devastation of domestic violence. Texas-based musical artists Shawn Colvin and Sisters Morales were part of the campaign's launch event that reached a younger audience. Doctora Isabel, a well-respected radio psychologist with a large Hispanic following, also joined the campaign by discussing family violence issues on her show.

REACHING THE ISOLATED

Jealous batterers often isolate wives and girlfriends, limiting or preventing contact with family members or friends, TCFV's communication director Kathy Miller said. "Isolation is their number one way to control women." Since victims then often become estranged from the very family and friends most likely to help them, campaign planning included unique private communication strategies to reach women who seldom venture from the watchful gaze of jealous partners. Such strategies would have to overcome monitoring of phone and Internet communication.

One technique TCFV created to meet this challenge was a "discreet" hotline card the size of a normal business card.

The small size allowed women to hide it easily. In one instance, a woman kept the card in her shoe for two years before she finally called, Miller said. More than 4 million of the little cards were distributed to Texans in the first two years of the campaign.

TCFV considered carefully how to distribute the hotline cards and flyers advertising the hotline number so that women would see them while husbands and boyfriends would not. "We thought of any place that a woman might go that her batterer might not," said Miller. Cards and flyers were put in public women's restrooms, and at hairdressers, grocery stores, break rooms, and pediatricians' offices. To reach victims via the Internet, TCFV's Web site alerted users that computers could be monitored; a message on the Web site encouraged them to use a safer computer, such as one located at a library or community center.

Beyond isolation, the shame and the pressure to keep a family together at all costs, especially in Hispanic families, was another obstacle. Vollmer said focus groups with Latinas cited the church as a "determining factor in the decision to break the silence." Focus group participants revealed that "because the Catholic Church is such a strong proponent of the family, when women consulted priests they were often encouraged to stay and try to work things out," said Vollmer.

A second phase of the campaign that ran in 2004 addressed the need for family and friends to speak out and support women in abusive relationships. The campaign's broadcast materials included bilingual radio and television public service announcements spearheaded by BRSG Advertising and CINCO Media Communications. A partnership with the Texas Association of Broadcasters boosted the campaign's statewide airtime through the use of noncommercial sustaining announcements for television spots worth at least three times the normal paid distribution fee.

A 30-second television spot entitled "Awakenings" featured a professionally dressed, attractive Hispanic woman:[14]

> **WOMAN (facing camera):** My husband used to hurt me . . . a lot. But I was silent because I thought I was keeping my family together. Until I saw how it was hurting my son.

The opening shot is followed by video of a young boy crouching in a darkened closet with angry voices in the background. The woman's narration continues:

> **WOMAN:** He was learning to be afraid . . . just like me.

The final scene shows the woman holding her child, both smiling. A female announcer closes the spot:

> **ANNOUNCER:** Break the silence. Make the call. 1-800-799-SAFE. Your call is anonymous.

Vollmer said the decision to depict an upscale Hispanic woman was intentional, to show that domestic violence can happen to anyone regardless of educational level or social status.

Another campaign goal was to overcome the common belief that victims share the blame for the abuse if they don't leave a relationship. Since emotional dependency on the batterer and lack of financial resources and information often deter victims from seeking help, Vollmer said family members, friends and coworkers may need to get involved. A television spot called "Phone Call" encouraged friends to intervene.

The 30-second spot begins with a young white man, pacing in his apartment, looking at a photograph of an attractive young white female.[15]

> **FEMALE ANNOUNCER:** Afraid of getting involved? Imagine how she feels.

The spot continues with the man nervously practicing with his phone as he repeats "Hi . . . Hi . . ." Finally, he makes the call.

> **MAN:** Hi. I've got a friend . . . I think she's being abused.

> **ANNOUNCER:** Break the silence. Make the call. 1-800-799-SAFE. Your call is anonymous.

The TCFV campaign also posted a "Guide for Family and Friends" on its Make the Call Web site. In English and Spanish versions, the guide explains how to recognize the signs of domestic abuse and how to get help.

The official launch of the campaign coincided with Domestic Violence Awareness Month in October.[16] Special events included a candlelight vigil with spokespersons in English and Spanish on the steps of the state capitol building in Austin. Shawn Colvin, a Grammy-winning recording artist, and Sisters Morales, one of whom was a victim of domestic violence, were also on hand to add music and star power for the occasion. The event also featured a powerful visual element to draw attention to the women killed by an intimate partner the prior year. Lining the steps of the state capitol building were 113 life-size wooden figures painted red, each bearing the name and story of a victim. The "Silent Witnesses" exhibit was a visual reminder that two women were killed each week in Texas as a result of domestic violence.

RESULTS

In the first phase of the 16-month bilingual "Break the Silence" campaign, responses to the national domestic violence hotline increased dramatically: 69 percent for English language calls, 93 percent for Spanish calls.[17]

In a post-campaign survey, half of the respondents remembered the advertising tagline "Break the silence. Make the call." Seventy percent of respondents could recall three definitions of domestic violence, compared to 50 percent prior to the campaign.

Seventy-two percent of those who recalled the campaign considered domestic violence a serious problem in the state.

More than 40 "grassroots advocates of understanding," including Texas colleges and universities and many Hispanic organizations, joined with 80 domestic violence shelters in spreading the word about the campaign and distributing materials.[18]

Business partnerships, including corporations such as Verizon Wireless and media outlets, were formed to help distribute campaign materials through payroll stuffers, billing envelopes, and point-of-sale locations. The campaign resulted in the formation of the Texas Business Alliance to End Domestic Violence. "With a network of partners that have multiple avenues to reach millions of employees," said TCFV Chief Executive Officer Cates, "the Alliance will have an unprecedented impact on domestic violence prevention efforts statewide by helping employees become aware of the assistance and services available to help them become safe."

Media partnerships, particularly with the Texas Broadcasting Association, extended the campaign's messages. From an investment of $160,000 the noncommercial-sustained advertising agreement yielded a $1.5 million value. The nonpaid on-air advertising netted an additional $3.9 million value.[19]

Questions for Discussion

1. How did precampaign research guide this campaign?

2. If you had to develop a domestic violence campaign in your state, whom would you choose as campaign spokespeople? Why?

3. What makes the campaign's slogan "Break the silence. Make the call." an effective message? What other slogans might work?

4. What were the strengths of the campaign's private (discreet) communica-

tion strategies? What other private communication strategies might be used?

5. Do you know of someone who has experienced domestic violence? What were the barriers he or she experienced in getting the help needed?

6. What new strategies for grassroots partners could be developed in this campaign? For example, what could your college or university do as a partner?

7. Beyond disseminating campaign materials, what other activities could a business partner be involved in?

8. This campaign used media partners to carry the campaign's messages to a mass public. It also used female anchors. What strategies could you develop for the news anchors?

9. How do nonsustained commercial advertising campaigns work in this case study?

Do Some Research

1. To be effective advocates for an organization, public relations practitioners need to become experts on a situation. Use your college's databases and the Internet to research your state or city's domestic violence situation. What facts and statistics were you able to find? Describe the state and local efforts to raise awareness about domestic violence.

2. Invite a representative from your local domestic violence shelter to your classroom. (Often, shelters' locations are secret to prevent batterers from finding victims, but a phone number is always available.) Discuss with the representative how the shelter promotes its activities and what special events it hosts to raise money. Based on this information and your research about the national and other state domestic violence efforts, devise a new special event that would raise awareness or help raise donations for the shelter.

Terminology
- domestic violence
- oversampling
- focus group
- grassroots campaign
- noncommercial sustaining announcements
- payroll stuffer
- celebrity spokesperson
- outdoor advertising
- private communication
- "discreet" hotline cards

Web Resources
- **Texas Council on Family Violence** www.tcfv.org
- **Break the Silence—Make the Call** www .makethecall.org (contains information for getting help, statistics on abuse, and campaign materials including posters, cards, and Web versions of the television and radio commercials)
- **National Center on Domestic and Sexual Violence** www.ncdsv.org (has many statistical and research resources on domestic and sexual violence)
- **National Coalition Against Domestic Violence** www.ncadv.org (contains information about the problem of domestic violence, public policy and education)
- **Vollmer** www.vollmerpr.com

National Rankings Fever
Enhancing Children's Hospital Boston's Reputation

Eight million children are hospitalized each year in the United States. When serious illness and injury are involved, parents are understandably determined to provide the best available care available—but how can they tell which hospital is the best?

For 13 consecutive years, Children's Hospital Boston was rated the number one hospital specializing in pediatric care in *U.S. News and World Report's* influential annual best hospitals survey. But Children's dropped to number two in 2003, 2004, 2005, and 2006 with Children's Hospital of Philadelphia narrowly taking the top spot.[20] The *U.S. News and World Report* survey, ranking only by reputation, asks board-certified pediatric physicians to list up to five hospitals that "they believe to be the best in their specialty without considering cost or location."[21]

Another nationwide survey of children's hospitals conducted by *Child* magazine similarly ranked Philadelphia and Boston as the top two children's hospitals in the country.[22] This biannual survey, which began in

2001, was based on self-reported information provided by nearly 100 children's hospitals. This survey included questions pertaining to survival rates, staff qualifications, nurse-to-patient ratios, research funding, the number of clinical trials, family services, and services that improve the overall care for children such as availability of playrooms, family resource libraries, and activities to help make children less anxious about their hospital stays.

Just as college rankings help parents make informed choices about higher education, hospital ratings provide patients with information that can guide their medical decisions. Rankings are important for two reasons. From a business perspective, competition drives organizations to provide the highest-quality products and services to maintain or dominate their market share. Quality products and services enhance an organization's reputation, which in turn helps it attract and maintain customers and the most qualified employees.

Children's Hospital Boston, established in 1869, has a tremendous story to tell as a worldwide leader in advancing pediatric care. The hospital has an impressive legacy of firsts and an unrivaled breadth and depth of expertise. It was the first hospital to successfully perform cardiac surgery on a child and the first to successfully treat pediatric leukemia. More recently, it was the first to successfully correct a congenital heart defect in a fetus. It has more pediatric surgeons than any other hospital in the world, many of whom are developing new techniques and employing the latest technology. The MRI Operating Suite was the first of its kind in this country. As the primary pediatric teaching hospital of Harvard Medical School, Children's is home to the world's largest research enterprise based in a pediatric medical center. More than 700 scientists, including eight members of the National Academy of Sciences and nine members of the Institute of Medicine, comprise its research community.

Additionally the hospital has the most sought after training programs in pediatrics, with 1,009 medical school graduates applying for 39 residency positions. Children's is known for training leaders, and estimates are that a third of the chiefs of pediatric departments and services nationally are trained at Children's.

Even though the hospital prides itself on being one of the best, if not *the* best, provider of high-level clinical subspecialty care, the leadership of Children's struggled with how much attention to pay to the rankings, even when the hospital was number one.

"Our own surveys showed that a large portion of parents did rely on these rankings to help inform their choice of which hospital to select," says Michelle Davis, vice president of Marketing and Public Affairs. "However, the techniques used to develop some of the rankings were not considered rigorous by scientific standards."

Despite this skepticism, the hospital leadership came to terms with the need to pursue strategies that increase the likelihood of improving its individual ranking as well as drive volume on a national basis.

More importantly, strategies to communicate and improve the reputation of Children's Hospital Boston among referring physicians on a national basis were consistent with the hospital's marketing strategy of promoting many of its unique higher-end services, such as the Advanced Fetal Care Center, its vascular anomalies program, and short-gut center.

STRATEGY

Ultimately, an organization's reputation is based on deeds, not just words. National survey rankings, while never perfect, have become a part of Children's overall quality improvement plan. In particular, *Child* magazine, whose biannual survey is based on assessing particular pediatric hospital services and statistical information, has provided new strategic areas to explore. For example, making medical appointments online and even the hospital's landscaping were considered.

Children's has been part of other mass media ranking vehicles including the *Boston Business Journal, Boston Magazine,* and *Fortune* magazine's best places to work surveys. A reputational survey conducted by Morrissey & Company, using the opinions of Massachusetts's corporate executives, listed Children's as the best medical institution in the state in 2004.[23]

Children's worked with a brand management and reputation firm, Arnold Worldwide, to help develop its brand strategy. A team of more than 40 people from Arnold Worldwide (account staff, writers, producers, directors, media buyers, and researchers) interviewed patients and staff from all levels of the organization and gathered direct and indirect consumer research. The top distinguishing attributes or characteristics were: "devotion, optimism and innovation." "These became the DNA for any new communication effort we undertook," said Davis.

From a communications perspective, the hospital's media relations team set a goal of doubling Children's media hits in top-tier news media. Over the course of a year, the hospital used a number of initiatives to increase coverage, including a survey of media on their top issues of interest, an audit of media worthy research at the hospital, the hiring of a science writer and an additional high-level publicist, satellite media tours, and the active promotion of experts of topics that were breaking news. Its medical experts were listed on EurekAlert's experts list, an international science-oriented database that is accessible to registered journalists in need of sources or background for their articles or broadcasts. The hospital's more research-oriented news releases' distribution was targeted to specific science media reporters using Bacon's MediaSource, an electronic media directory that constantly updates news media contact information.

Children's, for example, was featured in the *New Yorker* magazine, "The Pediatric Gap." The article included a gripping scene of Dr. James Lock, Children's cardiologist-in-chief, and another obstetrician trying to restore blood circulation to a fetus in a mother's womb.[24] The article's theme was lack of properly tested medications and precision surgical tools needed for operating on tiny fetuses and infants. With a circulation of nearly 900,000 highly educated and influential people, the *New Yorker* showcased Children's already considerable reputation in pediatric cardiac care and its Advanced Fetal Care Center, which was pioneering the research and development of appropriate medications and precision surgical tools for pediatric surgery.

Two Children's researchers, cancer pioneer Dr. Judah Folkman and nutrition expert David Ludwig, have brought international attention to the hospital.

Ludwig, for example, has been widely quoted in the national carbohydrates debate and its potential effects on childhood obesity. His animal studies showed a low glycemic index (low GI) diet—one whose carbohydrates are low in sugar or release sugar slowly—can lead to weight loss, reduced body fat, and reduction in risk factors for diabetes and cardiovascular disease.[25] Ludwig's research has been reported in *Consumer Reports*, the *New York Times*, the *Washington Post, Chicago Sun Times*, the *Times* (London), and *USA Today*, among others.

An Associated Press story that quoted Dr. Ludwig about keeping sweet drinks such as soda—and even juice—out of a child's diet was widely published in newspapers and broadcast on stations across the nation, increasing the profile of Children's as a pioneer in research, on children's nutrition.[26]

Other research, such as identifying reasons why clinicians don't screen teens for substance abuse and genetic studies of autism, along with reports of new medical firsts, including the first multivisceral (quadruple organ) transplant performed on an infant in New England, have kept Children's in the news.

The satellite media tour (SMT) helped Children's ramp up its nationwide broadcast media coverage. These live-interview opportunities offer radio and television stations across the country easy access to expert interviews on a variety of health and medical topics. Children's promoted its neonatal services by using a nurse practitioner from its Advanced Fetal Care Center. This expert was available during the three-hour morning drive time period for interviews from Children's broadcast studio or could be tape-delayed for a later broadcast.

Video of the center recorded earlier ("B-roll," as it's called in television) was also made available to participating news outlets. The value of the SMT is its adaptability and its third-party credibility. Children's experts can tailor their responses and interact with the local news broadcasters. These one-on-one interviews are viewed by audiences as highly credible; the news media like SMTs as well because they provide opportunities for local news anchors to interact with highly regarded national medical and science experts without leaving their studios.

A media audit conducted by Delahaye, a corporate communication consulting organization, compared Children's earned media coverage with its peers and competitors. It revealed positive results in the amount and tone of coverage.

During the past several years, the public relations team has increased the national target. In 2006, the hospital's already strong media relations efforts increased with a special activity. A day-and-a-half long press seminar attended by health reporters from *The Wall Street Journal, People* magazine, National Public Radio, the *Boston Globe*, and other top national media, provided an opportunity to showcase the hospital's impressive research and subspecialties; it resulted in 15 follow-up inquiries for stories—and stronger relations with reporters.

Communication strategies also focused on physicians. The hospital increased its physician messaging at specific events and through its publications. Children's took a more active role in major pediatric meetings, such as the American Academy of Pediatrics and National Association of Children's Hospitals and Related Institutions conferences. A physician newsletter called "Pediatric Views" is aimed at referring physicians in the Northeast; it includes the latest new developments at Children's and suggested guidelines for practice. "Children's Outlook," an electronic newsletter distributed nationally by e-mail, provides news on various pediatric practices.

Webcasting is another communication strategy to reach physicians locally and nationally. Children's, a pioneer in many new pediatric procedures, uses SLP 3D, a company that produces and delivers real-time video of operating and procedure rooms. From an educational perspective, Webcasts are a key strategy to build connections with

physicians nationally and increase referrals. Children's also offers traditional continuing medical education programs regionally for physicians.

A key to reaching consumers efficiently on a national basis is the hospital's Web site which contains more than 6,000 pages of medical content to help primarily family members better understand diseases, medical treatments, and procedures. The marketing team also focused on optimizing search engine visits through a variety of tactics: from making technical adjustments on the site to make sure that search engines could access content, to purchasing advertising on key search engine sites such as Google. These strategies paid off: Web traffic doubled in one year.

Every employee at Children's is considered a "brand ambassador." As such, communication with internal audiences is important. The CEO and COO host regular town hall-style meetings to get feedback from employees. Frequent e-mail communication, a monthly hospital newsletter, "Children's News," and a column on the hospital's intranet address new issues.

Employees and other stakeholders interested in the hospital's activities receive a magazine, *Dream, The Magazine of Possibilities*; and staff physicians receive "Faculty News." All the publications are available in electronic form, e-mail, and on the Children's Web site. The goal is to keep strategic publics—the community, employees, referring physicians, and the news media—constantly updated.

Finally, crucial to any strategy is an effective crisis communication plan. "One day of bad coverage can undo months of positive coverage," said Davis. The hospital communication team is proactive with anticipating and managing issues as they emerge. Should a crisis occur, "Our approach is do what's right; respond responsibly and communicate in a clear and transparent way."

Open Scenario Challenge

You are the media relations manager at Children's Hospital Boston. A researcher affiliated with CHB is just about to publish the findings of a significant new study on a cause of melanoma (see the CHB news release "When Does a Mole Become a Melanoma?" on its Web site, February 7, 2005). Because melanoma has become more common, the director of CHB's research center has e-mailed you asking if this announcement could get national coverage and if it could coincide with the research's publication in four weeks. He would like to discuss your ideas in two days.

Questions for Discussion

1. How do you define the concept of organizational reputation?
2. How do national rankings encourage proactive strategic efforts by organizations such as Children's Hospital Boston?
3. How does organizational reputation connect with an organization's branding efforts?
4. What is the role of public relations in reputation management?
5. Why does reputation matter to Children's Hospital Boston?

Do Some Research

1. Examine the Web sites of Children's Hospital Boston and Children's Hospital of Philadelphia. How does each Web site reinforce the hospital's brand concept? Provide three examples.
2. Look at each hospital's news release archive. Which news releases from the past year increased the reputation of the institution? Provide three examples.

Terminology

- brand
- brand ambassador
- electronic media directories (Bacon's MediaSource, Vocus)
- expert's list (EurekAlert!)
- intranet
- reputation management
- satellite media tour (SMT)

Web Resources

- **Children's Hospital Boston** www.childrenshospital.org/
- **Children's Hospital of Philadelphia** www.chop.edu/consumer/index.jsp
- *Child* **magazine's link to the 10 best ratings articles** http://www.child.com/
- *U.S. News and World Report's* **best hospitals** http://www.usnews.com/usnews/health/best-hospitals/tophosp.htm

Communicating in the Face of Tragedy

Tsunami Media Team Operational Analysis

The day after Christmas 2004, an enormous wall of water crashed onto the beaches of several Southeast Asian countries. The tsunami brought massive death and destruction and prompted a worldwide response from governments, organizations, and individuals. As word of the disaster spread on the day after Christmas, many reporters turned to World Vision's media relations team in pursuit of quotes and interviews from staff in affected countries.

World Vision, one of the largest Christian relief and development organizations in the world, has a sophisticated global communication network.[27] In its fund-raising, or "support," offices, stationed in developed countries, media relations teams build awareness of World Vision's work and protect and strengthen its reputation. In its "field" offices, located in developing countries where World Vision works, communications teams host media and other visitors, as well as gather stories, photographs, and video resources in support of World Vision's awareness-building efforts.[28]

In addition, World Vision staffs two communications specialists on its Global Rapid Response Team. This team is on-call at all times to respond exclusively to global emergencies. The team's communications experts collect marketing resources, work with international journalists reporting on location, and conduct media interviews for outlets in countries where support offices are located; they also maintain internal communication to provide World Vision's global partnership with consistent information on the emergency.[29]

The U.S. media team of four full-time and four part-time staff literally worked around the clock during the early days of the disaster to alert the American public about what World Vision was doing.

A two-person marketing communication team also works with the U.S. media group to promote World Vision's fund-raising efforts such as televised fundraising events and partnerships with corporations, artists, and celebrity spokespersons.[30] Private individual donations make up more than one-third of World Vision's budget, with government grants and corporate in-kind donations comprising the other two-thirds.[31]

For what was clearly an enormous human tragedy, World Vision set a $50 million worldwide fundraising goal for relief and rebuilding.[32] The organization's experience had shown that potential donors are most likely to respond to a crisis in its first days.

The tragedy that claimed so many lives and touched millions around the world was an enormous challenge for the many emergency relief organizations that responded. World Vision met the challenge by meeting the needs of victims and, at the same time, introduced itself to the world by showing how donations were used to rebuild shattered lives.

WEEK ONE

Throughout the first week, the team worked 24-hour shifts. During the graveyard shift, staff pitched night editors at network radio outlets and contacted communications staff based in the affected countries during their business hours. The round-the-clock availability paid off with extensive media coverage. Twenty-nine news wire stories mentioned World Vision in the first 24 hours of the tragedy, including the Associated Press story the day the tsunami struck—"World Vision Mobilizes Earthquake Relief." Also, 49 broadcast shows, including CNN's *Paula Zahn Now*, Fox's *The O'Reilly Factor*, and National Public Radio, carried stories that mentioned World Vision's relief efforts. At the end of the graveyard shift, staff compiled a report of stories and developed new story angles from the field. This report guided the pitching efforts of staff that worked throughout the day contacting media.

During the first week following the emergency, major stories and angles included:

- *December 26, 2004:* Initial notification that World Vision was responding to the emergency and was raising money to support its response ("World Vision Mounts Massive Response: Death Toll Exceeds 10,000 in Asia").[33]

- *December 26, 2004:* Notification of World Vision's response and the deaths of 100 children sponsored through World Vision ("World Vision Launches Response to Tsunami Devastation: In India, 'Wall of Water So Strong Cars Were Thrown Like Toys'").[34]

- *December 27, 2004:* Local staff members depart for the tsunami zone. This provided a local angle for interviews to Seattle-Tacoma media, but the primary purpose of their trip was to collect photo and video resources. The video that resulted from the trip improved many national media pitches and fundraising appeals ("World Vision Staff Head to Asia for Earthquake/Tsunami Response: Federal Way-Based Agency Will Send Communications Team to India").[35]

- *December 27, 2004:* Two days after the tsunami, the fear of disease as a result of communities' inability to dispose of the dead quickly enough became a news topic ("Relief Officials Fear Diseases from Rotting Corpses: Bodies of People, Livestock Litter Asia's shorelines: Mass Graves Replace Traditional Funeral Pyres").[36]

- *December 28, 2004:* The transition occurring within the humanitarian community from scattershot groups working independently to professional agencies coordinating and communicating to develop holistic and effective responses ("From 'Do-gooders' to Better-Organized Relief Professionals: Aid Agencies Have Greatly Improved Coordination Over Two Decades").[37]

- *December 28, 2004:* Stories and quotes from individuals affected by the tsunami (specifically, non-westerners—"Notes from the Disaster Zone: Survivors Ask, 'Why Us?' They Wish They Had Been Swept Away").[38]

- *December 29, 2004:* A list correcting myths many Americans believe about aid work ("Top 10 Myths of Disaster Relief: Aid Groups Address Public Stereotypes about Overseas Disasters").[39]

- *December 30, 2004:* The availability of World Vision's emergency response communications manager for interviews ("Global Relief Efforts 'Just Scratching the Surface': World Vision Emergency Communication Manager Available for Interview").[40]

- *December 30, 2004:* Press briefing in Chicago on World Vision's response ("World Vision Experts to Conduct Chicago Press Briefing: World Vision Reports more than $8 Million from U.S. Donors: World Vision Worldwide has Raised Between $15–20 Million").[41]

- *December 31, 2004:* The setting of an organizational record goal to raise $50 million for the tsunami response ("World Vision Sets $50 Million Goal for South Asia Disaster").[42]

- *December 31, 2004:* Press availability surrounding an airlift of relief supplies from World Vision's Global Positioning Unit (GPU) in Denver. GPUs are warehouses stationed around the world where the organization stocks nonperishable relief supplies so they can be shipped immediately to an emergency site ("World Vision Relief Supplies Leaving Denver for Tsunami Zone: Press Availability Planned for Friday, December 31").[43]

- *December 31, 2004:* Advice to potential donors on choosing reliable, effective, and honest relief agencies for their tsunami-related donations ("Donors Should Insist on Responsible Use of Relief Funds: Generous Response to Tsunami Disaster Presents Opportunities for Aid Agencies").[44]

During the first week, World Vision put considerable effort into making sure the organization was "in the box"—that is, included in every media outlet's list of responding agencies and donor agency information lists. Per its usual emergency protocols, the media team notified InterAction that World Vision was responding. InterAction is an umbrella organization representing the community of nongovernment organizations in the United States. During most emergencies, InterAction compiles a list of responding U.S. agencies, which is commonly picked up by national media.

In addition, team members worked to make sure that correct contact information was listed on www.freedomcorps.gov, the online list of approved agencies promoted by former Presidents George H. W. Bush and Bill Clinton. Finally, World Vision retained contract staff from the public relations firm Greer, Margolis, Mitchell and Burns, which audited individual media to ensure that World Vision was included in the lists of responding agencies.

WEEK TWO

After New Year's, the staff went back to working days only, but maintained daily contact with field staff (usually early in the morning or later in the evening) and remained on-call around the clock.

Late in the first week, and moving into the second week, a growing number of media outlets called team members to inquire about fund-raisers for tsunami victims. Many radio stations, particularly Christian music and talk stations, did on-air auctions or held other broadcast fund-raisers; other groups organized golf tournaments ("Media Alert: Play Golf and Help Tsunami Victims; The Tsunami Disaster Affected Millions of Lives—Upcoming Fundraising Golf Tournaments to Benefit the Tsunami Survivors").[45] In addition, stories about fund-raisers, especially those organized by children, received substantial local and national coverage. In the Seattle area, fund-raisers by Tully's Coffee and local restaurants, as well as children who set up a hot chocolate stand, and others who sold Christmas presents on eBay, were featured prominently. Not surprisingly, the media gave substantial attention to large donations, especially those made by celebrities. Announcements of financial support for World Vision from the Bill and Melinda Gates Foundation, the Paul G. Allen Family Foundation, Nike, Tully's, and Cher resulted in solid local and industry-specific stories.

During the second week, World Vision focused its outreach to media on the U.S. financial and political response to the emergency ("America's Generosity 'Unprecedented and Overwhelming': Businesses, Church, Individuals Respond to Tsunami Tragedy" and "Bush Urges Aid Agencies to Protect Tsunami-Affected Children: World Vision and Other Aid Agencies Meet with President about Response" and "World Vision Implements Programs to Keep Children Safe from Sexual Exploitation in the Wake of the Tsunami: Relief Organization Sets up Child-Friendly Safe Centers to Protect children in Hardest Hit Countries").[46] World Vision's credibility on Capitol Hill gave it access to high-level leadership, including a meeting with President George W. Bush.

WEEK THREE AND BEYOND

Media interest dried up quickly during the third week following the emergency. However, World Vision attracted local coverage of two airlifts of relief supplies, one in the Seattle-Tacoma market ("Northwest Aid Agencies Fly Relief to Tsunami Victims") and the other in Billings, Montana ("From Billings to Banda Aceh: World Vision Sends Helicopters to Tsunami Zone: Cargo Choppers Will Help Relief Workers Bring Needed Supplies to Inaccessible Areas").[47] During the first three weeks of the response, World Vision held four news conferences from its U.S. offices and two satellite media tours:

- *December 27, 2004:* Tom Costanza, videographer, and Jon Warren, photographer for World Vision, discussed their mission to document World Vision's efforts during the crisis.

- *December 31, 2004:* Dean Hirsch, president of World Vision International, and

Richard Stearns, president of World Vision U.S., discussed the role of World Vision during the first five days of the crisis.

- *January 1, 2005:* Jules Lynn Frost, director of emergency response and disaster mitigation team for World Vision, and Mike Mantel, senior director of World Vision in Chicago, discussed relief coordination between agencies and with governments responding to the tsunami, as well as wisely choosing an agency for individual donations and medical issues surrounding disaster relief and recovery.

- *January 19, 2005:* Hirsch made himself available a second time to media upon his return from the affected countries. He discussed what he had seen and the need for long-term commitment to rebuilding and rehabilitation.

- *January 7 and 12, 2005:* Stearns was World Vision's spokesperson for a radio media tour January 7, 2005, and a satellite media tour January 12, 2005. Stearns focused on the devastation of the emergency, the money World Vision had raised, and the need for a three- to five-year commitment to rebuilding and rehabilitation efforts.

CONNECTING TO STORY TRENDS

Most of the news coverage involving World Vision focused on the immediate consequences of the disaster. Beyond relief and cleanup efforts, the following story topics developed during the second and subsequent weeks:[48]

Proselytizing

National media interest was piqued after initial reports indicated staff from some responding Christian agencies were sharing their faith with beneficiaries in culturally insensitive ways. This issue is often one to which World Vision must respond, especially in regard to its work in Muslim, Buddhist, and Hindu countries. As World Vision does

not proselytize, its name was mentioned minimally or not at all in these stories.

Excess Fund-Raising

Media attention was focused on the possibility that relief agencies might raise too much money, following the announcement by Doctors Without Borders that it had raised enough money for its tsunami response and was no longer taking donations for that emergency. While this did call into question World Vision's decision to continue fund-raising, it was an opportunity to explain the difference between emergency relief agencies and those that also engage in long-term development. Since World Vision was already operational in the affected countries and had the infrastructure to continue work through full recovery, the organization was able to make this a positive story.

Child Protection

The large numbers of children separated from adult relatives created widespread concern that other adults might try to exploit their vulnerability. This concern became rumor, and while few cases were confirmed, the issue did attract some media interest. Without raising undue alarm about the impact of the tsunami on child exploitation, World Vision took the opportunity to increase public awareness of the ongoing issue of child exploitation, particularly the trafficking of children into the sex trade. World Vision also focused on ways that governments and relief programs in affected countries could mitigate the possibility of exploitation.

Long-Term Plans

There was a relatively small amount of media interest in the long-term plans of agencies intending to remain in the region to do rehabilitation and recovery. World Vision international leadership held a strategic planning meeting on January 12, 2005, to establish some of those plans; staff produced a document that allowed the media team to succinctly explain the organization's three-year plan.

RESULTS

As was the case around the world, Americans stunned by the enormity of the emergency responded generously. Within a week of the tsunami, World Vision had raised $12 million in the United States. By the end of the second month, between $200 million and $250 million had been raised worldwide (nearly $49.5 million in the United States) by World Vision.

During the first three weeks following the tsunami, much of the media coverage of World Vision's work was responsive: Reporters called World Vision to find out what its workers were doing to help survivors. World Vision staff were quoted in about 350 radio and television interviews, more than 1,000 newspaper and wire service stories, including the Associated Press, Reuters, and most of the nation's top 100 newspapers.[49]

The media staff sent out 25 news releases during the first weeks of the disaster. These focused on updates of World Vision's programmatic response to the disaster, announcements of partnerships with corporations, such as Hasbro, collaborative agreements with financial institutions, and donations by organizations, such as the Bill and Melinda Gates Foundation.[50]

World Vision was the major focus of many tsunami-related broadcast news shows and stories: CNN's *Anderson Cooper 360*, ABC's *Nightline*, CBS's *The Early Show*, PBS's *News Hour with Jim Lehrer*, Fox News, and MSNBC.

Major daily newspapers covering World Vision's response to the tsunami included *USA Today*, the *Wall Street Journal*, *New York Times*, *Washington Post*, *Los Angeles Times*, *Chicago Tribune*, *New York Post*, *Newsday*, *San Francisco Chronicle*, and *Boston Globe*. Weekly news magazines that mentioned World Vision's efforts included *Time*, *Newsweek*, *U.S. News and World Report*, and *Life* (the Sunday supplement).[51]

Because of its religious mission, World Vision was also mentioned or featured in numerous religious media: *Christian World News, Family News in Focus, Christianity Today, World Magazine, Religion News Service, Mission Network News,* Moody Radio Network, and USA Radio Network.

World Vision's media success was helped by several factors, including the following:

Existing Quality Emergency Plans

World Vision offices in every country are required to compile an emergency response plan. While plans must be modified for specific emergencies, World Vision offices in affected countries had quality plans in place and began executing them immediately. Beyond its emergency response, World Vision is involved in social/community recovery, economic development, infrastructure recovery, and long-term development.[52]

Experienced Field Staff

In addition to its response programs, World Vision had excellent communications staff, both nationals and expatriate support staff, who were able to send relevant stories to the United States and other fundraising offices and were able to conduct interviews in English with U.S. and other Western media from the field.

Credible U.S.-Based Spokespeople

Staff members like Emergency Response Director Jules Frost and Senior Policy Advisor for Child Protection Joe Mettimano proved to be excellent resources for the media and were much easier to connect with journalists as they were often in the same time zone.

Open Scenario Challenge

Keeping World Attention Focused on the Story a Year Later

It was relatively easy to get the attention of the world media during the initial phase of the tsunami crisis. But attention spans are short, especially when Americans were exposed to the concerns of the day: the Iraq war, rising gas prices, and who would win the World Series.

As the coordinator of media relations for World Vision, it is your task to develop a communication plan that takes advantage of the expected spike of news media coverage at the six-month and one-year anniversaries of this tragedy. Americans have donated in record amounts but have yet to see what has resulted from those gifts. Decide what your communication goals and objectives will be, and develop a list of possible story ideas.

Questions for Discussion

1. Why was there a need to react quickly to this disaster from World Vision's perspective?

2. What was the role of the global response team?

3. What were the first information needs addressed by World Vision?

4. How did World Vision use its home support resources in this emergency?

5. What were the news hooks of the news releases issued by World Vision in this disaster?

6. What tactics did World Vision use effectively to get its messages reported in the news?

7. What reputation issues were addressed by World Vision during this crisis? Why?

8. How did World Vision maintain audience and media attention after the initial emergency phase?

9. What were some of the religious media targeted for World Vision's messages?

Do Some Research

1. Read the news releases issued by World Vision (located on the textbook's Web site), and discuss the communication strategy of their timing and content.

2. World Vision was just one of many religiously based nongovernmental organizations (NGOs) that responded to the tsunami crisis. Pick another NGO that provided aid to the tsunami crisis or some other major disaster and compare its media relations efforts.

3. Examine World Vision's campaign to stop the use of child soldiers in Uganda. What communication strategies has the organization taken to get this story heard?

Terminology

- tsunami
- field offices
- rapid response team
- in-kind donation
- celebrity spokesperson
- pitched
- graveyard shift
- "in the box"
- proselytism
- press briefing
- press availability
- radio media tour
- satellite media tour
- contract staff

Web Site Resources

- **World Vision** www.wvi.org/wvi/home.htm
- **World Vision, Asia Tsunami** www.wvi.org/wvi/asia_tsunami/asia_tsunami.htm
- **Freedom Corps** www.freedomcorps.gov
- **Central Intelligence Agency, *The World Fact Book,* Indonesia** www.cia.gov/cia/publications/factbook/geos/id.html

The "4Cs" of a Great Picture

Launching Kodak's High-Definition Film

Digital cameras rule today.

And while Kodak dominates consumer picture taking, when it was shifting its business focus from film to digital photography, Kodak was still a leader in film-based products.

The dominance of digital photography has made promoting these "dinosaur" products a real challenge. Kodak's high-definition film was seen as a new advance for an old technology. Generating excitement and understanding about the product among the media and buying public required a focused strategy. Kodak teamed with Ketchum, a respected international public relations firm, to develop this successful campaign that won an award of excellence in the silver anvil competition from the Public Relations Society of America.[53]

RESEARCH

Kodak commissioned questions in an omnibus survey to better understand consumer interest in clearer, better-quality pictures. The results were key to its high-definition film marketing campaign strategy, said Charles Smith, director of communications and vice president of Film and Photofinishing Systems at Kodak. Survey questions posed to consumers included:

Of the four characteristics that I am going to describe, which one do you believe is most important to capturing a great picture?

- *Clarity (clearer, less grainy appearance)*
- *Color (more vibrant colors)*

Composition (how the content is set up within the picture)

- *Content (subject matter)*

When you get a roll of 24 pictures developed, how many of the pictures do you usually consider to be great? [Open-ended response]

How interested would you be in a film that captures more detail to give you clearer pictures?

- *Very interested*
- *Somewhat interested*
- *Not very interested*
- *Not at all interested*
- *Don't know*

The omnibus survey revealed three-quarters of Americans believed that clarity was one of the two most important characteristics of a great picture; 45 percent deemed it the most important characteristic of a great picture. Americans were critical of their developed pictures with only 13 to 14 pictures per roll of 24-exposure film considered "great." Thirty-two percent of respondents said 10 or less were great pictures.

Nearly three-quarters (74 percent) of Americans were interested in film that captures more detail for clearer pictures. Women were even more interested (44 percent of female respondents were "very interested" compared with 35 percent of male respondents). Interest was higher among younger respondents and parents with children at home.

Proprietary research among photo-active women helped shape the media strategy for the campaign and identify the most relevant target media outlets. Studies showed women were more interested than men in film that captures more detail for clearer pictures, and that the desire to capture memories of any kind increased with parenthood. Women were the active picture takers/memory keepers in most households.

STRATEGY

Kodak partnered with Ketchum to develop its high-definition film public relations strategy.

Kodak's three communication objectives were to build awareness of high-definition film; generate understanding that high-definition film helps consumers get clearer, more vibrant pictures; and motivate consumers to try high-definition film.

Ketchum's recommended communication strategies included:

- Differentiate Kodak and define clarity in pictures for the consumer.
- Execute a media campaign designed to communicate the importance and value of clear pictures.
- Frame the product launch within a broader context using a quality-focused education platform to serve as message point and news hook to communicate product benefits.
- Leverage celebrity and professional photographers to serve as credible third-party spokespeople.
- Use tips from spokespeople and actual pictures taken with high-definition film to offer tangible proof of clarity claim.

PROGRAM CONCEPT

Kodak's creative concept played off the term *high definition* to provide the "definition" of a great picture. The campaign also borrowed from the diamond industry's well-known "4Cs" system for grading diamonds (clarity, color, cut, carat weight). The 4Cs of a great picture included clarity, color, composition, and content and was incorporated into the campaign's consumer education strategy. Its primary audience was women 18 to 49 who were "photo-active," were family-oriented, and enjoyed taking and sharing pictures. Its secondary audience was males 18 to 49 who were interested in purchasing products that would enhance their picture quality.

To capture the attention of the media and communicate effectively to its target audiences, Kodak sought spokespeople with photography credentials and credibility

in the eyes of consumers. Specific criteria included appeal to women, appeal to media, genuine enthusiasm and expertise in photography, and topicality. Research revealed that Sarah Ferguson, the Duchess of York, was an avid photographer, a devoted mom and "memory keeper," and the author of a new children's book series, *Little Red,* which provided a topical news hook for the media. Additional research identified Rick Sammon, a professional photographer with an established reputation in film photography and a strong reputation with media that cover photography.

CAMPAIGN

A downloadable Web-based guide, the "Definition of a Great Picture," was devised, describing the 4Cs alongside photographs taken by Sammon and Ferguson using Kodak high-definition film. Available free to anyone who visited the site, the guide included information on clarity (focusing on high-definition film), color, composition, and content.

Although Kodak had already launched two other products and services targeting the same media and consumer audiences, the high-definition film product launch had two positive elements working for its publicity: good timing and popular media-savvy spokespeople. Timing the publicity launch for August 2003 coincided with one of the biggest months for picture taking. Ferguson started with a career in public relations and was very comfortable dealing with the media as Duchess of York. She also was well known as the international spokesperson for Weight Watchers. Sammon was well known in the photography world, with more than 1,000 articles and 22 published books about photography, traveling, wildlife, and conservation.

Phase one of the campaign involved trade publicity: introducing the film at the Photo Marketing Association Annual Conference in March 2003. This photography trade show provided access to many in the media who covered photography. Tactics included a news release on high-definition film and spokesperson interviews with the media.

Phase two of the campaign included local and regional launches with professional photographer Sammon in August 2003. Kodak and Sammon developed volume one of the Web-based "Definition of a Great Picture" guide, which included samples of his work using high-definition film. Tactics included a press release about the guide, distribution of a video news release with Sammon explaining how to get extremely clear pictures, and live local-market interviews with Sammon.

Phase three of the campaign began in September 2003 and was tied to Ferguson's launch of her children's book, *Little Red,* which brought even more national attention. Volume two of "Definition of a Great Picture" featured Ferguson's picture-taking advice (with samples of her photos) and reinforced the benefits of high-definition film. Tactics included a news release announcing volume two of the guide and the role of high-definition film in clearer pictures. A national media tour in New York City provided opportunities to tell people about the new picture-taking guide and high-definition film.

RESULTS
The campaign's public relations effort was measured and evaluated using Ketchum's measurement system. This measurement program had three types of goals: qualitative (media ratings and coverage analysis), quantitative (total impressions secured), and target audience reach (percentage of target reached with product message).

Media placements were evaluated based on a number of criteria, including key message reach and audience, photography and/or demonstration, tone of coverage, topic or type of coverage, influencer/spokesperson, and relative mentions of Kodak versus its competitors.

Target audience reach was evaluated based on media mix product coverage and media impressions, including print (using circulation figures), television (using audience reach for networks and total households for cable), radio (listeners), and online visits to Kodak's Web site.

Three key messages identified during the campaign plan were evaluated as part of the media-ranking criteria. These messages included:

- **High-definition film provides clearer, more vibrant pictures.**
- **Kodak high-definition film reduces the film's "grain" for more details and clarity in pictures.**
- **High-definition film allows consumers to get clearer pictures to better capture the moment as they see it.**
- **Additional "bonus" messages were also evaluated.**

Kodak's objective to reach 55 to 65 percent of all American picture-taking adults with messages about high-definition film was met with more than 62 percent of the "snapshooter" adults targeted by the campaign receiving the message.

Specifically, Kodak's campaign generated awareness for high-definition film with more than 48 million impressions, including top-tier placements such as *CNN Headline News, Larry King Live, The View, Living It Up with Ali & Jack, Fox & Friends,* CNNfn, and *People.* Kodak's video news release featuring Sammon's photography advice was aired on 24/7 television stations including two syndicated programs. Ninety-seven percent of the media coverage contained two or more key messages.

Kodak's Web site traffic increased as a result of publicity from Sammon's and Ferguson's "Definition of a Great Picture" guides (volumes one and two). The local/regional launch featuring Sammon resulted in 200-plus visits to the Web site daily, with many visitors (40 percent) printing the guide. During the national launch with

Ferguson's publicity, Web site traffic increased 70 percent.

Kodak's objective to build understanding that high-definition film enhanced pictured clarity was achieved in media coverage; 84 percent of the messages connected the film to picture clarity. Its other objective to fuel product trial was achieved despite an industrywide downturn in film sales. High-definition film sales increased 17 percent two weeks following the national launch in the absence of paid advertising.

Questions for Discussion

1. What was the challenge facing Kodak's launch of high-definition film?
2. Why were women the primary target audience for the public relations campaign?
3. What were the two positive elements of the campaign launch? Were there any potential impediments?
4. What were the criteria for Kodak's high-definition spokesperson selection?
5. What would be the main media pitching points for Kodak's high-definition film?
6. What questions would you include in a spokesperson questions-answers sheet to help Sarah Ferguson and the media prepare for an interview?
7. How would you *specifically* advise Sarah Ferguson to switch from talking about her new children's book to talking about Kodak high-definition film?
8. In developing a video news release for Rick Sammon, how would you develop key messages about high-definition film? Would you actually say the product name? If so, how many times could you do this?
9. What were the criteria used in evaluating Kodak's media placement effectiveness? Are any criteria more important than others? Why?

Do Some Research

1. Research avid consumer and professional photographers who are well known and could be suitable spokespeople for Kodak digital products. Explain your rationale for selecting these people. Are there any potential problems with your spokesperson selection?
2. Read a journal research article on celebrity or other organizational spokespersons. What are the traits of a good spokesperson? How are spokespeople best used? What does it mean to "leverage" your spokesperson as mentioned in this case study?

Terminology

- product trial
- media placements
- trade publicity
- omnibus survey
- proprietary research
- memory keeper

Web Resources

- **Kodak's home page** www.kodak.com
- **Kodak's Taking Great Pictures** www.kodak.com
- **Kodak.com Presents Rick Sammon** www.kodak.com/
- **Rick Sammon backgrounder by Adorama** www.adorama.com
- **Sarah Ferguson backgrounder by the Biography Channel** www.thebiogr-phychannel.co.uk

Chapter Six

Crisis Communication

LOOKING FOR RISKS AND MANAGING ISSUES

Most crises are not unforeseen "acts of God," such as tsunamis, earthquakes, or tornadoes. If fact, hindsight shows that most crises simmered for months—even years—before boiling over onto the front page.[1]

Crises at Enron, Arthur Andersen, Adelphia, and Global Crossing all involved improper business dealings that hurt employees, investors, and customers. Nike was sharply criticized for worker exploitation in foreign plants. McDonald's was sued by an elderly woman who suffered third-degree burns from a coffee spill.[2] Intel's image took a beating when it initially refused to recognize that a problem with its Pentium chip should be addressed.[3] While much of Hurricane Katrina's devastation of New Orleans and the Gulf Coast could not be prevented, better planning and coordination of emergency services would have minimized the disaster.[4]

In recent years, public relations research has focused on more than what to do in a crisis. Minimizing an organization's risks and managing issues to prevent a crisis from happening have received much needed attention. There is a great deal of information available on issue management and crisis communication, online and in print. Here is a quick review of some key points to consider.

The first step in preventing a crisis situation is to conduct risk assessment, an internal activity that identifies potential problem areas within an organization. Public relations should be familiar with internal reports and customer relations activity. By learning from others' mistakes, organizations can potentially reduce their own risks. After Katrina struck, for example, other hurricane-prone communities reviewed their risks and vulnerabilities. The public relations office can address identified risks with appropriate risk communication efforts such as safety guidelines and user warnings for products.

Environmental scanning, an external activity, requires careful, objective scrutiny of an organization's outside environment. This monitoring activity looks for problems faced by the organization, similar organizations, and even by organizations in other industries. Monitoring can be as simple as reviewing feedback from customers via toll-free telephone call lines, letters, e-mails, or Web postings. Practitioners should also read industry reports, trade publications, and other information sources to keep current with industry trends that might reveal potential threats to the organization.

Because organizations can face a variety of problems and dissatisfied customers, public relations has a role in identifying, prioritizing, and managing problems that can become serious issues. Practitioners, along with management, need to decide which problems have the potential for becoming major issues that could escalate into crises if not managed properly.

By asking "what if" questions and thinking "worst-case scenario," organizations can begin to develop a crisis plan that anticipates possible scenarios—from severe crises, such as a product failure, facility destruction, or employee strike, to moderate or minimal crises with appropriate response options for each situation. Each crisis plan should include a crisis management team that taps key individuals responsible for carrying out portions of the plan. Public relations' role is to coordinate and manage the communication activity during the crisis. Other typical team members include the organization's head of facilities, human resources, technology services, and security.

Plans are worthless if they are shelved and forgotten. A crisis plan should be revisited by an organization on a regular basis and tested and updated through simulations. The crisis team must know its role and be able to react quickly. Hospitals and other emergency response agencies have been leading the way in crisis response simulations. Thorough testing reveals gaps and identifies areas in need of further development.

CRISIS RESPONSE STRATEGIES

When proactive strategies such as risk and issues management cannot prevent a crisis from occurring, practitioners can still manage the crisis based on research and best practices. Researchers such as Timothy Coombs have developed helpful typologies to describe organizational responses.[5] They have identified at least seven basic ways an organization can react in times of crisis. The response typology represents a range of strategies, from preemptive action strategies to strategic inaction.

Some researchers view organizational responses as a continuum from defensive to accommodative strategies. Reactive defensive responses include: "prebuttal," attack the accuser, embarrassment, threat, denial, excuse, justification, and strategic silence. Accommodative responses include: concession, ingratiation, concern, condolence, regret, apology, investigation, corrective action, restitution, and repentance.

Depending on each situation, an organization can try one strategy or move to another. When the public holds an organization responsible for a crisis, defensive strategies often do not improve the organization's image, and accommodative strategies are recommended.

The textbook *Strategic Planning for Public Relations* discusses the variety of reactive responses used by organizations:[6]

Preemptive Action Strategy

- **Prebuttal.** An organization tries to be the first one to tell the story and set the tone before other versions of the story are published.

Offensive Response Strategies

- **Attack the accuser.** An organization may decide to attack its accuser when its logic or facts are faulty or if the accuser is negligent or malicious.
- **Embarrassment:** This strategy uses shame or humiliation to lessen the accuser's influence.
- **Threat:** An organization threatens its accusers with harm with such things as lawsuits or exposure.

Defensive Response Strategies

- **Denial.** An organization can deny that a problem exists or that the organization had any role in the crisis.
- **Excuse.** An organization can minimize its responsibility for the crisis. Any intention to do harm is denied, and the organization says that it had no control over the events that led to the crisis. This strategy is often used when there is a natural disaster or product tampering.
- **Justification.** Crisis can be minimized with a statement that no serious damage or injuries resulted. Sometimes, the blame is shifted to the victims. This is often done when a consumer misuses a product or when there is an industrial accident.

Diversionary Response Strategies

- **Concession.** An organization gives the public something it wants, which is valued by both groups, as a step toward repairing its relationships with its publics.
- **Ingratiation.** Actions are taken to appease the publics involved. Consumers who complain are given coupons, or the organization makes a donation to a charitable organization.
- **Disassociation.** This strategy distances the organization from the wrongdoer who has ignored or exploited the company's policies.
- **Relabeling.** Sometimes, devising a new name for a product, service, or organization is used if the old one has negative connotations.

Vocal Commiseration Strategies

- **Concern.** The organization does not admit guilt but does show concern for the situation.
- **Condolence.** This is a more formal vocal response than the concern response. Condolence recognizes the sorrow of personal loss or misfortune experienced by others, but the organization does not admit guilt.
- **Regret.** This strategy, according to Ronald Smith, "involves admitting sorrow and remorse for a situation." An organization may or may not accept fault for the situation.
- **Apology.** The organization takes responsibility and asks forgiveness. Some compensation of money or aid is often included.

Rectifying Behavior Strategies

- **Investigation.** This is a short-term strategy to examine the facts that led to the situation. Depending on what is found, an organization can take further action.
- **Corrective action.** Steps are taken to repair the damage from the crisis and to prevent it from happening again.
- **Restitution.** The organization offers to provide publics with ways to compensate victims or restore the situation to its former state.
- **Repentance.** An organization fully accepts responsibility for the situation and offers to change its practices that led to the situation.

Strategic Inaction

- **Silence.** Every so often, an organization may choose to remain silent when it is under siege. This strategy has been used to protect victims' privacy or some other higher cause. Sometimes a short statement explaining why the organization will not respond is helpful. This strategy is not the same as "no comment," which usually implies some wrongdoing by the organization.

ACTIONS TO TAKE DURING A CRISIS

Researchers and experts in crisis communication have many suggestions for what to do in a crisis. *Public Relations Strategies and Tactics* and other books have created basic communication tactics in times of crisis.[7] Following are some of the most important actions related to the communication function.

Put the Public First

An organization should act to immediately minimize or stop any negative effects on the public stemming from the organizational crisis. Sometimes an organization may need to take a drastic step, such as recalling a product from store shelves. While this action may cause immediate economic hardship for the organization, in the long run customers will remember this act and respond favorably.

Take Responsibility

Whether or not the crisis is caused directly by the organization, the organization involved should take a leadership role in solving the crisis. Fix the problem first—determine the blame later. Such action demonstrates the organization is more concerned about stopping any negative impact on consumers, the community, or the environment than its own bottom line.

Be Honest but Don't Speculate

Stick to the facts as the situation unfolds. Often, in times of crisis, facts may be few at the onset, but an organization needs to be up front about what it knows. Public relations practitioners frequently work with legal counsel to determine what can be said in times of crisis without incrimination. A simple statement, such as "The cause of the accident is not known but an investigation is underway," is better than "no comment." People tend to view "no comment" statements as an organization's attempt to hide information. Resist the temptation to speculate on a cause or other unknown aspects of the crisis. Constant changing or rephrasing the "facts" makes an organization look disorganized or possibly incompetent.

Be Accessible and Accommodate the Media: Communicate Frequently

In today's competitive 24/7 news environment the news media and their companion Internet Web sites seek constant updates or new perspectives for their audiences. If an organization does not make itself available to the news media, reporters will go elsewhere for the story—sometimes to the detriment of the organization. If an organization's leadership is not available, for example, the news media may seek out employees as they leave work. If they have not been briefed on the situation, employees may speculate or discuss rumors that can lead to misinformation—or worse. The news media can also go to outside experts who may speculate on the situation. It is far better to participate in the news coverage than ignore it, even when the organization's motives are good and the leadership would rather work full time on resolving the crisis.

From the onset, an organization should come forward with its version of the facts as they are known. Legal counsel often guides the process to ensure that information released to the public is appropriate. Depending on the intensity of the crisis, including situations with ongoing threats to human safety, the organization's top leadership should meet frequently with reporters through news conferences. Its Web site should include video or transcripts of its news conferences, as well as news releases, and other available background material. Log all media requests and respond immediately to top-tier media, such as national newspapers, television news shows, and the Associated Press, along with the local news media. When possible, respect the news media's deadlines, although companion Internet sites are now making such deadlines largely irrelevant since news can be instantly posted.

Designate a Single Spokesperson

A crisis requires the active participation of the organization's leadership in solving the problem. To ensure that the perspective of the organization is reflected accurately during a crisis, a single spokesperson should be designated. During major crisis situations, the spokesperson should be the CEO or other high-ranking official. A single spokesperson, trained in media relations, can focus on the organization's positive steps and key messages. Having more than one spokesperson can result in conflicting messages or faulty information.

Monitor News Coverage

Since a crisis can make it difficult to find the time to monitor news coverage, this is a task that can be delegated to a news and Internet monitoring service or to a crisis communication firm. Analysis of news coverage can uncover how well an organization's key messages are penetrating the news media so that adjustments can be made during the peak interest period of the crisis. If erroneous information circulates, it is necessary to create a rapid response strategy to correct the errors. This involves directly responding to the information and explaining the inaccuracies with factual, confirmable information.

Communicate with Key Publics

During a crisis, public relations staff are so involved in meeting media requests that key publics are sometimes lost in the shuffle. Direct communication should be considered for investors, employees, retailers, and customers since they are stakeholders and actively seek information. Employees particularly need accurate information during a crisis since this information may play a part in effectively combating the crisis situation. Investors, as part owners of publicly held organizations, will want information about what the organization is doing to address the crisis and protect their investment. For product-related crises, retailers and customers will want specific information on affected products. Is the product being recalled, is it safe to use under certain conditions, and so forth. The organization's Web site can be especially helpful in creating distinct messages for these publics and can be used to interact with individuals through e-mail. Organizations should also consider a toll-free telephone number and a call center to respond to individual inquiries.

Consult Crisis Communication Experts

Crises are often overwhelming situations that require sustained around-the-clock effort to respond to countless media inquiries and key publics within a relatively short period of time. This effort can quickly exhaust staff, and their objectivity can be lost due to stress and internal pressures. Before a crisis strikes, organizations can develop partnerships with public relations firms that have crisis communication experience. This partnership can provide additional staffing, resources, and objective counsel during a crisis. Some businesses offer crisis communication Internet modules that can be remotely created and updated if a public relations practitioner is unable to reach his office or the organization's Internet service is disrupted.

Planning for the Unthinkable
CDC's Smallpox Communication Crisis Plan

Experts agree that smallpox would make an ideal biological weapon *if* terrorists could get their hands on it.

Smallpox has many qualities that make it an ideal terrorist weapon: About 30 percent of people who contract smallpox die; it has killed about 300 million people in the twentieth century alone.[8] It's a small, highly contagious virus that can be released in aerosol form or through the air.[9] Those infected with the virus don't begin to show signs until at least a week has elapsed, and it's hard to detect early since the first symptoms resemble flulike viruses, with the addition of a small rash.[10] And for most doctors, early diagnosis would be especially difficult since they've never even seen a case of a disease that was officially eradicated in 1980.[11]

Officially, only the United States and Russia possess samples of the smallpox virus.[12] But these few closely guarded research samples are not the only concern. The World Health Organization stirred debate when it requested creating a genetically modified version of the smallpox virus to develop an antidote—just in case terrorists get their hands on the virus.[13] In the mass media, realistic scenarios of a bioterrorist attack using smallpox, such as the BBC-TV's "Smallpox 2002: Silent Weapon," have raised questions about America's readiness. Real bioweapons and public health experts guided the production of the BBC docudrama set in New York City.

Since 9/11, the mailed anthrax attacks, the severe acute respiratory syndrome (SARS) outbreak, and talk of "dirty bombs" (also the subject of a post-9/11 docudrama), government efforts to prepare for the once unthinkable have greatly expanded. The Centers for Disease Control and Prevention (CDC), the lead federal agency responsible for protecting the health and safety of Americans, has ramped up its planning for a bioterror attack involving smallpox.

It provides an example of the careful research and planning required to respond effectively in a crisis, and it provides a template for local governments to modify their plans for their specific needs.

START WITH A PLAN

A single laboratory-confirmed case of smallpox would be considered a public health emergency and would require extensive communication activities at the federal, state, and local levels of government and among various organizations in the private sector.[14]

To assist in this massive undertaking, the CDC has developed a comprehensive response plan that state and local governments can use as a template to prepare for a possible smallpox outbreak.[15] The author of the current plan, Wendy Heaps, a health communications specialist for CDC's Immunization Safety Office, said the plan involved many subject matter experts (SMEs), such as physicians and other health care professionals, researchers, and prominent risk communication experts. The plan has several ready-to-go elements, such as scientific fact sheets, incident tracking forms, vaccination guidelines, and much more.

State and local governments are encouraged to test-drive their plans in realistic scenarios that involve health and emergency response entities, including mock patients and the news media. This information is shared with the participating agencies and also with the CDC so that new lessons can be integrated into the overall plan, said Heap.

One topic discussed in the development of a smallpox communication plan is how information should be released to the public. Issues such as when information is released, what is said, and how it's said can have a great effect on a population. There is a fine line between fear and panic. Most Hollywood disaster movies love to show scenes of mass panic with people acting irrationally. However, studies of people during hurricanes, tornadoes, and even the 9/11 terrorist attacks showed that people don't usually panic even under severe stress and fear. "People are actually quite calm and helpful," said Heaps. Health messages must elicit the right balance to get people to act appropriately depending on the situation without causing undue anxiety.

The 2003 SARS outbreak in Canada was a good example of what happens when the urgency of the situation is downplayed and some people are undermotivated to act on SARS-like symptoms. As a result, the containment took longer and more people were infected.[16]

The CDC plan cautions communication planners to prepare for public panic, apathy, and denial.

SMALLPOX RESPONSE PLAN AND GUIDELINES

The CDC's "Smallpox Response Plan and Guidelines" addresses eight areas, including a 27-page "Communication Plan and Activities." The plan covers:

- Goals and objectives for smallpox communications
- Key considerations for smallpox communication
- Guiding crisis communication principles
- Communication preparedness strategies
- CDC communications in the event of a smallpox outbreak
- Core communication functions and CDC's emergency communication system
- Key stakeholders/intermediaries
- CDC's key smallpox preparedness communications activities

The plan's key communication goals are to:[17]

- Provide accurate, consistent, rapid, and complete information to instill and maintain public confidence in the public health system.
- Establish and maintain a strong communications infrastructure that enables prompt, coordinated, and ongoing information dissemination to its key publics.
- Offer immediate, consistent, and clear information to health care providers and the public about how to protect their health during a smallpox outbreak.
- Minimize hostility toward and stigma of persons who have smallpox or are perceived as "contaminated."
- Address as quickly as possible rumors, inaccuracies, and misperceptions.
- Increase the factual understanding of smallpox disease, treatment, control, and prevention.

Planning is key to a massive national response plan; the CDC has begun forming relationships, educating key groups about its plan so that when a crisis occurs, a working relationship will already be in place. The CDC has targeted organizations within the media, the general public, public health workforce, including clinicians and medical experts, and policymakers. To reach the medical community ("clinicians"), for example, the CDC plan calls for establishing working relationships with the American Hospital Association, American Media Association, American Academy of Family Practitioners, American Academy of Pediatrics, American Nurses Association, Association for Professionals in Infection Control and Epidemiology, National Mental Health Association, Association of Academic Health Centers, and the Society for Healthcare Epidemiology of America.

"Such groups are especially valuable for their perceived credibility and ability to reach their constituents. Stakeholder partnerships can help ensure smallpox messages effectively reach and are accepted by their intended audiences," according to the plan. State and local planners are expected to identify specific key publics for their own communication efforts.

Early messages would "emphasize smallpox disease facts, how it is transmitted, what the symptoms are, the importance of smallpox vaccination as a way to prevent the smallpox before and after exposure to the disease, smallpox control strategies and the public health system's response to a smallpox outbreak."[18]

Communication preparedness strategies include getting more smallpox informational materials to key publics, including detailed descriptions of the steps that might be taken to respond to an outbreak (ring vaccination, isolation and quarantine, vaccination clinics, etc.), so that the public and other stakeholders have confidence in and a deeper understanding of the CDC's planned response.

The CDC's Public Health Information Network (PHIN) and Health Alert Network (HAN), for example, is a communication network that reaches more than 90 percent of state and local health care and emergency response workers with vital health information.[19] HAN's infrastructure supports the dissemination of that information at the state and local levels and beyond. The HAN Messaging System transmits health alerts, advisories, and updates to more than 1 million recipients.

In the event of a smallpox outbreak, the CDC would be the lead agency in communicating to the public, through CDC spokespeople, the Health and Human Services' overall response, including antiviral and vaccine supplies, distribution, quarantine, and isolation measures. The CDC communication team would act as the liaison to other key communication officers with local, state, federal, and international agencies involved in responding to an outbreak.

A single laboratory confirmed case of smallpox found in the United States would trigger the Emergency Communication System (ECS).[20] The nationwide system was developed after the anthrax events of 2001, when the CDC was criticized for not providing clear and accurate information to the

news media. The ECS centralizes communication coordination to promote consistent messages and recommendations, manage information better to expedite its release, and respond rapidly to public inquiries.

The CDC plan incorporates suggested communication activities before, during, and after a smallpox outbreak. It also provides communication activities for a highly suspected but not confirmed case of smallpox. Some of the preparedness activities for implementing its communication plan include:[21]

- Keeping the plan updated and consistent with the CDC's "CDCynergy" emergency communication training tool
- Placing key aspects of the federal smallpox plan into visual, at-a-glance formats such as posters
- Conducting regular communication research with public health workers and clinicians to improve its plan
- Updating and developing new key messages
- Updating and developing new communication materials
- Ongoing satellite broadcasts, conference calls, webinars to train clinicians and public health personnel about smallpox preparedness and response
- Implementing tabletop and infield exercises to test the communication plan and draft messages and materials
- Developing mock smallpox Web sites and testing them for usability and accessibility with primary target audiences

If smallpox is confirmed, the CDC's plan triggers numerous actions, including the Emergency Communication System. For example, communication team members would monitor CDC hotlines (public and clinical), Web sites, and public opinion polls to identify emerging issues and information needs.

One regular media communication activity would be daily press briefings to meet the constant information demands of media in the age of an endless 24/7 news cycle. CDC spokespeople would provide important instructions to the public, morbidity and mortality figures, geographic location of cases, number of persons in quarantine and isolation, locations of immunization clinics, number of doses of vaccine available, and number of people immunized, among other information.[22]

For clinician communication, the CDC would conduct conference calls and webinars as needed with clinician organizations to identify their concerns and unmet needs. It would also use Listserv, Web sites, and other channels, such as the Health Alert Network, to rapidly send information to clinicians and public health professionals.[23]

The CDC's efforts to prepare for a smallpox crisis emphasize the importance of crisis planning. Without a plan, organizations are likely to lose credibility with their stakeholders and incur long-lasting damage to their reputations. In scenarios such as a smallpox outbreak, it is literally a life-or-death situation.

Appendix 4 Guide E Smallpox Response Plan and Guidelines: Communication Plan and Activities

Sample Public Service Announcements

Public Service Announcement #1

A Single Case of Smallpox in the U.S.
183 words
Hello I'm [name] with important information on smallpox. The CDC confirmed [number] cases of smallpox and the federal, state and local health officials are working together to quickly find, vaccinate, and treat people who may have been exposed to the smallpox virus. Smallpox normally spreads from person to person through close contact. A close contact is a person who has spent at least several hours within 6.5 feet of an infected person who has a high fever, more than 101°F (38.3°C) and a rash, especially on the face, hands, and feet. Smallpox is an infectious disease. To help prevent smallpox it is important that anyone who thinks they have had contact with a person who has smallpox, or visible signs of smallpox such as high fever and a rash, immediately call this number [#] or your doctor for information on what to do. Vaccination is most urgent for people who may have been exposed to the smallpox virus. For more information on smallpox please go to www.cdc.gov or call the CDC hotline: English 888-246-2675 | Español 888-246-2857 | TTY 866-874-2646.

Key message points covered in public service announcement #1

- What has happened.
- There is a plan. Fed/state/local working together.
- How it is commonly spread.
- Smallpox infectious symptoms.
- Whom to call if you have smallpox.
- Vaccination is high priority for people who may have been exposed to the smallpox virus
- Call your doctor or others for instructions.
- Where to go for more info.

Note: This case study was based on interviews with CDC communication specialists and "Smallpox Response Plan and Guidelines: Guide E—Communication Plan and Activities," which can be found at www.bt.cdc.gov/agent/smallpox/response-plan/index.asp (and is the basis of the following questions). Several parts of the plan were reproduced directly from the report in this case study.

Questions for Discussion

1. Why is smallpox an important health issue since it's been eradicated?
2. Why are preparation and planning key to the smallpox communication plan?
3. What research is necessary to develop an effective smallpox communication plan?
4. Examine the CDC's communication goals for a smallpox outbreak. Why would a strong communication infrastructure be an important goal?
5. How does communication research fit into the CDC plan?
6. The plan refers to subject matter experts (SMEs) within the information management activities. Who are they and what is their role?
7. Why is rapid information dissemination necessary in a competitive 24/7 news environment? Why does this pose problems for the CDC?
8. The CDC's Information Management Team comprises eight communication teams (CDC Smallpox Response Plan and Guidelines, Guide E, Appendix 1). What are the challenges of coordinating these teams during a crisis?
9. The CDC offers a communication plan template provided by their CDC's CDCynergy emergency communication planning tool at www.cdc.gov/communication/emergency/erc_training.htm. Evaluate its media relations program. What are some of its key points?

Do Some Research

1. Read the sample public service announcement (Smallpox Response Plan and Guidelines, Guide E, Appendix 4). What are the pros and cons of these releases? Read the early warning signs of smallpox provided by the Centers for Disease Control. Based on your research, develop a public service announcement that describes the early symptoms of smallpox and what listeners should do. Develop a 60-second and a 30-second script.
2. Examine the efforts of your own state's or city's emergency response plan. What are its strengths and weaknesses from a public relations viewpoint?
3. Read the Web column entitled "Fear of Fear: The Role of Fear in Preparedness . . . and Why It Terrifies Officials" by Peter Sandman and Jody Lanard at www.psandman.com. Discuss the fear factor of crisis communication—the fine line between "useful" fear and panic.

Terminology

- subject matter experts (SMEs)
- bioterrorism
- CDCynergy
- infield exercises
- tabletop exercises
- Listserv
- Health Alert Network (HAN)
- conference call
- webinar

Web Resources

- **Centers for Disease Control and Prevention** (the CDC's home page) www.cdc.gov/
- **Centers for Disease Control and Prevention: Emergency Response and Preparedness—Smallpox Preparation and Planning** (contains the overall smallpox preparation and response

guidelines including Guide E, the communication plans and activities) www.bt.cdc.gov/agent/smallpox/prep/index.asp.

- **Centers for Disease Control and Prevention: Office of Communication** (has current fact sheets and news releases of concern to public and community health professionals) www.cdc.gov/od/oc/media/
- **Centers for Disease Control and Prevention: Emergency Response and Preparedness** (contains support material for other types of emergencies, such as agents, diseases, and other threats) www.bt.cdc.gov/
- **Centers for Disease Control and Prevention: Emergency and Risk Communication Training** (provides training curricula modules for public health workers in emergency and risk communication and includes crisis planning, crisis communication, media relations, and other aspects of public health communication) www.cdc.gov/communiction/emergency/erc_training.htm

- **Centers for Disease Control and Prevention: Health Alert Network** (describes the national infrastructure for disseminating health information messages to health care and emergency response workers) www.phppo.cdc.gov/han/
- **Department of Homeland Security, Emergencies and Disasters, Planning and Prevention** (provides the federal government's national response plan for emergencies and disasters and includes the Fact Sheet Community Emergency Response Team Program) www.dhs.gov/dhspublic/display?theme=15&content=4269
- **The Peter Sandman Risk Communication Web site** (contains many articles on risk communication) www.psandman.com
- **The Society for Risk Analysis** www.sra.org/
- **CDC Communication Training in PowerPoint** www.bt.cdc.gov/agent/smallpox/training/overview/ppt/communications.ppt

Hidden Camera Captures Chicken Abuse
Animal Activist Group Targets Company

The *New York Times* broke the story—and buried it.[24] The tale of chicken abuse at a processing plant only made it to page 2 of the *New York Times* business section, but graphic video images made it a top story for television news that evening.

A hidden video camera, installed by an undercover investigator for the animal rights group People for the Ethical Treat-

ment of Animals (PETA), recorded in grainy black-and-white detail numerous incidents of animal abuse by employees at a Pilgrim's Pride chicken processing plant in West Virginia.[25]

The video was so shocking that all three network television anchors cautioned viewers before airing their respective reports on July 20, 2004.

CBS *Evening News* reporter Mika Brezinski's story began:[26]

Some call it one of the worst cases of animal cruelty captured on videotape; shocking scenes of slaughterhouse workers kicking, stomping and throwing live chickens at a plant owned by Pilgrim's Pride, the country's second-largest poultry processor, a supplier to fast-food chain KFC.

ABC's Ned Potter, reporting for *World News Tonight with Peter Jennings:*[27]

The pictures, shot with a small, hidden camera, purport to show plant employees hurling chickens against a wall, stomping on them to kill them. Kicking them like footballs, and committing other acts of cruelty. It's a far cry from the way the industry says things are supposed to be done. Workers are supposed to stun the birds before slaughter.

CNN's Anderson Cooper, host of *Anderson Cooper 360 Degrees,* began his story this way:[28]

It's enough to make a carnivore turn vegetarian, enough even to make Ozzy Osbourne from his bat-eating days gag. Caught on videotape, workers at a chicken-slaughtering plant in West Virginia torturing live birds for sport. It's the Pilgrim's Pride slaughterhouse, and right now the company is anything but proud. Both Pilgrim's Pride and the company it supplies, Kentucky Fried Chicken, say they are appalled. You'll quickly see why.

The PETA investigator who took the video images also provided eyewitness testimony to other acts of cruelty. According to the *New York Times*, the investigator[29]

saw "hundreds" of acts of cruelty, including workers tearing beaks off,

ripping a bird's head off to write graffiti in blood, spitting tobacco juice into birds' mouths, plucking feathers to "make it snow," suffocating a chicken by tying a latex glove over its head, and squeezing birds like water balloons to spray feces over other birds.

Similar stories about the chicken abuse at Pilgrim's Pride ran in hundreds of local and national television programs and newspapers in the week after the *New York Times* story.

The gruesome video was quickly offered to PETA Web site visitors, appearing in a section titled "Exposé: Cruelty in the KFC Slaughterhouse."[30] The stark black-and-red Web pages included video stills from the hidden camera video. But that was just the tip of the iceberg for the curious. Visitors to the site were provided an array of information about the Pilgrim's Pride situation, including:[31]

- A link to PETA's ongoing boycott campaign against Kentucky Fried Chicken (KFC) called "Kentucky Fried Cruelty."

- A two-page description of what the undercover investigator claimed to have seen.

- Three pages of quotes from leading and highly respected animal welfare experts and government and meat-industry advisors about their reactions to the chicken abuse, including Dr. Ian J. H. Duncan, Dr. Temple Grandin, and Dr. Bernard E. Rollin.

- PETA's letters to the Pilgrim's Pride chairman and KFC's chief executive officer detailing, among other things, the results of the undercover investigation and a plea for the use of more humane slaughter technology called "controlled-atmosphere killing."

- PETA's 17-page letter to the prosecuting attorney for Moorefield, West Virginia, containing 35 specific incidents of animal cruelty, excerpts from leading animal welfare experts commenting on the videotaped abuse, a review of slaughterhouse policies that allegedly created an environment of abuse (the letter claimed that the undercover employee did not receive training in killing methods until five months on the job and there was no mention of animal welfare policies in the employee handbook), and a request for an official investigation of the alleged violation of the state's cruelty to animals statute.

- PETA's two-page letter to the U.S. Department of Agriculture requesting an investigation of alleged violations of poultry products inspection regulations.

- Links to free videos or downloads for "Meet Your Meat," narrated by actor Alec Baldwin, and "Chew on This," which alleged health risks and inhumane practices of how 27 billion animals (including fish) are raised and killed for food in the United States. "The Hidden Lives of Chickens" discussed the science of chicken cognition (chickens do better than dogs or cats on scientific tests, according to PETA) and equated chicken consumption with eating dogs or cats.

- For those repulsed by the videos and information provided, PETA offered links to a free vegetarian starter kit, reasons for eliminating animals from a healthy diet, an explanation of veganism, and a link for donations to animal rights causes.

- PETA's home button on the "Exposé: Cruelty in the KFC Slaughterhouse" was linked to numerous other animal rights projects, including how to organize a demonstration against KFC, and downloadable print ads and billboards supporting a KFC boycott.

PILGRIM'S PRIDE RESPONSE

Pilgrim's Pride issued a four-paragraph statement from O. B. Goolsby, president and chief operating officer the day before the *New York Times* broke the story; the message was intended, in part, to alert Pilgrim's Pride employees that media coverage of the situation was about to occur:[32]

You may see coverage in the media in the coming days about a video reportedly taken in one of our chicken processing plants showing inhumane treatment of our birds. We are appalled at the treatment of the animals that was depicted in the video.

Let me make this very clear: Pilgrim's Pride will not tolerate any mistreatment of our animals by any of our employees. Any employee who is found to have mistreated animals in violation of company policy will be immediately terminated.

Pilgrim's Pride strictly follows the animal welfare program recommended by the National Chicken Council (NCC). This program covers all aspects of broiler chicken welfare and was developed by industry experts in consultation with academic experts from leading universities.

Pilgrim's Pride will continue to adhere to a program of animal welfare that is designed to eliminate unnecessary harm and suffering for animals in the day-to-day operation of our production processes, and we remain committed to the highest levels of humane treatment of the animals we raise for food.

In the *New York Times'* July 20 account, an unidentified Pilgrim's Pride spokesperson said that "the company had an anonymous report about poultry mistreatment at the plant in April 2004 and had made it clear to its workers that 'any such behavior would result in immediate termination.' In light of the tape, the company said, it will reopen its investigation."[33]

The same day, Pilgrim's Pride issued another statement by Goolsby entitled "Response to Allegations regarding Animal Welfare Practices in Moorefield, West Virginia."[34] The statement opened this way:

Pilgrim's Pride (NYSE: PPC) is appalled and outraged by the animal welfare allegations concerning our company's Moorefield, West Virginia, plant. The actions described are in complete and direct contradiction to Pilgrim's Pride animal welfare practices and policies regarding the humane treatment of poultry.

The statement also attempted to shield Pilgrim's customer, KFC, from criticism, noting the alleged animal abuse incidents "are totally unrelated to KFC, and we regret that they've been unfairly identified in this incident." The scandal only added to KFC's troubles with PETA, which had earlier called for a boycott of KFC restaurants because of its commercial connection to animal housing and slaughter practices.

The July 20, 2004, Pilgrim's Pride statement went on to list four specific steps taken by Pilgrim's Pride to resolve the crisis:[35]

- Pilgrim's Pride had launched an "aggressive" investigation the day before when it had first been made aware of the PETA videotape, and Goolsby noted that one employee already had been suspended and three others were under investigation. The statement declared that any employee found to have violated the company's policies on animal welfare would be immediately terminated.

- Goolsby issued a stop production order affecting 25 plants that handled live animals, directing that every employee on every shift would review "our previously-established animal welfare policies and practices." Pil-

grim's Pride would require "signatures from every employee who works with live animals indicating that he or she reaffirms their understanding of the policies."

- Pilgrim's Pride would create an independent task force to "assure the adequacy of monitoring and safeguards of animal welfare and to provide independent oversight of the Moorefield investigation."

- Pilgrim's Pride hired Dr. Temple Grandin, a leading expert in the field of animal welfare, to review Pilgrim's Pride's animal welfare practices.

The next day, July 21, 2004, Pilgrim's Pride issued a third statement entitled "Pilgrim's Pride Terminates 11 Employees Based on Moorefield, West Virginia, Investigation."[36] Among those terminated were three management-level employees and eight hourly workers. Goolsby said:

While we are making considerable progress with our investigation, we will continue with this investigation until we're confident that every employee—regardless of rank—who had knowledge of these incidents has been held accountable for their actions. . . .

He also reported that Pilgrim's Pride had placed quality assurance monitors on both shifts at the Moorefield facility to continuously audit handling practices and processing in connection with its ongoing investigation.

In addition to updating the public about its actions, Goolsby took the opportunity to question why the undercover employee failed to report the incidents sooner to plant management or to an employee hotline. The statement noted the employee received animal welfare training: "Had he reported the incidents to plant management and to the employee hotline, as he had been instructed during the company's animal welfare training he received on September 3, 2003, corrective and disciplinary actions would have been taken many months ago, and chickens would have been spared from suffering the types of abuses shown in the video."[37]

A Pilgrim's Pride statement sent to Associated Press reporter Vicki Smith August 3, 2004, further questioned PETA's undercover tactics. It confirmed that Pilgrim's Pride had received an anonymous report April 29, 2004, of alleged mistreatment of poultry at the Moorefield facility. It also reiterated:[38]

At that time, we promptly stopped production, addressed the allegations, and communicated the severity of these allegations to our employees, making it clear to them that any such behavior would result in immediate termination . . .

It is important to note that the "investigator" worked at the Pilgrim's Pride Moorefield plant for more than eight months, from mid-September to May 2004, and claims to have taken several hours of videotape. However, he chose to withhold this videotaped evidence from Pilgrim's Pride management until last month.

Additionally, the anonymous hotline report was not made until April 29, one day before the "investigator" showed up for work for the last time on April 30 . . . Had he presented the additional videotaped evidence earlier, corrective and disciplinary actions would have been taken many months ago, and chickens would have been spared from suffering the types of abuses shown in the video.

PETA claimed its investigator twice reported the abuse and said that the plant supervisor came by regularly and witnessed the abuse.

KFC'S RESPONSE

Kentucky Fried Chicken's response was also immediate. A statement entitled "KFC Response Statement to Pilgrim's Pride Incident" released July 20, 2004, the day the story broke, also used the term "appalling" to describe KFC's reaction to the chicken abuse video.[39]

The four-paragraph statement said KFC would terminate its business with the Moorefield plant until Pilgrim's Pride could "definitively assure us there are absolutely no abuses taking place."[40] It also noted that an inspector, trained by animal welfare expert Dr. Grandin, was at the Moorefield plant to monitor activity, a thorough investigation was underway that would identify the workers responsible, and that "Pilgrim's Pride will fire any individuals involved in this alleged activity."[41] The statement concluded as it had begun: KFC was committed to the humane treatment of animals.

The next day, at a news conference, KFC president Gregg Dedrick read a longer statement. In addition to the actions outlined in KFC's first statement, Dedrick called for the installation of security cameras at the Moorefield plant, and he noted KFC had sent a letter to all its suppliers to remind them to "strictly enforce" industry animal welfare guidelines.[42]

Dedrick took aim at PETA for what he characterized as unfair pressure tactics. For example, KFC purchases only 15 percent of the Moorefield facility's product, yet PETA called it a "KFC facility," instead of a Pilgrim's Pride facility. He said that KFC sells "about 5 percent of all the chicken in America today" yet is singled out by PETA because its name "is synonymous with chicken."[43]

Dedrick also mentioned examples of PETA's ongoing campaign of "distortion, deceit and duplicity" along with PETA's harassment of senior executives (including those of its parent company, Yum! Brands), their families, and neighbors. "This is not your warm and fuzzy animal rights group. This pressure through intimidation, harassment and invasion of privacy should not be tolerated. It is nothing short of corporate terrorism."[44]

The statement ended with a recapping of the actions KFC had taken to resolve the animal abuse situation at the Pilgrim's Pride plant, including its pledge to increase audits with all its suppliers to ensure standards were met.

Both KFC statements were posted on its Web site. The KFC home page contained a link "KFC Sets Record Straight on Pilgrim's Pride Incident" that sent viewers to the July 21 news conference statement. The KFC Web site also had a description of its parent company's (Yum! Brands) animal welfare program that contains guiding principles, advisory council, progress and goals, and experts' quotes. The site also contains a Yum! Brands supplier code of conduct.

THE GOVERNMENT'S RESPONSE

The U.S. Department of Agriculture (USDA) conducted a thorough investigation. According to an Associated Press article, the plant had a veterinarian and 10 USDA inspectors present. A USDA spokesperson said the investigation concluded the inspectors were not aware of the abuse because their work was inside the plant and the abuse supposedly occurred in the unloading area. As of August 11, 2004, the USDA had not concluded if any federal laws had been violated since the federal Humane Methods of Slaughter Act does not cover poultry.[45] However, in 2005 the USDA did issue a notice to poultry slaughterhouses that pursuant to the Poultry Product Inspection Act, "live poultry must be handled in a manner that is consistent with good commercial practices, meaning they should be treated humanely."

State statutes in West Virginia make animal cruelty either a felony (if the acts involve mostly torture) punishable by up to three years in prison or a misdemeanor punishable by up to $1,000 in fines and six months in jail.[46]

LIFE GOES ON

Media interest in Moorefield (population 2,400) began to peter out a week after the story broke. However, on July 27, 2004, an Associated Press article noted that Moorefield's annual West Virginia Poultry Festival, complete with a wing sauce cook-off, beauty pageant, golf tournament, carnival, and a chicken barbecue, had taken place as scheduled. In a week's time, the story had gone from outrage to irony.[47]

Criminal charges were never filed against the 11 employees who allegedly abused the chickens and were terminated by Pilgrim's Pride. After hearing a two-hour presentation by a special prosecutor and the undercover PETA investigator, a grand jury refused to indict four former workers PETA hoped would be convicted of felony animal cruelty.[48]

Open Scenario Challenge
Role-Playing Activity with Top Management

You are the director of public relations for Pilgrim's Pride. On a Friday, a senior manager tells you that you might get a call from the *New York Times* about an incident at one of the plants. There are no further details provided to you. Monday, a journalist from the *New York Times* calls you and shares with you an exclusive PETA-provided Internet link to the alleged video of animal abuse at the Moorefield plant. He wants the company's response today for an article that will run in the next day's edition. The video is shown during an emergency meeting of top management, which includes you. What are the first steps you would recommend to your CEO after seeing the video?

Come to class prepared with actual oral comments on how you would advise top management. Another student or the teacher should play the role of Pilgrim's Pride O. B. Goolsby, president and chief operating officer.

Questions for Discussion

1. What crisis communication concepts and practices were used in this situation?

2. Analyze the communication responses of Pilgrim's Pride and KFC during the initial phase of the crisis. Which one was more effective? Why?

3. What role does risk communication play in this situation? What might have prevented this crisis from developing in the first place?

4. The Internet played a major role in this incident. Explain how Pilgrim's Pride, KFC, and PETA used their Web sites to communicate. Would you do anything differently? Why?

5. PETA has been criticized as being too sensational and distorting the truth at times. What is your impression of its Web communication tactics?

6. Was it right for an undercover PETA investigator to stand by while animal abuses were taking place? How do you think PETA justified this action?

7. Should organizations and activists attempt to resolve their differences in ways other than those illustrated by the Pilgrim's Pride case? What role should public relations play in this effort?

8. Many activist and protest groups use visual communication to get their point across. Provide some examples of effective visual communication used in protest events.

Do Some Research

1. Compare the Pepsi syringe hoax case (see Web link below) with the Pilgrim's Pride case. What were the main differences in these cases? What approach did they take?

2. Why do visual images have a greater impact on audiences than text does? Provide some examples of other still or moving images that have left an indelible mark on the viewing public.

Terminology

- PETA
- hidden camera video
- controlled atmosphere killing
- cruelty to animals statute
- boycott campaign
- pressure tactics
- animal welfare experts
- veganism
- corporate terrorism
- supplier code of conduct
- Humane Methods of Slaughter Act

Web Resources

- **People for the Ethical Treatment of Animals (PETA)** www.peta.org/
- **Pilgrim's Pride** www.pilgrimspride.com
- **Pilgrim's Pride** The company's animal welfare policy www.pilgrimspride.com/aboutus/animalwelfare.aspx
- **KFC** www.kfc.com/
- **National Chicken Council** www.nationalchickencouncil.com/
- **National Chicken Council Animal Welfare Guidelines and Audit Checklist** http://www.nationalchickencouncil.com/aboutIndustry/detail.cfm?id=19
- **Pepsi crisis response, the syringe scare, silver anvil award entry** www.metapr.com/info/crisis/sa1994_1.html

Blogger Video and Internet Postings
Crisis Response in an Instant Internet World

The pen is mightier than the sword—and it's a pretty good bike burglary tool too.

Leading bicycle lock manufacturer Kryptonite of Canton, Massachusetts, found itself at the center of an Internet storm when bike owners discovered some tubular cylinder U-locks could be easily opened with a plastic Bic pen.

While the security vulnerability applied to many tubular cylinder U-locks, such as locks for vending machines and laptops as well as other manufactured bicycle locks, national coverage of the security problem focused on industry leader Kryptonite partly due to its revered brand status and because initial customer reports focused on Kryptonite locks.

It all started when bike enthusiast Chris Brennan told a friend about the recent theft of custom-made wheels from his 2004 Bianchi bicycle. His friend asked if Brennan knew that a Bic pen could open Kryptonite locks.[49]

Brennan didn't believe it—at first. But when he tried it at home on his Kryptonite Evolution 2000 lock, it worked. In fact, he said it was as easy as using a key and took less than 30 seconds on his first try.[50]

THE INTERNET POSTING

Brennan's disbelief soon turned to anger and then concern. If this security flaw affected him, it also affected thousands of other cyclists who relied on bike locks to protect their property. He sat down at his computer and typed out an urgent post late that night on an Internet bike site called Bike Forums (www.bikeforums.net) where hundreds of bike enthusiasts swap information about all things related to cycling.

Brennan's headline to a new Bike Forum discussion thread warned: "Your brand new bicycle u-lock is not safe!" The September 12, 2004, post, under Brennan's username Unaesthetic, stated:[51]

This is the most absurd thing I've seen in a long time.

As you guys might remember, I recently had the nicest set of wheels I've ever had stolen from me. Today, I was hanging out with a friend and we got to talking about that—he said his friend showed him just recently how to open a U-Lock with a ballpoint pen.

Of course I didn't believe it. That is until just thirty seconds ago when I opened my own Kryptonite Evolution 2000 with a Bic ballpoint pen.

This has to be the most absurd thing I've sever seen. Try it. Take the end off the pen, jam it in the lock, wiggle around and twist.

Please tell everybody you know and make sure they do something about it right away. The thieves probably already know this trick but from what I've heard it's fairly new. I figure the information is going to get out anyway and so it's better to let the honest people know first and hope this problem gets fixed.

Word spread quickly as the Internet post began to attract other postings; the forum's discussion thread circulated via e-mail and was easily pasted into other Internet bicycle sites. According to *Bicycle Biz*, a digital cycling magazine, an estimated 340,000 readers had read the Bike Forums postings during the first week.

Within the cycling community there was early debate and lingering doubt about Brennan's claim. Subsequent postings that followed in the first hours of Brennan's post claimed they also replicated Brennan's Bic trick, while others said they couldn't get it to work.

Soon a Bike Forums poster successfully "bic-ed" his bike lock, recorded the feat with a digital camera, and e-mailed the video to Kryptonite's customer service department by 12:18 p.m., just about 14 hours after the original post appeared. A copy of the video was sent to another Bike Forums member named Benjamin Running, who volunteered to host the video on his blog site. It was a big hit.

Brennan, who wrote the original thread post, aptly summarized the first 23 hours in his 26th posting about the bike lock flaw: "I think I opened a very big can of worms."[52]

THE BLOGGER VIDEOS

Early the next morning, September 14, Running successfully opened his bike lock with a ballpoint pen—to his utter amazement. Running also decided to re-create the feat on camera. He digitally recorded the "bic-ing" with his small digital camera, and posted it to his blog, Thirdrate.com, alongside the other digital video bic-ing. Running made both videos available on Bike Forums with Internet links. His September 14 blog entry started this way:[53]

9.14.04 take this quiz

kryptonite bike locks are:

- *the best on the market*
- *the most secure*
- *the most indestructible*
- *open-able in a few seconds with a 10 cent bic pen*

and the correct answer is "open-able in a few seconds with a 10 cent bic

pen." details of how to pen any bike lock using a cylindrical key (including most kryptonite locks) has been blowing up a number of bike websites and discussion boards in the last few days and sure enough, it's easy as pie.

check out this quicktime video of me cracking my $90 kryptonite EV disc lock in about 20 seconds [link].

bike owners beware, that same bright yellow lock that once said 'don't screw with me' now screams 'steal me!' obviously, i post this information as a warning to lock owners—not as a how-to. stealing is bad. stealing bikes is worse.

The next day, his blog chronicled the growing interest in his QuickTime movie:[54]

so. This kryptonite lock deal: is getting big. i called kryptonite on tuesday morning and was called back by a customer service rep who assured me that they are working on this and will come up with a solution of some sort within 48 hours (like . . . tomorrow?).

meanwhile, back at the web: the lock cracking videos that i and another guy recorded are linked from everywhere and have been downloaded over one hundred and twenty thousand times in 48 hours (um . . . damn?)

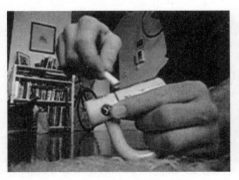

Video digital stills courtesy of Benjamin Running.

i'm going to have to unload these soon.

Actually seeing Running's Bic pen easily unlock the Kryptonite lock within seconds made believers out of doubters at Bike Forums and other Internet sites. The video was posted on various Web sites, including Bike Forums. According to *Bicycle Biz,* the video was downloaded 3 million times within days of its posting as word about it was spread by numerous media reports including CNN.com, Wired.com, many broadcast cable and local network news affiliates, CNN, the *Boston Globe,* and the front page of the *New York Times.*

KRYPTONITE: TOUGH WORLD, TOUGH LOCKS

Kryptonite, a Massachusetts company owned by Ingersoll-Rand, is widely recognized by cyclists as the premiere bike lock business. It's slogan "Tough World, Tough Locks" and its reputation for building theft-proof locks were legendary. Its Web site recounts how the legend was born in 1972:[55]

> *The Second Avenue Bicycle Shop in New York City, under Kryptonite founder Michael Zane's direction, locked a three-speed bicycle to a signpost in New York City's Greenwich Village. Like a lamb awaiting slaughter, the bicycle remained for thirty days and thirty nights. All removable parts of the bike were immediately stripped by marauders, but a month later the lock and the bike frame were still in place, even though it had been mauled by repeated break-in attempts. Publicity from this event gave Kryptonite the boost it needed, forever changing the face of bicycle security.*

The company's reputation continued to grow when Zane returned to New York in 1994 to once again pit his latest innovation, the New York Lock, against the city's toughest streets. Once again, an expensive, shiny

new bike stayed put for 48 hours locked to a parking meter in the East Village. The bike frame and lock were secure. The experiment, witnessed by a *New York Post* employee, was also tried in other high-crime New York neighborhoods with the same result.[56]

In addition to the street test, the *New York Post* ran its own battery of tests using common bike theft tools: "a 4-foot bolt cutter, a crowbar and a hammer. The non-Kryptonite locks cracked in seconds, but all methods failed on the New York Lock, even the monstrous bolt cutter, which ended up useless with large dents in its jaws."[57]

INTERNET POSTINGS ATTRACT TRADITIONAL NEWS MEDIA

Since Brennan's first Bike Forums message posted before midnight September 12, 2004, information about Kryptonite's tubular cylinder U-locks' vulnerabilities circulated quickly within blogs, e-mails, and Internet communities; it wasn't long before the mainstream news media became interested in the story. Kryptonite's Public Relations Manager Donna Tocci was designated to develop the media relations response.

Kryptonite began issuing official public statements September 15, 2004.

Meanwhile media calls had been pouring into Tocci's office.She responded to all news media e-mails by creating a distribution e-mail list of those who had e-mailed or called with questions. "I felt it was important to respond as quickly as possible even if we didn't have specific details about our plan at that time," she said. "Our message was that we were aware of their concerns and that Kryptonite would be responding with a plan within 48 hours . . . Please bear with us."

When communicating with the people most affected—owners of its tubular cylinder locks—Kryptonite's customer service department handled the consumer questions, including telephone and e-mailed questions, on a daily basis.

Kryptonite's headquarters, which employs 25 people, did not have a formal crisis communication plan, especially one that dealt with an inconceivable product failure. Tocci said a response team was immediately assembled comprising about 15 Kryptonite administrative staff people, including representatives from customer service, marketing, product management, and the general manager. The goal was to "provide constant and honest communication" and resolve the problem in a responsible way, she said.

KRYPTONITE'S MEDIA RELATIONS RESPONSE

Tocci, a one-person public relations office responsible for Kryptonite's public relations efforts worldwide, received more than 100 calls from the media in the first days of the crisis. Because of the sheer volume of phone calls and her need to be away from her desk in executive crisis management meetings, Tocci changed her voice mail message asking the media to leave a name, phone number, and e-mail address so that she could respond to requests by telephone or via e-mail. "I was taking my laptop home and responding to e-mails usually until midnight during the first week."

Information for the media was developed by the response team Kryptonite set in place.

"For me, it was a big deal to get back to [media and consumer information] requests," she said. "It's okay to say you don't know—just get back to them." Requests from top-tier media, such as the *New York Times* and *San Francisco Chronicle*, were answered in person. Tocci functioned as the company's main spokesperson, although other executives were also quoted in stories. Second-tier media were either answered in person or by an individual or group e-mail. "We actually got compliments from the media," Tocci said. "Major news organizations couldn't believe we got back to them," including one busy reporter who received three messages from Tocci.

According to the Internet cycling magazine *BikeBiz*, when it contacted Kryptonite September 14 for a comment, "the company said it was aware of the Bikeforum debate and wanted 24 hours to formulate a response."[58] The next day another media call came from the *Boston Globe*, Kryptonite's local paper with a national reach. Tocci decided to call *Globe* reporter Ross Kerber, whom she had dealt with before and who, she knew, would "listen and tell the story the right way"— fairly. "PR is all about relationship building," Tocci said.

Kryptonite issued a written statement September 15, 2004, which was reprinted by *BikeBiz* and other sources the following day:[59]

We understand there are concerns regarding tubular cylinders used in some Kryptonite locks. The tubular cylinder, a standard industry-wide design, has been successfully used for more than 30 years in our products and other security applications without significant issues.

The current Kryptonite locks based on a tubular cylinder design continue to present an effective deterrent to theft. As part of our continuing commitment to produce performance and improved security, Kryptonite has been developing a disc-style cylinder for some years. In 2000, Kryptonite introduced the disc-style cylinder in its premier line of products, the New York series. In 2002, Kryptonite began development of a new disc cylinder system for both its Evolution and KryptoLok product lines, which currently use the tubular cylinder design. These products are scheduled to be introduced in the next few weeks.

We are accelerating the delivery of the new disc cylinder locks and we will communicate directly with our distributors, dealers and consumers within the coming days. The world just got tougher and so did our locks.

The *Boston Globe* story that ran September 16, 2004, quoted from the statement mentioning the company had accelerated plans to upgrade the KryptoLok and Evolution lines of U-locks which were prey to pens.[60] The story included a quote from Tim Clifford, Kryptonite's director of sales, noting: "Unfortunately, this takes the thunder out of the launch at Interbike [trade show], but we'll do what's right by the bicycle community."[61]

The Associated Press also issued several versions of its story September 16, 2004, including one with this headline: "Bike Lock Can Be Picked with a Pen." The Associated Press article was picked up by hundreds of newspapers and broadcast media around the country. The *New York Times* ran an article titled "The Pen Is Mightier than the Lock" with video still frames from Running's homemade "bic-ing" video on September 17, 2004.[62] Out of a lengthy 1,142-word article, Kryptonite only received 68 words in the story based on an e-mailed statement from Kryptonite saying the company was aware of the problem and was working on a solution.

A slightly modified news release statement, developed the day after Kryptonite's initial statement, was distributed by Business Wire on September 16, 2004:[63]

Kryptonite Issues Statement on Tubular Cylinder Lock Consumer Concerns

CANTON, Mass., Sept. 16, 2004

For more than 30 years, Kryptonite has focused on delivering innovative advances that establish the benchmark for lock technology, product performance and enhanced security.

In light of recent demonstrations on the Internet that explain how to criminally defeat tubular cylinder lock technology, which has performed

successfully for more than three decades, Kryptonite intends to expedite the introduction of its upgraded Evolution and KryptoLok lines. These products will have the disc-style cylinder that has the same technology as the company's famous New York Lock.

Specifically, Kryptonite will provide the owners of Evolution and KryptoLok series products the ability to upgrade their cross bars to the new disc-style cylinder, where possible. This new cylinder provides greatly enhanced security and performance. Kryptonite is finalizing the details of this upgrade process and will publicly communicate these details as soon as possible.

The national news media and its Web sites were used to carry Kryptonite's messages during the crisis with mixed results. For example, the focus on solving the problem quickly was not the message contained in company officials' quotes. A *New York Times* article mentioned that Tocci said the "locks made by other manufacturers shared the same vulnerabilities,"[64] and another Kryptonite spokesperson talked about how this problem would not affect earnings.[65]

Kryptonite used Business Wire to disseminate two additional news releases September 17 and 22. The first formal announcement about Kryptonite's broad upgrade exchange program came September 17, five days after the initial problem was identified by Brennan, the cyclist. The statement said the company would begin providing "free product upgrades for certain locks purchased since September 2002."[66]

Kryptonite Offering Free Upgrade Worldwide for Consumers' High End Tubular Cylinder Locks

CANTON, Mass., Sept. 17, 2004

Kryptonite today announced it will provide free product upgrades for certain locks purchased since September 2002, in response to consumer concerns about tubular cylinder lock technology. Consumers can visit the company's Website (www.kryptonitelock.com) on Wednesday afternoon, September 22, 2004, to learn how they can participate in the security upgrade program.

Consumers who have purchased an Evolution lock, KryptoLok lock, New York Chain, New York Noose, Evolution Disc Lock, KryptoDisco or DFS Disc Lock in the last two years are eligible for a product upgrade free of charge from Kryptonite. Customers will need to have either registered their key number, registered for the Kryptonite anti-theft protection offer or have proof of purchase to qualify.

Specifically, Kryptonite will provide for free cross bars featuring the company's new disc-style cylinder lock technology to consumers who have purchased Evolution and KryptoLok series products. In addition the company will replace for free recently purchased Evolution Disc Locks on New York Chain and New York Noose with its "Molly Lock," a heavy duty solid steel padlock. Kryptonite also will upgrade recently purchased disc locks.

Consumers who have had one of the Kryptonite locks mentioned with a tubular cylinder for longer than two years will be eligible for a sizeable rebate on the upgraded products. This program will be administered through Kryptonite dealers and distributors.

A distributor and dealer swap program will be rolled out through direct communication from Kryptonite to all its partners.

Full details about this unprecedented program will be available on Kryptonite's website by afternoon Eastern Standard Time, Wednesday, September 22, 2004, at www.kryptonite.com.

Confusion about the exchange program and growing complaints from owners whose locks were not included in the exchange program led Kryptonite to expand the offer to anyone who owned a Kryptonite tubular cylinder lock. The full details of the exchange program came on September 22 when Kryptonite said in a news release and on its Web site that it would offer free product exchanges to "all customers who are concerned about the security of their tubular cylinder locks." The upgraded models used disc-style cylinders in which cuts in the key are angled, providing a more secure design.

Not everyone was happy with Kryptonite's response.

Frustrated lock owners accustomed to rapid communication and a "fast-food" lifestyle did not understand the seemingly slow response of Kryptonite, said Tocci. Many customers told Kryptonite, "We want our new lock today." Kryptonite's steel locks are made in Asia, and the unscheduled need meant a newly designed lock that took weeks, not hours, to manufacture, ship, and distribute, said Tocci. Even though people live in an age of instant communication, manufacturing is not instant—"steel locks can be made only so fast," said Tocci. Fortunately, production for an upgraded product line that had been scheduled to hit stores in January was accelerated to accommodate the rush orders.

Other problems also hindered Kryptonite's response. Kryptonite's phone system crashed during the initial days of the crisis due to the large volume of calls, the Web site crashed (and the webmaster was out of the country), and Tocci's personal laptop broke.

INTERNET RESPONSE

Kryptonite chose not to respond directly on Bike Forums, where Brennan's original post started the crisis, or other Internet sites. Tocci said the potential flood of questions and comments that a posting could generate would easily overwhelm Kryptonite's ability to respond responsibly. "We didn't want people to think Kryptonite was ignoring them [by not answering]."

This decision also meant rumors and inaccurate information that appeared in some Internet forums and blogs were not responded to although they were monitored. Instead, Kryptonite relied on its Web site, the mainstream media, and its Business Wire statements to communicate with its customers and other key publics. Tocci noted that minutes after an official statement was released to the media, it would appear on Bike Forums, posted by a user with access to the information.

Bloggers presented a new problem for Kryptonite. Running's site, Thirdrate.com, basically came out of nowhere. Blogs were a relatively new communication phenomenon at the time. And Running's blog was not considered a credible source of information by Kryptonite; it wasn't even a cyclist's blog. It was just Running's thoughts about his everyday activities that sometimes included thoughts about cycling. Still, its video "bic-ing" wreaked havoc for Kryptonite.

Unlike the mainstream media, which follow strict journalistic standards and ethical practices, bloggers are accountable to no one. There are no fact checkers or senior editors to complain to if a blogger errs. "You are left with no recourse other than trying to build relationships with them," said Tocci.

Another problem was determining which blogs were legitimate with influential audiences. "We were asking ourselves, 'Who are these bloggers? Are they 15- or 16-year-olds, experts or people who just think they're experts?'"

At the time, Kryptonite decided not to formally communicate with Running and his blog, just as it had decided not to communicate directly with Bike Forums.

MONITORING THE ENVIRONMENT

Tocci was not familiar with Bike Forums prior to the crisis, but she routinely monitored many cycling Internet sites. Her Internet and traditional media monitoring usually took an hour or more each morning. Kryptonite executives kept an eye on other sites and passed along pertinent information. Tocci also routinely scanned dozens of magazines and newspapers. Keeping up is a challenge, she said, because Kryptonite also caters to motorcycles plus power sports such as ATVs, snow mobiles, scooters, skies, and snowboards. Another niche area for the company is in mobile security.

While Kryptonite had two media tracking services in 2004, they did not monitor Internet and blog activity. Kryptonite was considering such a service in the future to help manage the ever-expanding Internet universe, said Tocci.

EPILOGUE

According to *PR News,* by February 2005, the lock upgrade program had cost Kryptonite about $10 million with about 40,000 locks affected.[67]

In an interview with *PR News,* Steve Down, Kryptonite's general manager, spoke about the lessons he learned from the experience with blogs:[68]

> *This was a totally new experience for me and my team, and I don't think anything can fully prepare you for this. We tried to communicate as much as possible up front, but could we have communicated a little more? Yes, I'm sure we could have. But the difficulty was that [being tripped up by the blogosphere] wasn't only new to our company but to our industry and all industries. We wrestled with the*

idea of going out in a clandestine way to try and influence the blog but felt that wasn't the right thing to do because we could have damaged ourselves even more.

When asked, "How do you think blogs have started to impact the ways in which companies communicate with their various stakeholders?" Down responded:[69]

When you are dealing with traditional media, there are some balances. The difficulty with Weblogs is that anyone can put out information in an anonymous way. [But] for any business, Weblogs are a reality, and companies have to look at what they do and be able to respond adequately to concerns that are raised in such a forum.

Questions for Discussion

1. What is an Internet forum? What is an Internet community?

2. What problems does the Internet pose for organizations faced with a crisis? What are the benefits for an organization?

3. How did Bike Forums ignite Kryptonite's crisis?

4. What is a blog? How did the blog Thirdrate.com make the crisis even worse for Kryptonite?

5. Evaluate Kryptonite's mainstream media relations response to the crisis. In your opinion, did Kryptonite have key messages communicated? Would you do anything differently? Explain.

6. Evaluate Kryptonite's decision not to respond to Internet postings or blogs. Would you do anything differently? Explain.

7. How might the trend of participatory journalism, the decline of traditional media readers and viewers, and the demand for information customization affect organizational responses similar to the Kryptonite case?

8. How can public relations practitioners monitor the Web effectively?

9. What key messages would you stress if you were the public relations manager for Kryptonite? Beyond customers and the media, would you target other key audiences? Why?

Do Some Research

1. Research the concept of "e-fluentials" and their role in influencing others into action. An e-fluentials study by Burson-Marsteller at www.efluentials.com will start this exploration.

2. Using the Internet or a newspaper database, such as Lexis-Nexis, research a company that issued a product recall or offered an exchange program. Describe and evaluate the public relations strategy and communication tactics.

3. Research a company such as PR Newwire's eWatch that provides Web monitoring services. Explain how these services work and what benefits they provide to public relations practitioners.

Terminology

- Internet communities
- Internet posting
- discussion boards, forums
- distribution e-mail list
- blog
- QuickTime movie
- response team
- top-tier media
- upgrade exchange program
- fact checkers
- media monitoring
- media tracking service

Web Resources

- **Kryptonite** www.kryptonitelock.com/
- **Bike Forums** www.bikeforums.net/
- **Thirdrate.com blog** www.thirdrate.com/

"Crazy for You" Bear

Mental Health Advocates Criticize Cuddly Toy

At the Vermont Teddy Bear Company, business was booming. With end-of-the-year holiday orders for adorable fuzzy bears up 29 percent, the company was looking forward to its busiest season, when consumers reach out to their loved ones with cards, candy, and—most important of all if you're a teddy bear company—stuffed animals.

Vermont Teddy Bear Company's comprehensive Valentine's Day line of teddy bears had bears for diverse tastes, and almost every imaginable romantic sentiment: Gangster of Love, Heart Racer Bear, Kissing Cowboy, Horny Devil, and even a Love Me Tender Elvis bear. Among the 35 Valentine's bears to choose from was something new for 2005, a Crazy for You bear—so called because of its unique outfit described on its Web site:[70]

> Dressed in a white straitjacket embroidered with a red heart, this Bear is a great gift for someone you're crazy about. He even comes with a "Commitment Report" stating "Can't Eat, Can't Sleep, My Heart's Racing. Diagnosis—Crazy for You!" Trust us. She'll go nuts over this Bear.

Far from the romantic reactions the company hoped to spark in customers, the 15-inch toy bear, priced at $69.95, attracted emotions of a different kind from mental health advocates soon after its January 1, 2005, Web site debut. Their objection was depicting a teddy bear in a straitjacket encourages

stereotypes and misperceptions about mental illness.

Jerry Goessel, executive director of the National Alliance for the Mentally Ill (NAMI), Vermont, faxed a letter to the customer service department of the Vermont Teddy Bear Company January 10, 2005:[71]

> I was dismayed this morning to learn of your company's use of involuntary psychiatric treatment to promote the sales of a Valentine's Day product. As advertised on your web page, the "Crazy for You Bear" is a tasteless use of marketing that stigmatizes persons with mental illness. The marketing use of a straitjacket, which is an instrument utilized at times to prevent a person in severe psychological crisis from injuring his/herself or others, sends a message to the general public that is contradictory to treating persons with mental illness as persons first.
>
> Further, your use of a "Commitment Report" devalues the legal system's use of psychiatric commitment proceedings as a means of temporarily involuntarily committing to psychiatric treatment an individual whose symptoms at the time preclude him/her from making informed decisions on his/her own behalf.
>
> Please remove this product from the marketplace. Your products

have long been associated with quality, caring and comfort. To continue to market this particular item undermines that integrity.

Sincerely,

Jerry Goessel

Executive Director

Goessel said the letter was also sent to his board of directors and to a limited e-mail list of NAMI Vermont members. He also sent a copy of the letter to a small coalition of mental health advocates in Vermont. The Vermont Teddy Bear Company reacted two days later with a statement released to the news media on January 12, 2005:[72]

We appreciate and acknowledge the concerns raised by the National Alliance for Mental Illness regarding the Crazy for You Bear. The Vermont Teddy Bear Company fully appreciates the serious nature of mental illness and the bear was not intended to diminish mental illness in any way.

We recognize that this is a sensitive, human issue and sincerely apologize if we have offended anyone. That was certainly not our intent. This bear was created in the spirit of Valentine's Day and as with all of our bears it was designed to be a light-hearted depiction of the sentiment of love.

This bear was developed just for Valentine's Day and is not a permanent addition to our product line. This bear will remain an offering for Valentine's Day. The Crazy for You bear was created to help guys convey how they feel about their significant others, that they are smitten with their wife or girlfriend.

All new products go through a product development process that involves a customer survey. We

received overwhelmingly positive feedback from our customers regarding this bear. Thus it was added to our Valentine's Day 2005 product line.

Vermont Teddy Bear has a long history of providing unique gifts and individualizing its bear offering so that customers can make very personal gift choices for their loved ones. That is exactly what sets VT Teddy Bear apart from the other bears that are being imported in mass quantities to this country.

Goessel did not initiate contact with the news media, but responded to the Vermont News Bureau when it approached him for comment the day after his first letter was written. News reports said the Vermont Teddy Bear Company had decided not to remove the Crazy for You bear from the market despite some criticism. Vermont Press Bureau's report, including excerpts from Goessel's letter, subsequently went national through the wire services.

When NAMI executive director Goessel had not received a direct reply from the company, he faxed a second letter January 13, 2005, to Vermont Teddy Bear Company president Elisabeth Robert (pronounced *roh-BEAR*). This letter was signed jointly by Goessel, Vermont state representative Anne Donahue, executive director Ken Libertoff of the Vermont Association for Mental Health, and treasurer David Fassler, M.D, of the Vermont Psychiatric Association:[73]

Dear Ms. Robert:

We are frankly very surprised and disappointed that the Vermont Teddy Bear Company has decided to choose profit margin over public sensitivity, through its decision January 12 to continue to market its "Crazy for You" teddy bear. Despite your acknowledgment that it was an *"edgy" marketing strategy and that it is offensive to some people, you are moving forward with the product.*

As such, we are asking that you meet with us at your earliest convenience so we can attempt to help you understand why this marketing strategy is so damaging to persons with mental illness. Specifically, the use of a straitjacket and commitment papers as symbols of love minimizes the plight of those who suffer from mental illness, and their loved ones. From our perspective, the campaign is insensitive, demeaning and wholly inappropriate for a company with a previous history of socially responsible behavior.

In the interim, we ask that the company immediately pull this product from its shelves, and in so doing apply a standard of good taste that would be associated with any other serious illness.

Vermont Teddy Bear Company CEO Robert called Goessel after the second letter was received. Goessel said that Robert "stated strongly that they would not pull the bear 'for a principled set of reasons' and that they had 'taken the position that we will not get together (with mental health advocates) until after Valentine's Day.'"[74]

Robert also told Goessel that the company is "absolutely willing to be educated" about mental illness and the impact that the product has had—but not until after Valentine's Day.[75]

January 13, 2005, Statement from the Vermont Teddy Bear Company[76]

We have responded to the letter sent by the Vermont chapter of NAMI [National Association of Mental Illness] asking to meet with representatives from the Company to discuss the issue of stigmatization further. The Vermont Teddy Bear Company welcomes the opportunity to meet with them and have agreed to do so. No date for that meeting has been set.

Goessel responded to Robert with a third letter on January 17, 2005. In it, he appealed to the company's civic-minded nature and continued his efforts to educate the company about the symbolic effects of the straitjacket and commitment papers; he repeated his request that the company pull the product:[77]

Dear Ms. Robert:
I want to thank you for personally responding to my complaint to the Vermont Teddy Bear Company regarding your marketing of the Crazy for You product: a teddy bear that comes outfitted with a straitjacket and commitment papers. In your telephone call of January 13 you indicated a willingness to enter into a dialogue with myself and other mental health advocates on the unintended, yet serious social statement the Crazy for You bear has made in Vermont and nationally. Your decisions, however, to neither meet with us prior to February 15, or to pull the item from your product line until after Valentine's Day are extremely disappointing. In standing by your principles, it appears that you have chosen to ignore the adverse social impact the product has had on Vermonters affected by mental illness.

An editorial in the state's largest newspaper has called for the company to "Retire the Teddy," pointing out that what some might view as "adorable" is actually offensive to many people—not just persons affected by mental illness. Similarly, Governor James Douglas has stated he hopes your company will pull the bear in light of the "dramatic and inappropriate statement" the toy makes about mental illness. By now you have also received more than simply a few calls, letters and other contacts imploring you to remove the product from your product line—many of which included poignant personal stories to underscore the negative impact this product has had on the public.

Straitjacket and commitment papers are symbols of involuntary commitment and treatment of persons with mental illness. In deciding to further your marketing of these symbols in association with the "Crazy for You" teddy bear, you will continue to offend a significant population—many of whom are your customers and neighbors. Like the Governor and others, I am in no position to, nor would I, demand that you remove the product from the market. Instead, I again respectfully ask you to do so voluntarily. I am counting on you to see this issue in light of your company's history of being responsive to civic and social concerns—of which this product is neither.

Ten days later, the company demonstrated that it had rethought its "after Valentine's Day" position:

January 27, 2005, News Release[78]

Shelburne, VT. The Vermont Teddy Bear Company announced today a meeting has been scheduled with officials from the National Alliance for the Mentally Ill (NAMI), prior to the Company's busiest holiday season, Valentine's Day. Officials from NAMI's Vermont office and Vermont Teddy Bear Company President and CEO, Elisabeth Robert are planning to meet on Tuesday, February 1st. In addition, representatives from the national NAMI office located in Washington, DC have been invited to the Vermont Teddy Bear Company headquarters on Tuesday, February 8.

"At this time, we are not sure of the scope of each meeting or all the parties involved," said Elisabeth Robert, President and CEO of The Vermont Teddy Bear Company. "But our doors are open to discuss the issue of stigmatization."

The Company has also set up a toll-free phone line and an email account designated for comments on the controversial "Crazy for You" Bear. Comments on the bear are being recorded daily. . . .

ADDITIONAL CASE BACKGROUND

The Vermont Teddy Bear Company's public relations manager Nicole L' Huillier explained the company's new product development was a systematic and deliberate process involving input from many customers and employees.

The process to develop new teddy bears begins six months to a year before production with a large employee brainstorming session representing the production, marketing, shipping, and retail employees, L'Huillier said. The product development team works with 20–25 of the most creative ideas and eventually 10–12 make the final cut. The finalists go to the company's product evaluation group, and many people within the company review the proposed products.

An e-mail survey was sent to approximately 10,000 customers with pictures of the proposed products. In the case of the Crazy for You bear, "it scored better than any others in the group," said L'Huillier. A small percentage responded that the bear was offensive. Based on the survey and no obvious red flags, the Crazy for You bear was forecasted to be a big seller and was positioned for prominent print, catalog, and radio advertising.

The Vermont Teddy Bear Company was cautious about offending potential customers. Three years before, the company had received several phone calls and some protests about the Gay Pride bear and, to a lesser extent, its Play Boy and Playmate bears.

Other factors playing into this decision included overwhelmingly positive feedback from key members of the company's national live radio advertising campaign. DJs from 100 radio stations were asked how they felt about the Crazy for You bear and to voice any concerns to the company's media buyers or advertising representatives; virtually no one complained. Robert also asked employees for their opinion; their response was to stick with the bear: "Don't let someone else tell us what to do." Heavy coverage of the controversy in the state fueled local criticism; many Vermont residents expressed anger as well as support over the company's actions.

By the end of the first week, the company's Contact Center combined with a comment line the company set up to allow people to voice their opinions and an e-mail address specifically created for this controversy had received about 3,000 comments with about 1,500 opposing the Crazy for You bear. In addition, by the end of the first week over 3,000 of the Crazy for You bears were sold through the company's toll-free number and its Web site www.VermontTeddyBear.com.

The Vermont Teddy Bear Company on January 12, 2005 pulled the Crazy for You bear from all its national live radio advertising promotions and from its home page and requested that radio personalities not discuss the controversy. The company also committed to halt further production of the bear for future holidays.

EPILOGUE

Robert met with Goessel and other members of NAMI February 1, 2005. According to the company's February 3 news release, Robert said:[79]

> We sat around a Vermont kitchen table and talked. From the respectful, human discourse I learned a lot about the significance of stigma in the mental health community and the plight of real people who suffer from mental illness. Again, we are truly sorry if we hurt anyone with this bear. We sincerely hope that the dialog with the mental health advocates can progress so that we can all continue to learn.

The same news release announced that its Crazy for You bear had sold out and reiterated the promise not to produce more of the popular gift bear.

The following week, amid calls for her removal as a board member of the state's largest health care facility in Vermont, Robert resigned from the post noting the controversy was detracting from her ability to serve effectively.[80]

Open Scenario Challenge
Face-to-Face Meeting between Vermont Teddy Bear Company and NAMI of Vermont

You are a one-person public relations/community relations office for Vermont Teddy Bear Company. Your direct boss is the vice president for marketing whose media strategy after a few days of negative stories about the Crazy for You teddy bear controversy is to stop talking to the media. Today you have provided information to 52 television stations and 24 papers from across the country; you don't think that's the right approach.

You have been with the company for three years following eight years as a broadcast journalist and know how the media business works. Although you report to the vice president of marketing, you also have direct access, as necessary, to company CEO Elisabeth Robert for public relations and media relations issues. The CEO's secretary calls you. Robert would like you to attend a conference the next morning to plan for the meeting with NAMI officials. How would you prepare for your meeting with representatives of the National Association for the Mentally Ill? What are Vermont Teddy Bear Company's options during the meeting? What should the media relations strategy be? How do you address the vice president for marketing's desire to stop talking to the news media?

Questions for Discussion

1. Advocates of the mentally ill who opposed the Crazy for You bear said the product encouraged stigmatizing behaviors. Explain what that means.
2. While this case does not present any legal problems, does this case have any ethical considerations? Explain.
3. Analyze Vermont Teddy Bear Company's overall crisis response. List the actions the company took to respond to the situation.
4. Evaluate Vermont Teddy Bear Company's statements and news release. Would you do anything differently?
5. The first two statements issued by Vermont Teddy Bear Company are not attributed to any individual. Choose a spokesperson and explain your choice.
6. Vermont Teddy Bear Company CEO Elisabeth Robert justified her company's decision not to pull the controversial bear product due to the company's "right of free commerce." Since there

were no legal issues involved, is there a problem?
7. Do you think this crisis has a silver lining for Vermont Teddy Bear Company? Explain.
8. How could Vermont Teddy Bear Company prevent further criticism of future bears or products?
9. Another teddy bear from Vermont Teddy Bear Company issued for Mother's Day in 2006 was called "Bear-Foot and Pregnant." Why have some people called this bear offensive?

Do Some Research

1. Find another example of a controversial consumer product that has been criticized by organizations and activist groups. How did the company respond to or resolve the conflict?
2. Name three products, advertisements, or media coverage examples that you think reinforce stereotypes. Explain your selections.

Terminology

- NAMI
- commitment report
- activist group
- stigmatizing behaviors
- live radio advertising
- right to free commerce

Web Resources

- **The Vermont Teddy Bear Company home site** www.VermontTeddyBear.com
- **The Vermont Teddy Bear retail site** shop.store.yahoo.com/vtbear/
- **National Association for the Mentally Ill home site** www.nami.org/Hometemplate.cfm

Living in a Post-9/11 World:

Controversial Campus Speaker Ignites Furor

Freedom of speech is a cherished cornerstone of American democracy, but it has its limits. As a Supreme Court justice once observed, free speech does not mean you can shout "fire" in a theatre where there is no fire.[81]

Similarly, academic freedom is one of the building blocks of university tradition dating back hundreds of years. But as proponents of both principles learned in 2005, free speech and academic freedom are no protection from controversy.

BACKGROUND

Hamilton College in Clinton, New York, is a nationally respected liberal arts college founded in 1793 by Samuel Kirkland, a missionary to the Oneida Indians. In 2004, its student enrollment was 1,750 of which most were Caucasian (77 percent), according to its Web site. The student body was a 60:40 mixture of public and private school graduates—and well educated (the middle 50 percent of accepted students had SAT scores between 1,340 and 1,450 out of a possible 1,600 points).

Hamilton College invited Ward Churchill, a professor of ethnic studies at the University of Colorado, Boulder, to speak on a panel about prisons.[82] The Hamilton campus is situated on the ancestral territory of the Iroquois Nation in upstate New York.

Churchill's speaking invitation was part of the college's Kirkland Project, which included weekly lectures, workshops, book and poetry readings, concerts, exhibits, and films. Nationally known novelists Dorothy Allison and Lorene Cary and racial advocates and researchers Jonathan Kozol and Dalton Conley were part of the Kirkland Project's 2004–05 events.

Churchill, who had given numerous talks on campuses and at community centers across the country, was described as a Keetoowah Band Cherokee and outspoken Native American scholar and expert on indigenous issues.[83] As the college was about to discover, "outspoken" was accurate—and an understatement.

OTHER FACTORS

Two months before Churchill's visit, Hamilton College had launched a $175 million capital campaign called the Excelsior Campaign to renovate buildings and increase both its endowment and annual fund. Hamilton's loyal alumni were ranked among the top 10 colleges nationally for alumni support, according to the college's Web site.[84]

Alumni support was resilient too—alumni supported Hamilton College in 2002, amid news that its president at that time resigned after he admitted plagiarizing parts of a convocation speech.

However, two years later and six weeks before Churchill's visit, Hamilton College's Kirkland Project made news headlines when a 1960s radical, Susan Rosenberg, was hired as an artist-in-residence for a memoir-writing seminar. She had served 16 years in prison for possession of weapons and more than 600 pounds of explosives; she also had been linked to a 1981 robbery of a Brink's armored car in which a guard and two police officers were killed, but the charges were later dropped against her.[85]

The *Washington Post* reported that some faculty members were protesting Rosenberg's visit in a news brief November 12, 2004. However, the *Wall Street Journal* wrote a lengthy and scathing commentary December 3, 2004 entitled "Meet the Newest Member of the Faculty" that recounted the Brinks incident and more recent invitation to Hamilton College. The article quoted Hamilton professor Nancy Rabinowitz, coordinator of the college's artist-in residence program, saying

Rosenberg was an "'exemplar of rehabilitation' whose 'story is about how you can make something productive out of something that was really awful.'"[86]

Word of Rosenberg's sensational past coupled with protests from professors and alumni eventually caused the one-time radical and now reformed prisoner to decline her position at Hamilton College.[87] Her resignation was reported in another major New York newspaper, the *Daily News* on December 10, 2004.

THE CHURCHILL CONTROVERSY

Following the Rosenberg controversy, a Hamilton College government professor began checking up on future Kirkland Project speakers.[88] His Internet search turned up some of Churchill's writings, including a little-known essay entitled "Some People Push Back: On the Justice of Roosting Chickens," which contained a political bombshell.[89] In the essay Churchill compared the financial workers killed in the 9/11 World Trade Center attacks to the Nazi technocrat Adolf Eichmann, notorious for his organization of the infamous "Final Solution," which resulted in the deaths of millions of Jews in World War II.[90]

Writing shortly after the 9/11 attacks, Churchill described America's history of military interventions, which he said had resulted in violations of international law and fundamental human rights. In the essay "Some People Push Back," Churchill said the victims of 9/11 were far from innocent and got their just desserts:[91]

> They were too busy braying, incessantly and self-importantly, into their cell-phones, arranging power lunches and stock transactions, each of which translated, conveniently out of sight, mind and smelling distance, into the starved and rotting flesh of infants.
>
> If there was a better, more effective, or in fact any other way of visiting some penalty befitting their par-

> ticipation upon the little Eichmanns inhabiting the sterile sanctuary of the twin towers, I'd really be interested in hearing about it.

The Hamilton College professor sent the offending essay to the attention of the college's administration on December 14, 2004, with the request that Churchill's invitation be rescinded.[92]

Although Churchill had spoken publicly hundreds of times, and at dozens of colleges without incident after the 9/11 terrorism attacks, Hamilton College was cautious of stirring up new controversy.[93] A meeting between Hamilton College president Joan Hinde Stewart, the dean of the faculty, and the Kirkland Project director on December 17, 2004, resulted in dropping Churchill's prison topic and changing the focus of the panel discussion to "confront Churchill's views."[94]

A month later, the January 21, 2004, edition of the campus student newspaper reported the controversy of Churchill's upcoming visit. The article carried direct quotes from the offending essay and was accompanied by a photo of Churchill outfitted with a camouflage jacket, beret, sunglasses, and assault weapon.[95] Theodore Eismeier, the professor who brought the essay to the administration's attention, as well as the student campus newspaper editors, said in the student article:[96]

> The Kirkland Project and the College may try to spin this event as constructive dialogue. I think such an effort won't pass the laugh test on or off campus. It seems akin to inviting a representative of the KKK to speak and then asking a member of the NAACP to respond.

A local newspaper picked up the story with a front-page article January 26, 2005,[97] which was featured the same day in a well-read conservative blog called "Little Green Footballs."[98] The blog entry also included excerpts from Churchill's controversial essay.

The blog entry was bombarded with hundreds of posters outraged by the essay and Hamilton College's decision to host Churchill. The blog, with its national reach, spurred traditional national media coverage.

The college issued two news releases on January 26, 2005. One provided biographical information on each panelist, including Churchill. Panel topics included "Some People Push Back" (Churchill), "Criminalizing Dissent" (Churchill's wife, Natsu Taylor Saito), and "Pragmatic Pacifism" (Hamilton College's Richard Werner).[99]

The second statement acknowledged that some people would view Churchill's ideas as "repugnant and disparaging":[100]

Kirkland Project Speaker to Appear Feb. 3

In the days and weeks immediately following September 11th, Hamilton joined with the world community in denouncing the terrorist acts of that tragic morning. We all share deeply in the pain of the families who lost loved ones. Many people view Ward Churchill's comments concerning 9/11 as repugnant and disparaging the 3,000 people killed that day, including three Hamilton alumni and the father of a current Hamilton student.

Hamilton, like any institution committed to the free exchange of ideas, invites to its campus people of diverse opinions, often controversial. The opportunity to encounter and respond to people from outside the college community in their intensity and their immediacy is among the key attributes of a liberal education. The views of speakers are their own. We expect, as a matter of civil discourse, that the members of this academic community, as well as visitors, respect the dignity of reasoned and principled debate. It is in this setting that the substance and credibility of a speak-

er's views are established as being worthy of support, or not.

We expect that many of those who strongly disagree with Mr. Churchill's comments will attend his talk and make their views known. This is the process of both academic freedom and freedom of speech.

The Churchill remarks outraged many alumni, faculty, and students; three Hamilton College alumni died in the 9/11 attacks. Days before Churchill's scheduled visit, some students and faculty planned a protest.

Two days later Bill O'Reilly, host of a Fox network conservative news show called *The O'Reilly Factor*, highlighted the controversy, attributing to Churchill the viewpoint that "the Americans killed on 9/11 deserved to be murdered, and that al Qaeda is correct in trying to kill anyone who buys into the American economic system."[101] O'Reilly interviewed Matthew Coppo, a Hamilton College student whose father—a municipal bond trader—was killed in the Twin Towers attacks, and a Hamilton College professor who reluctantly backed Churchill's visit on the grounds of free speech. O'Reilly ended the segment saying:[102]

I don't want anybody doing anything crazy to Hamilton College. I don't want any threats going in there. I don't want any of that. Feel free to write or e-mail the college with your complaints. And you alumni at Hamilton, do not give them a nickel if that man appears.

Hundreds and hundreds of e-mails and calls flooded into the campus, including e-mails from parents and spouses who lost children, husbands, and wives in the 9/11 attacks. In addition, alumni and parents whose children were considering or planning to attend the college responded. A few of their e-mails follow:

I have a son who is a junior in high school. We have been considering Hamilton College. After hearing about the anti-American hate monger you are giving a forum up there to spew his venom, we will be looking at more responsible schools to educate our son.[103]

I am a student looking at different options right now; your school was my number one choice, but after a segment I viewed on Bill O'Reilly, I will never speak the name Hamilton again. Just thought you should know. Thank you for showing me your schools colors before I attended.[104]

Your college is actually going to provide a person like Ward Churchill with a forum? Why not get some of the most vile Nazis or irrational Muslim terrorists and let them share the microphone? To spice things up, why not dredge up some of the old-line KKK types and let them scream the "N" word at the top of their lungs? And spare me the twaddle about "the First Amendment," "free speech," "diversity of ideas", yadda, yadda. Mindless, irrational hate speech does not need a public forum at a place that holds itself out as an institution of education.[105]

In several news accounts, Hamilton College's president defended the college's actions on grounds of academic freedom and free speech principles. She also noted that college was a place for students to learn how to be independent and critical thinkers.

A memo to the campus community from Hamilton College president Stewart on January 30, 2005, updated the situation and explained the reasoning behind the decision to continue the event despite growing negative publicity. At that time, more than a thousand e-mails and hundreds of telephone calls had been received. Most protested Churchill's impending visit and asked Stewart to

cancel the event. Instead, she said in her memo:[106]

However repugnant one may find Mr. Churchill's remarks, were the College to withdraw the invitation simply on the ground that he has said offensive things, we would be abandoning a principle on which this College and indeed this republic are founded. Free speech is put to the test precisely in circumstances like these when the speech in question is abhorrent. As Justice Brandeis put it, "If there be time to expose through discussion the falsehood and fallacies, to avert the evil by the processes of education, the remedy to be applied is more speech, not enforced silence."

The controversy about Churchill's visit reminds us all of the pain and suffering of the 9/11 attack. Our hearts go out to all the victims of this vicious attack for their fate is to me deplorable.

The next day, January 31, 2005, Churchill resigned as chairman of the ethnic studies department at the University of Colorado at Boulder. His resignation was accompanied by a press release posted on the university's Web site. In it he said the recent coverage of his controversial comments had resulted in death threats. He tried to clarify several points that he felt had been inaccurately portrayed in the media including the following:[107]

The piece circulating on the internet was developed into a book, "On the Justice of Roosting Chickens." Most of the book is a detailed chronology of U.S. military interventions since 1776 and U.S. violations of international law since World War II. My point is that we cannot allow the U.S. government, acting in our name, to engage in massive violations of international law and fundamental human rights and not expect to reap the consequences.

I am not a "defender" of the September 11 attacks, but simply pointing out that if U.S. foreign policy results in massive death and destruction abroad, we cannot feign innocence when some of that destruction is returned. I have never said that people "should" engage in armed attacks on the United States, but that such attacks are a natural and unavoidable consequence of unlawful U.S. policy. As Martin Luther King, quoting Robert F. Kennedy, said, "Those who make peaceful change impossible make violent change inevitable."

. . . Finally, I have never characterized all the September 11 victims as "Nazis." What I said was that the "technocrats of empire" working in the World Trade Center were the equivalent of the "little Eichmanns." Adolf Eichmann was not charged with direct killing but with ensuring the smooth running of the infrastructure that enabled the Nazi genocide. Similarly, German industrialists were legitimately targeted by the Allies.

Churchill's news release said he did not advocate violence. He also recounted U.S. Ambassador to the United Nations Madeleine Albright's 1996 response to the death of 500,000 Iraqi children as a result of economic sanctions as "worth the cost."

That night on Fox's *O'Reilly Factor*, a professor of law at the University of Colorado was interviewed about the Churchill controversy.[108] O'Reilly called Hamilton's president and the Kirkland Project director "villains" and recounted the embarrassing Rosenberg incident, another Hamilton College invited speaker who had spent 16 years in prison for possessing explosives. The professor explained the legalities of freedom of speech

as it related to the Churchill incident. O'Reilly concluded the segment by giving Hamilton College's toll-free phone number and President Stewart's e-mail address.

A Hamilton College news release the next day, February 1, 2005, announced the panel discussion had been moved to a new location—the college's field house—to accommodate expected large crowds. It also revealed a new panelist, Philip Klinkner, a Hamilton College professor of government.[109]

President Stewart had learned through Churchill's wife that Churchill had received more than 100 threats.[110] He planned to bring two bodyguards and wear a flak jacket and sit apart from the other speakers.[111]

Early the morning of February 1, the college switchboard received two calls that threatened violence, including "one who threatened to bring a gun to the event."[112]

Later that morning, a brief news release was issued:[113]

Kirkland Project Panel Cancelled: Public Safety Cited

Feb. 1, 2005, 11 a.m. Cancellation of Panel Discussion on Limits of Dissent.

We have done our best to protect what we hold most dear, the right to speak, think and study freely.

But, there is a higher responsibility that this institution carries, and that is the safety and security of our students, faculty, staff and the community in which we live.

Credible threats of violence have been directed at the College and members of the panel. These threats have been turned over to the police.

Based on the information available, I have made the decision to cancel this event in the interest of protecting those at risk.

Joan Hinde Stewart
President

EPILOGUE

Hamilton College president Stewart sent a lengthy open letter to the Hamilton community on February 9, 2005. The letter explained in detail the chronology of the controversy and explained her decision making process. A portion of the letter included the following:[114]

So why was I still prepared to allow the invitation to Ward Churchill to stand? Academic freedom means that faculty members are free to express differing views in their classrooms and in their scholarly research, and by extension so are speakers brought to campus. Inviting visiting lecturers has long been primarily a faculty prerogative. Such autonomy remains fundamental to our educational mission. . . .

Moreover, in college, young people learn to be independent, critical thinkers. There have been many controversial speakers on campus in the past, and students have benefited from the discussions they provoked. The cancellation of the event was, therefore, an educational loss. Our students and faculty will not have the opportunity to confront and challenge Mr. Churchill's views. As a society, we lose as well; if one of the best colleges in the country can be bullied into restraining academic freedom, we are all less free. Intellectual freedom has suffered a blow, and I worry that this tactic will be used again against us and other colleges and universities. . . .

Hamilton will continue to invite speakers with widely divergent views. At the same time, we must have speakers who are thought-provoking and not merely provocative, who challenge us intellectually as opposed to being merely outrageous. The point of academic free-dom is, after all, to pursue truth and explore serious and difficult questions with our students, holding ourselves and our students to the highest intellectual standards. Academic excellence and intellectual diversity must go hand in hand. . . .

Hamilton College's president also met with about 150 alumni and parents February 17, 2005, at a previously scheduled New York City fundraising event. She discussed the controversy and answered questions.

The following year, the number of applications to Hamilton College dropped slightly from 4,445 to 4,186, but full-time enrollment actually grew by 37 students.[115] Its 53 percent alumni giving rate in 2005, which declined 5 percent from the previous year, placed the college in the top 1 percent in participation with a record $5.45 million contributed by alumni, parents, and friends. The College's Excelsior Campaign had reached the $100 million mark by January 2006, well on its way to making its 2008 goal of $175 million.[116]

The college's ranking by *U.S. News & World Report* moved up four places to #15 for the liberal arts colleges category in 2006, thanks in large part to a higher "academic reputation" rating.[117]

Calls for Churchill's resignation or removal at the University of Colorado, Boulder, were numerous. In 2006 he was accused of allegedly plagiarizing the work of others and violating the most basic standards of scholarly research.[118] Churchill responded that the report[119]

is designed to send a clear message to all scholars: Lay low. Do not challenge orthodoxy. If you do, expect to be targeted for elimination and understand that the University will not be constrained by its own rules—or the Constitution—in its attempts to silence you.

In June 2006, the interim chancellor at the University of Colorado at Boulder issued a notice of intent to dismiss Churchill.

Questions for Discussion

1. Define organizational reputation. Why is it important?

2. What reputation problems did the Ward Churchill incident present for Hamilton College?

3. What techniques are there to manage an organization's reputation?

4. There's a saying that any publicity—even bad publicity—is good. Would you agree with that in this case study? Explain your reasoning.

5. Assess the public relations strategies and techniques used to respond to this crisis. What would you have done differently? Why?

6. If the event had been held, how would you have handled protests at it?

7. Many colleges, including Hamilton College, were unaware of Ward Churchill's more controversial writings. How could a college prepare for future invited speakers?

8. Why did Hamilton College mention academic freedom and principles of free speech in its defense of Ward Churchill? What are their values in a liberal arts education?

9. Why did some people consider academic freedom and free speech weak defenses within the context of the 9/11 terrorists attacks three years earlier?

10. Media coverage widely quoted the "little Eichmanns" statement in Ward Churchill's essay. Should Hamilton College have put this quote into a broader context?

11. How should Hamilton College have communicated with its key publics, especially alumni, in this situation?

12. Was Hamilton College president Joan Hinde Stewart an effective spokesperson? Why?

13. In a follow-up letter to Hamilton College to faculty, staff, alumni, and other college supporters, how would you present this controversy?

Do Some Research

1. Find three credible sources of information that deal with the legal limits of freedom of speech.

2. Research what academic freedom means on your campus. Come prepared to discuss your findings in class.

3. Research a past controversy at your college. Come prepared to discuss how you would handle this situation from a public relations perspective.

Terminology

- academic freedom
- freedom of speech
- reputation

Web Resources

- **Hamilton College** (the college has maintained some of its news releases on the Ward Churchill incident in its news section) www.hamilton.edu/news/wardchurchill/

- **Hamilton College, the Kirkland Project** academics.hamilton.edu/organizations/kirkland/

- University of Colorado at Boulder, (several news releases about the Ward Churchill matter, including "Report on the Conclusion of Preliminary Review in the Matter of Professor Ward Churchill") www.colorado.edu

- **First Amendment Center** (information relating to freedom of speech issues) www.firstamendmentcenter.org/

- **American Civil Liberties Union** (background information on freedom of speech issues) www.aclu.org/FreeSpeech/FreeSpeechMain.cfm

- **Foundation for Individual Rights in Education** (background information about academic freedom) www.thefire.org/

Minicase

Camp Leech-A-Lot

Summertime is a time when kids across the country head off to summer camp, where they can discover all those things that make nature and camping a perfect growing experience: hiking, arts and crafts, campfires, S'mores, sing-alongs, swimming, and leeches.

Leeches?!

At Camp Pine Trees, the spring had been unusually wet and warm. By the time hundreds of campers arrived in early summer, vegetation along the camp lakefront was thick, green, and home to a large leech population—a totally new wilderness experience for first-time and veteran campers. On day one of camp season, it was not long before a camper emerged with two leeches affixed to her leg, causing a sensation among the population of naturally curious and talkative little girls.

Fifty miles away at the headquarters of the camp's sponsoring organization, Samantha Snow, public relations specialist, received a visit from the executive director. "I just spoke with the camp nurse. We have leeches on the waterfront, and at least one girl had them on her," the director said. "We need to decide how we're going to handle this. I'm in a meeting right now. Could you get more information and come to my office in an hour so we can plan what we're going to do?"

"You bet," said Snow. "Is the girl okay?"

"Yes. The nurse says leeches are gross but not really harmful. Swimming is off limits until we get rid of them," said the director.

Leeches! Ugh! Snow's first thought was of slimy, bloodsucking pests attaching themselves to campers. She didn't know anything about leeches except what she'd seen in scary movies when people emerged from swamps covered with the critters.

With just an hour to go, Snow got down to business.

Questions for Discussion

1. If you were Samantha Snow, what would be your first action?
2. How would you get more information?
3. Whom would you communicate with?
4. What are the pros and cons of going to the news media with this story?
5. What short-term and long-term strategies would you implement?

Chapter Seven

Consumer Relations

Consumer relations embodies two areas of concern: (1) supporting marketing communication efforts to build consumer demand for products and services and (2) maintaining mutually beneficial and lasting relationships between the organization and consumer. Inherent in the concept of consumer relations is safeguarding against questionable promotional efforts and looking out for the long-term interests of the consumer. Essentially, public relations should always take a longer view of the organization's activities to ensure consumers are not taken advantage of by shortsighted, deceptive practices or misguided policies that offend customers and noncustomers alike.

The connective power of the Internet has had a major impact on the ability of individuals to quickly raise an issue and organize disparate individuals around the world into formidable activist groups. A disgruntled customer or other stakeholder today can use an activist Web site to wage a one-person battle that will appear to be a full-fledged organizational effort. The result can be unwanted negative publicity and turned-off customers.

By paying attention to consumers' needs and concerns, organizations can develop a long-term relationship resulting in repeat patronage and valuable word-of-mouth endorsements from the consumer sphere of influence. Public relations practitioners can work with activists and other stakeholders who are unhappy with the organization to build understanding and minimize hostile attitudes.

MARKETING COMMUNICATION SUPPORT

Marketing has traditionally relied on paid advertising to reach the consumer market to build a customer base for products or services. While effective advertising does attract attention, its expensive production and placement costs are multiplied and complicated by an increasingly fragmented audience that gets information and entertainment from myriad sources. Clutter, the enormous number of advertisements that confront consumers daily, is also a concern. With so many advertisements assaulting the senses today, many consumers have become expert in tuning them out or using technology that removes them. Also, younger consumers are spending less time with traditional entertainment advertising sources, such as television, and more online, instant messaging friends or playing video games.

To combat these concerns, marketing has increasingly valued its partnership with public relations. Its expertise in media relations and special event planning is a valued part of the marketing mix for product launches and lengthy campaigns. The basic informational tactics of brochures, newsletters, direct mailers, and Web site material, such as backgrounders and technical specifications, are also the shared responsibility of the marketing and public relations staff.

Media relations efforts involve product mentions in the news media to raise awareness. Public relations practitioners pitch the product to reporters or editors with a news release/media kit or through personal contact. The goal is to gain the attention of the media gatekeepers and persuade them that the product or service is newsworthy and interesting enough for their audiences. A product that is favorably mentioned in the news portion of a publication or broadcast is usually perceived by consumers as a credible, independent endorsement (third-party endorsement) deemed worthy of extra attention. The fact that the product is mentioned by a credible outside source, when other competitors' products are not, helps establish its superiority. This is a relatively inexpensive publicity tactic to draw attention to the product and heighten consumer awareness.

Associated with media relations is speaker and media training. Public relations can help CEOs and other managers become effective spokespersons for their organizations. CEOs who participate in various high-profile industry gatherings as convention keynote speakers and panelists are often covered by the media. In addition, CEOs can be invited as talk show guests or interviewed for news and feature stories. All these efforts, if focused on the organization's mission, can help build its reputation as an industry leader.

Special events also focus or refocus consumers' attention on the product, especially when the product or service is not that much different from other competitors' products. Gala store openings, stunts, and celebrity guest appearances are some of the tactics used to attract attention. The goal of designing the right special event is to logically connect it with the product's attributes. A hybrid electric auto, for example, could travel across the country to draw attention to advances in the company's electric car line. A cake mix company might make a large White House–replica cake for a birthday gift to the president. To promote chess playing, a top-ranked chess player might play 20 young competitors simultaneously in a timed competition. Celebrities are used frequently in special events or as product endorsers because they attract attention just because of who they are; companies want those star qualities transferred to the product or service. For example, the U.S. Postal Service's sponsorship of Lance Armstrong, a seven-time Tour de France winner, helped connect speed, quality, and a winning image of U.S. mail service with the world's top cycling athlete.

When a consumer's attention is captured and he or she seeks more information about the product or service, appropriate tactics can connect with those active information seekers. A stand-alone product Web site or a part of the organization's Web site can provide a multimedia source for video, audio, and text information. Some of the most effective examples of product Web sites today are those promoting Hollywood's latest offerings. The 2005 version of *King Kong*, for instance, used its Web site to provide weekly production videos and updates on the making of the big-budget film. A blog carried the latest news, including tidbits from key movie executives. The site also featured games and promotional items, as well as memorabilia from the original 1933 film. Web sites frequently contain electronic versions of media kits with news releases, fact sheets, questions and answers, backgrounders, features, photos, and logos that further inform information seekers.

While emotional appeals to consumers' self-interests are all important, informational tactics should also provide information that allows consumers to comparison shop. When it comes to consumer electronics, for example, specification sheets can offer detailed technical information that advertisements do not have room to carry. Often these sheets use unfamiliar technical language, particularly for technology products. While it is acceptable to use technical terminology, it is a good idea to have a glossary of terminology to help beginners.

Once a product or service is purchased, communication efforts should continue. Many companies include short satisfaction surveys in registration materials or mail them to the customer soon after his or her purchase. Other helpful consumer relations efforts include toll-free telephone numbers or Web-based customer representative chat rooms to guide customers with any product-related problems or concerns. Letters written to an organization regarding product problems should be answered and monitored for potential patterns of problems.

BEYOND THE CONSUMER

Public relations seeks to build relationships with many stakeholders to ensure the long-term viability of the organization. While the customer is a primary stakeholder for any organization, shareholders, employees, government officials, and others concerned with policies and actions of an organization are important to public relations.

In addition, public relations is concerned with identifying and managing issues from all stakeholders, including consumer complaints, that could have a negative impact on the organization. This is done by monitoring its environment and public opinion. Public relations ultimately should help organizations grow while maintaining mutually beneficial relationships with its stakeholders. This delicate balancing act is not always an easy task; it often requires organizations to look beyond their monthly earnings reports and see their connections to others.

Mashing the Low-Carbohydrate Craze
A Healthy Helping of Potato Promotion

Its demur brown countenance and decidedly earthy background aren't exactly glamorous.

And to add insult to injury, it contains carbohydrates.

Ah . . . the poor potato.

It wasn't always that way for the most popular dinner side dish. Hauled home from the grocery store in 5- and 10-pound bags, the potato was a mainstay at the American dinner table and was served mashed, whipped, fried, chipped, roasted, and baked.

In fact, the popularity of the potato hit an all-time high of 145 pounds per capita in the late 1990s (thanks to Americans' love affair with French fries, the most popular potato form). But fresh potato consumption declined 24 percent in the 1990s.[1]

Some of the reasons for the decline, according to an industry study, were:[2]

- Busy households that wanted quicker and easier meal preparation.
- The decline of traditional families, the core of fresh potato consumers, who are now a minority.

Get the skinny on America's favorite vegetable:

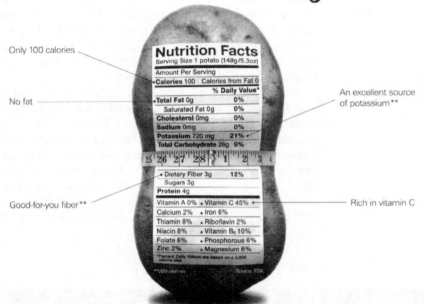

Only 100 calories

No fat

Good-for-you fiber**

An excellent source of potassium**

Rich in vitamin C

Nutrition Facts
Serving Size 1 potato (148g/5.3oz)

Amount Per Serving	
Calories 100	Calories from Fat 0

	% Daily Value*
Total Fat 0g	0%
Saturated Fat 0g	0%
Cholesterol 0mg	0%
Sodium 0mg	0%
Potassium 720 mg	21%
Total Carbohydrate 26g	9%
Dietary Fiber 3g	12%
Sugars 3g	
Protein 4g	

Vitamin A 0%	• Vitamin C 45%
Calcium 2%	• Iron 6%
Thiamin 8%	• Riboflavin 2%
Niacin 8%	• Vitamin B₆ 10%
Folate 6%	• Phosphorous 6%
Zinc 2%	• Magnesium 6%

*Percent Daily Values are based on a 2,000 calorie diet.

**With skin on   Source: FDA

The Healthy Potato.

Potatoes aren't just good; they're good for you. Just check the label. America's favorite vegetable is naturally fat free, only 100 calories, rich in vitamin C and potassium and a good source of fiber. No wonder leading nutrition experts like Harvard Medical School's Dr. George L. Blackburn and Registered Dietitian Ann M. Coulston, past president of the American Dietetic Association, recommend potatoes as part of a healthy, balanced diet.

UNITED STATES
Potato
BOARD

www.healthypotato.com

Courtesy of the United States Potato Board..

- The growth of one- and two-family households that eat out frequently and aren't buying 5- and 10-pound. bags of potatoes anymore.
- Consumer demand for new and different eating experiences, especially for ethnic foods.

During the 1990s *Dr. Atkins' New Diet Revolution* became a controversial best-seller that endorsed a high-protein, high-fat, low-carbohydrate diet. The potato's 26 grams of carbohydrates per 5.3-ounce serving were out. By the early 2000s, the low-carbohydrate diet had grown into a significant trend and subsequently affected attitudes toward the healthfulness of potatoes.

The downward trend in potato consumption required action, and the U.S. Potato Board (USPB), an industry association, rose to the challenge. It created a sustained national information campaign in 2004 that highlighted the many nutritional benefits of the potato. USPB, with its national representation of 6,000 potato growers and handlers nationwide and its long history of promoting potatoes generically since 1971, sought to reposition the potato as a healthy food choice.[3]

Extensive research sponsored by the USPB, including focus groups and a national survey, revealed that consumers didn't know how healthy a potato could be. "The good news is that once consumers were shown the actual FDA nutrition label for potatoes they were thrilled. They wanted to be able to eat potatoes, one of their favorite foods, and once they knew the facts, they intended to eat more of them," said Tim O'Connor, chief executive officer of the USPB.[4]

According to the Healthy Potato Web site:[5]

Only 6 percent of those polled knew that potatoes are an excellent source of vitamin C, when in fact, a medium-sized (5.3-ounce) potato provides 45 percent of the recommended Daily Value of this essential nutrient. Only 34 percent of respondents considered potatoes with skins to be rich in potassium, when they are actually an excellent source of this mineral— higher than broccoli, spinach, or bananas. Two in five consumers didn't know the number of calories or the amount of fat in an average potato (correct answer: 100 and 0 grams, respectively). Worse yet, only 4.2 percent thought potatoes were BOTH rich in potassium AND vitamin C.

Beyond consumers' lack of awareness about the potato's health benefits, low-carbohydrate dieters were being warned away from certain carbohydrates identified by their high glycemic index values (foods such as potatoes, white rice, bagels, and many breakfast cereals that are digested quickly and cause a rapid rise in blood sugar). A few small research studies pointed to increased risk of heart disease and diabetes due to foods with a high glycemic index.[6]

To combat its image woes, the U.S. Potato Board approved a $4.4 million (and later an additional $1.6 million)[7] nutritional campaign to carry the "healthy potato" message directly to consumers with the help of Fleishman-Hillard (FH), a nationally respected public relations firm.[8] Linda McCashion, vice president of public relations for the USPB, said Fleishman-Hillard recommended a proactive and integrated marketing program that focused on the positive nutritional message of potatoes.

THE STRATEGY

In addition to consumer advertising, the campaign included a national publicity program, a partnership with Weight Watchers, research, food service, and retail elements.[9]

The "Get the Skinny On America's Favorite Vegetable" advertising campaign targeted national news outlets including *USA Today*, the *New York Times*, the *Washington Post*, as well as *Time, Parenting*, and *People* magazines.[10] Advertising emphasized the nutritional value of potatoes with a nutrition label pointing out all its laudable qualities. A follow-up fall advertising buy included *People, Good Housekeeping, Ladies Home Journal, Better Homes and Garden*, and National Public Radio.

This limited advertising campaign, along with the research that directed its creative strategy, served as the news "hook" to capture media attention. An umbrella theme was created for the entire campaign: "The Healthy Potato, Naturally Nutritious, Always Delicious," which emphasized the nutritional value of potatoes. A press kit was sent to major newspapers across the country, and Fleishman-Hillard staff called many food editors to offer assistance in developing potato articles. For smaller newspapers, a high-quality two-column ready-to-use feature ("mat release," a term that refers to "matte" and its association to old printing techniques) was developed, allowing papers to easily insert the material without resetting. Fleishman-Hillard also targeted several magazines (*Food & Wine, Good Housekeeping, Glamour, Woman's Day, Country Living, Parade, Redbook, Self,* and *Family Circle,* among others) located in New York City for "deskside briefings" with key editors. Fleishman-Hillard's on-staff nutrition expert, Katherine Beals, Ph.D., R.D., joined each meeting to answer any questions related to potato nutrition, low-carbohydrate diets, and research studies related to potatoes.[11]

Radio and video news releases featured registered dietitians explaining the nutritional benefits of potato consumption.[12]

A major component of the public relations effort was the creation of an informational Web site called Healthypotato.com. The site created a one-stop resource center for consumers, health educators, and the media about the benefits of potatoes. Pull-down menus entitled "Nutrition and Information," "Heath Educators," "Foodservice," "Recipes," "Media Center," and "About Us" provided a wealth of factual information.[13]

The Nutrition and Information section of the Web site included downloadable nutritional handouts, written by nutritionists, that responded directly to some of the tough questions consumers had about potatoes; these concerns resulted in downloadable information products entitled "Childhood Obesity," "Heart Disease," "Athletic Performance," "Carbohydrate Basics," "Hunger, Appetite and Satiety," "Potato Storage and Care," "Glycemic Index," and "Starch Sources." In "Carbohydrate Basics," for example,

the brochure notes that "carbohydrates are so crucial to the body that if you severely restrict or eliminate them, your body will begin to make them!"[14] The publication notes the USDA's food pyramid recommends a "diet based on carbohydrate foods" (including potatoes). The publication attacks the misconception some people hold that to lose weight they need to reduce their carbohydrate intake. "But mainstream science advises that excess calories are to blame for weight gain, regardless of what foods they come from."[15]

Included on the Web site is a "Healthy Potato" consumer brochure—that highlights the nutritional benefits of the potato and provides health preparation ideas created by Robin Vitetta-Miller, MS, contributing editor to *Health Magazine,* and frequent contributor to *Shape, Men's Fitness,* and CNN.[16]

Also part of the Nutrition and Information section was a call for research proposals on the positive nutritional effects of potatoes.[17] Part of the Potato Board's strategy was to develop research about the satiety and satiation value of potatoes. Foods that are more filling, the theory goes, would increase the time in between eating, thus reducing the number of calories consumed in a given day.

The Web site's section for health educators included PowerPoint presentations on potatoes' nutritional benefits with speaker cards.[18] The carbohydrate debate was also directly addressed in a "Carbohydrate Confusion" Q&A fact sheet.[19]

To increase the use of potatoes within the home, delicious potato-centered recipes were available on the Web site in a simple and easy-to-use searchable database based on menu category, main ingredients, or prep/cook time.[20]

The Web site's media center featured a news release detailing the National Academy of Sciences' recommendation for increasing potassium intake from 3,500 mg to 4,700 mg per day.[21] The release noted that skin-on potatoes had 750 mg of potassium, the number-one source for potassium, higher than broccoli, bananas, tomatoes, or orange juice. The media center also included the healthy potato consumer brochure, what top chefs were saying about potatoes, a potato varieties fact sheet, and a backgrounder on the USPB.

Beyond the Web site, an important partnership was developed with Weight Watchers in which potatoes were featured in its new "Pick of the Season" educational program that stressed the importance of fresh fruits and vegetables in a healthy lifestyle.[22] Participating grocery stores, such as Schnuck's Markets chain in St. Louis, Missouri, featured in its produce areas the Weight Watcher's brochure "The Truth about Carbs" and the USPB brochure "Healthy Potato." One million Weight Watchers clients received potato recipe cards and nutrition information in their local Weight Watchers meetings during the promotion.

THE RESULTS

According to the USPB's annual attitude and usage study—participants' detailed mentions regarding the "best things about the health/nutrition of potatoes"—there was a 23 percent gain in favorable health/nutrition associations for potatoes (40 percent in 2004 versus 17 percent in 2003), and in this same study there was a 9 percent gain in respondents who cited that potatoes contained important vitamins and minerals (11 percent in 2004 versus 2 percent in 2003).[23]

The Healthy Potato public relations campaign generated nearly 62 million impressions in national print and broadcast consumer media within six months. The "Get the Skinny" ad with its nutrition label on a potato also generated media interest; newspapers such as the *New York Times* and *USA Today* reprinted the USPB's ad art as part of the news article that positioned the nutrition label before the public. According to Fleishman-Hillard, 28 million listeners heard the Healthy Potato message from the radio media tour (RMT) and radio news release (RNR).

Traffic to the Healthy Potato Web site doubled and more than 250,000 people requested the Healthy Potato brochure during the campaign.

With the goal of repositioning the potato as a "nutrition powerhouse," USPB sought opportunities to expand its message.[24] When the National Academy of Sciences recommended consumers increase their potassium consumption, a "potassium subcampaign" was launched to highlight the potassium content of potatoes ("potatoes rank highest among the 20 top selling fruits and vegetables.")[25]

Open Scenario Challenge
New Research Effort Examines Low-Glycemic Diets

You are a communication specialist for the U.S. Potato Board. In your media monitoring, you run across a news release from a research hospital entitled "New Data Validates Low-Glycemic Diet" by a top glycemic index researcher. The study notes that people should avoid foods with a high glycemic index rating. You know that potatoes have a high glycemic index rating. The news release also announces plans for a human trial of a low-glycemic diet. Interested, you do thorough research to better familiarize yourself with the glycemic index and how the USPB has previously responded to this issue. Further investigation convinces you that action may be needed. You e-mail the director of communication to set up an appointment.

Step one: Read the news release "New Data Validates Low-Glycemic Diet" at www.childrenshospital.org /newsroom/Site1339/ mainpageS1339P0.html

Step two: Read the U.S. Potato Board's glycemic index fact sheet at www.healthypotato.com/downloads/ GlycemicIndex.pdf

Step three: Do additional research, and then develop talking points for USPB about the research effort or the glycemic index issue. Present your ideas in writing, and come prepared to deliver them orally in class through a role-playing activity.

Questions for Discussion

1. Was an informational campaign the best strategy for the potato industry's problem? What other communication options were there?
2. What, in your opinion, was the most effective tactic of this information campaign?
3. What third-party endorsements did the U.S. Potato Board (USPB) get for its information campaign?
4. How would you make potatoes appealing to the college-age market and to young children?
5. Explain the purpose of the mat release, RNR, RMT, and VNR as media relations communication tactics for the Potato Board's promotional campaign.
6. What would you do if you were assigned to do the desk-side briefings for the information campaign to newspaper and magazine editors?

Do Some Research

1. What other foods and beverages are suffering image problems today? How are those problems similar to or different from the image problem that potatoes faced? Develop a communication strategy to solve the problems.
2. The USPB has one of the most extensive libraries of potato information in the industry. Several marketing research studies and reports are available on its Web site www.potatoes.com. Examine how marketing research or long-term planning reports are invaluable for developing strategic communication programs.
3. Extend your knowledge of marketing practices. Examine the Potato Board's use of point-of-sale materials, packaging, and merchandising as it relates to increasing sales in grocery stores. Information about in-store promotion is available at the Potato Board's Web site www.potatoes.com.

Terminology

- *Dr. Atkins' New Diet Revolution*
- high-protein, high-fat, low-carbohydrate diet
- industry association
- generic promotions
- consumer brochure
- nutrition label
- food pyramid
- focus group
- glycemic index
- satiety/satiation
- desk-side briefings
- repositioning campaign
- radio news release (RNR)
- radio media tour (RMT)
- video news release (VNR)
- mat release

Web Resources

- **U.S. Potato Board** www.uspotatoes.com
- **U.S. Potato Board's Healthy Potato site** www.healthypotato.com/index.asp
- **Food and Drug Administration's food pyramid** www.fda.gov
- **United States Department of Agriculture** www.usda.gov

Freedom, Flexibility, and Fun!

Trade Association Puts Record Gas Prices in Perspective

Retirees love them, and some environmentalists hate them: recreation-vehicles (RVs). If you've ever passed a huge RV on the highway, you've probably thought: "What a gas guzzler! It must cost a fortune to run."

Understandably, gas prices are a concern for those considering the purchase of a recreational vehicle. As a consequence, they're also on the minds of sellers and manufacturers—and the Recreation Vehicle Industry Association (RVIA), a national trade association representing more than 550 U.S. manufacturers and component suppliers.[26]

Smart business people not only know the merits of their product but its weaknesses as well. Effective organizations often use a strengths, weaknesses, opportunities, and threats (SWOT) analysis to determine what's good about their products and services as well as any weaknesses or potential problems. Such organizations are also outward-looking, scanning the environment to take advantage of opportunities and to plan for potential threats.

As a trade association, RVIA promotes the $14 billion "Made in America" recreation vehicle industry nationally to supplement the efforts of its manufacturer members and their local dealers.[27] While gas prices might be a psychological barrier for some potential RV buyers, RVIA sought to put rising gas prices into perspective during summer 2004. Higher gas prices, it argued, affected all modes of transportation and were just one small factor to consider when purchasing an RV.

"With the media's spotlight on rising fuel prices, our public relations and marketing team initiated a proactive, research-driven media outreach program to demonstrate to RV owners and potential buyers the exceptional value and other advantages of RV travel despite the higher cost of fuel," said Gary LaBella, RVIA vice president of public relations and advertising.

RESEARCH

RVIA used research extensively to build credibility in its media relations strategy. Three studies in particular were commissioned by RVIA and referenced in its media efforts:

- PKF Consulting, an international consulting firm with expertise in travel and tourism, found that a family of four can spend up to 70 percent less on RV vacations compared to vacations using other modes of transportation, such as cars, planes, and cruises.[28]

- The annual Spring/Summer Campfire Canvass Survey of 500 RV owners conducted in March 2004 by Robert Hitlin Research Associates on behalf of RVIA found rising fuel prices were of little concern to most RV owners and that most RV owners planned to travel even more than the year before.[29] For those concerned about higher gas prices, the respondents said they planned to take shorter trips or travel to closer destinations.[30]

- The third study focused on industry growth predictions and was conducted by Dr. Richard Curtin of the University of Michigan Research Center. Entitled "RV Roadsigns," this quarterly study predicted a new quarter-century record for RV shipments with 364,900 units shipped to dealers, up from 320,800 units in 2003. (The final percent sales unit increase for 2004 was 13.7 percent.)[31]

Dr. Curtin's study noted that RV sales would continue to benefit from the aging baby boomers—the 50+ age range in which RV ownership is the highest. By 2010, the number of consumers aged 50 to 64 will total 57 million, 38 percent higher than in 2000.[32] The number of RV-owning households was projected to rise 15 percent between 2001 and 2010, outpacing overall U.S. household growth of 10 percent, according to the University of Michigan study.[33]

The number of RVs owned by those 35 to 54 grew faster than all other age groups, bolstered by an industry advertising campaign aimed at the coveted baby boom generation.[34]

STRATEGY

When dealing with 2004's record pump prices, RVIA's defense was to mount an aggressive offense. Research confirmed that fuel prices had little impact on RV sales or travel. For most owners, the advantages of RV travel vastly outweighed the higher cost of fuel.

Working with public relations agency Barton Gilanelli & Associates, RVIA developed a multifaceted media relations program that emphasized two key messages: (1) RVs offer a great travel value and (2) sales of RVs were expected to reach their highest level in 25 years.[35] The program included other ongoing themes, including RVs are hip, RVs are family friendly, and RVs are "just plain fun."[36]

Media relations efforts were important to launching the overall advertising campaign and maintaining consumer interest through news and other national media outlets. RVIA's "Go RVing" national advertising campaign of print, television, radio, and Internet ads targeted adults 30 to 64 with the message of "Pursue Your Passions." Working with the advertising agency the Richards Group, the RV industry spent $20 million on its "Go RVing" campaign in 2004, including $14 million on national media.[37]

The centerpiece of RVIA's media relations program was its strategic spokesperson program, led by RVIA's president and travel expert David Humphreys. An authoritative and credible spokesperson for industrywide trends concerning recreation vehicles, Humphreys was widely interviewed and quoted by the national media.

RV historian David Woodworth, owner of the largest-known collection of antique

RVs, attracted attention wherever he roamed in his 2004 motor home towing a 1916 Telescoping RV.[38] During his 60-day National RV History Tour, sponsored by RVIA, Woodworth offered local media interviews about the ageless appeal of recreation vehicle travel—an American original with a tradition dating back nearly 100 years.

Representing Generation X, authors and RVIA media spokespersons Brad and Amy Herzog traveled from California to the East Coast in a motor home with their two small children.[39] They focused on how recreation vehicles provide young families with stress-free and affordable vacations.

Spokesperson Media Talking Points

Eleven media talking points were faxed to RVIA member company spokespeople and RVIA spokespeople on April 12, 2004, addressing the impact of rising fuel prices on RV travel as the main buying season approached.[40] The talking points emphasized research by PKF Consulting, an international consulting firm with expertise in travel and tourism, and the Spring/Summer Campfire Canvass Survey of 500 RV owners conducted in March 2004 by Robert Hitlin Research Associates:[41]

- **RV trips are less expensive than flying, driving a car, taking a train or bus, staying in a hotel, or taking a cruise, even when fuel prices increase. RV travelers spend only about $24 per night for a site at a full-service campground. They tend to buy groceries and cook many of their meals in the RV instead of paying high restaurant prices. A family of four can spend up to 70 percent less on RV trips compared to other forms of travel.**

- **Despite increased fuel prices, nearly three-fourths of RV owners indicated they planned to travel more in the spring/summer compared to the prior year. A fourth of the respondents said they would travel the same amount in** spring/summer as they did a year ago. Of those respondents expressing concern over fuel prices, a third indicated their RV trips would be shorter and a quarter said they would stay closer to home.

- Even when fuel prices increase, the difference isn't enough to keep RV travelers at home. For a 200-mile RV trip at 10 mpg, for example, the added cost of 20 gallons of fuel would only be $20 if the cost per gallon rose by one dollar.

- With 16,000 campgrounds nationwide, RV travelers have options and are in control of when and where they go, unlike other forms of mass transit such as airlines.

Other media talking tips focused on the record growth of the RV industry. The April talking tips noted factory-to-dealer deliveries of RVs were expected to set a new quarter-century record in 2004.[42] The reasons cited were low interest rates, an improving economy, low inflation, rising home values, the stock market revival, population trends, and concerns about the safety of international travel. The growth prediction was based on March 2004 research by Dr. Richard Curtain of the University of Michigan Research Center's March 2004 Survey of Consumers.

Reporters could do their own research by experiencing the benefits of RVs through the RVIA vehicle loan program that included a Winnebago Sightseer, Coachmen Santrara, and other units provided by member companies.[43] For example, a business reporter from Reuters News Service rode in a motor home from her Chicago office to Elkhart, Indiana, to visit two different RV factories for a "made in America" story.[44]

Other top journalists from *Motor Trend, National Geographic Traveler,* and *Arthur Frommer's Budget Travel* participated in RVIA's Media Luncheon program, which treated journalists to a drive and catered lunch aboard a motor home.

Beyond the media spokesperson program and traditional media pitches, RVIA's public relations efforts created a "halo effect" with hot entertainment programs and movies incorporating RVs into their plots.[45] RVIA worked to achieve this in two major ways: through the front door (by pitching producers and scriptwriters directly) and through the backdoor (resulting from the news media exposure generated by RVIA—what some call art imitating life).[46] Hollywood had noticed how RV travel was booming in popularity and wanted its works to reflect what's happening in contemporary American life, said LaBella. *Simple Life 2: Road Trip,* starring Paris Hilton and Nicole Richie, was a prime example. FOX's smash hit featured the two twenty-something pop icons traveling the country in an Airstream travel trailer pulled by a hot pink pickup. Two other primetime shows, *ER* and *The Bachelor,* depicted RVs as a glamorous "ride" for a date. This idea was also incorporated into the teen drama *Everwood* on the Warner Brothers network when its main characters went to the prom in a rented RV.[47] Based on television's lead, RVIA began pitching RVs as teen transportation to top teen magazines.

Meet the Fockers, Universal Studio's sequel to the comedy hit *Meet the Parents,* featured an RV for a cross-country road trip by the movie's lead characters portrayed by Hollywood stars regarded as influencers and hip trendsetters.

RVs grew in popularity with professional and amateur athletes, particularly professional golfers. In 2004, 19 PGA players were traveling to tournaments via motor homes—and many of them were talking to the media about their reasons for traveling by RV.[48] In *Golf Digest's* eight-page profile of professional golfer Davis Love, he cited a more comfortable "home" feeling.[49] The visibility of pro golfers with their RVs was a powerful influence for 37 million amateur golfers.

NASCAR had also raised the profile of RVs through its fans and drivers who traveled to races with their RVs.[50]

Closely associated with sports is the tailgate party. In previous years, RVIA had sent its guru of tailgating and media spokesperson Joe Cahn on the road to show how RVs are the ultimate "kitchen on wheels."[51] In 2004, a presidential election year, RVIA turned Cahn into a presidential candidate running on the platform of the Tailgating Party.[52] As *U.S. News & World Report* alerted its readers: "There's a presidential candidate headed to your football stadium, and his party is one everybody can embrace: the Tailgating Party!"[53]

Cahn's RV-1 motor home—decked out in bunting and banners—served as the Tailgating Party headquarters, including the "Rectangular Office." RVIA's initial public relations effort was timed to benefit from the media buildup to the Democratic and Republican conventions and the NFL kickoff in August. After the campaign, Cahn continued his annual trek to professional and college football stadium parking lots to promote RVs as the ultimate tailgating vehicle. His garrulous personality and his delicious tailgate recipes attracted news and food reporters alike.

RESULTS

The proactive media relations efforts of RVIA throughout 2004 kept attention focused on the positive aspects of RVs, despite the high gas prices. Key messages emphasized the industry's record-breaking sales and the freedom, flexibility, and fun that RVs offered to a post-9/11 society seeking greater control and more traditional, hassle-free family activities.

Positive publicity from its media pitches, news releases, press kits, RV loaner program, and media spokesperson program netted top-tier media coverage that continued throughout the year.

Family-theme RV stories, for example, were timed to hit around key holiday weekends such as Fourth of July. A pitch letter sent in the spring noted that families don't have to sacrifice comfort while getting back to nature: "RV travelers can enjoy all the comforts of home while they're on the road.

RVs are loaded with elegant features and state-of-the art entertainment and communication systems, including designer interiors, gourmet kitchens, satellite TVs, DVD players and living rooms and bedrooms that slide out at the push of a button to create extra space."[54]

The following is a sampling of media hits generated by RVIA staff and agency's focus on the family and recreation vehicle theme:[55]

- *NBC Today:* Correspondent Mike Leonard's multigenerational RV trip was the focus of a four-part series airing July 12–15. The segments highlighted the theme of family bonding.

- *Good Morning America* (ABC): The show's new weekend host Bill Weir took his family on a cross-country RV road trip. The three-part series aired in August and revolved around the family discovering America in an RV.

- *CNN Sunday Morning:* In May CNN began weekly updates on the Sprys, a young RV couple from California who were traveling the country in an RV with their four-year-old son.

- *New York Times:* In a July feature story on RV camping, RVs were lauded for promoting family togetherness in an age of overscheduled lives. "It's the last great family-oriented activity left," observed one RV owner.

- *Washington Post:* Kids Post, a page written for younger readers, enthusiastically recommended RV vacations. "Kids like RV travel because it makes the trips seem shorter: Along with watching the scenery they can read (often without headaches), write, watch TV and play games."

- Associated Press: A reporter chronicled her family RV trip to a NASCAR race in July. "As NASCAR fans, my husband and I couldn't have picked a better first trip in the RV," she wrote.

- *CBS Evening News:* Over Memorial Day weekend, CBS devoted a two-minute profile to an active retiree who travels the country in her motor home. Anchor Dan Rather noted that many babyboomers were deciding to hit the road by RV.

- *Wall Street Journal:* In July, RV book author Bernice Beard gave summer travel tips. "RVing surely ranks among the most rewarding of leisure pursuits," the *Journal* declared.
- *Sunset* and *Midwest Living* magazines: In June these magazines conducted hands-on research and chronicled family RV trips with photo-filled spreads.
- Travel Channel: Its new *Travel Gear* program devoted a segment to RV purchasing tips in June. The show noted that there are "RVs for every budget" and focused on the growing popularity of traveling by RV among families with children.
- *NBC Nightly News:* On Easter Sunday, the news featured RVs in its Made in America segment.[56]

Questions for Discussion

1. Why are fuel prices such a concern for the Recreation Vehicle Industry Association? What are the other factors involved in purchasing an RV?
2. Apply SWOT analysis to RVs.
3. What key publics are the Recreation Vehicle Industry Association attempting to reach? Explain the rationale for each.
4. If you were the media relations coordinator for the Recreation Vehicle Industry Association, how would you develop key messages that appeal to the youth generation, including Generation Y, Generation X, teens, and "tweens"? If you were pitching to a women's magazine, what would you emphasize? If you were pitching to a health magazine, what would you emphasize?
5. Analyze the Recreation Vehicle Industry Association's spokesperson program. What are the strengths of

this program? Provide three examples representing different perspectives on the recreation vehicle industry.

Do Some Research

1. Consumer RV trade shows are an important aspect of an RV dealer's marketing efforts. Industry research shows 31 percent of most likely new buyers and 32 percent of former buyers attend a local show. Research how trade/consumer shows work.
2. Research how to put together an effective show booth. What are some tips for successful show booths? Provide a strategic plan for your RVIA booth space. It should be a visually interesting space with a wide variety of collateral material.

Terminology

- SWOT analysis
- national trade association
- media spokesperson program
- top tier media
- talking points
- loaner program for reporters
- PR halo effect
- market expansion program

Web Resources

- **Recreation Vehicle Industry Association** (contains RVIA news releases, fact sheets, photos, media industry reports, surveys, and consumer information) www.rvia.org
- **Go RVing** (contains consumer information about how to rent and purchase an RV, including searchable dealer and campground directories, RV shows, publications, and clubs; Web visitors may order online a free DVD featuring testimonials from RV owners and RV travel tips) www.GoRVing.com
- **United States Department of Energy, Energy Efficiency and Renewable Energy** www.fueleconomy.gov/

Kansas, as Big as You Think
Making a Blank State a Strong Brand

What do you think of when you think of Kansas?

Dorothy and Toto? Tornadoes? Or nothing at all?

The question is one that prompted the Kansas Department of Commerce to create a promotional plan intended to communicate the essence of Kansas and the state's positive qualities to the outside world.

The meaning of Kansas in the minds of Americans arose when the governor held "prosperity summits" across the state in 2003 to discuss opportunities for and barriers to economic growth.[57] In the course of the summits, participants identified the state's image problem as a top priority.[58]

The Kansas Brand Image Task Force was created, comprising statewide business development and tourism industry leaders.[59] Image consultants from Callahan Creek and Ruf Strategic Solutions began by asking what Kansas stood for in the minds of Kansans. This image would become the Kansas brand—not just a logo or a slogan but a summary concept of the feelings, the emotional connection Kansans had with their home state.[60]

Consultants said "selling" a product, service, or location was no longer enough—states with strong brands ("Virginia is for Lovers," "Oklahoma: Native America," and "I Love New York") communicate a clear, consistent message that links the wants and needs of all target audiences. States with a strong brand or image distinguish themselves from other states with a positive impact on everything from economic development to tourism.

The Kansas Department of Commerce wanted to be a leader in the trend toward developing a single, cohesive state brand rather than separate brands for tourism, economic development, and other individ- ual governmental units.[61] For example, tourism had used the tagline "Simply Wonderful," while the business development used "Built on Character."[62] In addition the department wanted to promote the adoption of a single Kansas brand beyond state government, for the use of local governmental and nongovernmental organizations.

RESEARCH

Uncovering the unique characteristics of Kansas was no easy task, and the Kansas Image Task Force started the brand image development process with in-depth research. Its intent was to identify core values, attitudes, perceptions, and misperceptions from both in-state and out-of-state audiences; findings would provide a solid foundation for articulating the state's brand image.[63] The idea was to create synergies instead of disjointed, independent efforts.

Research included a qualitative study involving Kansas state legislators as well as out-of-state business development people, travel writers, and consumers. While Kansans viewed their state as the center of America where people can still trust a handshake and get things done, a survey of business development people who had never been to Kansas revealed a number of negative perceptions: slow paced, not sexy, flat and boring landscapes, and blends into other Midwest states.[64] Also, some respondents described a complete lack of awareness statement: "blank state."[65] However, after these businesspeople visited, their appreciation of Kansas's finer points improved their perceptions: more green rolling hills than imagined, history piques interest, honest, trustworthy, and hardworking, and "America—the way it's supposed to be."[66]

Tourism research found historic attractions, outdoor recreational activities, the western frontier, and agricultural themes were the most enjoyed by visitors.[67] When prospective visitors were asked what their image of Kansas was, the majority said "flat" (24 percent), "plains and grasslands" (13 percent), "don't know" (11 percent), "rich history" (10 percent), "friendly/loyal people" (9 percent), "hot and dry" (7 percent), and among the 18- to 34-year-olds, 10 percent answered "Wizard of Oz."

The main reasons potential visitors from out of state gave for not visiting Kansas included "nothing to do" (26 percent), "rather go somewhere more interesting and fun" (22 percent), "don't know what there is to do" (21 percent), "don't travel" (13 percent), and "never been there" (6 percent).

When asked about the state's personality, the majority of respondents (35 percent) didn't know. Others thought of "boring/dull, Average Joe" (19 percent), "friendly" (15 percent), "relaxed, quiet, easy-going" (10 percent), "wide open"(9 percent), and "exciting, adventurous, fun" (7 percent); smaller numbers selected "farmer, rancher," "nice, happy, content," "conservative," and "rugged, down to earth."

Secondary research found that the upcoming 2005 travel season was expected to surpass the record level set in 2000.[68] A post-9/11 stay-at-home mentality and recession and war resulted in reduced tourism nationwide in 2002–2004. But experts projected 2005 would change all that. Tourism research showed there was a "pent up" demand to get out and unwind; family travel showed special promise. A phrase called "togethering" explained why people were turning to family and friends for comfort in a challenging world. Eighty percent were traveling with extended family or friends. And "grand travel," the anticipated arrival of baby boomers with lots of time and money on their hands, could only mean opportunity for states catering to their needs.

The research revealed travelers were seeking historic, cultural, and "experiential travel."[69] More than half of tourism involves trips to see cultural, art, historical, or heritage sites, activities, and events. Agritourism had become increasingly popular, with its back-to-nature opportunities including farm visits and stays, corn mazes, and u-pick operations; in a processed food world, more "city slickers" were seeking a direct connection with the earth and their food. Geotourism also connected people with nature's wonders, as travelers attracted to geotourism sought to experience preserved natural, historical, and cultural sites or just the outstanding natural scenery.

While Kansas did not have neighboring Missouri's Gateway Arch, New York's Fifth Avenue, or Florida's Disney World, it did have many strengths to build on. It was, after all, an "authentic" place where people could come to unwind and find those special small wonders. Its slower pace promised to deliver more lasting enjoyable memories than an exhausting trip to a well-worn tourist destination.

STRATEGY

To take advantage of its strengths, Kansas needed to define its position—an important part of the branding process. Positioning would demonstrate Kansas's unique qualities to the world and place images in people's minds to fill in the blank response researchers found in many people outside the state.

A positioning statement to convey Kansas's unique qualities and aspirations was developed based on the research:[70]

In Kansas, our wide open spaces give people the freedom to dream and make big things happen.

The positioning statement served as the image campaign's platform for the communication strategy that would drive home one consistent message for business, development, tourism, and other entities in

Kansas. In the past, the state's tourism department had developed its own tagline, "Simply Wonderful," which competed with the business development tagline "Built on Character." The new branding effort communicated one consistent message for Kansas, not just for tourism and business development, but for the entire state. This single message was for all state agencies, businesses, and communities big and small.

The core creative strategy for establishing the new Kansas brand included a new Kansas tagline—"Kansas, as Big as You Think"—and an accompanying logo, along with standardized colors, typography, and graphic elements.[71] The campaign would use beautiful, open panoramic photos of Kansas landscapes that emphasized big skies. Key messages illustrated the state's open spaces and big thinking, and the campaign would include stories on big Kansas thinkers, both historical and contemporary.

The image campaign rollout started at home to educate leaders and average citizens about the statewide brand. As one Department of Commerce question-and-answer backgrounder described the effort:[72] "Strong brands are built from the inside out. The goal is for Kansans to take pride in and appreciate the many benefits of living, working, and traveling in the state. It is important to keep talented, educated, and trained Kansans in the state, and educating them on the many opportunities the state holds for them may motivate them to stay."

The Kansas legislature appropriated $700,000 for the state image work and $1 million more from its internal marketing budgets. The $1.7 million paid for research and development of the overall brand image; development of an overall marketing plan for in-state promotion and out-of-state business development and tourism promotion; television, radio, theater, and print advertisements; media placement in-state and out-of-state for

2005; development of a state Web portal (www.thinkkansas.com); and other public relations and marketing materials.

The budget breakdown included:[73]

- **$1.1 million (64.8 percent) for advertising, Web site, marketing activities and materials**
- **$261,500 (15.4 percent) for strategic planning and final creative production of numerous advertisements**
- **$181,500 (11.3 percent) for qualitative and quantitative research and development of the brand image campaign slogan**
- **$137,000 (8.5 percent) for travel and tourism research**

The Brand Image Task Force and the Department of Commerce announced the launch of the image campaign January 7, 2005. Their stated goals were to:[74]

- **Begin to change the way Kansans talk about Kansas.**
- **Change the way out-of-state people think and talk about Kansas.**
- **Ultimately create new jobs and new capital investments and increase the economic impact of tourism on the state.**

The in-state campaign focused on famous Kansans whose lives had been shaped by living there: "Kansans who dared to think big and make a difference in the world."[75] Initial campaign ads featured U.S. President and World War II supreme allied commander Dwight Eisenhower and pioneering aviator Amelia Earhart. Future ads would highlight other well-known Kansans, past and present.

For the tourism audience, ads would emphasize the state's historical sites, off-the-beaten path adventures and experiential trips, such as working ranches. Ads would be placed in travel-related publications, such as *The Official 2005 Getaway Guide* and the *Great Outdoors Guide*. Ad space was purchased in 17 magazines including AARP, *Good Housekeeping, Country Living, Reader's Digest,* and *AAA Tour Book.*[76]

The task force's research had revealed some useful information from the business side of the equation. Businesses were seeking bottom-line performance. While incentives were important, they didn't guarantee new business. Instead, "a positive, well-balanced offer featuring the Kansas lifestyle and unstinting work ethic" was a better approach.[77] The campaign's business development strategy included trade shows and advertising featuring Kansas companies and entrepreneurs, such as Garmin International, makers of GPS devices, and Cobalt Boats, maker of some of the best fishing and luxury boats, who dared to dream big and created successful companies in Kansas. Innovative products and services produced in Kansas as well as unique destinations such as the Kansas Speedway and Samuel Dinsmoor's Garden of Eden would be featured in campaign ads.

The new state Web portal provided a single location for everything about Kansas: travel and tourism, business and economic development, wildlife and parks, transportation, higher education, health and environment, the governor, legislature, and "Access Kansas," a link to the state's disability rights center. The new home page featured a rotating dominant photo with scenes representing all that Kansas has to offer: its historical and cultural heritage, rural landscapes, and city skylines.

EVALUATION

Especially important to the campaign rollout was an evaluation component. The new Web portal contained an online survey that asked readers how they had heard of the new image campaign and www.thinkkansas .com. It also asked, "After seeing or hearing the advertising and/or news story about Kansas, please indicate how much you

agree or disagree with the following statements":

1. I'm more proud to be a Kansan.
2. I believe Kansas has a rich history.
3. My interest is piqued to learn more about Kansas.
4. It's of value for people to hear this message about Kansas.
5. My perception of Kansas is improved overall.

Soon after the image campaign launch, Scott Allegrucci, director of Travel and Tourism Development Division, suggested metrics to measure his division's efforts including:[78] leads generated based on Web site visitation and use analysis, fulfillment/call response, advertising conversion studies, standardized industry reporting, and surveys.

Open Scenario Challenge
Extending the Publicity Dollars

Kansas's 2003–2004 state tourism office budget was $4.3 million; the state ranked 40th out of 46 states reporting data.[79]

The Kansas brand image campaign cost about $700,000 to develop, and an additional $1 million was budgeted for advertising materials, media placements, and distribution costs.

Budget conscious watchdogs criticized the campaign for its cost, while others questioned the slogan's effectiveness due to a rather vague metaphor. Still, the budget was relatively modest compared to many state branding campaigns. Working with limited budgets, the Kansas Commerce Department, which is responsible for the campaign, sought ways to extend the campaign through naturally occurring positive events involving Kansas and its citizens.

One such naturally occurring opportunity came soon after the campaign's launch in March 2004: It was Steve Fossett's daring attempt to be the first person to circumnavigate the globe on a nonstop, no-refueled solo flight in a technologically sophisticated Virgin Atlantic GlobalFlyer. He planned to depart from Kansas's Salina Municipal Airport April 30 and return four days later.

This would be a true aviation milestone and was a perfect fit to another great aviator—native Kansan Amelia Earhart. The adventurer Fossett had selected the Kansas destination for its location in the middle of the United States and its long 12,000-foot runway.

Your job is to connect this potentially historic event to Kansas and leverage the publicity that would be generated by worldwide press attention.

You start by doing some research.

Questions for Discussion

1. What image problem is the Kansas Image Task Force trying to overcome?
2. How did research guide the campaign plan?
3. What is a brand? In the case of Kansas, what does the brand strategy hope to achieve?
4. What does a position statement do in relation to the brand? What is Kansas's positioning statement? Do you feel it is an effective positioning statement?
5. What is the new Kansas slogan? Do you feel it is an effective slogan? Why or why not?
6. Why did the Kansas Task Force start its image campaign initiative within the state?
7. Analyze the text of the two 60-second radio commercials "Dwight D. Eisenhower" and "Amelia Earhart" presented on this page and the next. (Note that shorter versions of each were presented on television.) What messages are they trying to convey? What kinds of people would be a receptive audience for the messages in these commercials?

Do Some Research

1. Name some the basic facts about Kansas: population, economy, geography, history, and famous historical and contemporary Kansans.
2. Examine your state's tourism imitative. How is it similar to or different from the Kansas imitative?
3. Using a news media database, such as Lexis-Nexis, find three articles or columns that feature the coverage of the Kansas Image Task Force's campaign announcement. What did the news coverage focus on? What were the negative aspects that resulted from this coverage? How would you counteract that information?

Terminology

- image campaign
- branding
- agritourism
- geotourism
- positioning statement
- slogan or tagline
- graphic standards
- gampaign rollout
- Web portal

Web Resources

- **Kansas, As Big as You Think tourism portal** www.thinkkansas.org/
- **Kansas, As Big as You Think tourism advertising materials** www.thinkkansas.com/newsroom/
- **Virginia Tourism Corporation** www.vatc.org/pr/Prnews/35VIFL.htm
- **Virginia Is for Lovers** http://www.virginia.org/

"Amelia Earhart": 60-Second Radio Spot

Born and raised on the river bluffs of Atchison, Kansas, Amelia Earhart was beckoned by the open sky.

When you come from a place that's 90% sky, is it any wonder you would want to fly around the world?

Amelia Earhart of Atchison, Kansas, dared to go farther. Find out more about Kansas at www.thinkkansas.com.

KANSAS as big as you think

Courtesy of Kansas Department of Commerce

In a day and age when women could barely find a reasonable job, Amelia learned to fly. But even that wasn't enough for her. Amelia cut her own trails through the uncharted skies. Her record-breaking excursions were not mere daredevilry.

In her own words they provided proof that men and women were equal in jobs requiring intelligence, coordination, speed, coolness and willpower.

In 1937 in an attempt to fly around the world, she was lost. But this Kansas daughter will never be forgotten. Her spirit showed the world how Kansas carves a certain kind of person.

When you grow up in a place where 90 percent of what you see is sky, what else would you want to do? But touch the clouds.

Kansas—As Big as You Think.

Find out more at thinkkansas.com.

"Dwight D. Eisenhower": 60-Second Radio Spot

During WWII the enemy looked at our troop strength, ships and aircraft . . . even the fuel mileage of our tanks. It made no difference to them that the Supreme Allied Commander, Dwight D. Eisenhower, hailed from Kansas.

It should have.

The enemy had no idea that a Kansan would set an impossible goal, and then by sheer force of will achieve that goal—even if it meant putting more than 150,000 troops in Normandy . . . in 10 hours.

They had no idea how Kansas carves a certain kind of person.

How growing up in a place with no boundaries makes everything seem possible.

They had no idea what a Kansan would do if asked.

Kansas—As Big as You Think.

Find out more at thinkkansas.com.

From Last Year's Styles to Now
Payless ShoeSource Repositions Itself as Fashion Focused

With a name like "Payless," it's no surprise Payless ShoeSource has always been a favorite of consumers looking for a bargain. The company's own consumer research revealed consumers liked Payless's value pricing and self-shopping, two of the brand's foundational pillars. But those same consumers wanted something else too: "on-trend fashions."

The world of fashion moves fast—driven in large part by celebrities, the red carpet, and the fashion runway. Operating in this highly competitive environment, shoe retailers like Payless must anticipate where accessory trends are headed and react quickly to stay in the game. In the 1990s, many Payless shoppers often encountered fashions that were a season to a whole year behind the trends. Shoppers wanted on-trend fashions—the same styles that were seen in higher-end department stores and worn by Hollywood stars and other celebrities—available at the same time at great prices in Payless stores.

The research guided the company's repositioning efforts to create a new brand personality that meant on-trend fashions at value prices. Initial marketing efforts included advertising and hiring trendsetters "Diva of Shoes" Star Jones, one of the hosts of ABC's *The View*, and Ana Maria Canseco, a host of the Spanish language morning show *Despierta America*, as brand spokespeople; these paid spokespersons help spread the Payless message from 2001–2004.

"Indulge in the latest styles, guilt free," was the message delivered by Jones, Payless ShoeSource's new chief of consumer style.[80] And Americans did. With more than 200 million pairs of shoes sold annually, the company is America's largest footwear retailer with about 4,600 stores nationwide.[81]

Public relations was viewed as a powerful tool to augment the advertising message and to build on the equity created by Jones and Canseco. Previously, the company's consumer-focused public relations effort was nearly nonexistent, said Mardi Larson, public relations consultant and public relations team leader at Payless. The new strategy centered on "fashion influencers" to share the news of the new Payless, its focus on fashion, and its on-trend products.

Legions of fans and fashion connoisseurs followed the celebrity moves and styles of Paris Hilton, Jennifer Aniston, Jennifer Lopez, and Amber Tamblyn, among many others, for guidance on what was cool and hip. What they said, did, and wore made news. To move the Payless brand to a higher fashion status, Payless had to pay attention to these and other influencers who drive the fashion industry, said Larson.

Payless ShoeSource was established in 1956 in Topeka, Kansas. It is the largest specialty shoe store in the country and sold more than 187 million pairs of shoes in fiscal 2004, generating $2.66 billion in net sales, down from $2.78 billion the previous year.[82]

The company developed a three-prong strategy to compete. It repositioned itself to be the "merchandise authority" through "product, messaging and execution."[83] The strategy emphasized "clear and consistent" messaging that conveyed its "merchandise authority" and "value."[84] The strategy also called for a balance between external media, including television, free standing inserts at key selling periods, and product placement in news and fashion press.[85] The first task was research to identify the most important fashion influencers in the rapidly expanding fashion universe. The research led to several important categories, including the fashion media, high-profile fashion events, celebrities (and the stylists that dress them), and the designer community, said Larson. The fashion media became the first priority area of focus. This group is extremely influential in helping women decide what to wear and where to buy each season. It includes the fashion and women's general interest monthly magazines; style and fashion pages at newspapers across the country; fashion wire services; and TV fashion programming on morning news programs, daytime, and on fashion-focused networks like the Style Network.

Within each category there were numerous opportunities to pursue. For example, the Style Network offered a full line of fashion programming, including *Fashion Police, The Look for Less, Fashiontrance, Style Court, Style Essentials,* and *How Do I Look?* The programs were always looking for new material—and trendy shoes and accessories to feature on their shows.

Morning news shows and daytime talk shows, such as *Good Morning America, Oprah, The View,* and *Live With Regis and Kelly,* carried fashion segments put together by outsourced stylists and trend experts. Tight show budgets created the need to reach out to stylists, who make their living going on TV to do fashion segments. Building a strong relationship with this group was an important factor in Payless's publicity success.

In the early days of the publicity program, once the top fashion media influencers were identified, the next challenge was to figure out how to get media gatekeepers to notice Payless, a brand that was not yet considered trend-right and worthy of media coverage. Larson's strategy was "go to them" and she conducted a media tour with desk-side, face-to-face meetings with editors at top magazines like *Lucky, Glamour,* and *Marie Claire* for her and Payless's senior vice president of the women's collection. In just 30 minutes they quickly understood and saw how Payless was changing.

The time was right for Payless. "Editors were attentive not only because the shoes were on-trend, but they offered value too," Larson said. "Today, the editor's job is to track and report on the trends, but also to show consumers how they can get the latest look at varying price points from $500 to $20." The dot-com bust of 2001 and the recession that followed had many magazine readers in the mood to consider what was chic and trendy—for less than $20. "Accessible fashion really resonated with the editors so they were willing to talk to us right off the bat."

At desk-side briefings Larson delivered what the editors now refer to as the "shoe bible"—a "look book" featuring photographs of products in the upcoming Payless collection. If the editor was interested, he or she could "call-in" the product (by number) for fashion shoots. Payless partnered with GCI, a public relations firm based in New York City, which later managed the day-to-day contact with fashion editors and maintained the crucial Payless sample "closet," critical for the tight deadline requests.

The Payless closet had been located at the company's Topeka, Kansas, headquarters, but was moved to New York City to meet the often same-day deadlines of publications, the bulk of which are located in New York City. The goal was, over time, to establish Payless as a reliable source for on-trend accessory samples and information for fashion editors. GCI's New York office handled strategic seasonal outreach and made certain that shoe samples met often frenetic production deadlines.

Because magazines in particular work four to five months in advance of their publication date, an important part of the reliability factor was ensuring that the color, detail, and the shoe itself would be exactly as presented to consumers in the stores, said Larson. "We work with the Payless Product Procurement Team at corporate to confirm that the product sample would be the same when it hit the stores months later and that it will be available in stores when the magazine hit news stands—coordinating this is critical to preventing lots of consumer frustration both at the store level and at the Payless call center."

From eight editors for the first media tour, the number grew to 15 publications for the second tour and more than 20 for the third tour. Once the gatekeepers' doors began to open, the Payless public relations team began working on an even better way to showcase the Payless product collections—the "Payless Showroom" events, held twice each year.

Traditionally, product showrooms are places where buyers from retailers go to review a brand's collection to consider carrying it in their stores. The company planned a one-day event to showcase the excitement of the Payless brand persona with live products that could be seen and touched by New York City's fashion editors. Starting with a showroom event that drew about 30 editors, Payless now attracts more than 75 editors and stylists. The Payless Showroom event has become a must-attend fashion event among the influential fashion media in New York City.

The focused strategy on fashion editors has resulted in about 60 sample requests a month. Product placements in influential fashion magazines were an important place to start. It not only built massive awareness among consumers but also brought heightened awareness among other news media influencers and fashion stylists. This group's attention to the new Payless and its fashion-forward styles led to incorporating Payless product into their own personal fashion choices or their TV program segments.

While celebrities were not a high-priority strategy at the time for the Payless public relations effort, whenever a star mentioned Payless or wore the brand in media interviews and other appearances, a thank-you gift was sent to the celebrity to encourage the continued support and to help maintain the relationship. High-profile awards ceremonies, such as the Oscars, Grammys,

Emmys, Fashion Week, and others are major fashion events and will likely become a more formalized part of the overall Payless public relations strategy in the future. In March 2005, Star Jones Reynolds of *The View* wore a pair of Payless shoes on the red carpet at the Oscars. The Payless public relations team coordinated a red carpet photographer and issued the news on the wire service, securing significant coverage.

Cause-related marketing, in which Payless sponsors a nonprofit organization with a fundraising event, is a growing public relations effort. Larson said Payless is a philanthropic organization and has supported the United Way for years. Because the company's primary audience is females 18 to 44 years old, in 2004 Payless teamed with Susan G. Komen Breast Cancer Foundation to raise money to fight breast cancer. Payless developed a brooch with a trendy shoe charm that could be purchased for $2; all net profits from the brooch sales were donated to the Komen Foundation. A considerable public relations effort was launched to secure awareness of the program, including a letter personally signed by Star Jones Reynolds, and samples of the brooch were sent nationwide to female news anchors who wore them and publicized the fundraising program on air. News releases were issued, celebrities received packages, and news coverage was significant.

The Payless public relations team was recognized with the Sabre Award for this public relations program for its creativity and strong business results. The public relations effort cost $80,000 to execute and delivered 45 million impressions with a public relations value of $388,900, said Larson. With no advertising support in the first two weeks of October, media coverage alone drove awareness and sales of more than 185,000 brooches in just four days. Ads hit mid-October, and by the end of the program, Payless sold nearly 90 percent of its inventory, generating nearly $570,000 for the Susan G. Komen Breast

Cancer Foundation.[86] Payless conducted the program the following year with another exclusive brooch design.

For Payless, the public relations efforts have paid off; in 2004 the company's public relations efforts resulted in 826 million media impressions in targeted fashion media outlets, said Larson. The third-party credibility generated from the placements exceeded an estimated $6.4 million equivalent advertising value. During 2005, the company doubled its impressions and tripled the public relations value with 1.6 billion impressions with a public relations value of $19 million. Payless plans to build on its influencer strategy and cause-related marketing efforts with a few new twists. The company plans to pursue designer alliances to create designer collections featuring original designs that hit the fashion runway at New York Fashion Week and then are available in stores for the season; other strategic alliances will be pursued to elevate the brand image.

"The public relations strategy has been successful because we did the research to identify the right mix of fashion influencers and set our priorities. We let the amazing product tell the story, we leveraged our celebrity spokespeople whenever we could, and we had a sophisticated and reliable news bureau and product sample process that responded to the media's always tight deadlines," Larson said.

Open Scenario Challenge
Fur Fashion Week

You are a fashion public relations account executive working for a respected New York City public relations firm. Your firm has been hired by the trade association for furriers, designers, and fur animal farmers in America called Fur Information Council of America (www.fur.org/) Your job is to strategically promote fur fashions, and some of the major events include Fashion Week in New York City and high-profile media placements of fur fashion. There is also an educational component to the association's communication efforts that is reflected in the frequently asked questions section of the Web site.

Because well-organized activist groups oppose the use of animal fur for clothing and fashion accessories, Fashion Week special events for the Fur Information Council have been canceled in recent years. It is a tough promotional assignment. Critics ask why fur is needed when fur-substitute materials are available.

Conduct research into fur animal farming techniques today. Is there any way to justify fur farming today? Is there an educational component that can be leveraged? How would you promote this luxury product that continues in popularity worldwide?

Question for Discussion

1. What are the basic elements of the public relations strategy for Payless ShoeSource?

2. Who are fashion influencers? Why do they matter?

3. What basic communication theory is tied to the concept of influencers?

4. What is cause-related marketing? What public relations benefits does an organization get from this activity? Describe Payless's efforts in this area.

Do Some Research

1. Pick a niche industry and a related product, such as fashion and shoes, and develop a list of industry influencers that you would want to target. Name the top industry publications that you would target for your communication campaign. Develop a cause-related marketing idea for your selected industry.

2. Read Payless ShoeSource's latest annual report at its corporate Web site. What are the challenges facing this organization, and how is the organization's leadership responding to these challenges?

Terminology

- fashion showroom
- look book
- media gatekeepers
- product placements
- sample closet
- influencers
- cause-related marketing
- red carpet photographer
- media impressions
- desk-side briefings

Web Resources

- **Payless corporate site** www.payless.com/en-US/Corporate
- **Payless catalog** www.payless.com/
- **Style Network** www.stylenetwork.com/
- **Susan G. Komen Breast Cancer Foundation** www.komen.org
- **Fashion Week** www.newyorkmetro.com/fashion/fashionshows/
- **WGSN fashion education site** www.wgsn-edu.com/
- **WGSN fashion research agency** www.wgsn.com/public/home/html/base.html

Of Muggles, Quidditch, and Bertie Botts

Keeping the Harry Potter Magic Alive

BOOK 5: *HARRY POTTER AND THE ORDER OF THE PHOENIX*

Harry Potter and the Order of the Phoenix, the fifth book of the incredibly popular series, was one of the most anticipated publishing events in children's literature.

The June 21, 2003, publishing date had been circled on millions of aspiring Hogwarts students' calendars. Author J. K. Rowling did limited international media interviews to support the astronomical initial print run of 6.8 million copies, which climbed to 9.3 million copies in a second printing June 24, 2003.[87] It was the fastest "selling book in history for its opening weekend. In the first 24 hours, it sold 5 million copies, breaking all publishing records."[88]

Even though the book had an established fan base owing to the popularity of the first four books in the series (*Harry Potter and the Sorcerer's Stone*, *Harry Potter and the Chamber of Secrets*, *Harry Potter and the Prisoner of Azkaban*, and *Harry Potter and the Goblet of Fire*) and three

Warner Brothers movies, a new level of anticipation in the United States was the result of Scholastic's multimillion-dollar marketing communication campaign.[89]

While keeping the book's contents secret until its release date helped fuel speculation about the plot and kept anticipation high for readers, Scholastic did release some tantalizing information—the book's opening lines as well as information alluding to some past mystery in Potter's life:[90]

> *The hottest day of the summer so far was drawing to a close and a drowsy silence lay over the large, square houses of Privet Drive. . . . The only person left outside was a teenage boy who was lying flat on his back in a flowerbed outside number four.*

The other excerpt shared by J. K. Rowling in a news release announcing the publication date was:

> *Dumbledore lowered his hands and surveyed Harry through his half-moon glasses.*

"It is time," he said, "for me to tell you what I should have told you five years ago, Harry. Please sit down. I am going to tell you everything."

Scholastic's campaign, according to a company news release, included "national advertising and publicity, billboard promotion, partnerships with four Major League Baseball teams, promotional giveaways, and thousands of midnight parties at retail locations across the country celebrating the June 21 publication date."[91] Scholastic also held a national essay contest that sent 10 lucky winners on an all-expenses-paid trip to London for a world-exclusive J. K. Rowling event at the Royal Albert Hall.[92]

The marketing theme for the in-store promotions was "Is Harry Ready? Are You?" Promotional materials for retailers included:[93]

- 3 million mini-bumper stickers
- 400,000 buttons
- 50,000 window clings
- 9,500 easel backs
- 24,000 standees with a countdown clock
- 15,000 event kits to plan midnight events, including "Readiness Review" which offered 20 questions based on the first four books

The Major League Baseball partnership involved Harry Potter theme days at four games across the country. Each team held various costume contests, raffles, and promotional giveaways of 75,000 bookmarks to fans.[94] Baseball players dressed up as characters from the book and were displayed on the stadium video boards.[95] A week before the book's release, a signed copy of the book was flown under tight security from Scotland (the author's homeland) to a secret New York City location. It was presented to officials at the New York City Public Library the day before its midnight release.[96] Midnight parties at thousands of retail stores on its release date and many public library events generated enormous publicity. Virtually every news outlet carried pre-stories and first-day stories.

BOOK 6: *HARRY POTTER AND THE HALF-BLOOD PRINCE*

The sixth book in the series, *Harry Potter and the Half-Blood Prince,* was released July 16, 2005. The announcement came December 20, 2004, on Rowling's Web site as "an unexpected Christmas present" for legions of Potter fans anxious for any news.[97] A Scholastic news release cleverly dangled bits of tantalizing information from the author about the sixth book, including the revelation that the half-blood prince is neither Harry nor Voldemort. The release also noted that the opening chapter of the book "has been brewing in J. K. Rowling's mind for 13 years."[98]

Open Scenario Challenge
Keeping the Magic Alive for Book Seven

As a member of the Scholastic public relations and marketing communications team, you are asked to develop a publicity plan for the launch of the seventh and final book of the series. Based on your research of past Potter book launches, how would you promote the new book to the news media and help generate local coverage for retailers?

In particular, research the launch publicity campaign for *Harry Potter and the Half-Blood Prince,* the sixth book of the series. If you have read the books, recall what excited or interested you most about them. These experiences can help direct your communication activities to an audience of young readers, as well as Harry Potter's large adult readership.

Rowling, known as a "shy sorceress," does only limited interviews with top-tier publications, such as *Time, Newsweek,* and the *New York Times.*[99] Her Web site, www.jkrowling.com, does offer opportunities for direct communication with fans.

Develop a complete public relations launch plan for the book with an overall communication strategy, communication objectives, campaign tactics, and a timeline. Include how you would evaluate your plan's effectiveness.

Questions for Discussion

1. Why are Harry Potter books popular with children and adults?

2. What do you think is unique about the success of the Harry Potter books?

3. What are some of the potential public relations problems that could occur with the author or the book series itself? How would you prepare for them?

4. Book tours are a common promotional activity for new books and their authors. J. K. Rowling does very few personal appearances. What other options are there?

5. What promotional events did Scholastic sponsor for the latest editions of Harry Potter? What did Scholastic do differently for book six, *The Half-Blood Prince*?

6. A primary audience for Harry Potter books is children. What communication issues do you need to consider when promoting a new book to this audience?

7. How has the Scholastic Web site for Harry Potter books tried to cater its content to a younger audience?

8. How can Scholastic leverage the popularity of Harry Potter books to its product line?

9. Beyond its author, who else could serve as a credible spokesperson for this product?

Do Some Research

1. Some religious groups have criticized the Harry Potter books. What are the issues with this book series, and how have these groups or individuals communicated their issues?

2. Research book promotions. What are the various promotional tactics used? Try to find one book promotion that has used stunts or other unusual tactics to attract media attention.

3. Another popular book, Dan Brown's *The Da Vinci Code*, has received some negative attention by various groups. How did the publisher and author deal with the criticism? The book also created a travel boon for certain locations mentioned in the book. How could these locations take advantage of the attention?

Web Resources

- **J. K. Rowling's official Web site** www.jkrowling.com
- **Scholastic publishing** www.scholastic.com/harrypotter/
- **Warner Brothers studios** harrypotter.warnerbros.com/main/homepage/home.html

"A Monument to Decadence"
Introducing Hardee's Monster Thickburger

The health and fitness craze created a niche for some fast-food companies looking to satisfy customers tired of diets and small portions but with big appetites. Hardee's created a product launch combining marketing and public relations elements for the corporation's new menu item: the Monster Thickburger.

THE NEWS RELEASE

The public relations efforts included a news release to generate initial buzz in the news media for the product. The news release started off this way:[100]

> First there were burgers. Then there were Thickburgers. Now Hardee's is introducing the mother of all burgers—the Monster Thickburger. Weighing in at two-thirds of a pound, this 100 percent Angus beef burger is a monument to decadence, yet still a throwback, as it features lots of meat, cheese and bacon on a bun. Available at all Hardee's restaurants starting today, the Monster Thickburger is certain to crush the hunger pangs of even the most famished burger lovers.

Paragraph two of the release mentions how the Monster Thickburger was based on a previous burger product and was now back by popular demand—but improved.

The release provides a basic description of the burger, including its astonishing proportions:

> Like all Hardee's burgers, the Monster Thickburger features 100 percent Angus beef patties. In this case, it's got not one but two 1/3-lb. charbroiled patties, topped with no less than four strips of crispy bacon, three slices of American cheese, and some mayonnaise—all on a buttered, toasted, sesame seed bun. The result is an updated version of the classic that requires two hands, a firm grip and a serious appetite.

The massive burger sold for $5.49, or $7.09 for a combo meal including medium fries and a medium drink.[101] The release referred "lovers of bodacious burgers" to the Monster Thickburger Web site for a coupon and more information.

Not mentioned in the news release was the Monster's calorie count, 1,410, and its fat count, 107 grams.[102] It was clear that this product was not for the faint of heart.

Open Scenario Challenge
Launch Event Strategy

While the sheer magnitude of the Monster was guaranteed to attract media attention, you want to create a special event that would extend the media hype beyond the initial product announcement and complement the ongoing advertising campaign.

Hardee's public relations agency, Weber Shandwick, proposed a charity event featuring "massive" NFL players in 10 markets who would work the drive-through of a local Hardee's for two hours. Proceeds from every Monster Thickburger sold at the designated locations would be donated for the player's charity of choice.[103]

You want a different launch event strategy for smaller markets, and you call your agency representative to talk it over. The potential negative publicity that this product might generate from advocacy groups or health-conscious experts, such as dietitians, needs to be considered. Hardee's menu does include low-fat and low-carbohydrate options.

With help from your agency, you devise the following plan that includes public relations launch activities for smaller markets and a strategy to deal with potential negative publicity from health advocates.

Questions for Discussion

1. Beyond a news release, what other press kit materials could you offer the news media?

2. What did you notice about the writing style of the news release?

3. What would you do differently in a news release for this product?

4. How would you verbally pitch this new product to the news editors or food editors of top-tier media? Write out what you would say in a phone conversation.

5. To generate publicity, what kind of event launch would you suggest for

smaller markets? Your ideas should play off the "massive" theme.

6. What would you do to counteract potential negative publicity from health-conscious experts and organizations?

Do Some Research

1. The product launch advertising campaign for the Spicy BBQ Burger garnered attention for its edgy subject matter: a "hot," sexy Paris Hilton washing a Bentley in a revealing swimsuit while eating a Spicy BBQ Burger. Some critics said that although the ad cut through the clutter, it didn't necessarily sell more burgers. What do you think?

2. Hardee's took advantage of the hot commercial by creating a Web page that included downloads of the commercial, an extended 60-second commercial version, an interview with Paris Hilton about making the commercial, and interviews with a Hardee's marketing official, an advertising agency representative, and the commercial's director. There was a downloadable version of the commercial's song, "I love Paris," an updated Cole Porter tune sung by Eleni Mandell. From the still gallery, viewers could download a desktop image or e-mail the stills to a friend. At the bottom was a button to print a coupon or find a Hardee's restaurant. Is this an effective advertising strategy? Why or why not?

Web Resources

• **Hardee's home site** www.hardees.com/ home

Chapter Eight

Sports, Entertainment, and Travel

While leisure time or entertainment public relations has a strong connection to consumer relations and often falls under the umbrella of corporate public relations, these industries deserve a separate look because of their cultural impact on our society and the attention they get from the mass media.

Simply put, the sport, entertainment, and travel industries are major players in determining how Americans spend their spare time and money. Nearly 13 million Americans were employed in the leisure and hospitality industry in 2005.[1] The Travel Industry Association of America estimates that travel and tourism generates $1.3 trillion in economic activity in the United States annually.[2] The video game industry alone contributes more than $18 billion to the U.S. economy.[3] These industries span the performing arts (dance, drama, and music), sports, books, movies, art, video games, and travel to various destinations for leisure-time pursuits.

Sports are a growing part of what Americans do with their spare time. Plunkett Research estimates that the entire industry, including equipment and apparel sales, could range from $375 to $425 billion annually.[4]

Because our society loves its leisure, there are many business opportunities to market these commodities to their fullest. High-profile opportunities need creative and sophisticated marketing communication campaigns to generate buzz and fight for attention from the news and entertainment media.

The second concern of entertainment public relations is maintaining the business's or entity's reputation. The entertainment world's exciting dimension of star power adds a certain amount of volatility, however. People can be all too human, and their foibles and eccentricities get top billing in the media. After all, inquiring minds want to know what is happening with Sean Coombs, Paris Hilton, Oprah, Martha Stewart, Brad Pitt, Kobe Bryant, and Allen Iverson.

Entertainment companies hire public relations professionals to polish their reputation; celebrities have publicists, who can also function as spokespeople, publicity agents, and special events coordinators.

Entertainment-related organizations are eager to attract consumer attention to spur sales of event tickets or merchandise. A marketing communication approach (see Chapter 7, "Consumer Relations") is used to create awareness and interest in the product. In addition to advertising, media relations and special event planning are major components of this coordinated communication effort.

The 2004 season lockout of the National Hockey League (NHL) required a major promotional effort to bring back fans who spent an entire strike-canceled season finding other things to do with their time. The NHL's fan strategy emphasized media relations including media training for 30 teams. Coaches and players learned how to effectively interact with the media to boost positive media coverage, which included talking up the game's exciting rule changes. Individual teams also developed their own season-opening special events to encourage fan participation.

Celebrities are, in reality, products that project their own image, and this image changes depending on what the celebrity does or doesn't do. In the textbook *Public Relations Strategies and Tactics,* the authors suggest the following for conducting a personality campaign:[5]

Interview the client. This first step helps the publicist find "interesting and possibly newsworthy facts about the person's life, activities, and beliefs" that often are unrecognized by the individual for their publicity value.

Prepare a biography of the client. Based on the interview and other sources, assemble a short biography with the most interesting or newsworthy information mentioned prominently so editors and producers can locate the information easily. Photos of the client and other material can be included in a media kit.

Plan a marketing strategy. Similar to any strategic marketing communication plan, identify the public relations goals and what audiences to reach.

Conduct the campaign. Based on the public relations goals and defined publics, the next step is to determine which tactics will meet the campaign's objectives. This includes news releases with hooks about the client's activities, interesting photographs of the client, public appearances, awards, and nicknames or labels.

The last three tactics are unique to celebrity promotion. Celebrities are often asked and paid to attend organizational events (i.e., public appearances) to generate interest in an event. The client may be asked to talk at a meeting or sign autographs and chat and pose for photographs with fans.

Awards given to the client also generate publicity. It is acceptable to put forward the name of a client for awards or even suggest that an award be created for the client.

Nicknames and labels that emulate a client's special qualities can help create fun and memorable aspects of the celebrity brand. A Web site, www.pr.com, runs a contest on the best celebrity nicknames. In 2005, the top 10 picks were Regis Philbin ("Big Daddy"), Arnold Schwarzenegger ("The Governator"), Sean Combs ("Puff Daddy"), Madonna ("The Material Girl"), Dwayne Johnson ("The Rock"), Britney Spears ("Pinkey"), Jennifer Lopez ("J. Lo"), Michael Jackson ("Wacko Jacko"), Donald Trump ("The Donald"), and Kelly Ripa ("Brown Sugar").[6]

Some additional tactics include fans clubs and a celebrity Web site with a blog, with musings directly from the celebrity, and other informational items. Another growing tactic is book writing, such as Donald Trump's *How to Get Rich* or Rudolph Giuliani's *Leadership,* both best sellers.

DAMAGE CONTROL

Under the relentless glare of the media spotlight, it is not *if* but *when* a celebrity will make a gaffe that could potentially hurt or even ruin the celebrity's reputation. Fortunately, history shows time and again that fans usually forgive their celebrity heroes. Most realize that celebrities are human too and will make mistakes. In some cases, such as hotel heiress Paris Hilton's sex video and supermodel Kate Moss's alleged drug use caught on video, bad publicity eventually led to new ventures as edgy "bad girl" icons.

According to *Public Relations Tactics and Strategies,* "Experts suggest immediate response so that the momentum of subsequent stories is minimized. A brief, honest statement of regret for bad behavior or denial of rumors works well. . . Then the celebrity needs to disappear from sight and take care of personal matters."[7]

Supermodel Kate Moss, who was videotaped allegedly snorting cocaine in her boyfriend's studio, apologized to her fans and checked herself into a rehab clinic.[8] Her "bad girl" image actually helped the model rebound with new contracts and a cover photo on British *Vogue.*

All celebrities are not equal in their ability to attract buyers for products, according to a study, "The Celebrity Influence Study," conducted by NPD Group. While Ty Pennington of ABC's *Extreme Makeover: Home Edition* or Tour de France repeat winner Lance Armstrong actually helped sell products, some celebrities, such as Paris Hilton, Britney Spears, and Kobe Bryant, who scored well on awareness indicators, did not help product sales.[9]

CRISIS COMMUNICATION

Organizations that are inexorably connected to celebrities can be embroiled in controversy that requires more than damage control's quick-fix tactics. Consider these examples: the Los Angeles Lakers and Kobe Bryant's alleged sexual misconduct; Martha Stewart Living Omnimedia and Martha Stewart's prison time for lying to federal investigators. The tourism industry as well could be severely damaged by man-made and natural disasters such as the appearance of SARS in Toronto or monster hurricanes churning through the Gulf States.

These major problems can cause considerable apprehension and sometimes even anger toward the organization or destination involved. Customers and investors may shy away. Such incidents require a well-thought-out plan of action based on crisis communication principles (see Chapter 6, "Crisis Communication").

Special concerns of the travel and tourism industry, according to *Public Relations Strategies and Tactics*, include addressing terrorism fears, the growing use of the Internet to provide information and travel arrangements, and the appeals to target audiences, such as families and seniors.[10]

Despite the problems with celebrities and the fickle nature of consumers whose attention does not seem to last that long, organizations will continue to seek out opportunities to partner with the next big thing—celebrity, destination, or sport. It's up to public relations practitioners to manage the entity's communication and reputations proactively, ethically, and responsibly.

Queen of Talk Walks the Talk

Oprah Winfrey with Angel Network Tackles Katrina Needs

The devastating hurricane that ravaged the Gulf Coast in the last days of August 2005 left many Americans feeling helpless and frustrated—and for good reason.

The devastation left in the wake of Hurricane Katrina had never before been seen in the United States. Consider these facts from "The Federal Response to Hurricane Katrina: Lessons Learned":[11]

- Hurricane Katrina was the most destructive natural disaster in U.S. history.
- Katrina's hurricane force winds extended 103 miles from its center; it affected 93,000 square miles across 138 parishes and counties.
- The flooding destroyed New Orleans, the nation's 35th largest city; many other towns and cities in Louisiana, Mississippi, and Alabama were destroyed or heavily damaged throughout the Gulf Coast from wind, rain, and storm surge.
- An estimated 1,330 people died as a result of the storm; 71 percent of the victims were older than 60.
- Approximately 770,000 people were displaced by the storm; a total of 1.1 million over the age of 16 evacuated their homes during the storm.
- The economic cost including housing, consumer durable goods, business property, and government property was estimated at $96 billion; 300,000 homes were either completely destroyed or made uninhabitable.

Much of the news media's early Hurricane Katrina coverage focused on the inadequate response of local, state, and federal agencies, particularly to the plight of thousands of evacuees trapped in the New Orleans Superdome for days. With no light, air conditioning, working toilet facilities, or enough water and food, the Superdome quickly deteriorated into anarchy with gangs running wild and families desperate to leave.[12]

The human drama unfolding on national television drew heartfelt responses from many Americans, including celebrities and politicians. One celebrity was television talk show host Oprah Winfrey, whose efforts went well beyond mere words and quick symbolic actions.

Soon after the storm Winfrey made the rare decision to move her Chicago-based talk show to Houston, Texas, and produce it at the Astrodome, where many evacuees were temporarily relocated.[13] Winfrey and her production crew were on site to cover the stories that hadn't been told. She toured New Orleans, including a look inside the empty but still putrid Superdome, and the Houston Reliant Astrodome to assemble her first of two shows that aired a week after the storm struck the Gulf Coast.

"As this catastrophe unfolded, I watched like all of you and I felt helpless and I wanted to do something," Winfrey said during her show's introduction.[14] Winfrey used her reporting skills developed more than 20 years earlier when she was a television news anchorwoman in Nashville, Tennessee. She shared her reactions to the desperate scenes she witnessed: "I can tell you this: Even if you've been watching the news and reading the headlines, you have no idea what went on here. It is a travesty that is still unfolding. Nothing I saw on television prepared me for what I experienced on the ground."[15]

Her personal report with an emotional New Orleans Mayor Ray Nagin, who at one point had to walk away to compose himself, led Winfrey to tears and anguish about the situation she was witnessing:[16]

What's happened and didn't have to happen to children is pretty overwhelming. . .

This makes me so mad! This makes me mad. This should not have happened. This should not have happened!

At the Houston Astrodome, Winfrey talked to and comforted many survivors and reunited some separated families. The national news media covered Winfrey's visits to storm-devastated areas, noting she upstaged former presidents and senators when she entered the Houston Astrodome.[17]

The show was interspersed with reports from New Orleans, including reports on the medical facilities at the New Orleans International Airport and the efforts of celebrities such as Jamie Foxx and Faith Hill.

Directly after her show at the Astrodome, Winfrey traveled to Mississippi to prepare for a second show the following day that focused on Mississippi's recovery efforts, including the celebrity relief efforts of Chris Rock, Julia Roberts, Matthew McConaughey, and Lisa Marie Presley.[18]

During this time, a $1 million contribution to America's Second Harvest from Winfrey's foundation, Oprah's Angel Network, provided water, food, and toiletries for storm survivors.[19] Later, her Angel Network Book Club awarded $250,000 to support First Book's Book Relief effort that was collecting five million books to give to schools, libraries, and families affected by the storm.

Ten days after her visit to New Orleans and Houston, during her 20th anniversary show, Winfrey told an adoring audience that "I pledged to the survivors of Katrina that I would not forget them and I'm keeping my promise. I am personally today committing $10 million of my own money toward the rebuilding of people's lives."[20] The initiative was "Oprah's Katrina Homes," which would build and furnish homes for Katrina survivors. Her army of supporters would soon double Winfrey's donation. Within months, a new neighborhood called Angel Lane with 65 new beautifully furnished

homes sprouted in Houston.[21] And this was just the beginning. The Angel Network was making plans to put a total of 250 families in Katrina homes.[22] One show in February 2006 was devoted to showing grateful families their new homes, much like another popular show, *Extreme Makeover.*[23]

In November 2005, Winfrey dedicated her wildly popular "Oprah's Favorite Things" show to a surprised studio audience of Katrina volunteers—who thought they were there just to talk about their experiences. The "Favorite Things" show gave each audience member expensive gifts including a $2,000 Teslar diamond-encrusted watch, an Apple iPod, a fashionable Burberry coat, a Sony laptop, and much more.[24]

These Katrina-related events are typical of Winfrey, whose long list of good deeds and constant focus on living a life that makes a difference has earned her the title of America's Queen of Goodwill. She embodies her Web site's motto "Live your best life."

Winfrey's rags-to-riches story (she was raised in poverty in Mississippi and by 2005 had a net worth of at least $1 billion) made her one of the most recognizable and powerful women in America.[25] The *Oprah Winfrey Show,* which consistently focuses on positive, life-affirming content, had captured top talk show ratings since its inception in 1986.[26] Produced by her own production company Harpo (Oprah spelled backward), in 2005 it was seen in 215 domestic markets and 112 countries, with 49 million viewers each week, according to *Variety.*[27] Her media empire included her magazine, *Oprah,* with 2.6 million subscribers, and Oprah's Book Club with 700,000 members. Her charitable foundation Oprah's Angel Network had raised $35 million in its first eight years.[28]

Twenty years of good deeds and the determination to make a difference for righteous causes had built a mountain of goodwill for Winfrey's brand. Celebrity-based brands, such as Winfrey's, are often volatile business endeavors because the business is closely connected with the celebrity's public and private life. Intense public scrutiny of every action, including bad hair days and even mundane trips to the corner grocery store, are often too much for celebrities with all too human frailties.

Major indiscretions of drug abuse, illicit love affairs, and crimes, such as shoplifting or worse, routinely make the news and damage the celebrity's reputation and negatively affect the business connected to the celebrity's name. Martha Stewart, America's domestic diva, was jailed for obstructing justice and lying to investigators stemming from an alleged insider trading incident. A carefully planned image restoration campaign worked to Stewart's advantage. Basketball star Kobe Bryant lost valuable endorsements from McDonald's and Nutella following sexual assault allegations that were later dropped. It took three years and superlative on-court effort for Bryant to be featured once again in Nike ads.[29]

Open Scenario Challenge

Even Winfrey has fought threats to her professional reputation. Not long after Katrina, Winfrey selected author James Frey's memoir *A Million Little Pieces* for her Book Club. The book chronicled his "gut-wrenching nightmare of detox, the pain, the blood, the vomit."[30] It was a runaway best seller, with more than 3.5 millions copies sold. A large part of its success was due to being featured by Winfrey's book club.

A six-week investigation by The Smoking Gun, a Web-based organization that gathers government, law enforcement files, and court documents and conducts its own interviews, revealed that Frey's highly moving account of his recovery from drugs and alcohol abuse had "wholly fabricated or wildly embellished details of his purported criminal career, jail terms, and status as an outlaw 'wanted in three states.'"[31]

Despite the damning revelations by The Smoking Gun and extensive national news media coverage of the allegations, Winfrey

offered support to Frey during CNN's Larry King interview show featuring Frey. During the show Frey did admit he had embellished parts of his memoir but that the "essential truth" of his book was still valid. In a surprise call near the end of the show, Winfrey dismissed The Smoking Gun's allegations as "much ado about nothing."[32] She said: "that although some of the facts have been questioned. . . the underlying message of redemption in James Frey's memoir still resonates with me."[33]

Winfrey's support of Frey, however, only fueled the debate as more news media outlets independently corroborated The Smoking Gun's investigation along with Frey's admission of stretching the truth and fabricating some parts of it. For Oprah fans and critics, the debate also snared her. The question that arose was Did truth matter? Was Winfrey standing up for a liar? After all, if a book was published as nonfiction, even as a memoir, didn't readers expect to read the truth? What happened to the trust factor so many fans had for Winfrey?

You are Winfrey's publicist and trusted adviser. As the Frey controversy continues, she calls you to discuss what she should do. She knows it is damaging her reputation with her fans; many have posted to her Web site message board telling her they felt betrayed. She wants advice on what she should do.

Role-Playing Exercise

Using the above scenario, a student should assume the role of Winfrey's publicist and another student should assume the role of Winfrey. You are asked to come up with three options for responding to the controversy.

Questions for Discussion

1. How would you describe Oprah Winfrey's public persona?
2. What qualities make Oprah Winfrey a celebrity?
3. What specifically did Oprah Winfrey do in her Katrina response?

4. How did Oprah Winfrey's response to Hurricane Katrina enhance her reputation?

5. Why are brands based on individuals usually considered risky business ventures?

6. Overexposure is sometimes considered a problem for celebrities who are product endorsers. Why?

Do Some Research

1. Provide a recent example of a celebrity who has done a good job of enhancing his or her reputation and a celebrity who has not handled a controversy well. Describe their actions and why you think they helped or hurt their reputations.

2. Find a recent example of a celebrity who you think has done a good job of image restoration after a controversy.

3. Research how Oprah Winfrey actually responded to the James Frey incident. Do you agree or disagree with her response? Why?

Web Resources

- **Oprah Winfrey** www2.oprah.com/index.jhtml
- **Oprah's Angel Network** www2.oprah.com/uyl/oan_landing.jhtml
- **NPD Group's Consumer Response to Celebrity Endorsements** www.npd.com/dynamic/releases/press_060424.html
- **The Smoking Gun** www.thesmokin gun .com/
- **The Smoking Gun (The Man Who Conned Oprah)** www.thesmokin gun.com/archive/0104061jamesfrey1.html

A Big Hit in Tokyo—and Cooperstown
Baseball Shrine Courts Future Hall of Famer

In 1920, first baseman George Sisler's batting average was a whopping .407, with 257 hits for a single season—a record. That year Sisler was second only to Babe Ruth in home runs, base hits, and RBIs, and also second in doubles, triples, and steals that year.[34] And while Ruth's home run record had been surpassed by Roger Maris in 1961, Sisler's 257 hits for a single season eluded players for 84 years— till the fall of 2004.

That's when Seattle Mariners right fielder Ichiro Suzuki broke George Sisler's eight-decade single-season record of 257 hits. Reporters from the American and Japanese media were close at hand—and so was Jeff Idelson.

While he's not a major league player or a sports writer, Idelson's job often takes him close to baseball history in the making: He is vice president of communications and education for the National Baseball Hall of Fame and Museum in Cooperstown, New York. One of his jobs is to acquire historic baseball items for the museum.

So after the October 2004 game in which Ichiro matched and then broke Sisler's record, Ichiro met first with American and Japanese reporters. Then on his way back to the clubhouse, he happily greeted Idelson, and the two agreed to meet before the following day's game to talk.

Coming just hours after one of baseball's longest-standing records was shattered, this level of access to Suzuki did not happen overnight. Idelson's efforts to build a relationship with the rising star began three years earlier.

The following is the account of Idelson's relationship building with Suzuki that led to significant acquisitions for the National Baseball Hall of Fame and Museum as well as a museum exhibition. This account was condensed from Idelson's article entitled "Texas at Seattle, Oct. 1–3, 2004: Witness to History: Ichiro Breaks Single-Season Hit Mark."[35]

Prior to joining the Seattle Mariners in 2001, Suzuki was a major celebrity in Japan. During 13 years with Japan's Orix Blue Wave team he batted .347, won three MVP awards, and was named to seven All-Star teams and seven consecutive Pacific League batting titles. After completing his first successful season with the Mariners that included hitting .350 with 242 hits and helping the Mariners win the American League West Division title, one of Suzuki's postseason trips was to the National Baseball Hall of Fame and Museum.[36]

Suzuki wanted to immerse himself in the origins of baseball and arranged a three-day excursion with his wife and friends to this remote village in upstate New York. The visit was kept secret to safeguard Suzuki's privacy so that he could fully enjoy the museum's amazing treasures.

"He marveled at holding and swinging a game-used Babe Ruth bat and one of Shoeless Joe Jackson's famed 'Black Betsy' model bats, as it was Jackson's record for most hits by a rookie that Suzuki surpassed that year," Idelson said.

While visiting Cooperstown, Suzuki learned that he had been named Rookie of the Year. Idelson provided his office to Suzuki so national and international media could interview him by telephone. In the meantime, Idelson purchased a bottle of champagne for lunch with Suzuki and his companions.

Courtesy of the National Baseball Hall of Fame and Museum.

Suzuki presented the Hall of Fame with a game-used 2001 bat from his rookie season with the Mariners. As Suzuki and his party left Cooperstown to go home to Japan, Idelson knew "a lasting relationship was cemented between the superstar from Japan and the Baseball Hall of Fame."

Three years later, Idelson called Suzuki in the middle of September to let him know that he would be present at the record-breaking game. When the big event happened, Idelson met Suzuki at his locker the following day with gifts:

- A George Sisler S91-model Louisville Slugger bat, measuring 36 inches long and weighing 46 ounces, which was significantly different from Suzuki's 33-inch, 32-ounce Mizuno bat. The bat was compliments of Louisville Slugger, a Hall of Fame business partner.

- A binder that included a note of congratulations to Suzuki, a complete set of photos of Sisler from the Hall of Fame's massive photo archive, a set of photos from Suzuki's visit to Cooperstown, and plaque postcards of Sisler and Paul Molitor, the 2004 Hall of Fame inductee who was Suzuki's hitting coach. Later, a lifetime free admission pass to the Hall of Fame would also be presented to Suzuki.

During their conversation at Suzuki's locker, Idelson said the Hall of Fame was interested in developing a special exhibit in honor of him and his record-breaking season. Suzuki insisted that Idelson take the bat from his 200th hit of the season, when he became the first player to achieve 200 hits during all of his first four major league seasons.

Later, Idelson expressed interest in obtaining either Suzuki's bat from hit 258 or the bat from the final hit of the season, as well as spikes worn during either game. Suzuki agreed to donate the spikes and the bat with which he hit his final season hit (262), an event that occurred in the final regular season game the next day.

True to his word, Suzuki presented Idelson with the now-historic bat responsible for hit 262 in the dugout after the game, October 3, 2004. After posing for photographs with Suzuki, Idelson presented Suzuki with a lifetime pass to the Hall of Fame. At the clubhouse, Suzuki gave Idelson spikes, wristbands, batting gloves, elbow guards, and sunglasses—all from the October 3 game.

Idelson had also asked for and received the scorecard in Japanese kept by *Kyodo News* sportswriter Keizo Konishi; an "Ichimeter" sign, keeping track of Suzuki's hits by a fan from Algona, Washington; and a sign congratulating Suzuki in Japanese, the work of a sixth-grader from Renton, Washington. All these items, plus a road jersey worn by Suzuki in 2004 and tickets to the final three games of the Mariners' season, formed the Hall of Fame's "Suzuki Hits Record" exhibit, which opened November 8, 2004.

Questions for Discussion

1. Solid relationships are not generally built instantly. What steps did the National Baseball Hall of Fame and Museum take to establish a lasting relationship with baseball legend Ichiro Suzuki?

2. Why was it necessary for the Hall of Fame representative to be at the record-breaking games and speaking with Ichiro Suzuki?

3. Ichiro Suzuki gave the Hall of Fame several items related to his record-breaking hits. What did he get in return?

4. Instead of the Hall of Fame, what other organizations or people might vie for the historical artifacts?

5. From the Seattle Mariners's perspective, what type of special events, features, and news releases would you plan for the historical records that Ichiro Suzuki would break?

Do Some Research

1. What strategies work best for building long-term relationships? How can the public relations function assist?

2. Many nonprofit organizations, such as the Hall of Fame, rely on the generosity of donations for their survival. Although the Hall of Fame could not compete dollar for dollar in a competitive bidding for baseball artifacts, its reputation as the ultimate repository of baseball artifacts is unparalleled. Examine the operations of a successful and respected local nonprofit organization. What has this nonprofit offered instead of money to get what it needs?

3. Examine the Seattle Mariners's Web site news archive. How did the team cover Ichiro Suzuki's records? What other story angles could be included?

Terminology

- Hall of Fame
- "Ichimeter"
- George Sisler
- Shoeless Joe Jackson

Web Resources

- **National Baseball Hall of Fame and Museum** www.baseballhalloffame.org/
- **Seattle Mariners** seattle.mariners.mlb .com/NASApp/mlb/index.jsp?c_id=sea

Todd Bertuzzi's Sucker Punch

Violent Incident Sparks Debate among NHL Fans and Critics

Its critics have often described hockey as the most violent major league team sport in the country: a fast-paced game where—for some fans—a good fight is as much a part of the action as speed and skill on the ice. But many hockey fans were shocked by the March 8, 2004, incident in which one player grabbed an opponent from behind and struck him repeatedly, resulting in three neck fractures and a concussion.[37]

Fans and commentators alike were expecting the Vancouver Canucks to seek revenge on the Colorado Avalanche's Steve Moore; three weeks earlier the 25-year-old Moore sidelined the Canucks' team captain for three games with a concussion—and Moore was not penalized.[38]

Live-televised coverage (and endless replays in the days and weeks that followed) gave viewers an up-close look at Todd Bertuzzi's revenge. The 245-pound power forward with the Vancouver Canucks had stalked his prey on ice before he acted.

Two days later, during the uproar, a tearful Bertuzzi with his wife by his side responded at a news conference with direct statements for Steve Moore, his family, and hockey fans:[39]

This comment's for Steve: Steve, I just want to apologize for what happened out there. That I had no intention of hurting you; that I feel awful for what transpired.

To Steve's family: Sorry that you had to go through this. And I'm sorry again, about what happened out there.

I'm relieved to hear that Steve's going to have a full recovery. It means a lot to me to hear that that's going to happen.

I want to apologize to Mr. Burke and Mr. McCaw, the Vancouver Canucks organization, and my team-mates.

To the game of hockey and the fans of Vancouver, for the kids who watch this game: I'm truly sorry. I don't play the game that way; I'm not a mean-spirited person. And I'm sorry for what happened.

The next day, March 11, 2004, the National Hockey League suspended Bertuzzi for the rest of the 2003–2004 hockey season, including the 2004 Stanley

Courtesy of Rogers Sportsnet

Cup Playoffs, and fined him a half-million dollars of his $6.8 million annual salary for violating Rule 52, deliberate injury of opponent.[40] His reinstatement would be determined by the league's commissioner, based in part on Moore's health status, before the next season's training camp. The league characterized Bertuzzi's attack as a "blindside punch." According to the league's news release, Colin Campbell, NHL executive vice president and director of Hockey Operations, said:

> When Mr. Moore declined to engage Mr. Bertuzzi, Mr. Bertuzzi responded by delivering a gloved punch from behind the side of Mr. Moore's head, rendering him unconscious. Upon falling to the ice, Mr. Moore suffered additional serious injuries. We want to make clear that this type of conduct will not be tolerated in the NHL.

The National Hockey League also fined the Canucks organization $250,000. While the League noted that the Canucks bore no direct responsibility for Bertuzzi's actions, player comments following the previous Vancouver-Colorado game in which the Canucks' captain was injured by Moore should have resulted in more proactive efforts by the Canucks' management to prevent a retaliatory incident, according to the NHL news release.

But the team was quick to respond to critics who blasted Bertuzzi's behavior, tying it to their broader contention that professional hockey had become increasingly violent. Two days after Bertuzzi's news conference Canucks general manager Brian Burke called the "media's vilifying of Bertuzzi 'shameful.'"[41] Both Burke and team captain Markus Naslund agreed that Bertuzzi had made a mistake, but contended that he was being made a scapegoat. "We're going to use this as a motivating factor," Naslund said.[42]

One newspaper, the *London Free Press*, reported that Burke and Naslund were angry over stories that said Bertuzzi was reckless. "You've taken this opportunity to kick the crap out of him and it's been just shameful," Burke said.[43]

"Naslund was equally blunt. 'I'm very disappointed with a lot of the things that have been said about Todd,' he said. 'I know the guy.'"[44]

Moore, in a neck brace, addressed the media during a news conference March 29, 2004, about his progress:[45]

> *I'm feeling well and I've made some improvements and the doctors have passed along some good news. . . . I don't know whether I'll be able to play again, but I remain optimistic and I'm more fortunate just to be alive and take one day at a time from here on in.*

While he did not have any memory of the attack, he did talk briefly about the incident:[46]

> *I can't explain how scary it is to kind of wake up to a nightmare. I'm playing a game and the next thing I know I'm lying in a room with medical personnel standing over me and I have a neck brace on and I'm having my equipment cut off from me and I'm strapped down and I really had no idea what was going on. It's pretty scary.*

When asked about feelings of retribution for what happened he replied:[47]

> *Well, I think that type of stuff, you know, is—doesn't have any place in the game, and that's all I want to say about that. We have a tremendous game, this game of hockey, and I think this incident has made the image of this game suffer, and that's unfortunate, and I sincerely hope that nothing like this ever happens again.*

When asked if he would sue Bertuzzi, he replied:[48]

That's not something that I've really thought about. I'm more worried just about feeling better tomorrow than I do today, and hopefully moving towards a full recovery, so it's kind of enough on my plate just to deal with that.

That day, an official Canucks statement was issued following Moore's press conference, which expressed concern for the victim:[49]

Canucks Statement Regarding Steve Moore Press Conference

Vancouver, B.C. (Monday, March 29, 2004). Vancouver Canucks President and General Manager Brian Burke released the following statement after viewing Steve Moore's press conference today:

On behalf of the entire Canucks organization, I'd like to wish Steve a quick and full recovery. I was pleased to see him looking better today and we hope to hear good things about his status in the near future.

Although we appreciate the media's interest in this story, due to the time of year, our organization will refrain from commenting further on this matter until after the completion of the regular season and playoffs.

Three months later, Bertuzzi was charged with assault causing bodily harm; he pleaded not guilty, but the case was not destined to play out in court. On January 17, 2005, Bertuzzi agreed to the prosecutor's plea bargain: a conditional discharge with a year's probation during which time he could not play in a game that included Moore (who had not returned to hockey at the time).[50] Bertuzzi was also ordered to perform 80 hours of community service. According to news accounts, Bertuzzi, who had no prior criminal record, faced a maximum of 18 months in prison if a trial had resulted in his conviction. Before agreeing to the plea

bargain, Bertuzzi told the court in a videotaped statement:[51]

For the last nine months or so, my life has been turned upside down. I made a terrible mistake that I wish I could take back. I crossed a line that professional hockey players, like anyone else, should never cross. I hit a fellow player from behind with my gloved hand when he was not expecting it. I did not intend for him to be hurt as badly as he was. I apologized to Steve Moore and I do so again and continue to wish him a complete recovery.

I was so caught up in the intensity of the game that I lost sight of certain fundamental rules. I certainly don't think of myself as a criminal. What happened that night in March is not who I am.

Moore was not present in the courtroom but delivered this statement: "I have no desire to interact with [Bertuzzi] in any way," Moore said. "If I'm ever able to play again, I would ask that Todd Bertuzzi never be permitted to play in any sporting activity I'm involved in."[52]

For fans, the Bertuzzi-Moore incident has already passed into hockey lore: an isolated case of a player crossing the line.

For critics, the case was a grim illustration of the old joke: "The other night I went to a fight, and a hockey game broke out."

EPILOGUE

Bertuzzi missed 13 regular season games and the 2004 Stanley Cup playoffs, and was fined about $502,000 of his $6.8 million salary.[53] About 17 months after the incident, National Hockey League Commissioner Gary Bettman lifted Bertuzzi's suspension, and he was "eligible for reinstatement for play in the NHL."[54] He resumed playing hockey for the Canucks and was even selected for the Canadian Olympic team in 2006. However, a few months later, the Canucks traded Bertuzzi to the Florida Panthers.

Moore filed a multimillion dollar lawsuit against Bertuzzi in 2006 for damages resulting from the March 8, 2004, attack.

Questions for Discussion

1. Analyze Todd Bertuzzi's responses to the Steve Moore incident. Did they help his reputation in the court of public opinion? Why or why not?
2. What is your reaction to the Vancouver Canucks general manager and team captain's remarks in this case?
3. Because this incident was televised nationally and replayed later many times by national news outlets, the stalking images of Bertuzzi will linger in many people's minds. How would you rehabilitate Bertuzzi's image?
4. What is your opinion of the Vancouver Canucks' response to this incident?
5. How can the National Hockey League promote a less violent image of the sport?

Do Some Research

1. There is a broad range of response options available for entities or organizations involved in a crisis. In this instance, Bertuzzi offered a full apology during a news conference. Do you think it was acceptable that he waited two days to offer a public apology? Under what circumstances do crisis experts recommend an apology as the response?
2. In the sports media world, the individual, not necessarily the team, is the focus of most reporting. In an industry dominated by celebrity or at least high-paid players, how do players manage their reputations on and off the court or field? Examine your favorite professional sport team or players; what activities do teams and players engage in to build positive reputations among their fans? How has Bertuzzi attempted to rehabilitate his image?
3. What are the pros and cons of products or services dependent on a celebrity?

Terminology

- apology
- assault
- community service
- scapegoat

Web Resources

- **National Hockey League** www.nhl.com/
- **Colorado Avalanche hockey team** www.coloradoavalanche.com/index.asp
- **Vancouver Canucks hockey team** www.canucks.com/

From Blazer Mania to "Jail Blazers"
Portland Blazers Struggle to Reconnect with Community

For decades, fans adored the Portland Trail Blazers. Although the team had not won the National Basketball Association championship since 1977, for 21 straight seasons Portland played well enough to earn a postseason playoff spot.[55]

From 1976 to 1995, every home game (for 809 consecutive appearances) was sold out at the 12,000-seat Memorial Coliseum.[56] Fans followed the Trail Blazers when the team moved to a roomier home at the Rose Garden's nearly 20,000-seat arena.

But fan loyalty in this one-sport town began to flag as players' on- and off-the-court antics were routinely reported by Portland media and beyond. Eventually, Blazer mania gave way to widespread use of a much less flattering moniker, "Jail Blazers," as story after story of player misdeeds captured the headlines.[57]

Media coverage of Portland's problems included:

- One player told *Sports Illustrated* this about fans: "We're not really going to worry about what the hell [the fans] think about us. They really don't matter to us. They can boo us every day, but they're still going to ask us for our autographs. That's why they're fans and we're NBA players."[58]
- A player racked up an NBA record for 41 technical fouls in a single season and was suspended for allegedly threatening a game official after a game.[59]
- A player pleaded guilty to attempted rape charges, was convicted of misdemeanor assault for attacking a man who scratched his car, and was arrested on felony domestic abuse charges.[60]
- A player fractured another player's eye socket during practice. [61]
- Several players were cited for marijuana possession.[62]
- A player was suspended for animal abuse involving alleged dog fighting.[63]
- Players were suspended or fined for spitting, fighting, cursing at the coach, throwing towels and other items onto the court, and making obscene gestures to fans.[64]

After the embarrassing string of bad publicity, Trail Blazer owner and retired Microsoft billionaire Paul Allen issued a rare statement about players' behavior:[65]

As an owner, I take player behavior very seriously. We all expect a lot from our team, and the Blazers have to be accountable for doing what's right for the team, the fans and the community—and players will indeed be held responsible.

Let there be no mistake that unacceptable conduct will not be condoned. Everyone at the Blazers will tackle these issues head on—and we are prepared to suspend players, levy heavy fines and trade or release a player if that becomes necessary.

The community deserves a team of which we can all be proud and I am fully committed to improving the Blazers' conduct on and off the court.

The team with new management also adopted a 25-point pledge to fans and followed through with stiff fines and suspensions for player misconduct. A news report quoted several players admitting they had not read the pledge or were ignoring it.[66] Some troubled players were traded. The first pledge was "To evaluate character along with basketball talent when selecting players."[67] Additional pledge items included:

- To establish a player code of conduct and to hold our players accountable for their actions both on and off the court.
- To help our players represent our team and community with pride by creating a player program and development position.
- To educate our players so that they will understand why Portland, Oregon is a special place to play and what it means to be a Portland Trail Blazer.

Fan attitudes did not change overnight. A new team president and general manager traded two temperamental players, and player misconduct began to lessen. Still, some minor incidents occurred; after a player threw a towel in the face of a fellow player, one frustrated fan said:[68]

When players don't play hard, and they thumb their noses at the fans, and they flip off the fans, and they get technical fouls, and the drug stuff . . . you just get sick of it. I'd rather see a mediocre team of over-achievers than a talented team of underachievers. And when they're underachievers and thugs to boot, you put up with it so long, and then you say, "Wait a minute. I'm stupid. I'm not giving any more of my money to these guys."

While player misconduct lessened during the 2004–2005 season, large multimillion dollar contracts, injuries, continued losing seasons, a young team, and a low community profile kept many fans away. A November 9, 2005, game against the New York Knicks was the lowest-attended game, with just 12,296 sold seats in an arena that seats 19,980.[69] The 2004–2005 season did have a few highlights, including Damon Stoudamire's new single-game-scoring record of 54 points and a new season record for 3-pointers with 181 points.[70] However, the team's season record of 27–55 equaled its third-worst performance since its first season of play in 1970 (also the fifth-worst NBA season record) and its lowest average attendance in 10 years.[71]

It would take time to convince fans that both performance *and* character were back to stay.

Open Scenario Challenge

One month before the 2005–2006 season opened, the Trail Blazers announced the hiring of former marketing communications consultant Art Sasse as the club's vice president of communications. (It was a newly created role. Previously, communications was combined with marketing.) Sasse had more than 20 years of experience in marketing communications, community relations, public affairs, media relations, and sports journalism.[72]

Lacking big-name talent, the new Trail Blazer's roster did not generate exceptional excitement during the 2005–2006 season. It was viewed by most as a building year. Still, positive signs were beginning to emerge.

Before the season started, a Blazer study reported that 71 percent of Portland respondents said the team was headed in the right direction.[73] Also ticket sales were up 21 percent from the previous season.[74]

You are the director of community relations. The Trail Blazers communication department has contacted you to discuss ways of raising the team's profile in the community through philanthropic efforts with various community nonprofit organizations. The goal is to reconnect players with old fans and establish new ties with family audiences; the team is interested in special events for schools and other kinds of outreach. He would like to discuss your ideas sometime next week. What are your ideas, and how will you prepare?

Questions for Discussion

1. How can an organization such as the Trail Blazers restore its credibility and respectability with fans?

2. What strategic public is most affected by the Portland Trail Blazers' past actions?

3. What was the organizational response to the bad publicity?

4. Who are the most credible spokespeople for this situation?

5. How effective is a 25-point pledge to fans by the players?

6. What other player actions in basketball and other sports have sparked controversy lately?

7. What type of community relations program would have the quickest impact on the situation?

Do Some Research

1. Portland Trail Blazer Mike Hansen, executive director for communication, said that the biggest challenge is getting the message out to fans about positive player deeds. Hansen said the team can't rely on the media to tell this story. How do you tell and effectively deliver that story to fans?

2. Examine another professional sports team that has experienced negative publicity. How did that team respond?

Web Resources
* **Portland Trail Blazers** www.nba.com/blazers/

* **Paul Allen Addresses Fans, April 5, 2003 (statement from owner)** www.nba.com/blazers/news/Paul_Allen_Addresses_Fans-71876-41.html
* **Trail Blazers Pledge to Fans** www.nba.com/blazers/features/Blazers_Pledge_to_Fans-81965-41.html

Witch Way to Go?
Going Beyond Salem's Witch City Persona

In 1692, the small Puritan village of Salem, Massachusetts, was caught in the grip of witchcraft hysteria triggered by a group of girls who dabbled in the occult and accused nearly 200 townspeople of witchcraft.[75] This peculiar chapter in American history raged for a year and resulted in 20 executions (19 hangings and 1 death by crushing).[76] The tragedy has captivated America's imagination for years.

Its mystique has grown ever stronger since playwright Arthur Miller wrote *The Crucible* in the 1950s (with a Hollywood film version in 1996) and several best sellers, such as *Witch-Hunt* that re-created Salem's mass hysteria.

More than three centuries after the gruesome events enshrined on stage and in film, Salem now attracts about a million visitors annually.[77] Nearly one-third visit in October, when a full slate of Halloween activities is offered: lantern-guided walking tours, a costume parade, and haunted storytelling.[78] Witch-related attractions—the historic Witch House (home to one of the witch trial judges), Witch History Museum, Salem Witch Museum, Witch Dungeon Museum, Spellbound Museum, and The Salem Wax Museum—all offer extended hours to accommodate enthusiastic tourists.

It is a city that has embraced its witchy history with gusto. Salem police officers wear badges embroidered with a witch on a broomstick; the local high school's athletic logo and mascot also feature the same, and the school student newspaper is called the *Witch's Brew*. The local brewery offers a Pumpkinhead ale, a Witch City Red amber, a Black Bat stout and a Devil's Mark porter. Salem even managed to capitalize on the Harry Potter phenomenon when the author mentioned Salem in one of her books; in 2005 the city hosted its first five-day Harry Potter literary conference, the "Witching Hour," sponsored by an international fan group.[79]

Tourism is a major economic engine for the entire state of Massachusetts, bringing in $11 billion annually and employing 124,800 people.[80] Salem, population 42,000, relies heavily on tourism as its economic foundation; restaurants, hotels, and shops all benefit from visitors. However, in 2004, 25 percent of Salem's tourism trade occurred in October.[81] People were fond of describing Salem as "dead" after Halloween.

As a result, business and civic leaders decided to explore moving beyond their broomstick-heavy image. As one of America's oldest cities with a scenic waterfront, there were plenty of other attractions that seemed to get lost among the witch industry. In 2005 it was named one of America's dozen distinctive destinations by the National Trust for Historic Preservation.[82] How could Salem leverage its history to build a year-round tourism trade?

Its tourism group, Destination Salem, hired a consulting firm to take a comprehensive look at Salem's attributes. A tagline, "Experience the Unexpected," cleverly incorporated the city's past with promises of more—including its rich literary, architectural, and maritime history.

Some of Salem's attractions found in its official guidebook include:[83]

- Peabody Essex Museum: A museum that chronicles New England's storied past as well as other cultural wonders. It houses one of the finest maritime art collections. Its $125 million renovation completed in 2003 has made it a major cultural institution in Salem.
- The House of the Seven Gables: The Turner-Ingersoll Mansion was made famous by author Nathaniel Hawthorne in his 1851 classic tale, *The House of the Seven Gables;* the home that Hawthorne was born in, circa 1750, is next door.
- McIntire Historic District: This area of Salem is home to hundreds of architecturally significant houses and buildings. Historic Chestnut Street, called "the most beautiful street in America," is lined with homes built by sea captains and merchants between 1800 and 1840. There are many examples of homes in the Federal architecture style. Some homes, such as the Witch House, even date back to 1642.
- Salem Maritime: The first national historic site in the National Park System, it was established to preserve and interpret the maritime history of New England and the United States. It has several historically preserved buildings.
- Friendship of Salem: A full-scale replica of a 171-foot, three-masted 1797 Salem East Indiaman.

- *Fame*: A full-scale replica of a 1812 privateer.
- Salem Harbor.
- Derby Wharf and the picturesque Derby Lighthouse.
- Pickering Wharf: a waterfront shopping and dining village.
- Ye Olde Pepper Candy Companie: The site of the oldest candy company in the country, established in 1806.
- New England Pirate Museum: Salem docks saw its fair share of pirates in the seventeenth and eighteenth centuries, including the nefarious Captains Blackbeard, Kidd, and others who prowled the coast looking for plunder.
- An online (and downloadable) visitor's guide (www.salem.org) details more of Salem's attractions.

Open Scenario Challenge

Destination Salem, the city tourism agency, has contracted with your marketing communication consulting company to expand Salem's tourism trade beyond its witch city image. Civic leaders are working to keep tourists longer so visitors can see more than just the city's historic witch trial attractions. The city wants visitors to recognize that Salem offers other significant tourist spots involving its maritime history, waterfront, literary history, and architecture. Develop a marketing communication strategy that addresses these concerns. In particular, Destination Salem is interested in your ideas about using a history theme that ties together its attractions.

Questions for Discussion

1. What is the historical significance of Salem, Massachusetts?
2. What types of events happen in October?
3. Why does Salem want to expand beyond its witch city image?
4. What groups might not appreciate the witch city heritage?

5. How could media relations play a pivotal role in changing Salem's image?

6. How could other public relations and marketing tactics change Salem's image?

Do Some Research

Many cities, states, and even countries must deal with image problems. Hurricane Katrina devastated New Orleans in 2005. In the aftermath of the hurricane's enormous destruction, its tourism industry needed to respond. Research news media accounts on how New Orleans Convention and Visitors Bureau responded after the disaster. How did the city market itself after extensive daily media coverage showing the hurricane's destruction? In particular, how did the city present itself to outsiders for the 2006 Mardi Gras just five months after the hurricane? What were its key messages and strategies? How is New Orleans marketing itself today?

To begin the research, visit:

- **New Orleans' Convention and Visitors Bureau** at www.neworleanscvb.com/
- **New Orleans Online** at www.neworleansonline.com/

Web Resources

- **Destination Salem, Salem Office of Tourism & Cultural Affairs** www.salem.org/index.asp
- **Official 2005/2006 Guidebook & Map Destination Salem Massachusetts** www.salem.org/pdf/visitorsguide.pdf
- **Massachusetts Office of Travel and Tourism** www.mass-vacation.com/jsp/index.jsp
- **Office of Travel and Tourism Industries, U.S. government agency** (contains market analysis research on travel and tourism statistics for the United States) tinet.ita.doc.gov/ and tinet.ita.doc.gov/research/reports/basic/index.html

Queen Mary 2's Unhappy Voyage
Luxurious Cruise or "High-Speed Passage"?

Americans love to cruise. They make up 79 percent of the global cruise line market, which has seen near double-digit growth since 9/11.[84] Cruise Lines International Association, the trade industry group, estimated that the cruise industry generated more than $32 billion to the U.S. economy.[85] In 2005 there were 8.6 million U.S. cruise embarkations alone.[86]

One of the crown jewels of the sea is the *Queen Mary 2* (QM2). When launched in 2004, it was the tallest, longest, largest, and most expensive cruise ship ever built.[87] Its sheer size and widely touted magnificence turned heads wherever it went.

Consider some of these fun facts from the QM2's press kit:[88]

- At 1,132 feet, the QM2 is twice as long as the Washington Monument, 147 feet longer than the Eiffel Tower, or just a bit shy of four football fields long.
- 17 decks tall, the QM2 sits 200 feet above the waterline, which is the equivalent to a 23-story building; from keel to funnel, it is 236 feet tall.
- It weighs 151,400 gross tons.
- QM2 offers a planetarium (the first at sea), one large indoor swimming pool and four outside pools, and a

20,000-square-foot health club; and it has the largest ballroom at sea. For those seeking intellectual stimulation, the QM2 offers educational lectures, discussions, and presentations organized by the University of Oxford.

- Pampered attention is guaranteed with more than 1,250 officers, crew, and social staff on hand to accommodate the needs of 2,600 passengers.

- Several restaurants, lounges, bars, and clubs.

- Other amenities include a casino, a showroom with seating for 1,105 guests, a children's playroom with nannies, a golf driving range, gymnasium, a kennel and pet park, and duty-free shops.

For many travelers, a cruise is a carefully planned dream vacation. When 2,500 passengers left New York on January 15, 2006, for a 38-day South American odyssey aboard the *Queen Mary 2*, expectations for a wonderful trip probably matched the equally high fares; according to Cunard's rate information "brochure fares" started at about $8,000 and rose to $80,000 and higher for its most exclusive luxury offerings.[89]

Just two days after leaving New York, the *Queen Mary 2* damaged one of four propeller motors while leaving a port near Miami.[90] This forced the ship back to port for safety checks, delaying the cruise two days. Traveling at a slower speed and behind schedule, the QM2 skipped stops at the Caribbean islands of St. Kitts and Barbados and Salvador in Brazil.[91]

Approximately 1,000 of the 2,500 passengers had purchased the 12-day cruise to Rio de Janeiro, Brazil.[92] When these passengers realized that the only port of call they would experience would be their port of destination, passengers were angry. Some had planned day activities at other ports; some passengers had planned to enjoy whatever amenities were available. Meetings were held with the captain, and a protest petition was circu-

lated garnering 1,300 signatures.[93] An offer of a 50 percent refund did not appease many.

According to news accounts a week after the ill-fated trip began, January 22, many passengers threatened a sit-in to protest by refusing to disembark when scheduled at Rio. Another 1,000 new passengers were expected to join the cruise in Rio.

The QM2's owner, Cunard, defended its offer as fair. "We obviously have missed these ports of call but our passengers have had 12 days on the most luxurious liner in the world and we felt there was value in that," said Carol Marlow, president of Cunard.[94]

One passenger, responding to a BBC request for passenger quotes on its Web site, said:[95]

This is not a cruise, it's a high speed passage from NY to Rio. We paid to see the Caribbean and Salvador and we have got 7 days + on a ship. We all want our money back!

Continued pressure by affected passengers and widespread news coverage of the developing event finally forced Cunard to reconsider its compensation offer. The night before the QM2 was to arrive in Rio de Janeiro, Cunard announced that it would give all passengers disembarking at Rio de Janeiro a full refund including airfare.[96] Those traveling beyond Rio de Janeiro would be refunded for the New York to Rio de Janeiro portion of the trip. Cunard president Marlow also flew into Rio de Janeiro to meet with passengers who were disembarking.[97]

Role-Playing Exercise

You are the public relations director for Cunard. President Carol Marlow would like your suggestions for her meeting with potentially angry passengers in Rio de Janeiro. She wants to practice some remarks and responses before she goes. Also, you want to prepare her for interacting positively with the media. Design some role-playing exercises to prepare Marlow for her difficult assignment.

Questions for Discussion

1. What is Cunard's reputation?
2. What makes *Queen Mary 2* special?
3. Why were some of the ports of call canceled on this particular trip?
4. Why were many passengers upset when *Queen Mary 2* did not make three scheduled port calls?
5. Did you feel the initial Cunard offer to passengers was sufficient? Explain Cunard's reasoning for its initial offer of compensation.
6. What type of organizational response did Cunard ultimately offer?
7. What effect did the negative publicity have on Cunard's reputation?
8. How could management actions and/or organizational policies have prevented this situation?
9. How would you have responded to this problem?

Do Some Research

In recent years, some negative incidents and issues regarding safety have arisen within the cruise line industry. How has the Cruise Lines International Association responded to these issues? What is its overall strategy? Do you agree with the strategy? Why?

Web Resources

- **Cruise Lines International Association** http://www.cruising.org/index.cfm
- **Cruise Lines International Association market research, industry trends, and news releases and press kits** http://www.cruising.org/Press/index.cfm
- **Cunard (company information)** www.cunard.com/
- **Cunard Queen Mary 2 press kit, news releases and other information** www.cunard.com/AboutCunard/NewsReleases.asp?Active=News
- **The Cunard Fleet** (provides facts and a virtual tour of its fleet including the Queen Mary 2) www.cunard.com/onboard/

Is It Live or Is It Recorded, Ashlee?
Managing Singer's Reputation after SNL Performance

It only took the push of a button—the wrong button—to create an instant crisis for singer Ashlee Simpson during a performance on NBC's *Saturday Night Live* (SNL).

On a show where everything is supposed to be "live," including the musical performances of guests, Simpson was caught off guard when her drummer accidentally activated the wrong backing tracks—which featured Simpson's prerecorded vocals.[98] Instead of "Autobiography," the opening beats of her hit "Pieces of Me" began playing, a song already performed earlier in the program. Her frantic

signals to stop the tape didn't work, and the band, trying to make the best of a bad situation, played along to "Pieces" for a second time.

The *Washington Post* characterized Simpson's next move as a "hoedown," a "very-odd 'Hee Haw'-esque dance."[99] After a few seconds of jumping around, Simpson left the stage and SNL went to a commercial.

At the end of the show Simpson blamed her band publicly: "I feel so bad! My band started playing the wrong song! And I didn't know what to do! I'm sorry! It's live TV! Things happen! I'm sorry!"[100]

The embarrassing lip-syncing incident (including rehearsal and backstage footage caught by a CBS *60 Minutes* crew) not only made the 20-year-old Simpson a pop culture laughingstock but also angered many music fans that expect only live performances from SNL.[101] The program has thrived for 30 years and attracted millions of fans because of its reputation for topical sketches and popular musical acts, all live in front of an in-studio audience.

For Simpson, the episode was a humbling experience. Just three months earlier, her debut album *Autobiography* reached number one on Billboard's Top 200 Albums Chart.[102] The younger sister of Jessica Simpson (also a pop singer and reality TV participant in MTV's hit *Newlyweds*), Ashlee was following and surpassing her sister's success as a pop star.[103] Ashlee's MTV's *The Ashlee Show* had chronicled this climb; SNL was a major performance for the early stages of Simpson's carefully choreographed career.

The lip-syncing debacle, a potential setback for her rising star, also raised larger questions and speculation about the music industry itself. If Ashlee Simpson was lip-syncing, then what about other supposedly "live" performances? With some concert tickets surpassing $100, was it really worth the money to hear prerecorded music and backing vocal tracks?

Simpson girded herself for the avalanche of negative publicity and decided not to hide.

Simpson kept her scheduled appearance at NBC's *Radio Music Awards,* just two days after the gaffe. She sang live and even tried to joke about the SNL incident. When the music began, she made a slashing gesture at her throat and said "Wrong song! This is the wrong song!" before adding, "Just kidding, you guys!"[104]

That day, Simpson's official Web site carried an announcement that Simpson would appear on NBC's *Today Show* the next day to discuss her SNL performance. Interviewed by Katie Couric, Simpson

explained the sequence of events that led to the fiasco.

She told a sympathetic Couric that she started the day with voice problems caused by acid reflux, a condition in which acid from the stomach rises up into the esophagus, that became even more apparent during rehearsal.[105] After consulting with her personal physician, Simpson said her father and manager recommended that she use backing vocal tracks so that she wouldn't have to strain and possibly damage her vocal chords. She told Couric:

> *I was singing with the track. Like on the first one, I was singing along, you know, with the track. But my voice wasn't strong enough to hold up the song alone, because I would have like—I mean, I didn't—my dad was the one who was like "Honey, you have to do it." He put my—Dr. Sugarman, my local doctor, on the phone with me. I was like. . . "You have to or you're going to ruin your vocal chords if you sing on them like this."*

She noted during the interview that many musicians do what she did, especially when they aren't feeling well, and that it was the first and only time she had used backing vocal tracks. She also said she did not blame her band, particularly her drummer, Chris Fox, for the mistake.[106]

Simpson: *And, you know, my drummer, you know, who I love and adore, accidentally, you know, pressed the wrong button and didn't set up the next song.*

Couric: *Is he still your drummer?*

Simpson: *Yeah, he is. You know, I love him. And everybody makes mistakes, you know.*

Thousands of her teen fans had posted mostly negative comments on Simpson's Web site. Simpson told Couric she had tried not to read them because "it's hard." Not long after the *Today Show* interview, a posting appeared on Simpson's Web site from her drummer who pushed the wrong button during the SNL performance. In the posting he took the blame for the music mix-up and then verified Ashley's voice problem, contradicting media reports that she had been lip-syncing:

In his posting titled "From Someone on the Inside" at 9:15:29 a.m., shortly after Simpson's *Today Show* appearance, he admitted that he had simply made a mistake and cued the wrong song. He refuted reports that Simpson was lip-synching:[107]

> *. . . SHE WAS NOT!!! I was there. Ashlee was having problems with her voice/throat that day. A couple hours before playing SNL. . . Your voice is almost gone. . .*
>
> *What do you do? A lot of performers may have gone the lip-synching route. But Ash trucked on through, singing her own songs, but with a backing vocal track for reinforcement. She did not "FAKE" anything. If you listen to the first performance, you can make out two voices. Hers, and that of the backing track. No, this is not something that she usually does. In fact, this is something that she NEVER does. But this was somewhat of an emergency. . .*

Later that day, Simpson also put up her own posting titled "Hey Guys!" on her Web site that thanked her fans for sticking by her and gave her version of what happened:[108]

> *. . . I have decided to speak openly and honestly about what happened on snl because I want you guys to know what really happened. My acid reflux started acting up and I know my real fans know that music and performing is my true passion and you support me for that. . . I couldn't control what happened that day. . .*

She admitted that the criticism of recent days had stung. But she ended her post by thanking her fans again and saying their support "makes me want to go back out there and continue to prove all the negative press wrong!"

A few days later, Ashlee and her family—sister Jessica, her manager-father, and mother—appeared together on ABC's *20/20*. The report focused on Ashlee's father's drive to manage and promote both daughters' careers, even if some said it compromised family values. Interviewed by Elizabeth Vargas, the lip-syncing debacle was replayed along with her publicized excuses for what happened: acid reflux and band error.

Having apologized, explained, and completed the main damage-control interviews, Simpson moved on with her career. Despite being booed at the Orange Bowl during a performance of her single "La, La" from her first album, she completed a national tour, a second season of MTV's *The Ashlee Show*, appeared in an independent film, and in October she issued a second album, *I Am Me*, which debuted at number one on Billboard's top 200 list and eventually turned platinum.[109] Nearly one year after her disastrous SNL performance, she was invited back and sang songs from her new album without a hitch.[110]

Questions for Discussion

1. Explain what happened on *Saturday Night Live* featuring Ashlee Simpson that ignited a controversy for the young star.

2. What steps did Ashlee Simpson take to explain her actions after the *Saturday Night Live* incident? Could she have acted more quickly?

3. Did Ashlee Simpson's decision to stay public after the *Saturday Night Live* incident help or hurt her image?

4. Analyze Ashlee Simpson's Web site postings, both hers and Chris Fox's.

Were they effective? What would you say differently? (Both postings are available from her Web site at http://www.ashleesimpsonmusic.com/.)

5. The *Saturday Night Live* video of Ashlee Simpson's performance is widely available on many Web sites along with some video lampoons. How should Simpson respond to this negative publicity?

6. From a publicist's viewpoint, what could Ashlee Simpson do in the future to garner good publicity? In particular, what kinds of images would it take to replace the mental images people have of Simpson's embarrassing gaffe?

Do Some Research

1. More celebrities, particularly musicians, are using their official Web sites to communicate directly with their fans with letters or message boards. Examine the Web site of a favorite musician or other celebrity, and look for direct communication efforts. Do you think these efforts are more credible than news releases? Explain.

2. Many celebrities enhance their reputations by performing good deeds in public, such as charity work. These efforts not only promote a positive image of the person but also gain the celebrity needed exposure. Examine charity work of two celebrities. Do you think there is a strategy involved in the types of charities celebrities choose? Explain.

Terminology

- lip-syncing
- prerecorded music
- vocal tracks
- MTV

Web Resources

- **Billboard's Top 200 Albums Chart** www.billboard.com/bb/charts/bb200.jsp
- **MTV's The Ashlee Simpson Show** www.mtv.com/onair/dyn/ashlee/series .jhtml
- **Saturday Night Live** www.nbc.com/Saturday_Night_Live/index.html
- **Ashlee Simpson official Web site** www.ashleesimpsonmusic.com/

Nazi Prince?
The Trouble with Harry's Poor Costume Choice

Big mistakes make big headlines, and some members of Britain's royal family often find themselves the subject of intense media scrutiny. A grandson of Queen Elizabeth II, Prince Harry, got more than the usual tabloid treatment when he was photographed wearing a Nazi uniform at a costume party—two weeks before the 60th anniversary of the liberation of the notorious Nazi death camp, Auschwitz.[111]

The photograph showed the young prince (who was 20 at the time) at a friend's party holding a drink in one hand and a cigarette in the other while sporting a red-and-black swastika armband and an army shirt with Nazi regalia.

As the embarrassing photo was reprinted around the world, it clashed with the somber Holocaust anniversary seen as particularly poignant because it was considered the last major gathering of Holocaust survivors; world leaders, including Queen Elizabeth, planned to commemorate the event.

The Nazi gas chambers, like those at Auschwitz, were part of a camp system that exterminated more than 6 million Jews and "undesirables"; millions more were subjected to imprisonment and forced labor during World War II.

In a two-sentence statement released to the media the day after the photo was published, Prince Harry said: "I am very sorry if I have caused any offense. It was a poor choice of costume and I apologize."[112]

The London-based *Jewish Chronicle* Editor Ned Temko was unimpressed with the apology:[113]

> It implied this was a wardrobe problem. Whatever further statement he makes, there has to be some reflection that a swastika armband isn't just a fashion item, that it symbolizes a lot more. One of the most dismaying aspects for Jews and non-Jews is that there seems to be an utter lack of awareness of the context of the Holocaust and the war.

Prince Harry did not make an in-person apology. Amid calls for Prince Harry to do more than apologize, the royal family ruled out his attendance at Auschwitz ceremonies. An official said:[114]

> It would be a distraction and a detraction from the importance of the occasion because it would become a different story in media terms. . . He recognizes he made a very bad mistake and he apologizes for that.

Question for Discussion

1. What do you think of Prince Harry's decision to wear a Nazi uniform to a private costume party?

2. What do you think about Prince Harry's decision to release a written statement of apology? What were his other options?

3. Analyze the wording of Prince Harry's written statement. Why did this lead to more criticism?

4. How would you initially begin to rehabilitate the prince's reputation?

5. What kinds of activities could Prince Harry do to show he is really a decent chap?

6. Images often leave a lasting impression. How can a celebrity or public figure, such as Prince Harry, visibly build a positive reputation?

Do Some Research

1. Using newspaper databases, such as Lexis-Nexis, find three articles since the initial January 13, 2005, story that provide evidence that Prince Harry is actively (or not) rehabilitating his image.

2. The Prince Harry gaffe sparked debate worldwide that the lessons of the past had not been learned by twenty first-century youth. Europe has seen a rise in anti-Semitic activity, and a number of genocide atrocities have taken place in several other countries since World War II. If a Jewish community organization came to your public relations agency, what kind of a campaign would you recommend that the Jewish community undertake to preserve the lessons of the Holocaust? What would be the main campaign elements, themes, and audiences?

Chapter Nine

Community Relations

"No man is an island," a famous poet once wrote—and likewise, no organization can succeed in isolation. Organizations constantly interact with and depend on all kinds of groups: employees, customers, members, government officials, other businesses, suppliers, educational institutions, and many others.

The traditional definition of community has included groups loosely or tightly associated through some unifying trait or issue such as ethnicity, politics, gender, work, and geographic location. Since technology and globalization have erased geographic barriers in the last generation, the definition of *community* has changed dramatically. Just as people of like minds are now easily connected through cyberspace communities, multinational organizations, while headquartered in one place, may have plants and other operations scattered across the globe.

Even though the meaning of community has expanded, the traditional definition based on geographic location still counts today because organizations rely on attracting good employees and operating in business-friendly environments.

BUILDING POSITIVE RELATIONSHIPS AT HOME

In either case, public relations seeks to build positive relationships with community groups whose activities can have an impact on an organization's reputation and livelihood. Issues such as pollution, working conditions, hiring practices, compensation, the economic impact of the organization on other businesses—even traffic, noise, and other quality-of-life issues—all can grow into major controversies that may disrupt operations and damage the reputation of the organization.

An organization can develop a good-neighbor approach to community relations that balances the needs and concerns of community partners with its mission. This approach, called *corporate social responsibility*, recognizes an organization's obligation to contribute to society in some way because it's the right thing to do. Many organizations have found that giving back to the community is good business and often leads to stronger consumer loyalty. Such activity can foster company pride and provide opportunities for employees to be involved in their neighborhoods.

An effective community relations program should be conducted purposely with goals and objectives. This starts with an examination of the organization's strengths and weaknesses, from facilities to human resources. While many businesses have big hearts and deep pockets, they want to see a benefit, even for charitable activities. An organization should inventory what it has to offer beyond money. For example, a professional baseball team could offer to run a baseball camp for underprivileged children, or executive leadership could be "loaned" to nonprofits for a year. Often organizations seek a natural fit that extends their brand recognition. Organizations should also consider employee interests. Employees are often willing volunteers for a good cause when their company provides the necessary resources.

Next, an organization needs to get acquainted with the community and its challenges. Organizational leadership should connect with elected community leaders and other organizations' executives by joining key civic or nonprofit organizations. Some of these could include the United Way, Rotary International, and cultural institutions.

Once an organization has examined its strengths and determined community needs, it must decide what it can do to help. Effective outreach may be as simple as a library that offers its meeting rooms to nonprofits, displays local artists' works in its lobby, or offers reading programs and craft activities for children.

Whatever an organization decides to do should be planned and executed with care. A poorly run program will reflect negatively on the organization. The same diligence that goes into planning a public relations campaign should apply to charitable events.

The good deeds of an organization should also be communicated to key publics through the contributing organization's own organizational media as well as community channels. Effective outlets can include the local news media, the organization's employee and community newsletters and Web site, the chamber of commerce newsletter, and the available communication channels of the organization receiving the help. A Girl Scout council that receives building materials for an office renovation project from a hardware store, for example, could be featured in the Girl Scouts' community publications or recognized at an annual volunteer dinner.

CORPORATE PHILANTHROPY

Similar to the good-neighbor concept of community relations is corporate philanthropy. By law, corporations are allowed to donate up to 10 percent of their earnings to charitable organizations. The authors of *Public Relations: The Profession and the Practice* suggest a strategic approach to philanthropy that considers the following factors:[1]

1. **Do no harm.** Contributions should not be made to any cause that may be contrary to the best interests of the donor or the recipient.

2. **Communicate with the recipient.** Effective grant making requires a close partnership between donor and the recipient.

3. **Target contributions toward specific areas.** Gifts should achieve maximum impact on the community and maximum benefits for the donor. In this regard, donations should go to areas where individual corporations have unique expertise not available in the nonprofit sector.

4. **Make contributions according to statements of corporate policy.** Fully developed policies of this nature should include the charitable aims and beliefs of the company, the criteria to be used in evaluating requests for funds, the kinds of organizations and causes that will and will not be supported, and the methods by which grants will be administered.

5. **Plan within the budget.** Corporate giving should be tied to a set percentage of net earnings.

6. **Inform all persons concerned.** Employees and the community at large should be fully aware of corporate activities.

7. **Do a later follow-up.** The corporation does a valuable service by demanding high levels of performance and proper financial accounting from recipients.

8. **Remember that more than money may be needed.** An effective corporate contribution program requires more than checkbook charity. Volunteer workers, managerial expertise, and corporate leadership are essential elements of an effective program.

EVENT SPONSORSHIP, IN-KIND CONTRIBUTIONS, AND CAUSE-RELATED MARKETING

Beyond general cash contributions, corporations sponsor events, do pro bono work, give in-kind contributions, and conduct cause-related marketing.

Event Sponsorship

Organizations may provide the financial backing for an event. David D'Alessandro, author of *Brand Warfare: 10 Rules for Building the Killer Brand,* said that sponsorships can be well worth the investment. "By contributing to something consumers value, you may win their interest and respect, perhaps even their gratitude. Ideally, they see the glamour, excitement, and emotion of the event or person you are sponsoring as attributes of your brand as well."[2] Transferring the positive attributes of an event or person to the organization or product can also build awareness among new audiences. Event sponsors gain the rights to having the company's name and logo prominently attached to advertising and other visible venues, including clothing associated with the event and decorations.

Pro Bono Work

Businesses that have specializations, such as legal expertise, can offer to help organizations by doing the work instead of subcontracting it for money. Many advertising agencies and public relations firms provide their services free for special nonprofit projects.

Cause-Related Marketing

Corporations have found that good causes are good buying incentives. Research from the 1999 Cone-Roper "Cause-Related Trends Report" found that 78 percent of adults would be more likely to buy a product associated with a cause they care about.[3] Cause-related marketing provides a portion of the sales receipts as a donation to a particular nonprofit organization. According to the Cone-Roper study, businesses have moved beyond short-term sales strategies to using cause-related marketing to build customer loyalty and stronger brands and reputations.

MANAGING ACTIVIST GROUPS

Activists are people who seek political, social, or organizational change by targeting organizational policies or institutional behaviors through vigorous campaigning. High-profile activist groups have focused on the treatment of animals used for food, particularly housing and slaughtering methods; products that cause pollution; foods that contribute to obesity; and national and international political, financial, and environmental issues. Just about anything or anyone in the public domain can become a target of activist groups.

The Internet and technology have leveled the playing field in some respects between activists and organizations. While organizations still have powerful resources of money, staffing, and political connections, activists today are much better organized and understand how to use the media to reach their goals. One-person crusades are possible if the person is Web savvy, dedicated, and has lots of spare time. Affordable cameras, camcorders, computer graphics, and low-run custom printing options can provide activists with a highly effective and credible-looking communications campaign.

PR Week offers some ways that companies can respond strategically to activist groups:[4]

- Identify the kind of protest groups you're dealing with. Some just want to damage the company, whereas others truly desire to effect mutually beneficial changes.
- Speak the truth and be open and accessible. Provide information.
- Keep your cool and don't become overly confrontational. Adopt a friendly tone.
- Know the strengths and weaknesses of your activist groups. Determine if they should become strategic partners.
- Consider policy changes to neutralize or placate hostile organizations.
- Provide employees with facts to allay fears and to be ambassadors for the organization.
- Don't underestimate the power of an activist group to damage an organization.

"It's the Real Thing"

Protest at the Jewish Museum

Art exhibitions sometimes attract criticism and greater public attention when individuals or groups find fault with the subject matter. In the case of the Jewish Museum in New York City, the uproar came before the exhibition had even opened.

Mirroring Evil: Nazi Imagery/Recent Art featured 19 works by 13 contemporary artists from 8 nations; many of the works used Nazi-era images and symbols in combination with pop culture symbols and consumer products to "raise questions about commercialization and iconic images of the Holocaust."[5] Using the imagery of the Third Reich and the challenging language of conceptual art, the artists led viewers of their work to question how images shape perceptions of evil today. Some of the offending art included:[6]

- *Giftgas Giftset*, by New Yorker Tom Sachs, replicated three Zyklon B gas canisters using the colors and logos of Chanel, Hermes, and Tiffany's. Zyklon-B, a commercial preparation of hydrocyanic acid, was used in the Nazi death camps.
- *LEGO Concentration Camp Set*, by Polish-born artist Zbigniew Libera, consisted of LEGO pieces used to construct small-scale models of concentration camps including barracks and crematoria. He created fake LEGO packaging that looked like packaging boxes for commercial LEGOS children's building blocks. The viewer saw a suite of these boxes, but not the actual models. The work was intended to remind the viewer of the Third Reich's propaganda aimed at children

as well as the pervasiveness of violence in children's products today.

- *Self-Portrait at Buchenwald: It's the Real Thing* was a Web image of artist Alan Schechner holding a Diet Coke digitally inserted into Margaret Bourke White's famous photograph of emaciated Jews in their bunks shortly after the liberation of Buchenwald concentration camp.

Four of the artists, including Sachs and Schechner, were Jewish; some were descendants of Holocaust survivors. Most were born after World War II; many were in their 30s or 40s. While the art did not approve of the Holocaust or suggest that it did not happen the way history records it, many survivors and descendants felt the works trivialized a horrific period in which 6 million people lost their lives. However, the exhibition and its accompanying art were

© Alan Schechner. Image courtesy of the artist.

not about the Holocaust; instead it was current social commentary.

The Jewish Museum, which celebrated its 100th anniversary in 2004, is considered a cultural gem that explores the intersection of 4,000 years of art and Jewish culture. Its exhibitions and educational programs appeal to people of all cultural backgrounds; 35 percent of its visitors in 2004 had no Jewish background. The museum attracts about 200,000 visitors annually and has about 11,000 members.[7]

While the Holocaust theme had been explored by the museum in other exhibitions, including the Holocaust-era paintings and drawings of Charlotte Salomon in 2000, the March 17–June 30, 2002, Mirroring Evil exhibition was the first show featuring works by a younger generation using Nazi imagery in combination with current pop culture themes and consumer products. The resulting works of art made powerful (and, for many, disturbing) comments about modern cultural issues. The exhibition's wall text described the approach: "This art is cautionary rather than memorial. It warns us not to take for granted the symbols of oppression that pervade our outlets of news and entertainment. It conveys a sense of wariness about techniques of persuasion, including those we encounter in the marketplace."[8]

CONTROVERSY

Ultimately, the aims of artists, the exhibition's curator, and museum alike were obscured by controversy. The negative public reaction followed the catalog copublisher's decision to release the exhibition catalog, complete with color photographs of the featured art, three months before accompanying educational materials were completed and before the exhibition was open to the public. Museum Director of Communications Anne Scher said at the time the decision would leave the institution "vulnerable" to criticism. She shared her concerns with the exhibition's curator

and deputy director but not with the museum's director.

In a city that boasts the largest concentration of Jews anywhere outside of Israel who had experienced the Holocaust firsthand, some found the works disrespectful and painful.

The 164-page catalog, edited by exhibit curator Kleeblatt, featured essays by well-known academic scholars who wrestled with the exhibition's aesthetic, historical, and cultural issues; short essays about each piece in the exhibit were also included.

In the museum's news release, Kleeblatt said the exhibit's artists represented a new generation and viewpoint that weren't exactly in line with traditional ways:[9]

A trend has emerged over the past decade in which younger artists have departed from the more traditional ways of addressing the Holocaust and have begun to find new ways to confront the evil of the Third Reich. Many of these artists base their works on material of popular culture, which is a potent source of information for their generation. Others wed Nazi imagery to coveted consumer products, warning us about the fragile boundaries between propaganda and promotion, desire and destruction. I believe all of these artists invite us to look at ourselves, to reflect on the role the Holocaust plays in our lives today—as memory, as point of reference, even as a subject for the entertainment industry—and to question the adequacy of our own response to evil.

Soon after the catalog's publication, a small educational program was held at the museum to discuss the upcoming Mirroring Evil exhibition, including the curator and some of the contributing catalog essayists. A few participants objected to the art during a question-and-answer session, and a few attendees, one of whom may have been a Holocaust survivor, walked out of the event, said Scher, who heard about the reaction from those attending the program.

A *Wall Street Journal* reporter heard about the program and began researching the exhibition. Scher provided information and sources for the reporter's story. The resulting January 10, 2002, article entitled "Coming Museum Show with Nazi Theme Stirs New York's Art World" drew a connection with a controversial 1999 shock art exhibit by noting in its lead the exhibit could be the "next art-world 'Sensation.'"[10] That exhibition included, among other highly charged works, a painting of the Virgin Mary splattered with elephant dung.

The *New York Daily News* ("Jewish Museum's Holocaust Storm: Show with a Lego Concentration Camp Hit for Trivializing Horror") picked up the story the next day as did the the the *New York Post*. The Associated Press released a domestic wire story entitled "Jewish Museum Exhibit Criticized for Lego Concentration Camp, Designer Gas Canisters" and another story for its state and regional wires entitled "Jewish Museum Exhibit Criticized for Including Nazi Art." Both AP stories quoted Menachem Rosensaft, a founding chairman of the International Network of Children of Holocaust Survivors, who criticized the exhibition, and the exhibition's curator, Norman Kleeblatt. The AP propelled the story nationwide and beyond.

ORGANIZATIONAL RESPONSE

Calls from reporters came flooding into Scher's office, which included just one other staff member. "There was a call every minute and we did our best to respond." Scher worked many late nights responding to media requests. "It was overwhelming."

An extensive press kit included a six-page news release, biographies of the artists, a backgrounder that described the museum's art holdings that related to the

Holocaust and its past Holocaust-related exhibitions, and a backgrounder on the museum.

To get its messages out, the Jewish Museum worked to place op-ed pieces or letters to the editors in such publications as the *Daily News*, *Jewish Week*, the *Washington Post*, and the *New York Times*. It provided third-party advocates to speak on its behalf in interviews for newspapers, magazines, and television news segments.

Joan Rosenbaum, Helen Goldsmith Director of the Jewish Museum, reiterated her support for every art object in the exhibition. In the news release announcing the exhibition, Rosenbaum defended the exhibit saying:[11]

As an art museum that presents all of Jewish culture, we are committed to showing works of contemporary artists who have used images of the Nazi era to make a powerful and timely investigation of the nature of evil. These artists ask each viewer to consider his or her responsibility toward civil society and to be vigilant about the bigotry and dehumanization that continue in the world more than fifty years after the Holocaust.

A small public relations firm helped Scher draft materials for the media, and its senior management served as a "sounding board" for strategy sessions. The firm's crisis management experience was limited, and Scher said the firm had never before experienced such a controversy.

One month before the exhibition's opening, the American Gathering of Jewish Holocaust Survivors, a national organization with ties to about 70 Holocaust survivor groups, urged a boycott if the museum did not cancel the exhibition.[12]

New York State Assemblyman Dov Hikind, whose mother survived Auschwitz, and a group of about 10 Holocaust survivors and children of survivors met with Jewish Museum representatives on

March 1, 2002, 16 days before the exhibit's opening to ask for the removal of the three most offending pieces.[13] The meeting lasted two hours and ended with museum officials agreeing to give more consideration to the group's request.

Three days later the Jewish Museum announced that it would post signs at the point where visitors are about to encounter the most troubling artwork. The sign would read: "Some Holocaust survivors have been disturbed by the works of art shown beyond this point. Visitors may choose to avoid the works by exiting the exhibition through the door to the left." Carpenters would also build a special exit from the gallery allowing visitors to avoid those works. And the museum would mount Schechner's "Real Thing" Buchenwald image on a computer that displayed it only after the viewer had read a content warning.[14]

Still, critics were unhappy. Hikind was quoted in a New Jersey newspaper six days before the opening:[15]

But I don't think they get it. When I saw that thing with the Coke can, hey, give me a break. I can't think of anything [the museum should do] to frame the art that would make it acceptable. I will be out in front of the museum with such a large group of protesters on March 17 when it opens.

Robert J. Hurst, chairman of the Jewish Museum and the son of a Holocaust survivor, said in a statement prepared for the news media that his initial reaction to Sachs's and Schechner's pieces changed once he saw them at a member preview showing:[16]

. . . When I heard of artist Tom Sachs' Giftgas Giftset—three gas canisters packaged in Chanel, Hermes and Prada—my reflex was anger. Confronting it in person, seeing it in context, made me think

about how in fact the Nazi party itself was "packaged" in a kind of inflated glamour that led otherwise rational individuals to buy into them in a way not dissimilar to how we buy into cult brands today. Another contentious piece, Alan Schechner's self-portrait at the Buchenwald concentration camp—where he inserts himself holding a Diet Coke can into an historic photograph of emaciated prisoners—also earned my ire before I saw it. But giving up my indignation I gained much more by considering—and in fact relating to—the way in which this artist tried to find his place in an oppressive past that claimed many of his family members. . . .

A week before the exhibition opening, a press preview event attracted about 150 people from the news media, including 12 television crews.

Nearly 100 protesters were on hand for opening day. From behind police barricades across the street from the Manhattan museum, protesters chanted, "Don't go in" and "Shame on you"; some held signs with messages such as "Nazi Museum."

A written statement released by the museum to the news media the opening day of the exhibition said:[17]

Mirroring Evil: Nazi Imagery/Recent Art is not an exhibition about the Holocaust. It is about the way some younger artists are commenting on today's society, using images taken from the Nazi era.

We feel that comments, both pro and con, should now come from the people who see the exhibition.

We hope that public debate will now move on to the issues the artists raise.

Beyond providing viewing options for individuals who might be disturbed by portions of the exhibit, the museum also developed a broad educational program, a major exhibition catalog publication, and another more traditional Holocaust exhibit during the time Mirroring Evil ran.[18]

At the museum's entrance gallery, an interpretive video by noted art historian Maurice Berger introduced the major themes of the exhibit and discussed Nazi images in popular films and television programs.

Some of the questions raised by the video included: Who can speak for the Holocaust? How has art used Nazi imagery to present evil? What are the limits of irreverence? Why must we confront evil? How has art helped break the silence?[19]

The second video, produced and directed by Maxine Wishner, was shown at the end of the exhibition. It contained commentaries and responses to the artworks, taken from interviews with the artists and with curators, educators, Jewish community leaders, and Holocaust survivors.[20]

Throughout the exhibit's 14-week presentation, the Jewish Museum sponsored public programs for adults, school groups, and educators organized in partnership with other institutions throughout New York City. Programming partners included the New York Public Library, New School University, Columbia University, and the National Jewish Center for Learning and Leadership.[21] Each program was designed to promote dialogue between the artists and the public on the ideas represented by the exhibition.

Hardly noticed in the media storm was a concurrent Jewish Museum exhibition entitled An Artist's Response to Evil: We are Not the Last by Zoran Music. The series of paintings and watercolors by Zoran Music reinterpreted the drawings of the dead that Music made during his two-year internment at Dachau concentration camp.[22]

Once the Mirroring Evil exhibition opened to the public and was reviewed by art critics—after several weeks—the intense scrutiny died down.

Questions for Discussion

1. What is the mission of the Jewish Museum? How does it relate to the controversial exhibition Mirroring Evil?

2. The release of Mirroring Evil's exhibition's catalog three months before the exhibition opening created unique problems for the Jewish Museum as the images were shown to the news media without the exhibition's context. Explain why the catalog's early release ignited the controversy.

3. The museum's director of communications had reservations about the early release of the exhibition's catalog. Analyze the director's actions in this situation, and suggest another course of action.

4. Analyze the museum's media relations response to the initial national media coverage after the initial *Wall Street Journal* article appeared January 10, 2002. What other course of action would you suggest?

5. What crisis communication tactics could be used in this situation?

6. Analyze the organization's accommodative response after meeting with Holocaust survivors and children of Holocaust survivors. Do you feel the accommodations were appropriate? Would you do anything differently?

7. What third-party advocates would you suggest the museum use to communicate its goals?

8. The Mirroring Evil exhibition was compared to another exhibit called Sensation. What was the controversy with Sensation? What were the similarities and differences with the two exhibitions?

9. Who can speak for the Holocaust? Can only survivors or descendants of survivors speak out?

Do Some Research
1. Explain the power of visual images over text in communication. What are some other powerful images that evoke emotional responses?
2. What First Amendment issue does this exhibition raise?

Terminology
- Buchenwald
- Holocaust
- popular culture
- propaganda
- shock art
- wall text (exhibition)

Web Resources
- **The Jewish Museum** www.jewish museum.org
- **First Amendment Center** (This site contains information about controversial art on college campuses) http://www .firstamendmentcenter.org/speech/ pubcollege/topic.aspx?topic=art _controversies
- **American Civil Liberties Union** http://www.aclu.org/index.html
- **Jewish Virtual Library, the Holocaust** www.jewishvirtuallibrary.org/ jsource/holo.html
- **A Teacher's Guide to the Holocaust, Art** (provides information based on the U.S. Holocaust Memorial Museum) feit.usf.edu/Holocaust/arts/art2.htm

Night Train to Nashville
Music City Pays Tribute to Its R&B Heritage

Nashville may mean "country" to many music fans, but there's more to Music City than cowboy hats and steel guitars.

While Nashville was establishing itself as country music's world capital, it was already known as a rhythm and blues (R&B) mecca. For example, legendary guitarist Jimi Hendrix and rock and roll pioneer Little Richard both paid their dues in Nashville's black rhythm and blues nightclubs.[23]

For nearly a quarter of a century after World War II, countless locally known and nationally recognized R&B artists performed in crowded nightclubs and recorded hot-selling records in Nashville. The city's R&B reputation spread nationwide as WLAC, Nashville's 50,000-watt radio station, carried R&B and jazz to nearly half the nation late at night.[24] Two pioneering television shows also showcased Nashville's extraordinary R&B talent.[25]

Over time, this rich chapter of Nashville's musical past slipped into obscurity. Many of the city's old theaters and nightclubs were torn down by new highway construction projects in 1970[26] and WLAC changed its influential late-night formats.[27] Eventually, the city's attention shifted toward the rising popularity of country music.

Fortunately for music lovers, Nashville's R&B heritage was revived when the Country Music Hall of Fame decided to create Night Train to Nashville: Music City Rhythm & Blues 1945–1970, the first major exhibition since the Country Music Hall of Fame's grand opening of its new downtown facility in 2001. The decision to host the exhibit and its accompanying educational programs and musical projects provided a powerful means of recognizing African-American contributions to Music City and to country music itself. It showed how Nashville and its musicians played an important role in the national desegregation movement.

Nine months before the exhibit's opening, a news release announced the exhibition plans and Museum Director Kyle Young explained why a country music organization was focusing on R&B music:[28]

For our visitors to fully appreciate the rise of Nashville as the capital of country music, which is part of the history of country music told in our permanent exhibit, we felt it important to look at the context in which that emergence took place.

In those years, Nashville was divided by segregation. In the early 20th Century, soon after the advent of commercial recording, record industry marketers drew a false color line when Southern vernacular recordings were divided and sold as "race" and "hillbilly" music.

So, as Nashville developed into a major recording center, it did so against a background of urban change and at a time when music was splintering racial barriers. Those barriers were repeatedly tested, and sometimes broken, on Nashville bandstands, in our studios, and on the radio when it was still risky to do so.

The 5,000-square-foot multimedia exhibition used photographs, text, artifacts, touch screens, sound recordings, and vintage television clips from "Night Train" and "The!!!!Beat" to tell the story of Nashville's contribution to R&B.

The news release also announced the creation of an advisory committee to guide exhibit planning, feedback, and outreach.[29] The committee included the senior director writer/publisher relations at BMI, the visual and performing arts coordinator of Metro Nashville Public Schools, a professor of music at Tennessee State University, the executive vice president of Danner Company, Nashville's state senator, the president of Killen Music Group, a professor of history at Fisk University, an executive principal of DreamWorks Nashville, and a principal of Nashville School of the Arts.

RESEARCH

A nonprofit educational institution with limited funds for research and marketing, the museum commissioned Nashville's Perdue Research Group to conduct a market survey during August 2002.[30] Researchers conducted 789 telephone and personal interviews, 329 with people who had visited the museum and 460 with nonvisitors. Among the findings were 77 percent of potential visitors (those who had contacted the visitors bureau for information about Nashville) were aware of the new Country Music Hall of Fame and Museum, and 78 percent of Nashville residents knew where it was located.

For potential visitors, the most important source of awareness about the museum was "family and friends" and seeing the new building (27 percent), but the Internet was almost equally important (26 percent).

The three most popular reasons given for going to the Country Music Hall of Fame and Museum were:

- Need for activities to do with family and friends.
- Hall of Fame and Museum is perceived as the "thing to do" in Nashville (similar to the Statue of Liberty in New York City).
- Hall of Fame and Museum offers country music lovers a chance to learn about their passion.

However, while 88 percent of potential visitors to Nashville were interested in visiting the Hall of Fame and Museum, just 39 percent of Nashville residents said they were interested in visiting. To draw local residents, researchers recommended that the museum consider reduced local pricing strategies, promote the use of the building for local functions, and increase public relations efforts to raise awareness locally.

In summary, the survey data provided a starting point for building on the museum's strengths and developing effective messages for the new exhibition. But the survey was not the only kind of research taking place.

The show's curators were beginning to piece together a fading era—Nashville's nightclubs and music halls were gone, and many of the musicians had moved away or died. From the start, museum public relations staff were involved with the curators' research and acquisition process. Over a two-year period, curators showed public relations staff core exhibit pieces as they were obtained; when R&B musicians came to visit, they were introduced to the public relations staff. "This proved very helpful later when we were promoting the exhibit to the media," said Public Relations Director Liz Thiels.

Beyond promoting the exhibition, the public relations staff wanted to increase awareness of the organization's nonprofit status, its educational mission, and its reputation as an accredited, highly regarded museum. It was also important to demonstrate that the exhibit had definite connections to country music's roots, a key component of the institution's mission.

STRATEGY

Thiels said the Night Train to Nashville exhibition provided "the best opportunity since the new facility's grand opening to increase visitor expectations, maintain and grow the number of national and local visitors who 'know about' the museum, layer more diverse audiences to current attendance, increase understanding of the serious nature of the subject matter and the institution's role as both a local and national history museum, and showcase the resources and expertise of the Museum Services staff."[31] The appeal to "more diverse audiences" was important; while Nashville's 1.2 million population is predominantly white, its nearly 200,000 African-American residents

(16 percent) were undoubtedly a new constituency with which the museum could potentially build positive relationships.

Thiels said the museum made significant efforts to reach African Americans in the community through community clubs, organizations, churches, and colleges.

The communication strategy involved partnering with three local organizations to execute the local and national publicity campaign: Commotion Public Relations, a publicity firm that specializes in music promotion; McNeely, Pigott & Fox, a small full-service public relations firm; and the Nashville Convention and Visitors' Bureau.

The Nashville Convention and Visitors' Bureau (NCVB) promoted the exhibition as part of its "coming soon" Nashville story for tourists and convention goers. Through the Florida-based Geiger and Associates public relations firm, which specializes in the travel industry, NCVB would also link trade and consumer travel journalists to the museum.

The public relations departments sent three different news releases designed to alert editors and producers that Night Train was a newsworthy story—one that needed to be placed on the media's editorial planning calendars.

One month before the exhibit opened, nationwide buzz began to build with the launch of the exhibit's same titled two-CD collection of 35 R&B recordings. Commotion Public Relations' expertise in music promotion was used to garner attention for this historically significant music collection. It included "sounds made mostly in Nashville studios for local labels like Bullet, Nashville's first notable independent record company, and Excello, now recognized as Music City's most important R&B label," according to a museum news release.[32] Advance review copies with liner notes were sent to the entertainment press.

Thiels said the usual competition among the media for an exclusive angle did not occur because there were so many artists and different angles to pursue. "Basically, we let the media look at the artifacts, decide what interested them and then we'd take their orders." The public relations staff provided reporters background information and helped steer R&B artists in their direction to build news and feature stories.

The 18-month exhibit, which ended December 2005, was constantly revitalized by a series of 22 scheduled educational and cultural R&B events promoted by McNeely, Pigott & Fox. The exhibit's opening events on March 27, 2004, included exhibit tours and a family concert, R&B for You & Me, with Hendrix's bass player Billy Cox, among others.[33] A panel discussion featuring Bobby Hebb, a Nashville songwriter best known for the hit song "Sunny," discussed the country-R&B connection. The day's festivities ended with a concert by another early Nashville R&B artist, Earl Gaines and his band.

Visitors also had the chance to learn dances done to classic R&B music and attend a workshop on hip-hop dance moves. Another program invited attendees to watch and discuss the groundbreaking R&B television shows "Night Train" and "The!!!!Beat," both of which predated "Soul Train" and originated in Music City in the mid-1960s. R&B songwriter Buzz Cason, who penned "Everlasting Love" (recorded by U2 and Gloria Estefan), and other songwriters held a songwriter session. Other programs covered segregation and desegregation in the music business and Jimi Hendrix's years in Nashville.

RESULTS

The media campaign was jump-started by the music industry press. Music reviews of the exhibit's CD collection representing Nashville's historical contributions to R&B were carried in 28 regional and national fan magazines, including *Blender* (circulation 250,000), *Rolling Stone* (1.2 million), *Downbeat* (92,990), *Country Music Today* (300,000), and *R&R, a music trade publication.*[34] General audience magazine *People* (3.5 million) and national music industry trade publication *Billboard* also tracked the CD's success. By January 2005, the CD collection had sold 30,000 copies. The *Night Train Vol. 1* CD was nominated for a Grammy

in 2004 and won it in spring 2005; the second *Night Train, Vol. 2* CD was also nominated for a Grammy in fall 2005. The Grammy attention guaranteed an even wider exposure beyond the music industry press.

National and international exposure came from stories in the *Boston Globe* (circulation 280,000), the *New York Times* (1.6 million), and, across the Atlantic, the *Times* of London, along with a story carried by the Associated Press and a CD review by the Knight-Ridder wire service. CBS and cable outlet CMT (Country Music Television) covered the exhibit. When CBS *Sunday Morning* correspondent Bill Flanagan, executive vice president of MTV Networks, shared with viewers his favorite CD of the year so far, the three-minute feature on *Night Train* caused an immediate spike in sales on Amazon.com, pushing the CD into its top sales slot, said Thiels.

Local newspaper, radio, and television media provided more extensive coverage with reports on the exhibit's educational and cultural programs carried in the *Tennessean* and its weekly *Nashville Scene,* Nashville's NBC affiliate WSMV, and CBS affiliate WTVF, along with radio interviews with the exhibit's curator, museum director, and veteran R&B artists.

Museum, travel, and convention industry media were also targeted and included *Group Tour Magazine.* AAA's *Going Places* (circulation 300,000), the auto club's national magazine, gave potential vacationers another reason beyond Nashville's country music attractions to visit.

The exhibition's media team also courted Web media. Web sites that covered *Night Train* included NowToronto.com, CMT.com, MSNBC.com, Allmusic.com, Jambands.com, and Popmatters.com.

The grand opening CD release party for museum patrons and musicians at Nashville's Tower Records was packed. Opening day activities drew more than 1,500 paying visitors.

More important than media impressions and paid admissions, however, was the immense impact the exhibit had on musicians from the Night Train era and on the community. "The artists just put their arms around us. They provided interviews and performed for our educational programs, and participated in fund raising events," said Thiels. "This exhibit helped redefine what Music City meant. Our organization took this important story— one that had been overlooked, forgotten and almost lost—and brought it back," she said. For the African-American community, the exhibit helped validate important music and important lives through a shared connection between country music and R&B.

Questions for Discussion

1. What did the market research survey reveal about the Country Music Hall of Fame and Museum?

2. What was significant about the museum's Night Train exhibition?

3. Why was initial concern expressed about moving away from the museum's mission?

4. What was the role of the community advisory committee? Why are community groups helpful for these types of events?

5. How did the museum reach out to its minority community for the Night Train exhibition?

6. What is an editorial planning calendar, and what was its importance to this exhibition?

7. How did the public relations staff at the museum provide a number of exclusive story angles for reporters? Why is story exclusivity important? In what way would exclusivity not work for certain aspects of the communication plan?

8. While the exhibition focused on the music of a particular period, what types of artifacts would be of interest to reporters?

9. The 18-month exhibition was revitalized by a series of special programs held at the museum. What other extended program celebrations have you seen, and how does the organization maintain media and public interest?

10. What other organizations did the Hall of Fame partner with to extend its message reach?

Do Some Research

1. Examine a grand-opening event for a local event or from a Web site. What are the communication elements and activities? What special events were planned? How was it organized? Was it a one-day event or longer?

2. How would you plan a CD release party, such as Night Train to Nashville?

Terminology

- desegregation movement
- race
- hillbilly music
- R&B
- "Night Train"
- "The!!!Beat"
- Music City
- market survey
- community advisory committee
- editorial planning calendars
- media impressions
- CD release party
- exclusive

Web Resources

- **Country Music Hall of Fame and Museum** www.countrymusichallofame.com/index.html
- **Nashville Public Library, Historic Nashville** www.library.nashville.org/Links/Nashville/nhistory.html
- **Jimi Hendrix and the Chitlin' Circuit** www.soul-patrol.com/funk/jh_chitlin.htm

FOR IMMEDIATE RELEASE   Contacts: XXX

NIGHT TRAIN TO NASHVILLE: MUSIC CITY RHYTHM & BLUES 1945-1970 TO OPEN AT THE COUNTRY MUSIC HALL OF FAME® AND MUSEUM NEXT SPRING

Major New Exhibit to Focus on Little-known Chapter in Music City History

NASHVILLE, Tenn., June 16, 2003 – *Night Train to Nashville: Music City Rhythm & Blues 1945-1970*, a media-rich, major exhibition focusing on a vibrant, little-known chapter in the affirmation of Nashville's title as the Music City USA, will open at the Country Music Hall of Fame® and Museum in the Spring of 2004.

The 5,000-square-foot exhibition, designed by New York-based ESI Design in collaboration with Nashville's 1220 Exhibits and the Museum staff, will remain open for 18 months.

The exhibit will illuminate a continually overlooked era in Nashville's music history, the quarter century after World War II, when

- cultural icons like Little Richard and Jimi Hendrix apprenticed on Nashville bandstands;
- Etta James recorded her scorching live album *Etta James Rocks the House* at the New Era club, and Arthur Gunther recorded the r&b classic "Baby Let's Play House" for the renowned Nashville blues label Excello Records;
- brilliant singers like Christine Kittrell and Gene Allison recorded powerful and timeless hits and other songs that should have been;
- 50,000-watt powerhouse WLAC blasted r&b across late night airwaves;
- station WSOK (later WVOL) was among the country's first to adopt an all-black format; and
- r&b singer-songwriters like Jimmy Sweeney collaborated with Music Row musicians like Hank Garland, Boudleaux Bryant, and Floyd Cramer.

"For our visitors to fully appreciate the rise of Nashville as the capital of country music, which is part of the history of country music told in our permanent exhibit, we felt it important to look at the context in which that emergence took place," said Museum Director Kyle Young.

"In those years, Nashville was divided by segregation. In the early 20th Century, soon after the advent of commercial recording, record industry marketers drew a false color line when Southern vernacular recordings were divided and sold as 'race' and 'hillbilly' music," he said.

"So, as Nashville developed into a major recording center, it did so against a background of urban change and at a time when music was splintering racial barriers. Those barriers were repeatedly tested, and sometimes broken, on Nashville bandstands, in our studios, and on the radio when it was still risky to do so. *Night Train To Nashville* will provide a unique vantage point from which to consider the era's conflicts and how they affected the making of music in Nashville and nationally. Joe Simon's r&b million-seller 'The Chokin' Kind,' for example, was written by quintessential country composer Harlan Howard. The sound of vintage Nashville r&b will guide visitors through the important story of this music and this time. These musicians and disc jockeys fostered nothing less than a reinvention of American taste and culture," he said.

A historic reissue recording, publications, and exhibit-themed Museum merchandise will support the exhibit. As with all Country Music Hall of Fame and Museum exhibits, the *Night Train to Nashville* exhibit will be enhanced by a full and ongoing schedule of public programs including live performances, panels, and opportunities to talk with musicians and others.

To assist with the development and programming of *Night Train to Nashville*, the Museum has formed an Advisory Committee including representatives from the Board of Officers and Trustees and leaders in the academic, educational, and music communities with a strong interest in the subject matter. The Advisory Committee includes: Thomas Cain, senior director writer/publisher relations, BMI; Carol Crittenden, visual and performing arts coordinator, Metro Nashville Public Schools; Dr. Charles Dungey, professor of music, Tennessee State University; Francis Guess, executive vice president, Danner Company; Thelma Harper, Senator, State of Tennessee; Buddy Killen, president, Killen Music Group; Dr. Reavis Mitchell, professor of history, Fisk University; James Stroud, executive principal, DreamWorks Nashville; and Bob Wilson, principal, Nashville School of the Arts.

Accredited by the American Association of Museums, the Country Music Hall of Fame® and Museum is operated by the Country Music Foundation, a not-for-profit 501(c)3 educational organization chartered by the State of Tennessee in 1964. The Foundation also operates CMF Records, the Museum's Frist Library and Archive, CMF Press, RCA's Historic Studio B, and Hatch Show Print.

The Ford Division of the Ford Motor Co. is a Founding Partner of the new $37 million Country Music Hall of Fame® and Museum, which opened on May 17, 2001, in downtown Nashville's new $1 billion entertainment district.

More information about the Country Music Hall of Fame® and Museum is available at www.countrymusichalloffame.com or by calling (615) 416-2096.

Courtesy of Country Music Hall of Fame and Museum.

Wells College
History, Tradition, and Now—Men

History remembers Henry Wells as a founder of Wells Fargo and the American Express Company, but he also gave his name to a small liberal arts college for women in 1868.

Historically, women's colleges were started as counterparts to exclusive male-only colleges, and for 136 years, Wells College's women-only admissions policy provided an environment focused on developing women's potential. In 2004, it was one of just 64 colleges nationwide that enrolled women only.[35]

Its advantages—small class sizes, ample opportunity for involvement and development of leadership skills—did not translate into growing enrollments. A lovely but isolated campus on the shores of Cayuga Lake in Aurora, New York, made recruitment a challenge; the closest city was 20 miles away, a distance magnified by upstate New York's snowy winter weather. Apart from its relative isolation, Wells College's single-gender policy was a significant recruitment obstacle. According to the College Board, only 3 percent of college-bound women at the time considered an all-women's college.[36] Apparently, most women want to go to college with men.

One Wells College news release outlined many attempts to increase enrollment, including reducing tuition 30 percent from $17,000 to $12,000, increasing student aid, adding new programs, and trying aggressive advertising campaigns to get the Wells College message to prospective female students.[37]

Two years before its decision, Wells College president Lisa Marsh Ryerson and the college's board of trustees developed a strategy to introduce the idea that change was necessary and build support for change. Ryerson and vice president for External Relations Ann Rollo made a concerted effort to visit in person or by telephone each honorary board of trustee member, former board chairperson, and the college's most significant supporters. Thirty-nine alumnae groups heard about the current state of the college and the need for change from Ryerson or Rollo in person. Class agents (volunteer alumnae representing specific class years) and board members were used to spread the word about the need to change. E-mail blasts and electronic newsletters were sent to alumnae to reinforce these messages.

The college's annual report and presidential speeches for two years preceding the decision characterized its financial situation as "fragile," not "viable."[38] The bottom line was that rising costs and declining enrollment required annual infusions of money from the college's endowment to cover operating expenses.

The 2002–2003 president's report hinted at the change coming:[39]

At Wells, we are compelled to find innovative solutions to share our future or we will be doomed to the constant struggles and dangers faced by those colleges that do not have the wisdom and courage to change.

. . . We have now reached a place where steadfast and unwavering adherence to a model established for the college over a century ago places us at odds with public sentiment and economic realities. The chronic issues that have re-emerged for decades in the arena of recruitment and retention must be satisfactorily resolved through the establishment of a new, sustainable model for Wells. The post-'70s paradigm of crisis has to be put to rest.

The new model would emerge from a committee called the Sustainable Wells Action Team, formed during the 2002–2003 academic year.[40] Its membership included board of trustees, faculty, and administrative members, including Ryerson. Its recommendations were presented to the Wells College board of trustees in October 2003. In the following three months, the board refined the team's proposals, which were shared with the college community in February 2004. One of those recommendations was to move forward with a "full examination of the possibility of a transition to coeducation."[41]

In her 2004 alumnae reunion address Ryerson noted:[42]

> *Our challenges in the highly competitive college recruitment market dictate that we must focus on core academic programs and consider the possibility of expanding the audience to whom we offer our programs. We cannot separate the two; program and audience are inextricably linked.*

The president also noted that men were already on campus, although in limited numbers, in special programs: the summer book arts programs, study abroad program, and cross-registration programs with nearby coeducational colleges.[43]

Alumnae discussions and research indicated small class sizes, close relationships with professors, and great friendships were what alumnae valued most about their educational experience, said Rollo. When asked what the determining factor was in selecting Wells, the most common responses were financial aid and a campus that many "fell in love with" when they visited, she said. Educational consultants said the all-female distinction had little value in the educational marketplace and recommended the college build on its reputation as a premiere liberal arts college. Wells College's mission would continue as a top-notch liberal arts college for women, said Rollo, but "it wouldn't be defined by who it excluded."

Faculty response was cautious, said Rollo. In addition to listening to the board's proposal, the faculty invited one of its members to share her academic research on other colleges that made the transition from female to coed. Many of the 50 full-time faculty members had lengthy tenures and were committed to the college's well-being. One faculty survey two years earlier indicated that the majority wanted a "vibrant academic community" foremost; its all-women mission was secondary, said Rollo. When a straw vote asked if the coed issue should be pursued, two-thirds of the faculty voted yes.

The personal outreach campaign backed by research, trends, and facts resulted in "incredible behind the scenes support," said Rollo.

These circumstances prompted Wells College's 18-member board of trustees to make the difficult decision to admit men, starting in the 2005 fall semester.

Wells College explained its action to the public as necessary because of recruitment challenges and fiscal realities. During the 2004–2005 academic year, 302 students lived on campus and an additional 100 students commuted or were involved in off-campus study abroad or internship programs. Wells College, the news release stated, needed "at least 450 students living on campus, along with more commuters and other part-time students, to grow toward fiscal stability."[44]

Wells College's president put it this way in a college news release:[45]

> *. . . All the evidence made it abundantly clear that we could not grow our enrollment by remaining in our present state. We looked at nearly 200 liberal arts colleges, including a number of women-only colleges, and found that in nearly every case, applications and enrollments went up for colleges that made the transition from single-sex to coeducation. That is what we need for Wells College.*
>
> *A continued focus on the advancement of women will remain a key objective in the college's new mission.*

Wells will always be a small, close-knit, high quality liberal arts college, with our rich traditions as a women's college. Even as we welcome more men to the campus, we will remain a college that honors women, and our deeply held values will still predominate . . .

Before the vote, alumnae letters were sent urging Wells to maintain its all-women traditions; previous reunions had attracted a small but vocal group of angry and disappointed alumnae. A protest Web site called "Wells for Women" contained a petition for the removal of Wells's president.[46] The anonymously run site provided links to student articles, local and national news media stories, and analysis of the administration's coed strategy.

Rollo's staff had prepared news releases and letters for three scenarios: accept, reject, or delay. After three days of trustee meetings, the college's trustees voted to admit men.[47]

The board's vote took place on a Saturday. With faculty and staff gone for the weekend, Rollo's staff, along with administrative staff, personally telephoned all employees the news. This was followed by a mass-distributed e-mail to all faculty and staff from the president. A letter to alumnae and other college supporters and a news release were also sent within hours of the board's decision.

AFTER THE VOTE

Emotions ran high following the vote. Students and other supporters gathered on campus to console each other. More than 150 angry students staged a sit-in at the main administration building for a week;[48] two students filed a lawsuit against the college on grounds the school had misled them when they enrolled.[49]

The national and local media covered the emotional confrontation: *USA Today* ("Women Rail against College's Coed Plans"), the Associated Press ("Wells College to Admit Men Despite Protests" and "Women Seek to

Save Single-Sex Schools"), National Public Radio ("Wells College Students Sue the School for Voting to Admit Men Next Year"), *Ms Magazine* ("When Wells Run Dry"), and the local news media.

Rollo's e-mail account filled up following the announcement. Two-thirds were supportive with messages of "congrats" and "chin up." Many senior alumnae indicated a tone of sad resignation about the decision; "they were sad but realistic . . . these are people who had already experienced a lot of changes and they saw this as just part of the scheme of life," said Rollo.

Predictably, there were a number of negative e-mails that ranged from "vile" ("the president should be shot!") to those who logically questioned the college's long-term strategy and motives, said Rollo. Legitimate e-mails received individual responses in which alumnae and others were thanked for "expressing your concerns." Rollo said the negative e-mails provided a glimpse of people's specific concerns. "We saw this as an opportunity to interact with people interested in the college on a one-to-one basis and to eventually gain their support."

A special faculty meeting was called to consider whether the board's decision should be called a "failure of leadership," a position that did not gain support. Rather, many faculty expressed support for the coed decision and, though some remained skeptical, most of the faculty seemed "ready to move on," Rollo said.

The Wells College Alumnae Association sent a letter on October 8, 2004, recognizing the conflicting emotions generated by the vote:

Members of your Association Board feel many of the same emotions you do over the Trustees' recent decision to transform Wells into a co-educational institution: heartbreak, disappointment, and sadness on one side; relief, hope and optimism on the other.[50]

An alumnae letter, posted to its Web site, noted the reasons for the board's decision and mentioned the board's 18-member composition included four members elected by the alumnae, two elected by students, and nine others who were either alumnae or alumnae spouses. The three other board members were recommended by alumnae for their special skills. Each trustee, the letter stated, were "connected to and love the college."[51]

It concluded by noting that "change happens" and, while difficult, the decision had the "potential to increase enrollment which will enable Wells to strengthen programs, support faculty in the fantastic work they do, provide quality facilities and equipment, and enable excellent, women-centered education."[52]

Wells College students and parents marched during Friends & Family Weekend in the fall.[53] The Collegiate Cabinet, a student governance organization, conducted a small informal poll that asked students to state if they agreed with a statement of no confidence in the school's president, which was backed by just 22 percent of the student body that voted.[54]

Three months after the decision to admit men, the protest Web site posted the results of an e-mailed survey of alumnae. About 371 out of 1,455 former Wells students responded to the eight-question survey including the question, "Do you believe that there are reasons for Wells to remain a women's college?" to which 84.2 percent checked yes.[55]

EPILOGUE

During the 2005–2006 academic year, Wells College enrolled 36 males—24 first-year and 12 transfer students; there were 380 women students.[56] After the first semester, just one student out of 14 cited the presence of males as the major reason for leaving the college.[57] While there was some discontentment among upperclassmen, for the most part students accepted the change or tried to ignore it. The male

students felt welcomed, according to news reports.

By January 2006, applications for Wells College had doubled compared to the same time period the year before.[58]

Open Scenario Challenge
Rebuilding Frayed Relationships

By the start of the spring semester, student protests had faded and Wells College was firmly committed to its new mission and recruitment strategy. To rebuild frayed relationships and create new ones, it needs to continue a proactive public relations plan to communicate to all its publics, including alumnae, prospective students, current students, parents, and faculty.

Of particular note is the upcoming alumnae reunion in early June. The four-day event includes many special activities, such as academic open houses and workshops, village tours, a wine tasting, a quilt exhibit, yoga, canoeing, the famed reunion parade (led by a Wells Fargo stagecoach and accompanied by the ringing of the bells), and the grand finale—the midnight reunion celebration gala overlooking Cayuga Lake.

Wells College President Lisa Marsh Ryerson will be active in several events, including a welcoming reception at her home. The Wells for Women activists, who oppose the president's and board's decision to go coed, have encouraged alumnae to attend the annual meeting.

How will you advise President Ryerson to take advantage of this time with alumnae to positively reinforce the board's decision to go coed and deal with potentially angry members who may disrupt the event?

Questions for Discussion

1. Explain the communication and public relations strategy of Wells College in preparation for its trustee vote to admit men. What are the strengths and weaknesses of the strategy?

2. Which key messages would you communicate to the media during the announcement of the board of trustees?

3. How would you communicate with students and alumnae before the trustees' vote? After the vote?

4. How can public relations help organizations adapt to major changes?

5. How would you help the first group of male students feel welcome at Wells College? Who would you involve in these decisions?

6. How will the marketing communication efforts (recruitment materials and advertising) change at Wells College?

7. Analyze the college's Web site. How has it communicated its new mission?

8. Has your college dropped a popular program or service? How did your college communicate this change?

Do Some Research

1. Randolph-Macon Woman's College in Lynchburg, Virginia, also changed its mission to admit men to its institution in 2006. How did its key publics react

to the decision? How was this college's situation the same or different from Wells College?

2. Read articles that discuss change theory. How can public relations be an integral part of organizational change?

3. Examine the Wells for Women activist site. What approach does it take to persuade readers of its issues? Does keeping its organizers anonymous hurt its credibility? Why? Read an article on an activist Web site. What strategy would you employ in dealing with this site?

Terminology

- class agents
- cross registration
- straw vote
- sustainable (economic) model

Web Resources

- **Wells College** www.wells.edu
- **Wells for Women** www.wellsforwomen.org

Creating Long-Distance Membership Value

The National Baseball Hall of Fame and Museum is located in picturesque Cooperstown, New York, next door to the legendary site of the 1839 Doubleday ballgame, which generally heralds the beginning of baseball.

Its mission is to preserve history, honor excellence, and connect generations to the game of baseball, said Brad Horn, the Hall of Fame's communications director. With 165,000 artifacts—including 130,000 baseball cards and 35,000 bats, balls, gloves and other items—and a library archive with 2.6 million items, including scrapbooks, photographs, and moving pictures, the Hall

of Fame is unmatched in the world of baseball memorabilia.[59]

By 2006, the Hall of Fame had welcomed more than 13 million visitors, making it one of the most popular destinations in the United States; nearly 350,000 fans visit each year.[60] Doubtless, those numbers would be greater if the hall and museum were not in a relatively remote location. Situated on the southern shores of Otsego Lake, the Village of Cooperstown is off the beaten track, more than an hour away from an airport or significant population center. Long and snowy winters also keep tourist numbers down in the off-season.

As a nonprofit educational membership institution, the Hall of Fame depends on tourists and membership revenue for a significant portion of its operating revenue.

The Hall of Fame and Museum sponsors many special events, including movies, plays, Sandlot Stories, staff and visiting experts discussing baseball history, and its biggest event—the Hall of Fame Weekend, with the induction ceremony. An annual Hall of Fame game has two major league teams playing an exhibition game at Doubleday Field. For those wishing to fulfill their ultimate baseball fantasy, there's the Hall of Fame Fantasy Camp ($7,995), where participants received batting and fielding tips from Hall of Famers George Brett, Eddie Murray, Ozzie Smith, Phil Niekro, and others.[61]

Communications Director Horn said the Hall of Fame emphasizes member relations through a variety of publications, events, and exclusive gifts:[62]

- Personalized membership card
- A bimonthly magazine entitled *Memories & Dreams*
- A deluxe, hardbound edition of the *Hall of Fame Yearbook*
- Complimentary admission to the Hall of Fame for one year
- Two Friends of the Hall of Fame lapel pins
- Free shipping on all orders from the Hall of Fame's catalog and Web site

The most expensive memberships have additional benefits, such as a limited-edition matted lithograph of a famous ballplayer and Hall of Fame induction weekend privileges. The Hall of Fame created a free electronic newsletter called "Inside Pitch," available to anyone, with more than 75,000 subscribers.

The National Baseball Hall of Fame and Museum also introduces itself to the next generation of fans through its educational programs, including distance education. One hour to half-day electronic field trips and videoconferences have been delivered

to more than 60 million students nationwide.[63] The museum's education department presents more than 300 educational events annually.[64]

The organization created a touring exhibition of 500 baseball artifacts from the museum. The Baseball as America exhibit visited 10 American museums during its four-year journey.[65]

Its Web site is a trove of information and outreach, including online exhibits, player statistics, and historical information for those who cannot make the trip to America's baseball shrine.

Open Scenario Challenge
Converting One-Time Visitors into Long-Distance Supporters

Because many fans come from great distances, a visit to Cooperstown may be their first and last. The membership director of the Hall of Fame wants to devise new strategies to interest one-time visitors or people who have never visited the Hall of Fame to join as paying members. The membership director asks for a meeting with Communications Director Brad Horn and his summer intern—you.

Horn asks for your suggestions on how to create exciting new opportunities for these potential long-distance members by next week. He wonders if there is any new technology communication tool that could be part of this strategy. You go back to your office and begin to research ideas.

Criteria for this group assignment will follow, including presentation guidelines. There should be *no direct contact* with the Baseball Hall of Fame.

Do Some Research

1. Virtually every sport now has a hall of fame and museum associated with it. To assist you with the open scenario project, look at what other sport museums are doing to attract and keep members. What incentives do they offer? What types of programs are offered only for members?

2. Investigate how to develop an effective direct-mail piece. What are the elements of effective direct mailers? Create a rough design of a direct mailer to promote membership to the National Baseball Hall of Fame and Museum.

3. If your college has a sports hall of fame, how does it promote its efforts? How could the program improve its

image or become more active with its key publics?

Terminology
- member relations
- educational membership institution

Web Resource
- **National Baseball Hall of Fame and Museum** www.baseballhalloffame.org/

Boston Marathon
John Hancock Uses Sports to Leverage Its Image

Mention insurance and many people will search for the nearest exit. Talk of annuities can make eyes glaze over. The truth is that the difference between universal and variable life policies doesn't excite too many people.

But one financial services company uses sport sponsorship to build awareness and create an exciting brand. It also leverages its world-class sport sponsorship to build strong ties with its community.

John Hancock Financial Services merged with Manulife Financial Corporation in Canada in 2004. As a subsidiary of Manulife, the fourth-largest global life insurance company, John Hancock generates nearly $9.9 billion in sales annually and employs about 4,000 employees at its headquarters in Boston.[66] According to the company's market research, 95 percent of U.S. consumers are aware of the John Hancock brand for financial services.[67]

HANCOCK SPORTS EVENT SPONSORSHIPS
Beyond traditional marketing efforts, John Hancock has pioneered sports event sponsorship with four major events: the Boston Marathon, the U.S. Olympic Team, "Fantasy Day" at Fenway Park, and the Champions

on Ice skating tour. All were developed under the leadership of John Hancock's former CEO David F. D'Alessandro.

Olympic Sponsorship
John Hancock became a sponsor of the Olympic Games in 1993. It sponsored the 2005 Winter Olympics in Turin, Italy, and is a worldwide sponsor of the Beijing 2008 Olympic Games.

Marketing strategists suggest that sponsorships of worldwide events such as the Olympics create a halo effect for the sponsoring organization. The excitement of the sport, winning athletes, and other positive attributes that radiate from the source include the sponsoring organization.[68] The Olympics provide a unique international marketing platform that can further match internationally renowned athletes with hometown events. Sponsorship of Olympic athletes provides relationship-building opportunities for important clients who appreciate the experience provided by the organization.[69] Athletes sponsored by John Hancock participated in speaking engagements, meet and greets, and Olympic-themed community outreach events.[70] For example, during the Turin Winter Olympics, various U.S. Olympic athletes were available daily at John Hancock–sponsored hospitality events so that clients had a chance to meet with Olympic superstars.

"Fantasy Day" at Fenway Park

Since 1991, John Hancock has teamed up with the Boston Red Sox to give die-hard Sox fans an opportunity to swing the bat at historic Fenway Park while supporting childhood cancer research and treatment.[71] Participants take aim at the "Green Monster," the left-field wall, take turns fielding, and receive a tour of the park, a reception at the 406 Club, an official team jersey and cap, a photographic memento, and the opportunity to dress in the visitor's clubhouse.[72] The day's events cost each team of five $11,000 ($2,200 for one player),[73] which is donated to the Jimmy Fund, the prime fundraising arm of Boston's Dana Farber Cancer Institute, dedicated to helping children fight cancer. John Hancock also donates $2,000 for each home run or $1,000 for anyone who hits the Green Monster. About 100 John Hancock employees volunteer at the event annually. One year, the event raised $220,000 for cancer research.[74]

Champions on Ice

Olympic superstars Michelle Kwan, Sasha Cohen, and many nationally and globally recognized skaters have headlined the multicity tour of Champions on Ice.[75] John Hancock's sponsorship was a way to provide an evening of glamour for company agents and their clients throughout the country. Special meet and greets with the show's star athletes further enhanced the relationship-building aspect of the event. Several athletes were also available to conduct radio media tours to promote the event and support its corporate sponsor.

Boston Marathon

John Hancock's longest sport sponsorship is the Boston Marathon, the world's oldest continuous marathon race.[76] The 26.2-mile event is held on Patriot's Day each April and attracts 20,000 qualified runners, including many Olympians. It starts in the nearby community of Hopkinton, Massachusetts, and ends at the doorstep of the John Hancock Tower in Boston's downtown Copley Square. While John Hancock has admitted the marathon doesn't attract high national television ratings (it's been broadcast on the Outdoor Life Network cable channel, which specializes in "outdoor adventure, action sports, field sports and bulls & rodeo"), signage opportunities are weak, and there hasn't been a top American contender in decades,[77] it's a keeper because of the massive community goodwill it generates. The company has pledged its support through at least 2018.[78]

John Hancock rescued an event that had lost its luster in the 1980s and grew it into a world-class sporting event that annually attracts many of the top distance runners in the world.

As lead sponsor of the event, John Hancock outfits elite runners for media events with company turtlenecks and vests. John Hancock logos are strategically placed on the neck and upper chest areas of the clothing so the company's name is captured in news media photographs and broadcasts.

In past years John Hancock has contributed up to $2 million to the Boston Athletic Association, which operates the event.[79] Part of the money goes to prizes for athletes. In 2005, John Hancock contributed $575,000 in prize money, plus other performance bonuses.[80] Communities outside of Boston that are part of the marathon route also receive assistance from John Hancock to cover the additional costs associated with the huge event. The company has more than 1,900 volunteers to assist with race-related tasks and provides its Copley Square facilities for race needs.[81]

John Hancock's corporate communications department handles the hundreds of local, national, and international media representatives who cover the event. Communications staff members create a media guide, coordinate press materials and credentials, and operate the press room at the finish line.

Despite John Hancock's massive support of the marathon since 1986, the company has not insisted on event naming rights, like nearly every other major sporting event today. It's still the Boston Athletic Association's event, although Bostonians know who keeps the marathon in top shape. Bostonians truly appreciate what John Hancock has done for the community through its annual marathon sponsorship. That goodwill ultimately transfers into business dividends.

John Hancock has also expanded its support for distance running beyond Boston by creating the John Hancock Running and Fitness Clinics.[82] This national education program seeks to inspire the next generation of distance runners. The program brings top athletes into area schools to demonstrate running techniques, training methods, and healthy lifestyles.[83] Several Boston marathon winners have worked as training staff for this program.

COMMUNITY OUTREACH

John Hancock uses its world-class sports sponsorships to benefit its community. Because many of the top Boston Marathon performers consistently come from Kenya, two events introduce students to this distant world: The Kenya Project and the Adopt-a-Marathoner program.[84]

The Boston Marathon Kenya Project teaches third-grade students about the Kenyan culture, tribes, Swahili language, geography, and a little history about the marathon itself. John Hancock volunteers and executives provide the lessons. It is held at the African Tropical Forest exhibit in Boston's community zoo and includes a visit from Boston Marathon Kenyan champions.[85]

In the community where the marathon begins, the Adopt-a-Marathoner program brings elite Kenya team runners together with students for a prerace pep rally at Elmwood elementary school. Students study Kenyan culture and welcome the athletes by singing the Kenyan national anthem at the rally. Some students get to go for a short jog

with the elite runners.[86] Every year, this event usually attracts local broadcast media and photographers from the print media.

EPILOGUE

When John Hancock was acquired by the Canadian company Manulife, John Hancock's new leadership announced it would reevaluate its sports sponsorships from a "purely business perspective."[87] While the Boston Marathon sponsorship was safe, because of its community relations value, company executives questioned local investments in advertising signs at Fenway Park and the Boston Celtics arena.[88]

The *Boston Globe* quoted James Benson, president and chief executive of John Hancock in 2005, saying, "It's hard to rationalize putting a disproportionate amount of brand development expense into a community where the brand is extraordinarily well known and respected."[89] The article also said that John Hancock's sponsorship of Major League baseball and the Olympics would be reviewed. Money might be redirected into more traditional marketing efforts—television and other media.[90]

Open Scenario Challenge

You are a public relations counselor at John Hancock. The sports sponsorship office is considering the sponsorship of a new golf tournament featuring top golfers. The office wants your advice on what type of community programs could be developed from the event. Create two community events that could be part of this golf tournament sponsorship. Remember to stick to the golf theme and assess with which nonprofit organizations your partnership would provide the most community goodwill. The cosmmunity events should be easy to host, and complement, but not overshadow, the major event.

Questions for Discussion

1. What are John Hancock's marketing communication challenges?
2. Why do companies like John Hancock sponsor a sport event?

3. How does a corporate sport sponsorship work?
4. What do companies, such as John Hancock, look for in a successful sport sponsorship?
5. How does sport sponsorship differ from traditional marketing tactics?
6. What nationally and internationally recognized sporting events has John Hancock sponsored in recent years?
7. How does John Hancock leverage its world-class sport contacts in the Boston area?
8. What are the community relations benefits of sport sponsorships and its community educational programs?

Do some Research

Provide an example of another successful sport sponsorship program and any related community relations programs. What are the benefits of the sport sponsorship and related community relations programs?

How would you evaluate the benefits of a sport sponsorship program?

Terminology
- sport sponsorship
- community relations
- media guide
- press room

Web Resources
- **John Hancock, Community Relations** www.johnhancock.com/about/abo_community.jsp
- **John Hancock Boston Marathon site** www.marathon.jhancock.com/
- **Manulife Financial Public Accountability Statement** www.manulife.com/
- Sport sponsorships sites:
- **Institute of Sports Sponsorships** www.sports-sponsorship.co.uk/
- **IEG Sponsorship Report** www.sponsorship.com/iegsr/
- **Sponsorship.com** www.sponsorship.com

2004 BOSTON MARATHON MEN'S CHAMPION TIMOTHY CHERIGAT LEADS BOSTON MARATHON KENYA PROJECT AT FRANKLIN PARK ZOO

Boston Third Graders Receive Introduction to Kenya and the Historical Race

BOSTON, MA–April 12, 2006—John Hancock Financial Services and its elementary school partners, the Samuel Mason Elementary School in Roxbury and Lucy Stone Elementary School in Dorchester, today hosted the sixth annual Boston Marathon Kenya Project. The event, which is held at the Franklin Park Zoo in the African

Tropical Forest exhibit, educates students about the Boston Marathon and the country of Kenya.

John Hancock executives and associates taught 60 third grade students subjects ranging from Kenyan culture and geography to the history of the Boston Marathon. The program included a visit from 2004 Boston Marathon men's champion Timothy Cherigat.

This year's Boston Marathon is scheduled for Monday, April 17, 2006. These students will have the opportunity to attend the Marathon and view the race from the finish line.

"We are always searching for new ways to teach children about different cultures from around the world," said Janet Palmer-Owens, principal of the Mason School. "The Boston Marathon Kenya Project offers a terrific opportunity for our children to learn about Kenyan culture from John Hancock volunteers. We know the Company has developed relationships with a variety of Boston public schools and we're thrilled to be partnering with John Hancock in this unique program."

The project's lessons support the curriculum of the Boston Public Schools, and have been designed by an education consultant with input from the teachers and principals. The Boston Marathon Kenya Project provides access to world class sporting events, athletes, and workshops for young people throughout the city of Boston. John Hancock also provides Running and Fitness Clinics, bringing top athletes into area schools to teach students about health and fitness.

"John Hancock is committed to developing innovative youth programs to help improve the education of children and the future of the Boston community," said Carol Fulp, vice president, Community Relations. "Due to our relationship with the elite athletes who compete at the Boston Marathon, we are able have Kenyan runners teach the students about their culture first-hand."

About John Hancock and Manulife Financial

John Hancock is a unit of Manulife Financial Corporation, a leading Canadian-based financial services group serving millions of customers in 19 countries and territories worldwide. Operating as Manulife Financial in Canada and Asia, and primarily through John Hancock in the United States, the Company offers clients a diverse range of financial protection products and wealth management services through its extensive network of employees, agents and distribution partners. Funds under management by Manulife Financial and its subsidiaries were Cdn$372 billion (US$319 billion) at December 31, 2005.

Manulife Financial Corporation trades as 'MFC' on the TSX, NYSE and PSE, and under '0945' on the SEHK. Manulife Financial can be found on the Internet at www.manulife.com.

-30-

Courtesy of John Hancock Financial Services.

Chapter Ten

Employee Relations

Management, human resources, and public relations are interested in developing an environment in which employees want to work and thrive. Employee relations are the actions undertaken to create that positive work environment. Paying attention to employees' welfare is worth the investment because satisfied employees can be more productive and perform higher-quality work.

Management, led by the CEO, is a major influence on the organization's culture, which researchers have defined as "the sum total of shared values, symbols, meanings, and expectations that organize and integrate a group of people who work together."[1] As the main decision maker, management will reinforce the organizational culture through its actions, which can be authoritarian or participatory.[2] Authoritarian cultures have a tight chain-of-command structure in which managers make the decisions and employees are expected to carry out their orders. These are closed systems that resist change from outside the organization.[3] Participatory cultures value teamwork and encourage employees to contribute their ideas. This type of organizational culture is open to new ideas inside and outside the organization.[4]

A study by the National Consumers League and Fleishman-Hillard found that 76 percent of American consumers "believed that a company's treatment of its employees plays a big role in consumer purchasing decisions."[5]

Human resources also plays a role in employee relations by carrying out fair hiring and termination practices and administering employees' pay and benefit programs. Of particular interest to organizations is attracting and retaining the best employees to ensure top worker performance and innovation. This becomes easier if the organization is known for its quality products and services and for being an industry leader—which is, of course, often the result of a good workforce to begin with!

PUBLIC RELATIONS CONTRIBUTES TO A PRODUCTIVE WORKPLACE CULTURE

The authors of *Public Relations: The Profession and the Practice* suggest that public relations can make three contributions to a productive workplace culture:[6]

- **Help create organizational communication policy based on organizational goals.** Workplaces would run better if employees were aware of and understood basic policies that codify workplace expectations and behavior about communication. Some examples include policies governing personal use of workplace computers and the use of the Internet (especially Web surfing and downloading of objectionable materials). Blogs and personal Web sites, even when owned and operated from a home computer, can create problems if the employee is communicating about his or her company. Related policies guide employees' personal communication while on the job: telephone calls, e-mail, and instant messaging. Other policies cover employee nondisclosure of confidential or privileged information. Employee handbooks explain policies and procedures for common work-related situations. More organizations include a code of ethics or an ethics statement that embodies an organization's values and standards.

- **Help design and implement organizational change programs.** Organizations are constantly changing; services and products are updated or dropped, buildings are renovated, and some are closed. Oldtimers retire; new people come and some go. Things just don't stay the same. Organizations must respond to competitive pressures and other factors that may require an organization to change in order to survive and thrive. Helping employees understand these factors and the necessity for change can maintain employee support even during difficult times.

- **Provide effective employee communication programs.** Many organizations today are dynamic and complex operations. Effective communication programs are needed to explain management actions, educate employees about new initiatives or safety concerns, acknowledge employee contributions, and keep employees informed during a crisis or dramatic change—a time of acquisition, merger, or restructuring. Public relations staff can also help keep a clear line of communication open with employee unions to prevent labor unrest, protracted negotiations, or strikes. Informing and explaining employee benefits is another important focus of employee communication programs. Employees are especially interested in health care and retirement savings options.

EFFECTIVE EMPLOYEE COMMUNICATIONS

The authors of *Effective Public Relations* note that "organizations miss out on a sizable share of their human resource potential because they do not put a high priority on effective, two-way communication—the foundation for management-employee relations and overall job performance."[7] Two-way communication assumes a feedback mechanism from internal constituents, including face-to-face interaction with lots of management listening, questionnaires, and focus groups. The textbook authors cite Opinion Research Corporation's tracking of employee opinions showing that most employees want to "know what is going on" and they want management to willingly "listen to their views."[8]

Just like undertaking any effective communication program, employee communication requires no less research, planning, careful implementation, and evaluation than a consumer information campaign. In fact, employees may be the most attentive and critical audience because they have a great deal invested in the company's success; they also understand the company better than management sometimes is willing to acknowledge. Intolerant of meaningless platitudes and empty promises, employees are usually the first to see a disconnect between what a company says and what it does. As a valued resource, employees deserve frank and honest communication that's timely; employees should not have to rely on the grapevine or local news media to find out what's happening at work.

INTERNAL COMMUNICATION

Public relations staff can be involved in numerous communication activities for internal audiences. *Effective Public Relations* describes four first-step communication activities that help organizations build their identities and operational frameworks:[9]

Vision statements: These statements are broad declarations of an organization's goals and are future-looking. The vision statement should answer the questions: "Why does the organization exist?" and "What would we like to accomplish?"

Mission statements: These statements are more specific than vision statements and answer the question, "How are we different from our competitors?" They focus on an organization's strengths and establish priorities.

Policy documents: An organization's rules and operational procedures are often found in documents such as employee handbooks. Other documents include the organization's code of ethics or an ethics statement (also called credos, principles, beliefs, values, or standards). These documents provide guidance for employee decision making in more difficult situations.

Training materials: No better time exists to introduce employees to the goals, operations, and expectations of an organization than when they are new. Orientation programs often provide new employees with face-to-face interaction with management and other key employees and lots of helpful information. Employees who understand "how things are done here" and the mission and expectations of an organization are better equipped to transition quickly into valued members of the organization.

INTERNAL MEDIA OPPORTUNITIES

The public relations professional has many tools that can help build an effective employee communications program. Organizational media's distinctive feature (and distinct advantage) is that their appearance and content are controlled by the organization.

Textual-based tactics include:

- Employee newsletters
- Letters, memos, e-mails
- Web-based intranet employee sites
- Inserts and enclosures
- Published speeches, position papers, and backgrounders
- CEO blogs, discussion/message boards
- Bulletin boards
- Posters

Nontextual tactics for reaching employees include:

- Face-to-face meetings with management
- Hotlines and toll-free numbers
- Teleconferences
- Video and film presentations
- Exhibits or displays of artifacts and other interesting or significant organizational items

Web Resources

- **Public Relations Society of America—Employee Communication** http://www.prsa.org/_Networking/ec/index.asp?ident=ec1
- **International Association of Business Communicators—Employee Communication Commons** http://commons.iabc.com/employee/

Sago Mine Tragedy
Garbled Message Turns Jubilation into Anguish, Anger

For many Americans, the hopeful arrival of a new year turned tragic as they watched and listened to tense news reports of a desperate rescue attempt in a tiny West Virginia mining community.

At 6:26 a.m. on January 2, 2006, 29 miners at the Sago Mine were arriving at work sites near the end of a long coal shaft, at places called "First Left" and "Second Left," when an explosion occurred, killing one miner and trapping 12 other miners.[10] Sago Mine's two-mile shaft gradually slopes into a side of a mountain; the 13 were deep in the mine at the time of the explosion. The miners caught in the explosion were located in the Second Left, near the mine's farthest point, next to an abandoned mine area that was recently sealed.

After 41 hours, only one miner was found alive—hanging by a thread. The bodies of 11 miners were found, together with the lone survivor, barricaded behind a makeshift shelter trying to maintain a pocket of good air until rescue teams arrived. Another miner's body was recovered by his workstation, nearer to the blast site.[11]

That morning, close to the time of the explosion, three lightning strikes were recorded in the vicinity of the mine—one was exceptionally powerful. Experts speculated at the time that the lightning might have ignited methane, triggering the explosion.[12]

Initial rescue efforts were hampered by the detection of dangerous levels of both methane and carbon monoxide. Rescue

Courtesy of AP Images (AP Photo/George Widman)

Ben Hatfield, ICG president and CEO, addresses questions from the news media during a press conference.

teams could not safely enter the mine until 11 hours after the explosion, and their progress was slow as searchers covered the mine on foot. After several hours of searching, the teams were forced to return to the surface after discovering that certain equipment was not de-energized; the rescue effort did not resume until nearly 24 hours after the explosion.[13] In the meantime, a drill hole near where the miners were trapped revealed high levels of carbon monoxide and no signs of life.

Whatever the cause of the explosion, mining is one of the most dangerous industries in America, according to the U.S. Bureau of Labor and Statistics, which tracks industry fatality trends.[14] Falling objects, such as roof collapses, cause most mining deaths, followed by explosions ignited by sparks from machinery or other equipment with combustible gases.

In 2004, 152 people died in mining accidents related to coal, oil, and gas extraction; 28 of those were coal related.[15] While other occupations such as construction and agriculture are also dangerous, coal mine disasters attract the most media attention due to dramatic rescue attempts that depict nervous families and friends awaiting news near the scene. Still, improvements in safety were

happening. Coal mine fatalities had trended downward since 1970 by 92 percent, while coal production had increased 83 percent during the same period.[16]

According to the U.S. Labor Department Mine Safety and Health Administration (MSHA), Sago mining operations had doubled the year prior to the January 2006 tragedy. The increased mining activity led to more monitoring by MSHA federal inspectors, who issued 208 citations, orders, and safeguards against Sago Mine—triple the number issued the year before.[17] Some of these included "significant and substantial" violations. In the fourth quarter report for 2005, 49 citations were issued with 18 considered "significant and substantial" that led to "withdrawal orders," shutting down mining activity in certain mine areas until health and safety actions were corrected.[18] At the time of the explosion, three of these violations were still in the process of being addressed by the mine's owner. The total penalties cited against Sago Mine in 2005 amounted to about $24,000.[19]

The alarming number of violations did prompt the company to "voluntarily invite MSHA's technical support group on incident reduction to help implement a new program to continually improve mine safety," said Ben Hatfield, ICG president and CEO.[20]

Sago Mine is located in the coal-rich hills of Tallsmanville, West Virginia, population 418. International Coal Group purchased the owner of Sago in November 2005. ICG controls 11 mining complexes in northern and central Appalachia.

The following timeline covers the first 44 hours of the mine disaster based on initial information provided by congressional testimony, MSHA's and ICG's Web sites, and supplementary information from news reports.

January 2, 2006

- 6:26 a.m. Explosion occurs as mining crew reaches its work destination.
- 5:25 p.m. First rescue team enters mine.

January 3, 2006

- 2:40 a.m. Rescue teams return to surface after discovering that one piece of equipment appeared to be energized; this situation deemed a hazard, the team was forced to return to the surface at 3:40 a.m.
- 2:45 a.m. Drilling a borehole begins for Second Left section of the mine.
- 5:35 a.m. Borehole punches into the mine.
- 6:22 a.m. Rescue teams reenter the mine.
- 6:50 a.m. Drilling for borehole for First Left section of the mine starts.
- 2:00 p.m. Rescue teams reach First Left section entries.
- 5:18 p.m. First miner found dead in the main shaft near the entry to the Second Left, but not identified.
- 7:12 p.m. Rescue teams begin Second Left exploration.
- 11:46 p.m. Command center gets first report from rescuers who have found the trapped miners; 12 miners erroneously reported alive.

- 11:50 p.m. Family members who gathered at Sago Baptist Church hear leaked information from the command center that 12 miners are alive.

January 4, 2006

- 12:30 a.m. Command center receives a second report from the "fresh air base" that the "lone survivor" has arrived. This report contradicts the earlier report; hope lingers that the remaining miners are not dead but comatose.
- Approximately 1:00 a.m. The lone survivor brought out of the mine, but is not identified at the time.
- Between 1:30–2:00 a.m. State police inform ministers at the church to caution family members that the information had not been confirmed.
- Approximately 2:30 a.m. Family members are told that all but one of the trapped 13 miners are dead.
- 9:55 a.m. All miners' bodies are removed from the mine.

THE EARLY MORNING HOURS OF JANUARY 4

Throughout the ordeal, the ICG president and others held frequent press briefings and communicated separately with family and community members distraught by the situation.

Shortly before midnight, January 3, an initial report came in from the rescue team to the command center saying that "12 are alive"; the news spread like wildfire. Family members, relatives, and supporters at the nearby Sago Baptist Church celebrated, ringing bells and sharing hugs.

According to Senate hearing testimony, a roomful of people in the command center overheard the initial transmission that came from the "fresh air base" at the mine. Information was being transferred by handheld radios that, because they operate in the line of sight, had to be transferred at least five times underground before it was relayed to the command center.[21] This transmission was being relayed from rescuers still in the mine who communicated through breathing masks and used code words to indicate the living and the dead. Somehow, the message got garbled.

When rescuers brought the one survivor to the fresh air base at 12:30 a.m., a second message was sent to the command center. At this point, the rescuers unencumbered by breathing apparatus directly reported that they had "the survivor." The rest were still in the mine. Hope still remained that the other miners might not be dead but comatose.[22] The command center requested that state police ask clergy to tell the families that the initial information was premature. That message did not reach the families.[23]

The families were informed at 2:30 a.m. that all but one of the miners had died.

According to witnesses at the church, when Hatfield addressed the families he explained that "there had been a lack of communication, that what we were told was wrong and that only one survived."[24] Afterward chaos broke out. Grief quickly turned to anger and dismay.

Responding later to the delayed communication to families, Hatfield said, "Based on our information, at least some of the clergy received that message," but it was not passed on to the families.[25] "That, we deeply regret. In hindsight, all I could have done differently is to go to the church and personally say, 'We have conflicting information. Please, let's just hold where we are.'"[26]

ICG's Web site provided a statement regarding the delay in notifying family members of the confirmed dead miners:[27]

Our goal throughout the day was to provide timely, accurate information. Unfortunately, we were not in the position to confirm or correct the initial report leaked to the families at the church until the mine rescue teams reached the surface with the survivor and were debriefed with their findings. This process delayed the formal family notification until about 2:30 a.m. There was never any intent to misinform, mislead or raise false hopes. We deeply regret the pain caused by that inadvertent disclosure.

An official statement released January 4 by ICG's Chairman Wilbur L. Ross said:[28]

A terrible tragedy has occurred and everyone at International Coal Group shares the grief of the families of the twelve miners who lost their lives despite the best efforts of our company, Governor Joe Manchin and the rescue teams. My heart goes out to these families. I personally understand their trauma since I lost my own father when I was a teenager and my widowed mother was left with three children, the youngest of whom was eight years old. I offer these families my heartfelt sympathy and my prayers.

No amount of money can take the place of a loved one, but the families do have financial needs as well. Therefore, International Coal Group has organized The Sago Mine Fund with an initial contribution of $2,000,000. People who wish to contribute to the Fund may do so by calling 1-800-811-0441.

Ben Hatfield, President and CEO of International Coal added, "This has been the most tragic period of my life. Our goal is always to see that our people get home safely each day and we will redouble our efforts to make sure that a tragedy like this never occurs again. Our management is working diligently with the government investigators to learn the cause of the explosion and we will report all findings in the hope that lessons learned here may help prevent similar problems at other mines. No amount of explanation can replace a loved one, nor can the Sago Mine Fund, but our fervent hope is that this will help. I reiterate the deep sympathy I have already expressed to the families. We regard our miners as part of our extended family and hope that many people will express their sorrow by contributing to the fund."

EPILOGUE

Not long after the Sago Mine tragedy, a fire at another West Virginia mine claimed the lives of two more miners. The state governor asked for legislative approval of new safety regulations, including electronic tracking of miners underground, faster emergency response, and storage of additional air supplies in mines. The legislature passed the bill in a record eight hours.

After an on-site investigation and repairs were completed, Sago Mine reopened March 15, 2006, for mining operations.[29]

Questions for Discussion.

1. Why do mining accidents garner so much media attention?

2. What was the main communication problem between Sago Mine owners and its employees and families?

3. Explain the logistics of the command center and the fresh air base and how critical information was communicated incorrectly. How could this communication problem between the organization and its employees have been averted?

4. If you were the Sago Mine president, how would you have handled the media relations during the mining accident?

5. The news media and some employees of Sago Mine criticized the mine owners for its numerous safety violations at the time of the mining accident. What is the best organizational response for this situation?

6. How can Sago Mine managers win back the confidence of employees in the aftermath of the mining disaster?

7. What is your impression of the two statements and news releases given January 4 expressing regret over the communications failure and announcing a Sago Mine fund?

Do Some Research

Mine Safety and Health Administration, part of the U.S. Department of Labor, is charged with creating a safe and healthy environment for workers. Go to its Web site (www.msha.gov/), and research how this organization has improved mine safety despite the deaths at the Sago Mine. While mining safety violations issued by the agency for mining operations have increased, some in the media say fines have not been substantial enough to force mining operations to take the violations seriously. How can this agency improve public perception of what it is doing?

Web Resources

• **International Coal Group (ICG) official Web site** www.intlcoal.com

• **U.S. Department of Labor, Sago Mine Information** www.msha.gov/sagomine/sagomine.asp

• **Mine Safety and Health Administration** www.msha.gov/

• **Mine Safety and Health Administration, Mine Safety and Health at a Glance** www.msha.gov/MSHAINFO/FactSheets/MSHAFCT10.HTM

• **Mine Safety and Health Administration, Historical Data on Mine Disasters in the United States** www.msha.gov/MSHAINFO/FactSheets/MSHAFCT8.HTM

Hallmark Writers on Tour
Meaningful Moments and Memories for Employees and Consumers

For nearly a century, Hallmark has been helping people express their feelings and touch the lives of others. As anyone who has received one knows, a greeting card can communicate love, humor, sympathy, and much more.

With an array of product lines that includes not only greeting cards but also ornaments and television entertainment, Hallmark netted $4.2 billion in 2005.[30] The company leads domestic greeting card sales with a 50 percent market share in the United States; it publishes products in more than 30 languages and distributes them in more than 100 countries.[31] Its 800 artists, designers, writers, editors, and photographers generate more than 19,000 new and redesigned greeting cards and related products each year.[32] Hallmark offers more than 40,000 products in its model line at any one time.[33]

Clearly, consumers understand the power and value of a greeting card; almost 90 percent of U.S. households use them.[34] According to the Greeting Card Association, the average household purchases 30 individual cards each year, with costs ranging from 38 cents to $10 per card.[35]

However, greeting card sales had slowed in recent years, in part because busy lifestyles can lead to forgetfulness and missed purchasing opportunities. Competition has increased with nearly 3,000 greeting card publishers in America.[36] The solution from a marketing standpoint was to develop a creative card-based advertising campaign to promote sales.

Hallmark also turned to its public relations staff for help. However, "cards in and of themselves are not news," said Hallmark's national campaigns manager Lydia Steinberg. Typical card news opportunities are usually limited to holiday times, such as Valentine's Day and Mother's Day, or when new card themes illuminate social trends. At other times of year, few holidays support card giving: Summer's most celebrated holiday, the Fourth of July, is not especially known as an occasion to send a greeting card.

STRATEGY

The public relations staff's creative solution to help grow the greeting card category was the Hallmark Writers Tour (later including Hallmark artists), which began in 2003. "It was an opportunity to express to consumers directly and through news stories the emotional benefit of greeting cards," said Steinberg. The program would take writers on the road, allowing them to interact with consumers through small events and creating media relations opportunities to share their work and solicit consumer memories about special greeting cards. These consumer stories could then be leveraged for additional news coverage.

"We wanted to remind consumers in person and through the news media of the emotional benefit of greeting cards," said Steinberg. Other objectives included reinforcing and personalizing the Hallmark brand and using the freshly media-trained creative staff and consumer testimonials to feed other promotional efforts. Hallmark

Courtesy of Hallmark Cards, Inc.

partnered with Fleishman-Hillard to develop the media tour.

Beyond the promotional benefits of sending its writers on tour, a secondary outcome happened: The customers and their stories inspired Hallmark employees. The tour became an effective employee relations program that helped renew employees' sense of purpose; by hearing directly from consumers how their daily work had affected others' lives, they gained new insight to feed future endeavors, said Steinberg.

The program was designed to allow people to share their stories about how cards have helped them connect with others in a meaningful way. "Whether you send greeting cards or write them, we all have experiences that speak to our spirits, that touch us in important ways," said Pat Daneman, Hallmark writing director. "Greeting cards are often part of those memories. We hope to gain inspiration and insight from others' stories, as well as share some of our own."[37]

One of the stories shared by a couple in Texas was posted to Hallmark's Meaningful Moments Web site and was also re-created in a television commercial. A customer's Web posting told about a Valentine déjà vu experience:[38]

During the second year of our marriage, my husband, Mike, was serving in the Army in Viet Nam. Anxious to find the perfect valentine, I searched diligently to find a card that expressed exactly how I felt in my heart during our separation. Finally, I found that special valentine, a large Hallmark card, and mailed it with the hope that it would arrive on time. Imagine my shock and disappointment when I went to the mailbox and opened a large card only to think, "Oh, no! My valentine to Mike was returned to me. He never got it!" After looking carefully at it for a moment, I realized that the card was actually from my husband. He had bought the identical card at the PX in Da Nang that I had bought in Beaumont, Texas! I have kept those cards to remind myself of the miracle of love and God's goodness to me. Those special thoughts I searched so hard to send to my husband, he had also sent to me.

Beyond inspirational moments, Hallmark writers discovered new consumer needs for greeting cards. At the Minneapolis–St. Paul tour stop, writers Scott Emmons and Molly Wigand, a city native, heard a need for more cards to help men, especially husbands and sons, to express themselves. Customers told them that in times of polarized opinions, there was also the need to help people say, "Let's agree to disagree."[39]

At a second stop in a cozy Twin Cities bookstore, the writers heard stories like this: Two women shared how they've often found a card so perfect for their friendship that they would send the same card back and forth for years.[40] Later that day at a coffee house, another woman talked about her long-distance relationship with a man who is now her husband. The pair never lived in the same town until they were married, but they got to know each other through the cards they had exchanged.[41]

The Writers on Tour market locations were selected for media receptivity, heavy consumer card purchasing, "hometown" connection between the writers and the market, and their nearby location to a Fleishman-Hillard office or other in-market resource.

Audiences were generated by invitations to Hallmark Gold Crown members, advance media relations stories, fliers in Hallmark Gold Crown stores, fliers at event venues, and affinity group outreach, said Steinberg. Writers on Tour was tested in Lawrence, Leavenworth, Leawood, and Topeka, Kansas, and Kansas City, Missouri. Pilot events allowed the public relations team an opportunity to tweak the "run of show" and help the writer pairs and host gain comfort in their roles.

The pilots also helped the team identify which program elements were meaningful to guests, which were extraneous or disruptive, and which venues worked best before the investment in travel was made. Official tour stops included San Diego, Cincinnati, Philadelphia, St. Louis, Nashville, Minneapolis–St. Paul, Las Vegas, and many other cities.

Steinberg said that sessions were purposely not held in Hallmark stores to keep the events from seeming too commercial. "We sought smaller, casual venues with engaged proprietors so that audiences would feel comfortable enough to tell very touching, personal stories in public." Typical venues were libraries, coffeehouses, tearooms, bookstores, community centers, and cafés. Writers were scheduled for three days and two nights in each market. This allowed time for media interviews, four to five event appearances, and retailer interaction and store visits.[42]

An event format usually included a host and two writers, an introductory video, writer presentations including background and sources of inspiration, a question-and-answer session, story sharing, and informational packets containing card samples, story forms, bookmarks, and gift cards.[43]

To give the initiative a year-round presence outside specific tour markets, the Hallmark Visitors Center, at the company's Kansas City headquarters, offered a display showcasing videos and card samples from the touring writers and seeking guests' greeting card memories. Hallmark launched a Web site for an additional source of consumer stories and to showcase the entire program.

Within 19 months, Writers on Tour made 77 appearances in 15 markets. "We laughed, we cried, and sometimes we scratched our heads ... but mostly we marveled at the way greeting cards touch people in strange and wonderful ways," Steinberg said.

Internally, the public relations staff used this project as a way to inspire employees about their company. Writer profiles and consumer stories were featured in employee newsletters. Hallmark employees, as well as CEO Donald J. Hall, Jr., were also solicited to share stories in the company newsletter and on the company's intranet site.[44] Weekly e-mails highlighting consumer stories to Hallmark writing staff and other employees allowed tour members to share their experiences and maintain enthusiasm for the program. The company made presentations to writers and editors to celebrate the program's success, and an all-employee meeting recapped the program and recognized everyone's contributions.[45]

RESULTS

In the first year, Hallmark writers talked face to face with more than 2,500 employees and members of the public, Steinberg said. The program netted about 600 written consumer stories from events, its visitors center, Web site, and mail. The program's Web site (Hallmark.com/meaningfulmoments) had more than 75,000 visitors.

The media helped tell the story: More than 131 million media impressions resulted from top-tier media coverage about the Writers on Tour project.[46] Major print and online clips included the *New York Times*, *Wall Street Journal*, *New Yorker*, *Philadelphia Inquirer*, *St. Paul Pioneer Press*, *South Florida Sun Sentinel*, *Kansas City Star*, and *Cincinnati Inquirer*. Some of the in-market articles, most notably in the *Nashville Tennessean* and *Salt Lake City Tribune*, were syndicated to other newspapers around the country. Twenty-one radio interviews reached 5.5 million listeners, and 17 television interviews reached 8 million viewers. Overall, the team was successful in generating one to three television appearances, one or more radio interviews, and a daily newspaper feature in each market.

Additional Writers on Tour messages fed other Hallmark campaigns, yielding 143 million more impressions.[47] Consumer stories were used in Valentine's Day publicity efforts, and media-trained writers were prepared to participate in a successful campaign supporting a relaunch of the popular Shoebox card line.[48]

Ninety percent of the news coverage carried the program's key message: "This tour is not only about sharing how we work at Hallmark, but also about listening to real people talk about how cards have made a difference in their lives."[49]

Those surveyed at Writers on Tour events enjoyed their time. When asked if the program helped them realize how important cards are to people, 83.5 percent strongly agreed. Participants said that their respect for what goes into the creation of a greeting card was increased (95 percent), and 50 percent said they had purchased or used greeting cards more than normal the week following the event.[50]

The success of Hallmark's Writers on Tour rested in its authenticity. "It was a campaign built around our DNA," Steinberg said. "It did not portray us as something other than what we are. The writers were able to completely be themselves, sincerely delivering the message about the benefit of greeting cards—because it is with their words that the magic begins. As a result, audiences had no problem with embracing the concept. It basically reinforced our brand promise."

The support of Hallmark employees was key, Steinberg said. When employees embrace a campaign, it becomes part of the corporate culture. As a result, "card planning teams began to ask for relevant consumer stories when assigning new projects to writers; the company's chairman referred to the program in his annual Thanksgiving letter to employees and many volunteered for the second and third years of the program," Steinberg said. "The stories were shared throughout Hallmark, reinforcing the importance of each job and improving morale," she said. Consumer stories also have been used in communication to Hallmark's independent retailers to reinforce their role in enriching consumers' lives as well.

Stories such as a single mother who spoke of her elation at receiving a card "To Mom on Father's Day" from her daughter and a woman who recalled the reassurance she felt on finding a card from her family tucked in her suitcase when she was headed away for a college semester abroad underscored the belief and values of Hallmark—to enrich people's lives through creativity, quality, and innovation.[51]

Questions for Discussion

1. What business problem did the Hallmark Writers and Artists on Tour program attempt to solve?

2. Why was it important that the Writers on Tour program be authentic—part of Hallmark's "DNA"?

3. How did the Hallmark Writers on Tour program create positive publicity for Hallmark?

4. How did Hallmark avoid overcommercializing Writers on Tour?

5. How did the Hallmark Writers on Tour program promote quality products?

6. How did the Hallmark Writers on Tour program promote employee morale?

7. What are some traditional ways that public relations practitioners build strong employee relations?

8. Analyze Hallmark's brand essence statement "Enriching Lives" available on Hallmark's Web site. What does brand essence mean? Why is it important for an organization to look inward and develop such a statement?

9. Analyze Hallmark's beliefs and values statement available on Hallmark's Web site. Why is it important for an organization to have such a statement?

Do Some Research

1. The Writers on Tour is a form of research called a "listening tour." How did the results of the first listening tour inform its product research?

2. Hallmark has a brand essence statement and a beliefs and values statement. How do these help companies? What is their function? Examine the mission or beliefs and values statements of other large organizations. Do you think they reflect the purpose of those institutions?

3. Investigate the employee relations efforts of your college or university. What does your organization do to create an institutional culture and improve employee morale? Are there better ways?

Terminology

- media impressions
- brand essence
- mission statement
- beliefs and values statement
- listening tour

Web Resources

- **Hallmark's home page** www.Hallmark .com
- **Hallmark's Writers and Artists on Tour** pressroom.hallmark.com/writers-artists_tour_release.html
- **Greeting Card Association** www.greet ingcard.org

Communicating Organizational Growth

General Motors' Strategic Integration of Internal-External Communications

By Gary Grates, president and global managing director of Edelman Change practice

By any measure, General Motors (GM) today bears little resemblance to the GM of 5 or 10 years ago. Despite financial troubles, its management team, including communication, has kept reputation and brand image management a major focus. Its strategy has included three key drivers:

- A focused business strategy, which began in the early 1990s with a new CEO, John F. "Jack" Smith, who strove to get the organization resubscribed to results and focused on, as he so often said, "deeds, not words." The approach has been evident in the latter half of the 1990s and now into the twenty-first century with Smith's successor, G. Richard "Rick" Wagoner.

- Building momentum for the business, which has been possible by concentrating on improvements and "game changers" in the key business areas of the auto industry, including quality, productivity, reliability, and design.

- Dynamic, real-time communications, which link internal and external activities to tell a holistic story. This case will deal principally with this component.

COMPANY'S ORIGINS

General Motors Corporation came into its own in the 1920s through the efforts of Alfred P. Sloan. He established the fundamental blueprint for the company, culminating in his "brand ladder" architecture ("a brand for every pocketbook")—a carefully crafted hierarchy built on distinct identities for Chevrolet, Pontiac, Oldsmobile, Buick, and Cadillac.

In 1962, GM boasted a North American market share of 50.7 percent, dominance never before or since equaled by GM or any other automaker. From there, GM's supremacy eroded, to the point where, by the early 1990s, GM had reached a crisis point. Its credibility and market share had fallen precipitously, and it was losing money hand over fist.

Though its current market share is well below its peak, GM is still the world's largest automaker, with 2005 global revenues of $192.6 billion, a North American market share of more than 28 percent, and a global market share of nearly 15 percent. It has manufacturing operations in 32 countries, with 349,000 employees designing, man-ufacturing, and marketing vehicles for sale in more than 190 countries.

Since the nadir of the early 1990s, GM and its vehicle brands have been revitalized and the quality of its products improved every year. GM's productivity is now unmatched by any other domestic manu-facturer and on par with the best in the world. Within the organization, there is a rediscovered sense of pride and urgency that had been absent for years.

The move toward a resurgent market position and a renewed future promise began with Jack Smith's focused business strategy, which aimed to remake GM from the inside by focusing on results through five business drivers:

1. **Achieving commonality of manufactur-ing methods and business processes**
2. **Rebuilding relationships with dealers, suppliers, employees, and customers**
3. **Recommitting to quality**
4. **Transcending GM's "not invented here" attitude and, instead, benchmarking itself against competitors**
5. **Bringing in outside talent for new, fresher thinking.**

Today, GM's resulting "deeds," as Smith would call them, are evident in an expanding roster of "gotta have" products, especially the revived Cadillac lineup that has reclaimed its ranking position as the luxury brand among luxury brands. Each division, in fact, is offering a range of compelling vehicles, successfully arresting the compa-ny's market share slide in 2001 and 2002. Since the Cadillac revival, a plethora of new models have flooded the Chevrolet, Buick, Pontiac, and Saturn lines. At the same, GM has continued to push the envelope with advanced safety technologies like OnStar, its in-vehicle safety, security, and commu-nications system and service, and Stabili-Trak, the brand name for GM's electronic stability control system.

The building momentum became obvi-ous in the key industry-recognized mea-sures. Quality went up, most evident with year-over-year improvements in the num-ber of vehicles and assembly plants rated highly by J.D. Power in its annual Quality Surveys. Similarly, as a testimony to the improving reliability of the company's vehi-cles, the number of GM vehicles among *Consumer Reports* annual "recommended buys" list has increased or at least held steady the past few years.

LETTING THE FACTS CHANGE PERCEPTIONS

The key to the strategic communications effort that helped drive GM's revitaliza-tion was a "GM story" built on the five key business drivers. The story let the facts themselves change the embedded internal and external perceptions that had been holding the company back. This was possible when communications became closely linked with the leader-ship's business strategy.

Most organizations are structured in a way that erects barriers between manage-ment and communications. For utmost effectiveness in the execution of the business strategy, communications must become inextricably linked to the way the business is run. With leadership's endorsement, that is what happened at GM.

After a major United Auto Workers strike in 1998, Wagoner recognized that improving and building relationships with employees would improve their chances for success. He and his leadership team started by crafting four cultural priorities around which they wanted the organization to rally:

- Act as one company.
- Push for stretch performance.
- Move with a sense of urgency.
- Focus on our products and customers.

They made internal communications a management priority to drive those core messages across the organization in a consistent, relevant, and meaningful way. The leadership team committed itself to what later became known as the *internal communications improvement process* (ICIP) for its North America operation to help ensure that it would happen.

INFLUENCING BEHAVIOR, OBTAINING RSULTS

ICIP, a systematic approach to communications at all GM facilities in North America, put communications professionals ("business communications integrators") in place at all 91 locations and overlaid a communications system that assured that the company could reach every employee every day with consistent messages.

The process focused on influencing behaviors and obtaining real results by building relationships between and among employees, managers, and leadership. Management's business objectives and cultural priorities were reinforced in all internal and external messages and became meaningful and actionable for each individual in the organization.

The effort played out in many ways, but especially in the actions and words of the company's leaders in their internal and external speeches, quarterly broadcasts

(internal television), media interviews, internal memos and letters, and meetings with employee groups. These coordinated internal and external efforts had a profound impact on employees' perceptions of both GM and their roles in its success.

As it evolved, ICIP developed four key strategies that sought regularly to engage the people in the business:

- **Create a cohesive story:** The story links the company's business objectives and goals with specific business strategies (marketing, product, and operational strategies), the company's values, specific initiatives that would achieve those ends, and the measurements by which the organization would determine its relative success at a point in the future. Telling a cohesive story enables a complete picture to emerge, take hold, and be understood by both internal and external stakeholders. It effectively explains and connects the what, why, how, when, and where of the business. It provides a common language to convey organizational values consistently to audiences, helping people engage emotionally, intellectually, and behaviorally in the company's success.

- **Discover versus sell:** Such communications provide context and relevance, which help people connect the dots for themselves. As the cohesive story begins to take hold, stakeholders better understand goals, and communications then evolve into a way for them to experience personally the changes needed and the true benefits of initiatives. The discover approach is built on the human truth that discovery carries more credibility than something that has been spoon-fed (sold). The discover versus sell approach plays itself out in many ways that involve active engagement of audiences, such as face-to-face meetings to ensure understanding of priorities going forward and manager briefings on strategic priorities. These and other forms of active engagement are reinforced by conventional communications and by leadership actions to ensure that decisions and actions match rhetoric.

- **Dynamic versus inert information:** This refers to meaningful, useful, and relevant information to the recipient, rather than impersonal information, disconnected from the recipient. Inert information addresses a topic without making it important or meaningful to the listener or reader. Dynamic information, on the other hand, helps the reader or listener make sense of a situation, better able to rethink what he or she is doing—modifying behaviors accordingly—and walk away feeling a bit smarter.

- **External validation:** This puts internal and external messages in sync, and such messages therefore are more meaningful. Communications are more effective when their various components work together synergistically. ICIP developed a more holistic approach to communications, which is now viewed as a complex, fluid management function rather than a group of separate, disconnected silos. ICIP linked all facets, including executive and financial communications, product communications, employee communications, and corporate communications. External communications strive for relevance in the marketplace, while internal ones try to make the business more relevant to employees. When all elements work together, this integration becomes formalized in the "situation room," a mechanism to regularize that integration by building consensus among communications professionals around the key external and internal drivers of the industry in general and the company in particular. In that way, the communications functions are better able to coordinate message content, spokespeople, media, and timing.

MOSAIC OF CONSISTENT MESSAGING

The chief communications vehicles through which these strategies were enacted comprise a mosaic of consistent messaging that reflects management behavior and leadership direction, including:

- "GM Leads": Bimonthly global and regional electronic messages that characterize leadership thinking
- External visibility: A daily, weekly, and monthly coordination of external and internal communications to reflect consistent themes and perceptions
- "Drive Time": A daily, 3–5 minute in-house television broadcast throughout North America that characterizes key competitive and company highlights
- "Four Common Processes": A template for conducting communications on a local level, including quarterly business updates, small group dialogue, weekly newsletters, and monthly supervisor support

This internal communications architecture engaged people in what had to get done, using information hubs to help employees gain greater awareness and understanding of:

- Marketplace conditions, GM's place within the market place, and the effectiveness of its efforts there.
- How GM is performing versus the competition.
- How each functional area is doing its part to realize goals.
- Feedback on what's working—and what's not.
- Failures—why and what can be learned from them.
- How organizations outside the industry have confronted similar challenges.
- Big accomplishments, as well as small wins and gains along the way.

- New ideas and new thinking on how to address priorities.
- Functional areas or policy barriers standing in the way of progress.

The starting point was (and remains) the philosophy that employees are intelligent, adept at applying diverse lessons from various internal and external sources to their own unique challenges. At its core, GM internal communications has become a reinvented function, its focus on opening and improving information channels for employees, encouraging their own unique learning processes, and providing information and sources such as those in the above list.

To achieve that, emphasis is placed on the informal face-to-face communications taking place at all levels of the organization, at all times. Conventional communication tools are consigned to their proper place: supporting and supplementing the real communications going on in the company.

Employee communications have thus been able to build global reach with local relevance, linked to the major business functions, to improve their ability to leverage functional expertise. Employee communications became results-oriented, striving to influence behavior and build trusting relationships between and among employees, managers, and leadership. In so doing, communications made management's agenda meaningful and actionable for each individual in the organization, thereby giving people a voice.

Internal communications built relationships at the local level, while reducing the "noise" that typifies most communications by focusing on relevant information that encourages discussion and allows people to discover the story. And because people were able to come to the company's story on their own terms—comparing consistent messages from multiple sources—the story had more credibility and personal meaning to them.

As a consequence, GM created more conducive internal and external environments in which it could, to an increasing degree, leverage its people, processes, and architectures—all its functional expertise—around the globe for a competitive advantage.

WORKING TOWARDS COMMON GOALS

In the midst of this evolving internal environment, where employees and management were increasingly working together toward common goals, GM's leadership has been better able to get the business focused on the key business drivers and cultural priorities, which in turn has begun to give people guidance for both what to do and how to do it.

This, then, has begun to produce results in various areas, such as the manufacturing systems that started to yield quality and productivity improvements and cost elimination. The vehicle development component saw the introduction of exciting new "gotta have" products at the concept stage. And the company began to achieve recognition from third parties, like Harbour Associates (productivity), J.D. Power (quality), *Consumer Reports* (reliability), and, the ultimate arbiters, consumers.

All the components then began to bear fruit as corporate communications told the story behind the business decisions that drove the transformation. Vehicles such as the Cadillac CTS, the Chevrolet Avalanche, the Pontiac G6, Buick LaCrosse, and the Hummer H2 were the tangible confirmation of the resurgence, winning plaudits from the auto enthusiast press and sales at the dealerships. At the same time, as noted, additional evidence was piling up in the form of market share growth, productivity improvements, stock price improvement, and continuing quality improvements.

As these strategies took hold in the organization, change became apparent.

GM built momentum by focusing on results, avoiding empty rhetoric, and finding its center of gravity in its people, products, and innovations.

GM allowed itself to be defined by its actions, not its words. Third parties—the media, ratings groups, customers, analysts, and so on—sat up and came to realize that GM had changed. So they, in fact, began to define the new GM. Because communications operated in a more holistic manner, the enterprise came to be managed in a manner more consistent with its brand promise.

WHAT DOES IT MEAN?

GM communications has, in actuality, begun to create a habit of communications. In so doing, it has built credibility for information while establishing a yearning for more information and much more robust information.

As GM proceeds along this path to realizing the full benefit of ICIP, the focus of the initiative has begun to shift from reinforcing a habit to creating a lifestyle change within its facilities. In this way, communications will become integrated into the unique culture of each facility. As a result of engaging in meaningful dialogue and feedback, people will become personally committed to helping create GM's story, contributing to its success and moving ever closer to realizing Wagoner's vision for GM: a fast, nimble, flexible, twenty-first century organization.

From this real-life situation, still unfolding at GM, what becomes apparent is the value in the alignment of internal and external communications to present a holistic view of the organization. This is the wave of the future.

The strategic integration of internal and external communications at General Motors is allowing a clear story of organizational growth to appear and, in effect, knocking down the cobwebs to create clear lines of sight—for employees to better see the marketplace and for the external audiences to better see the GM brand.

Questions for Discussion

1. What should be the central purpose of any employee communications effort?

2. What is the linkage between effective communications that build relationships and trust and that drive behavior change?

3. Why is it important for employees to understand their company's competitive environment?

4. Define "employee communications" in the context of a business environment.

5. What is the core role played by communications vehicles like newsletters, intranet Web sites, in-house videos, and the like, in helping fulfill the core mission of employee communications?

6. When developing messages for internal consumption, should those messages be in sync with external public relations, such as communications directed at investors and consumers? Why or why not?

7. What role does a company's business strategy play in employee communications? What is the role of employee communications in helping a company fulfill its business objectives?

8. Why is "discovered" information more meaningful to the recipient than "sold" information?

9. How does "external validation" help connect employees to the company and its business objectives? Cite some examples from your own experiences or readings.

Terminology

- cohesive story
- discover versus sell
- external validation
- dynamic versus inert information
- situation room
- habit versus lifestyle
- relationships
- behaviors

Web Resources`

- **General Motors Corporation** (complete information about General Motors and its many products and brands) www.gm.com/
- **Public Relations Society of America, Employee Communications Section** (information about seminars, teleseminars, and other resources on employee communications)www.prsa.org/ _Networking/ec/index.asp?ident=ec1
- **Ragan Communications** (seminars and conferences on employee communications) www.ragan.com/
- **Melcrum** (corporate case histories and related materials on employee communications) www.melcrum.com/

Big Brother Is Watching
Browsing on Company Time

Employees are important to the success of ComXSoft Corporation, a computer products company. ComXSoft's latest product, a handheld computer device tailored for the college student market, has been a huge seller.

ComXSoft, founded five years ago, employs 300 people, including software and hardware developers, assemblers, and sales and support staff. The average age of its employees is 35. Morale has been high as strong sales have led to annual raises and bonuses. ComXSoft prides itself on a fun and relaxed business environment.

The company's founder, Malcolm Middleton, is chairman of ComXSoft's board of directors. He started his company after a successful software engineering career at a Fortune 500 company. He wanted more freedom to create innovative products, and he knew he could have more fun and make more money building his own company. Based on his experience, Middleton has always operated under the assumption that a happy workforce is more loyal and willing to contribute its creative energy to the company.

As the company grew, Middleton handed over its day-to-day operations to an old business associate, CEO Kenneth Purdon. Middleton remained chairman of the board and spends time developing new markets for the company.

Nelson Perry, public relations director, has been on the job for six months. Based on thorough research and many discussions with the management team, he has begun to develop a comprehensive public relations program aimed at generating positive relationships with ComXSoft's primary publics: company employees and college students in the United States and, soon, several European countries.

There has been widespread acceptance of Perry's role within the organization. He does his homework and understands the mission of the company. He has worked well with the marketing and human resources departments, which are pleased with his ability to develop an active employee relations program and a successful third-party endorsement campaign within the national media for ComXSoft's new products. Perry has a secretary and a public relations assistant.

One day, Perry's assistant, Larry Meyers, steps into the office and shuts the door. He has a complaint about the new secretary:

"She spends all her time on eBay," he claims. "It slows down my work." Perry promises Meyers to have a talk with the new secretary, who reacts defensively, saying she is only on eBay during her lunch hour or during coffee breaks. Perry starts to pay more attention to the secretary's computer habits. As Perry enters the office, every now and then he thinks he sees eBay screens which are quickly replaced with work-related documents when his presence is detected. Just how much time does his secretary spend on eBay? Perry wonders.

Perry decides to ask for some advice from Paul Johnson, director of human resources. After he explains the situation about his secretary's possible abuse of office equipment for personal use, he tells him that other managers have voiced similar complaints. Johnson advises Perry to continue to counsel his secretary on workplace expectations and that use of office equipment is for work, except during lunch, breaks, and after work. He says it would be a good idea to establish an employee folder and jot down basic details, including the dates, of any conversations he has with his employees about this or other issues. He thanks Perry for stopping by and says he'll let him know if he has any other suggestions.

Three months later, Perry receives a call from the human resources director. Johnson wants to see him in his office. Johnson tells Perry that the company has been monitoring employees' computer use for the past two months with software technology that can record every Web site visited, file deleted, or data downloaded. As part of the employee computer surveillance, it was discovered that Perry's secretary has spent excessive time each day on eBay; in fact, records showed one day she was logged on to eBay for four hours during normal business hours. Johnson tells Perry his secretary isn't alone. Many employees have been surfing the Internet during business hours for obvious nonwork-related purposes. Johnson tells Perry that, so far, 20 employees have been identified as excessive abusers and have

been targeted for further workplace surveillance, including nonbusiness e-mail usage. It's only a matter of time, Johnson says, before some—perhaps all—of the 20 will be terminated based on the accumulating evidence.

Perry's reaction is one of shock and disbelief. Immediately, he wonders, "Am I under surveillance too?" He had never considered that his employer was monitoring everyone's computer activities. "Is this legal?" he asks. Johnson replies that laws such as the federal Health Insurance Portability and Accountability Act of 1996 and the Sarbanes-Oxley Act of 2002 had actually resulted in many new record keeping and investigative burdens for companies that could be held accountable for the misconduct of their employees. Johnson told him more than a third of workers at major American companies were monitored in one way or another.[52]

Open Scenario Challenge
Creating a Positive and Productive Work Environment

Perry leaves Johnson's office extremely uneasy. For the rest of the day, Perry (wearily) conducts computer research on the role of public relations with employee relations and a new field called *human resource forensics*. On his way home after work, he begins to form a plan of action based on this employee relations issue that he hopes to present at the next management meeting.

Questions for Discussion

1. Why should employee relations be important to companies? What return on investment is there when a company invests in its employees?

2. Perry knew his own personal computer and phone habits during office time were within the acceptable range, but who was defining this "acceptable range"?

3. While Perry knew the company had a right to terminate unproductive

employees, it bothered him that the company was monitoring its employees. What effect might these impending terminations have on the company and its employees? How can Perry help the company avoid a backlash of employee anger once the corporate snooping technology is revealed?

4. Because it is a new company that has grown rapidly in five years, assume ComXSoft has no company policy for employee use of office equipment. Why are company policies and clearly defined job expectations important? If you were developing such a policy, how would you go about getting employees to "buy into" corporate spying? What other types of communication policies might be helpful?

5. Do you think spam and personal e-mail can have an effect on an employee's productivity? What are the other hidden costs of nonwork e-mail?

6. Have you ever gotten an e-mail that was sent to you in error? Or perhaps an e-mail with an offensive joke or message in it? What kinds of concerns would employers have about these types of messages?

Do Some Research

1. Go online and search for workplace privacy or employee monitoring information. What are the current trends?

2. How can an employee's personal Web site or blog (operated from home) that discusses his or her company's business actually result in being terminated? Provide an example and why the employee was terminated.

3. Interview a human resources manager at a local business or organization. Find out what the organization's computer usage policy is and how the company monitors employee productivity. Also ask for an employee policy handbook. Does this publication offer guidance on work-based or home-based computer use?

Terminology

- spam
- surfing the Web
- Health Insurance Portability and Accountability Act of 1996
- Sarbanes-Oxley Act of 2002
- human resource forensics

WEB RESOURCES

- **Sarbanes-Oxley Act of 2002: Frequently asked questions** www.sec.gov/divisions/corpfin/faqs/soxact2002.htm or (commercial site) www.sarbanes-oxley.com/

- **B Net: Employee management resources** http://www.bnet.com/

- **U.S. Government** (This site allows you to search for state and federal government information, legal decisions, and examples of employee computer use issues, workplace privacy issues) www.fedworld.gov/

- **Personnel Systems Associates** (This commercial site contains links to many Internet resources relating to human resources issues) www.personnelsystems.com/links.htm

- **Fulcrum Financial Inquiry: A commercial site that specializes in computer forensics** www.fulcruminquiry.com/

Note: This case study is a composite based on news accounts.

Chapter Eleven

Governmental Relations

In the United States, government is a vast enterprise encompassing federal, state, county, and local municipalities responsible for providing programs and services that are either too important or impractical for individuals or businesses to address.

Government provides for our security through the armed forces, police and fire departments—even through the repair and maintenance of roads, highways, and bridges. Social programs care for and protect our most vulnerable populations in a variety of ways, including health research and food safety testing. Government also develops guidelines and enforces laws governing many aspects of how individuals and organizations behave and conduct business. With hundreds of billions of dollars involved, government is a major force in our lives. In fact, it is hard to find any aspect of our daily lives that is untouched by government activity.

In a democracy, citizens play a major part in determining the role government should play in their lives and judging its effectiveness in meeting their needs. This is mostly accomplished by electing and interacting with political representatives. Direct contact with government programs and services is another way that citizens can influence change within government. Because government officials, appointed and elected, are responsible to citizens, government must keep them informed.

In general, the relationship can be viewed from two perspectives: governmental relations and public affairs in government. In both, the public relations function responsible for the necessary relationship building and communication activity is often called *public affairs* instead of public relations.

GOVERNMENTAL RELATIONS

Governmental relations is an organization's efforts to build and maintain a working relationship with elected politicians or appointed government officials. The goal is ensure that the organization's concerns and needs are known to appropriate governmental representatives and their staff members to ensure the long-term success and the survivability of the organization. And organizations often provide valuable feedback for officials considering proposed legislation; an organization, for example, might know very well what a proposed new law or regulation would do and what positive or negative effects it might have. Organizations invest in research and outside experts to bolster their arguments.

The public affairs specialist may write factual informational letters, op-ed pieces, position papers, and newsletters and create and place advocacy advertising to convince government officials of the virtue of their organization's point of view.[1] This person may also visit government officials and their staffs to discuss issues directly or provide testimony for public hearings.

When information dissemination of a particular point of view is not enough, organizations often resort to lobbying, which is a persuasive campaign to support, defeat, or amend legislation that the organization deems necessary to its own interests.[2] Lobbying efforts are characterized by continuous and strategic pressure advocacy tactics at every opportunity and are orchestrated by lobbyists who are well connected to those whom they choose to influence. This intense effort sometimes results in unethical and illegal behavior to buy influence through expensive gifts, travel, or other perks to politicians.

Some organizations will try to enlist the help of average citizens, by encouraging them to band together and participate in grassroots lobbying efforts. This tactic, often orchestrated by industry groups or individual organizations, involves calling legislators, letter writing, and even holding rallies or protests. In some cases, critics will say the organization's support of such activity may cross the line of ethical behavior.[3]

Another area of concern is the use of front groups for grassroots lobbying, called *stealth lobbying,* wherein the organization hides its involvement.[4] For example, an organization such as Citizens for the Right to Smoke might give the appearance of concerned citizen participation but in reality is financed and operated by a tobacco company. This would be dishonest and, consequently, unethical behavior.

PUBLIC AFFAIRS IN GOVERNMENT

The other function of governmental relations is government's need to inform its publics about its programs and services, respond to inquiries, and gauge public opinion of its efforts. Every federal agency, such as the U.S. Department of Defense, Health and Human Services, Census Bureau, the Bureau of Labor Statistics, the Centers for Disease Control, the Department of Commerce, and the National Endowment for the Arts, has its own unique information needs. This is also true at the state, county, and local government levels.

In addition to the title of public affairs, other titles used include public information officer, press secretary, administrative aide, and government program analyst.[5] Most public affairs jobs are located within government agencies, in the offices of elected officials, and in the military.

Public Affairs and Informational Campaigns

Many of these agencies or departments must alert constituents of new services or changes and seek feedback. The informational campaigns require the same research, planning, implementation, and evaluation that corporations use to reach target audiences. Many campaigns require creative strategies to reach their audience, such as outreach programs for minority or rural immunization services. But accurate message creation and dissemination and awareness building are just the first steps, according to the authors of *Effective Public Relations*. Other goals include ensuring active cooperation and support for government programs, serving as the public's advocate to government administrators, keeping government employees informed, and handling media relations duties.[6]

There are legal limits to the information role of governmental communication. Federal law prohibits taxpayer money "for publicity or propaganda purposes designed to support or defeat legislation before Congress."[7] This means that while information programs can be highly creative to effectively reach an intended audience, government agencies cannot take sides to support or attack a particular legislative initiative. Propaganda refers to covert communication attempts, lies, half-truths, and other unethical tactics to persuade others to endorse a particular point of view.

Public Affairs and Elected Officials

Elected officials are in the same position as government agencies and offices; they must tell their constituents what they are doing on their behalf and respond to their needs and concerns. Often, politicians have press secretaries and other support staff who help coordinate the communication and relationship building activities required for winning elections and staying in office. Media relations is a major component of this specialty. Special event planning and logistics are also important because politicians interact with many groups regularly. Among a politician's constituents are nonprofit organizations, businesses, colleges, industry groups, and others who band together to advocate for their causes. Election campaigns particularly require public relations expertise to strategize, fundraise, and communicate effectively. Many governments have laws and regulations concerning the separation of government employees' official duties and their political activities.

Public Affairs and the Military

According to *Effective Public Relations,* "Military public affairs is geared toward boosting public opinion about the armed forces, maintaining or improving personnel morale, procuring financial support for its programs, and nurturing public understanding and support."[8] The military, due to its sheer size, complexity, and sometimes controversial activities and policies, attracts a great deal of media coverage, particularly in times of war. The practitioners in charge of military public relations often go by the title of public information officer (PIO) or public affairs specialist.

One of the main challenges of military public information officers is maintaining professional and open lines of communication between military commanders and the news media during difficult times. Journalists want complete and timely information, while sometimes the military, for security or other reasons, cannot release the information requested. During times of conflict, such as the Iraq war, tensions can run high and test everyone's patience. Cool heads need to prevail to maintain the effective image of authority, power, and control needed in wartime.

Another unique challenge for public information officers is the frequent change in command due to retirements and reassignments. These leadership and PIO disruptions can lead to confusion, slow response, or gaps in communication that can damage the military's credibility.

An article in *Military Review* raised another potential problem with combining all military information services together, including public affairs, information operations, and psychological operations. Information operations and psychological operations use persuasive techniques to achieve military objectives, such as changing audience perceptions for behaviors. Public affairs officers use a public information model, and they develop relationships with the news media to disseminate factual information. The authors noted that public affairs should keep its independence and report directly to the commanding officer instead of competing for attention alongside information and psychological operations.[9]

The use of news conferences, news releases, news articles, media tours, Web sites, television and radio programs, magazines, newsletters, and full transcripts of news conferences and other interviews, and embedded journalists within fighting units has helped create a more transparent organization. Still, the military has more than 1 million soldiers, and with that many individuals, conflict is bound to occur.

Military public affairs works with politicians, military advisers, and the White House. The president, as commander in chief of the armed forces, is often communicating to the American public to garner support for his military decisions. Actions taking place in faraway lands are being analyzed and commented on in Washington when complete information may be unavailable and key messages can be uncoordinated. The goal of effective military public affairs is to provide accurate and timely information. It also strives to coordinate its communication efforts so that consistent messages are reinforcing the military's strategy and actions.[30] Elizabeth Cooper, "Base

Base Closings and Realignment
Strategic Planning and Lobbying Protects Military Assets

Was history repeating itself?

To the dismay of community and state leaders, it certainly looked that way on May 13, 2005, when U.S. secretary of defense Donald Rumsfeld presented his sweeping national proposal for military base closures and realignments.[10]

The Department of Defense (DoD) figured it had about 20 percent more physical infrastructure than it needed.[11] More efficient use of its existing military facilities could save billions of dollars and allow the Pentagon to reconfigure its forces for future threats.[12] To accomplish the mammoth task, DoD scrutinized thousands of domestic military installations, everything from massive submarine bases to small Army Reserve units.

Buried deep within the pages of Rumsfeld's thick proposal were a few lines that had big consequences for one small community: Rome, New York (population

35,000). The closure and realignment recommendations would eliminate about 500 jobs from an Air Force Research Lab and a large military accounting process center.[13]

While small in comparison to other proposed large-scale closures, it would be a major blow to an area hard hit by previous military cutbacks. In 1993 a DoD proposal effectively closed Griffiss Air Force Base, the economic engine of the military-based economy in the Rome area. This meant 4,529 civilian and military jobs were lost—a devastating blow that accelerated a staggering population decline.[14] From 1990 to 2000, Oneida County, New York, where Rome is located, experienced a 6.1 percent drop, or 15,000 people in population, a rate among the nation's highest.[15]

Overall, the 2005 DoD proposal requested closing 180 installations, including 33 big bases, and hundreds of other consolidations and reductions that affected every state. Military planners said the recommendations would save $5.5 billion annually for a net savings of $48.8 billion over 20 years.[16] Since the restructuring process began in 1988, the government had closed or realigned more than 450 installations, including more than 130 bases in five major reviews.[17]

The restructuring was necessary to eliminate waste and refocus military resources on new threats from terrorism and evolving challenges in technology. The goal, according to Rumsfeld, was to create an agile and flexible military response force.[18]

The military restructuring process includes a full review of the DoD recommendations by an independent panel, the Base Realignment and Closure and Commission (BRACC). Its recommendations go to the president and Congress for final approval. Criteria for recommendations include an installation's military value to meet current and future mission capabilities, the condition of the land or facility, the ability to accommodate future needs, and the cost of operations.[19]

THE STRATEGY: LEAVE NOTHING TO CHANCE; TAKE NOTHING FOR GRANTED

Still recovering from the impact of the Griffiss base closure announcement, community leaders in Rome were hit two years later with a 1995 DoD recommendation to close another major military asset—Rome Laboratory, later known as Air Force Research Laboratory (AFRL). The community overcame the threat by challenging DoD's contention that the closure would save money, and the lab remained in Rome. Another government recommendation resulted in some good news—a military finance and accounting center would move into the new business park that was once Griffiss Air Force Base.

The close call over Rome's lab was a sobering experience. The lab was the lynchpin for the region's economic revitalization plan. It employed top scientists and computer engineers who developed cutting-edge technology for the Air Force, including combat communication systems, cyber security, and other warfare technologies. The lab's work rippled through the community's economy; partnerships with outside technology contractors that located nearby brought more technology businesses to the area.

Much of the technology developed at Rome lab had immediate practical applications for air combat missions. Special operations forces in Iraq used Rome-developed technologies to identify patterns of insurgent activity. Intelligence analysts also used new technology to intercept and crack terrorist communications.[20]

Having overturned the 1995 BRACC proposal, business and community leaders realized as BRACC 2005 approached that a strategy and a plan were needed to keep this economic engine in Rome. Nothing could be left to chance and nothing taken for granted. The region's chief economic development agency, Mohawk Valley Economic Development Growth Enterprises Corporation (EDGE), took the lead role in developing the strategy.

In addition to the research lab, the Rome region had two other military assets that needed protection—the Northeast Air Defense Sector and the Defense Finance and Accounting Service. Together the three facilities provided 1,600 jobs, not counting hundreds of additional private sector industry jobs. The regional economic impact was $246 million annually. All three military operations were located at the now closed Griffiss Air Force Base.[21]

The Rome research site of the Air Force Research Lab (AFRL) is one of 10 AFRL locations across the country and is headquarters for the AFRL Information Directorate, a high-tech cyber systems research center. It also housed a smaller unit of the AFRL Sensors Directorate that conducted research on radar systems for the Air Force. More than 100 large and small businesses and 95 universities were under contract with the Rome research site in 2005.[22]

The Northeast Air Defense Sector, operated by the New York Air National Guard and also located at the now closed Griffiss Air Force base, tracked all aircraft flying into and through the northeastern quadrant of the United States. Its mission and value were easier to understand after the terror attacks of 9/11. It was not a likely target for realignment or closure by the DoD.

The Defense Finance and Accounting Service center, however, was a target for consolidation because there were other finance and accounting centers that could absorb the work. Defense staff analysts felt that it could save money by moving this facility to another one. This military operation processes military payroll and travel vouchers and pays military contractors. The DoD proposal recommended that the 24 centers be consolidated into three megacenters and that 21 centers, including Rome, be closed.[23]

LESSONS LEARNED

As the target of two previous base closings and realignment recommendations, the community, led by EDGE, developed a comprehensive plan involving political and community leaders. Anticipating Rome would be the target of a future closure proposal, it had focused for years on meeting the military's criteria: efficiency and military value.[24]

Creating highly cost-efficient military operations was accomplished through unique partnerships with local government and the private sector. The city of Rome offered to maintain the Griffiss water and sewer lines and its roads, including winter plowing. To further reduce costs, the electricity and steam heat at Griffiss Business and Technology Park were privatized. Further partnerships were established through the creation of a nonprofit organization called the Griffiss Institute, which worked with colleges, private companies, and the government to address common problems involving cyber security issues.

The Rome AFRL was updated in 2004 by consolidating the lab's previous 10 aging buildings scattered over the former base into a more compact three-building complex with two new state-of-the-art buildings as its hub.[25] For the first time in years, its engineers and scientists were in a modern building together, further increasing work efficiencies. The building was funded through a unique federal-state partnership aided by congressman Sherwood Boehlert, who obtained $13 million in federal funds, and state grants that provided $12 million.[26]

Boehlert and U.S. senators Hillary Clinton and Charles Schumer of New York obtained an additional $120 million in federal allocations to fund projects at the three facilities,[27] and New York governor George Pataki designated the Rome lab a key partner in building a state emergency preparedness center in the region. The battlefield technology AFRL developed, officials said, could also be used in the war against terror. In the

Courtesy of Mohawk Valley EDGE

New York Senators Hillary Rodham Clinton and Charles Schumer and Governor George Pataki provide testimony to BRACC commissioners.

10 years since Griffiss Air Force Base closed, more than $252 million in private and public money had been invested in Griffiss Business and Technology Park.[28]

Military value was demonstrated by clearly articulating the importance of each facility as it related to the DoD's criteria. A war chest was developed to hire experts to defend Rome's military assets. Some traditional tactics were not considered. Efforts such as the massive 20,000-person rally held in the early 1990s when Griffiss Air Force Base was scheduled to close had little effect on BRACC's ultimate decision. What mattered were facts, not emotions.

Instead, the community was asked to invest their energies in raising money for number crunchers, military analysts, public relations specialists, and lobbyists. An $800,000 campaign fund was assembled from private, local, and state partners, said Steven J. DiMeo, Mohawk Valley EDGE president.

The region's elected officials and governor invited high-ranking military officials to tour the new facilities at the lab. Area officials also traveled to Washington, DC, to meet with others involved in the decision-making process to reinforce the military value of Rome's operations.

Other factors such as an abundant workforce, affordable housing, several area colleges, available space for expansion, and continued support from local and state governments were other efficiencies communicated to decision makers.

RUMSFELD'S RECOMMENDATIONS

Secretary of Defense Rumsfeld's May 13, 2005, recommendation included:[29]

- Moving 130 jobs from the Air Force's Sensors Directorate at Rome to the sensors headquarters at Wright-Patterson Air Force Base in Ohio. Other labs in Arizona and Texas were also recommended to relocate to Wright-Patterson.
- Moving 380 jobs from the Defense Finance and Accounting Service to three planned megacenters. Several similar facilities throughout the country were affected.

Rumsfeld's recommendations were forwarded to the Base Realignment and Closure Commission. Members of the BRACC visited many sites and held public hearings and teleconferences with local leaders.

ROME'S RESPONSE

Rumsfeld's recommendations were potentially devastating, but this time Rome was ready with a plan. Rome's response was aided by several high-profile lobbying and law firms specializing in BRACC issues, including the Washington, DC, lobbying firm Hyjek & Fix and the Akin Gump law firm. Akin Gump had influential people such as former congressman Bill Paxon, former chairman of the National Republican Congressional Committee, with active political ties. Another consulting and lobbying firm, Park Strategies, included former U.S. senator Alfonse D'Amato.

"We learned from past BRACC investigations that we had to be more strategic," said DiMeo, president of Mohawk Valley EDGE, the lead organization in the campaign to save military jobs. Information is power in these types of investigative situations. The goal was to provide accurate and persuasive information to the analysts and other staff members working for BRACC during their investigation.

The challenge was to build positive relationships with the people who were in charge of analyzing and assessing Rome's military facilities. "When a staffer seemed interested in what we had to say, we kept feeding that person more facts to boost our case," DiMeo said.

Mohawk Valley EDGE managed to form relationships with two of the nine BRACC commissioners during the investigative phase of the commission: Samuel Skinner and General Lloyd "Fig" Newton. A staff member of Newton seemed particularly sensitive to the economic impact the closure of the finance and accounting center could have on the local economy, DiMeo said. "We knew we were on Newton's radar screen when he came to visit . . . he was hearing our arguments."

The relationship with Skinner began when a law firm associate of Skinner arranged a teleconference between Skinner and members of the community team. After talking, Commissioner Skinner offered

DiMeo his unpublished e-mail address, the one he personally paid attention to for his BRACC work.

State and local elected officials did their part to gather information about the ongoing investigation, reinforce key messages, and refute any errors in the DoD's original proposal. Congressman Boehlert, Senator Clinton, and Governor Pataki talked to nearly every commissioner about the merits of Rome's military facilities. Senator Schumer also lobbied two commissioners. State Assemblywoman RoAnn Destito, representing the Rome area, helped set up the teleconference with Skinner. Other opportunities to address four commissioners face to face came at a regional BRACC conference held in Buffalo, New York, and during a visit to Rome by Commissioner Newton.

Mohawk Valley EDGE's vice president of marketing and communications Rob Duchow coordinated the communication strategies with the help of the Marino Organization, a New York City public relations agency, and HR&A, a public policy and consulting firm. HR&A helped develop the core arguments while the Marino Organization assisted with developing the talking points that were repeated in numerous support documents and publications.

The research and facts to support Rome's military assets had to be simple and easy to grasp since BRACC commissioners were trying to sort through hundreds of other arguments from other communities. To coordinate the communications effort and drive home the value and importance of the Rome lab (AFRL) and DFAS to the community and military, several communication tactics were used:

- White papers on economic impact and military value
- Economic impact analysis reports
- Fact sheets with graphics and photos on talking points
- PowerPoint presentations for BRACC commission presentations

- Rome research facilities informational DVD and posters
- Local media relations

During the commission's investigation, hundreds of communities fought to protect their military assets, a process that often pitted one community against another. For example, one community with a larger Air Force base floated a plan to take Rome lab's (AFRL) entire information research mission (with the sensors division moving to another base). To sweeten the pot, that community also promised to build a $410 million base if its proposal was accepted.[30]

Mohawk Valley EDGE, the economic development agency for the region, developed a rapid response strategy to counteract outside threats. It hired consultants to track any new proposals coming from other communities or any new BRACC activities, such as visits to other communities with similar military installations. This information was shared with elected representatives who lobbied decision makers.

Rome supporters also carefully examined their opportunities and made their own counterproposals. In particular, Rome supporters questioned the rationale for sending 125 cyber systems research jobs at Wright-Patterson Air Force Base to another base when the Rome lab was the designated national headquarters for that research and had room to accommodate the extra jobs.

The Griffiss Local Development Corporation created an "issues paper" (white paper) that argued for both the cyber and sensors research missions staying at Rome because it had the most cost-efficient and effective research teams in the country. The proposal was vigorously lobbied among BRACC members and the commission's staff.

BRACC'S FINAL RECOMMENDATION

The hard work paid off. When BRACC voted August 25, 2005, it was mostly good news for Rome. While BRACC did not reverse DoD's recommendation to ship 125 jobs connected with sensors research division from Rome to Wright-Patterson Air Force Base, it did agree that another 140 cyber-related research jobs also at Wright-Patterson AFB should not go to Hanscom Air Force Base in Massachusetts, but should go to Rome research lab (AFRL) instead.[31] BRACC also agreed that Rome's Defense Finance and Accounting Service facility was efficient and should, in fact, expand. It was recommended that the facility grow to no fewer than 1,000 jobs, an addition of 620 new jobs from another facility.[32]

TIMELINE

- 1993: BRACC recommends the closure of Griffiss Air Force Base in Rome, New York.
- 1995: Griffiss Air Force Base in Rome, New York, closes.
- 1995: Department of Defense and BRACC recommend closing the Air Force's Rome laboratory (AFRL). The lab successfully defends itself to BRACC and remains open; the Department of Defense recommends creating a military finance and accounting center at the redeveloped former Griffiss Air Force Base.
- Post 1995: Redevelopment of the now closed Griffiss Air Force Base includes building on the existing strengths of its Air Force Research Lab, its military finance and accounting facility, and the Northeast Air Defense Sector. The local redevelopment agency created many private and nonprofit synergies by partnering them with the Air Force Research Lab. Additional businesses also occupy the former Air Force base.
- May 13, 2005: Initial Department of Defense military recommendations; Rome's research lab and finance and accounting center are targeted.
- June 22, 2005: BRACC Commissioner Lloyd Newton visits Rome, New York.

- June 27, 2005: Griffiss representatives present information to four BRACC members at the regional BRACC hearing in Buffalo, New York.
- July 2005: Griffiss officials give teleconference presentation to BRACC's Samuel Skinner.
- July 25, 2005: Griffiss Local Development Corporation sends issues paper to BRACC (colocation of both research directorates "enhances military value" because the Rome lab is one of the most cost-effective installations in the country).
- August 25, 2005: Final recommendations of BRACC sends 125 jobs from the Sensors Directorate to Wright-Patterson AFB in Dayton, Ohio. The 140 Information Directorate jobs located at Wright-Patterson were relocated to Rome. The Defense Finance and Accounting Service facility in Rome would remain and grow to no less than 1,000 jobs, an addition of 620 jobs.

Questions for Discussion

1. What were the initial Department of Defense recommendations that involved the Rome, New York, area? What military assets were threatened by the proposal?

2. What is the role of the Base Realignment and Closure Commission?

3. What was the strategy to protect the community's military assets?

4. What were the community's strategic publics?

5. What role did research and communication play in this effort to protect the military assets? Describe specific tactics used.

6. What was the result of this public information campaign for Rome's military assets?

Do Some Research

Find the nearest military installation that has been the target of the Department of Defense and the Base Realignment and Closure Commission for closure or realignment. Examine the marketing communication and public relations strategies to protect the military installation. Compare the strategy to that used for Rome lab. What were the unique and effective characteristics of the campaign?

Terminology

- AFRL
- BRACC
- DFAS
- economic impact analysis
- lobbying
- Mohawk Valley EDGE
- realignment
- talking points
- white paper

Web Resources

- **Defense Base Realignment and Closure Commission** www.brac.gov/
- **Department of Defense Base Realignment and Closure 2005** www.defenselink.mil/brac/
- **Air Force Research Lab, Information Directorate at Rome, New York** www.rl.af.mil/
- **Mohawk Valley EDGE** www.mvedge.org/index.asp
- **Griffiss Business and Technology Park** griffiss.mvedge.org/index.asp
- **Rome, New York** romenewyork.com/index.asp

Welcome to Your New Job

Rebuilding a City's Damaged Reputation

You are the mayor's newly appointed public affairs director for your small city. The city has never had a person in charge of public relations before. Until your arrival, the job of communicating with the news media had been delegated to individual city offices with varying degrees of success. Usually, news releases were issued by individual department secretaries—or not at all. However, a string of small crises involving problems with city services led to several embarrassing stories in the local media. The lack of coordinated, responsive communication left the city looking incompetent at best and open to expensive legal action at worst.

The mistakes (many unintentionally humorous) had spread beyond the local media. The Associated Press picked up and distributed some of the more unfortunate stories, sending them to a national audience.

The bad publicity had demoralized a mostly dedicated, hard-working city hall staff and infuriated business leaders and concerned residents. The situation prompted the city council to approve funding for your position. With most council members constantly looking for places to cut the city budget to keep taxes low, creating a new position in the mayor's office is seen as a significant step.

You are responsible for developing and providing basic information about the city and being on call whenever the news media want information on city services. Duties include researching and writing news releases about city council activities and city departments, and providing information for the city's Web site. You also are in charge of a monthly employee newsletter. While funding for your office is limited, the bad publicity has made the council and mayor very receptive to the concept of good public relations. In this climate, your ideas will be heard and seriously considered.

You are a graduate of the local college's public relations program. At a recent community event, you see one of your former public relations teachers, and she asks how things are going with the new job. As the discussion progresses, she invites you to visit her class next semester to talk to students about public relations in city government. This gives you an idea: You ask if the teacher would be interested in involving her class in a project. After hearing your ideas, she enthusiastically agrees. The class will be divided into two teams, and each will be given a challenge. Hopefully, the team approach to problem solving will give you some valuable ideas that you can put into practice.

TEAM CHALLENGE ONE—THE INTERNAL CHALLENGE

The mayor and city council expect the creation of your position will result in improved city employee morale. Since the city's public affairs office is new and unfamiliar to most employees, you need a plan to explain what your office does and how employees should use your services. As a one-person department, you can't do everything—so how would you:

- **Manage to provide coordinated and effective public relations services internally? What communication policies would you implement so that the city communicates with one voice?**

- **Establish good working relationships with city departments? How would you build employee morale?**

- **Keep the mayor and city council members informed of your activities so that they know they are getting a good return on investment?**

- **Do research that would help you?**

Your team needs to create a plan for handling all these questions. To assist you with this project, look at your own city's structure and public affairs office. If you cannot locate a public affairs function in your own city government, you may have to look at larger cities or state government departments with a public affairs function for potential models for your plan.

TEAM CHALLENGE TWO—THE EXTERNAL CHALLENGE

The mayor and city council expect to see the city's image improve as a result of creating the public affairs office. One of the first tasks is to begin establishing good media relations and provide positive stories to the media on a regular basis.

- **How will you create a strong media relations program? You are also** expected to work with the city's economic development department to attract new businesses and promote successful companies already located in the city.
- Since there is no official tourism department for the city, you will also need to fill that role. What could you do to get the ball rolling for the city's tourism efforts? What research will help you with these tasks?

To assist you with this project, look at your own city's structure, especially its public affairs office. If you cannot locate a public affairs function in your own city government, you may have to look at state government departments with a public affairs function for potential models for your plan.

Abu Ghraib: Part 1
Public Affairs and the Iraqi Prisoner Abuse Scandal

During Saddam Hussein's reign, Iraqis had good reason to fear Abu Ghraib prison. Located approximately 20 miles west of Baghdad, it was the final stop for thousands of Iraqi political prisoners and other enemies of the regime; ordinary Iraqis viewed it as a loathsome symbol of Saddam's notorious system of torture and repression. After the U.S.-led coalition's invasion, the prison's death chamber and its double hanging room were displayed to the world as damning proof of Saddam's cruelty.[33] U.S. officials estimated that as many as 30,000 criminal and political prisoners were hanged during the Saddam years.[34]

When graphic photographs of Iraqi prisoner abuse by American soldiers were shown on television around the world a year later—it seemed unbelievable. But seeing was believing. For critics of American policy in the region, the depraved situations

Courtesy of Salon.com's Abu Ghraib Files

depicted in the photos provided evidence of an occupational force that was cruel and seemingly no better than Saddam's reign of terror.

Part 1 of this case study examines the background factors leading up to the abuse, the subsequent investigation launched, and how the Army public affairs staff handled the information dissemination strategy.

BACKGROUND

As part of the war on terror, Operation Iraqi Freedom began with massive air strikes against Baghdad on March 19, 2003.[35] Within six weeks, the American-led multinational force had taken control of Iraq's cities, and major combat operations were declared over.[36] Organized Iraqi resistance, however, continued with daily attacks against American, British, and other multinational coalition troops. It was a dangerous and chaotic place.

Abu Ghraib became one of several coalition detention centers used to contain thousands of detainees held on suspicion of anti-coalition activities. The chaotic nature of the war often meant there were no formal charges against detainees and their access to relatives and lawyers was restricted.[37] Military officials at the time said detainees were treated in accordance with international law and had access to the International Committee of the Red Cross.[38]

Abu Ghraib detainees included both suspected insurgents and common criminals. Those labeled "MI Hold" were interrogated by military intelligence (MI), seeking information about insurgent leaders, their networks, and plans of impending attacks.

Military police (MP) in detention centers were trained to maintain security and order and provide detainees' basic needs. During normal interaction with detainees, passive intelligence gathering, such as overheard conversations, was encouraged and passed onto military intelligence for use during interrogations.[39]

The 800th MP Brigade, comprising eight MP battalions, had been stationed at another Iraqi detention facility during the initial phase of the war. When major combat operations ceased in May, many soldiers thought they would be sent home.[40] Instead, the brigade was given a new mission: management of the Iraqi penal system and several detention centers, including Abu Ghraib.[41]

Abu Ghraib was a tough assignment for the 320th Military Police Battalion of the 800th MP Brigade that took charge of between 6,000 and 7,000 detainees in late May 2004.[42] Official investigations would later note the battalion lacked effective leadership, was severely under strength for an overcrowded detainee population, inadequately trained for detainee operations, and was often under attack from mortar shells, small arms, and rocket-propelled grenades.[43] Not surprisingly, morale was low and discipline was lax.[44]

Despite earlier reports of detainee abuse by four members of the 320th battalion at its previous assignment at Camp Bucca, Iraq, later investigations could find no evidence that MPs received adequate training on the requirements of the Geneva Conventions, which govern prisoner of war and detainee treatment.[45]

A growing insurgency at the time increased the demand for "actionable intelligence" from suspected insurgents under control of U.S. forces.[46] According to later investigations, this already troubled battalion was further compromised when MPs began to aid the interrogation process by setting "favorable conditions for subsequent interviews" of high-value detainees for the military intelligence brigade at Abu Ghraib.[47] While the "softening up" of detainees ran counter to the MPs' mission to maintain order and security at the detention facility, conflicting commands from superior officers blurred the fine line between military police and military intelligence stationed together.[48]

The combination of circumstances made a difficult wartime environment chaotic and set the stage for excessive detainee abuse between October and December 2003 at Abu Ghraib.

In October 2003, 24-year-old Army Spc. Joseph Darby, a member of the 320th Military Police Battalion, arrived in Abu Ghraib. According to the *New York Times* and military documents, shortly after his arrival, a friend showed him an image captured by a digital camera: The photo showed a naked prisoner chained to his cell, his arms above his head. The soldier told Darby how he enjoyed the abuse.[49] It didn't take long for Darby to discover this was not an isolated incident. Knowing the treatment was morally wrong, he reported the detainee abuse on January 13, 2004; his initial report included a CD full of photos. The next day, the military's Criminal Investigation Division (CID) launched a criminal investigation.

Internally, the seriousness of the CID's ongoing investigation prompted Lt. Gen. Ricardo Sanchez, commander of Joint Task Force-7, to request a high-ranking investigating officer to conduct a broader administrative review of the 800th Military Police Brigade's detention and internment operations. Led by Maj. Gen. Antonio Taguba, the probe would be followed by several other military and independent investigations.

The first news release came January 16, 2004, from Headquarters U.S. Central Command (Centcom) with a Baghdad dateline:[50]

An investigation has been initiated into reported incidents of detainee abuse at a Coalition Forces detention facility. The release of specific information concerning the incidents could hinder the investigation, which is in its early stages. The investigation will be conducted in a thorough and professional manner. The Coalition is committed to treating all persons under its control with dignity,

respect and humanity. Lt. Gen. Ricardo S. Sanchez, the Commanding General, has reiterated this requirement to all members of CJTF-7.

During the initial Taguba investigation, completed at the end of February, there were few news media reports about detainee abuse, although reporters were hearing rumors. Reporters knew something was afoot when 17 U.S. soldiers were suspended from duty pending the outcome of an alleged prisoner abuse investigation February 23, 2004. More information was delayed due to the ongoing investigation until the March 20, 2004, Coalition Provisional Authority briefing in Baghdad by General Mark Kimmitt:[51]

As you know, on 14 January 2004, a criminal investigation was initiated to examine allegations of detainee abuse at the Baghdad confinement facility at Abu Ghraib. Shortly thereafter, the commanding general of Combined Joint Task Force Seven requested a separate administrative investigation into systemic issues such as command policies and internal procedures related to detention operations. That administrative investigation is complete; however, the findings and recommendations have not been approved. As a result of the criminal investigation, six military personnel have been charged with criminal offenses to include conspiracy, dereliction of duty, cruelty and maltreatment, assault, and indecent acts with another.

The coalition takes all reports of detainee abuse seriously, and all allegations of mistreatment are investigated. We are committed to treating all persons under coalition control with dignity, respect and humanity. Coalition personnel are expected to act appropriately, humanely, and in a manner consistent with the Geneva Conventions. Lieutenant General Sanchez has reinforced this requirement to all members of CJTF-7.

Kimmitt's opening remarks led to the following questions from the news media:[52]

Question: General, when were those six MPs charged? What are they alleged to have done? Were they all in the same unit? And what's the maximum penalty for these crimes? And anything else you want to tell us about it.

General Kimmitt: I'll take the first two questions on. They were charged with those crimes today. Those charges were preferred on them. There were six involved. And as I said in the statement, the charges were, as I said, they were all separate articles in the Uniform Code of Military Justice. We'll be able to provide that after the press conference.

I don't want to at this point because the charges have only been preferred and not referred. In other words, we have not done the military equivalent of a grand jury investigation at this point. That is the point, at the end of that Article 32 investigation, that grand jury, if those charges are referred for trial, that would be the point at which we would start providing information with regard to their unit, their names, so on and so forth. But it's just not appropriate to do it at this time.

Question: But they're going to an Article 32, and they're all charged in the same episode, sir?

General Kimmitt: They are all being charged—I don't know if each one is being charged with all the same counts. We can have a lawyer sit down with you perhaps in a day or so and

go over which ones are being charged. Nonetheless, I don't believe they're— all six are being charged with all those counts. It's just a range. And, again, I'm not a lawyer—I have no idea what the maximum penalty for all of that is . . .

Question: Were the six people—were they doing abuse on the same person, or is it six different cases of abuse? And also, what are the—where are they at the moment? Are they being held in detention?

General Kimmitt: We believe that this was a small number of detainees, less than 20, that were involved in this. The persons, as we talked about a couple of months ago, they have been suspended from their duties.

They are working administrative duties. They are still here in country, and they have been moved over to other duties pending the outcome of the investigation, and now pending the outcome of any further deliberations.

Question: Sir, it's Guy from CNN. A question for General Kimmitt. What's the reason for the shut down of the Abu-Ghraib prison, not allowing any journalists in to see what is—what's actually happening inside? It's sort of seems to be getting a similar sort of reputation to what it had during Saddam's time in the moment.

General Kimmitt: We—we traditionally treat—we don't legally classify, but we treat the detainees similar to the manner that we would treat enemy prisoners of war. The Geneva Convention, which is our guideline for that, specifically prohibits making detainees, making prisoners of war subject to public curiosity and humiliation, and so that's why we feel it's important that we follow the procedures and allow the ICRC in for routine investigation, routine inspections—health, welfare— to assure that we're doing everything in accordance with the Geneva

Conventions, but it is not a matter of practice to allow journalists into those kinds of facilities.
Question: Just a follow-up—Jim Clancy with CNN. I mean, if you're treating—are they de facto, then, prisoners of war under the Geneva Conventions? They are not, are they?
General Kimmitt: They are not, but they are being—
Question: Well, then why—you know, in any other democracy, you would allow journalists into a prison to examine the conditions, if there were large public issues involved—and I think that there are large public issues involved just because of this investigation you've announced. So—
General Kimmitt: What I would—what I'd ask you to do is go to the International Committee of the Red Cross. They would be more than happy to provide you with their findings, that they do on a regular and routine basis. And I think that you would find from their investigations that that is not the case.

One news report at the time quoted Kimmitt's characterizing the alleged abuse as "the kind of cancer that you have to cut out quickly. You've got to address it very, very quickly."[53]

Two days later, when a reporter told Kimmitt during a coalition news briefing session that the Red Cross had a policy of not speaking "specifically because they know that they will be denied access if they do," Kimmitt replied:[54]

. . . if that's their policy, that's their policy. It remains our policy that we will not subject the detainees in Abu Gharib or any of our detention facilities to public humiliation or ridicule. And as a result, we will continue to treat them in a manner consistent with that, as we treat enemy prisoners of war under the Geneva Conventions. . .

In February, the International Committee of the Red Cross (ICRC) issued a confidential report about unlawful Iraqi detention conditions to top coalition authorities.[55] Based on ICRC observations and private interviews of detainees at Iraqi prisons, including Abu Ghraib, from March through November 2003, the report noted:[56]

According to the allegations collected by the ICRC, ill treatment during interrogation was not systematic, except with regard to persons arrested in connection with suspected security offences or deemed to have an "intelligence" value. In these cases, persons deprived of their liberty under supervision of the Military Intelligence were at high risk of being subjected to a variety of harsh treatments ranging from insults, threats and humiliations to both physical and psychological coercion, which in some cases was tantamount to torture, in order to force cooperation with their interrogators.

The February 22-page ICRC report provided specific instances of abuse:[57]

In certain cases, such as in Abu Ghraib military intelligence section, methods of physical and psychological coercion used by interrogators appeared to be part of the standard operating procedures by military intelligence personnel to obtain confessions and extract information. Several military intelligence officers confirmed to the ICRC that it was part of the military intelligence process to hold a person deprived of his liberty naked in a completely dark and empty cell for a prolonged period, to use inhumane and degrading treatment, including physical and psychological coercion, against persons deprived of their liberty to secure their cooperation.

The ICRC's report also noted that some detainees were humiliated when forced to wear women's underwear over their heads "while being laughed at by guards, including female guards, and sometimes photographed in this position."[58]

CNN quoted a Pentagon source on March 20, 2004, saying the CID had seized some computer drives in search of photographs and other evidence of prisoner abuse from the accused.[59] Other news reports said the photographs contained partially nude prisoners and "inappropriate physical contact between soldiers and detainees."[60] Subsequent coalition briefings by Kimmitt did not reveal more details about the investigation.

The secret Taguba investigative report, which built on the CID's initial investigation, was completed and began circulating up the "chain of command" on March 3. The report said "numerous incidents of sadistic, blatant, and wanton criminal abuses were inflicted on several detainees." Incidents cited by the report included:[61]

- Videotaping and photographing naked male and female detainees
- Forcibly arranging detainees in various sexually explicit positions for photographing
- Forcing detainees to remove their clothing and keeping them naked for several days at a time
- Forcing naked male detainees to wear women's underwear
- Forcing groups of male detainees to masturbate themselves while being photographed and videotaped
- Arranging naked male detainees in a pile and then jumping on them
- Placing a dog chain or strap around a naked detainee's neck and having a female soldier pose for a picture
- Using military dogs (without muzzles) to intimidate and frighten detainees and, in at least one case, biting and severely injuring a detainee

Taguba's report also found other credible detainee accounts and supporting evidence on other abuses:[62]

- Breaking chemical lights and pouring the phosphoric liquid on detainees
- Threatening detainees with a charged 9 mm pistol
- Sodomizing a detainee with a chemical light and perhaps a broom
- Threatening male detainees with rape

Because the report was classified secret, the public and the news media were unaware of the extreme graphic depictions of abuse. Apparently, the photos' implications were not known by the White House administration or Secretary of Defense Donald Rumsfeld.[63]

With little to go on, the news media were busy investigating. The CBS newsmagazine *60 Minutes II* was the first to obtain and broadcast copies of the elusive photos.

Citing severe repercussions the story might cause for U.S. troops on the ground in Iraq, the Department of Defense and chairman of the Joint Chiefs of Staff general Richard Myers asked CBS to delay airing its story.[64] CBS held off for two weeks until April 28, 2004, just before other stories were printed or aired.

The first effort by the military to manage the story came from General Mark Kimmitt in Baghdad during a Coalition Provisional Authority news briefing hours before *60 Minutes II* aired its story:[65]

General Kimmitt: Finally, as you remember, in January it was announced that a criminal investigation was initiated to examine allegations of detainee abuse at the Baghdad confinement facility at Abu Ghraib. The Criminal Investigation Division began when an American soldier reported and turned over evidence of criminal activity to include photographs of detainee abuse. CBS television has acquired these images and may show some of the evidence tonight on 60 Minutes II.

Shortly after the criminal investigation began, Lieutenant General Sanchez, the commanding general, requested a separate administrative investigation into systemic issues such as command policies and internal procedures related to detention operations. That administrative investigation is complete. Lieutenant General Sanchez has also directed a follow-up investigation of interrogation procedures in detention facilities, and that investigation is ongoing.

Again, as a result of the criminal investigation, six military personnel have been charged with criminal offenses.

The coalition takes all reports of detainee abuse seriously and all allegations of mistreatment are investigated. We are committed to treating all persons under coalition custody with dignity, respect and humanity. Coalition personnel are expected to act appropriately, humanely and in a manner consistent with Geneva Conventions.[66]

Question: Can you give us more information and detail about those people?

General Kimmitt: . . . I'm afraid I don't have any more details than what was initially reported this afternoon, that—as I stated earlier. With regards to the six personnel that were charged with criminal counts against them back in January, we can go over that, along with Christine, after this press conference so I can get all that information for you. We typically do not reveal their names. As we've said in the press conference when this was announced, we would wait until the Article 32 investigations were complete before a decision was made whether their names would in fact be revealed.

Question: Is it true that we have reports that some of them have just used pictures in torturing the detainees? What is your role in order to take care of those detainees? And where is the security, your security, especially giving them chances to have all these pictures and also to show it to the public? So can't you just tell us why this happened?

General Kimmitt: Yeah. And that's exactly why we had the investigation. Let's start from the beginning. In early January, a soldier came forward at Abu Ghraib Prison. That soldier said, "There are some things going on here that I can't live with. I am aware of some activities that are being conducted by the guards and some of the interrogators that are inconsistent with my job and inconsistent with my values as a soldier." That soldier came forward. He presented evidence to his chain of command. The chain of command brought it forward. General Sanchez, upon hearing it, immediately started a criminal investigation.

I don't remember the exact date I stood in front of this podium and talked about the outcome of that investigation. So that outcome is now—has resulted in criminal charges being levied against six soldiers.

To answer your other question, this does not reflect the vast majority of coalition soldiers, vast majority of American soldiers that are operating out of Abu Ghraib Prison. We have had thousands, tens of thousands of detainees in Abu Ghraib. We have understood that a very, very small number were involved in this incident, and of the hundreds and hundreds of guards they have out there, a small number were involved in the guards.

I'm not going to stand up here and make excuses for those soldiers. I'm not going to stand up here and apologize for those soldiers. If what they did is proven in a court of law, that is incompatible with the values we stand for as *a professional military force, and it's values that we don't stand for as human beings. They will be tried before a court, and then those decisions will be made.*

CBS's *60 Minutes II* "Abuse of Iraqi POWs by GIs Probed" showed many startling photos of the detainee abuse at Abu Ghraib.[67]

One photo showed a hooded detainee on a box of meals ready to eat (MREs) with wires attached to his hands. According to the broadcast, he was told he would be electrocuted if he fell. Other photographs showed naked prisoners hooded and piled in a human pyramid, next to smiling female MPs.

Not only had photographs been leaked to the press, but the top-secret Taguba report had been as well. Soon after the CBS *60 Minutes II* report, excerpts of Taguba's report showed up in the news media, including the highly regarded *New Yorker* magazine; its article entitled "Torture at Abu Ghraib" was written by Seymour M. Hersh, the Pulitzer Prize winner who investigated Vietnam's My Lai massacre. His article had detainee abuse photos and contained an in-depth analysis of the Taguba report that revealed severe "institutional failures of the Army prison system."[68]

Questions for Discussion

1. How would you characterize the public relations model used by the military staff in this case?

2. What constraints do military public affairs officers work under? In times of war, what are some of the special considerations?

3. One military news release announcing the abuse investigation was released just prior to the April 28, 2004, CBS report. Why? What was the communication strategy?

4. The coalition briefings led by military spokesperson General Mark Kimmitt provided little information about the

investigation in his introductory remarks. He did provide more information when directly asked by reporters. Was this an effective communication strategy?

5. Reporters knew investigations were underway about the detainee abuse, and rumors about detainee abuse photos began to circulate in news reports on March 20, the day of the announced criminal charges against six soldiers. Do you think the military had a plan for the potential leak of these photos or the investigative reports? What would you do differently?

6. CBS and the *New Yorker* magazine were the first to obtain detainee abuse photos and the military's classified Taguba report. What would be your planned response to these reports? Who would you select as the main spokesperson? What would you say? Who would be the primary audiences you need to reach?

7. The military and government are known for their reliance on euphemisms to mask some of the unpleasant realities of war. Provide some examples from this case study or from news releases.

Do Some Research

1. The majority of official information about the Abu Ghraib scandal came from oral briefings between military spokespersons and the news media. There was just one news release issued by U.S. Central Command that announced on January 16, 2003, the detainee abuse investigation. What, if any, communication techniques would you use to communicate the U.S. government's story? Explain why.

2. Research both sides of the debate on interrogating prisoners of war and suspected insurgents or terrorists in the global war on terrorism. Is there ever a time when extreme interrogation practices (those not sanctioned

by the Geneva Conventions) could be justified?

Terminology

- military police
- military intelligence
- public affairs
- Geneva Conventions
- Uniform Code of Military Justice
- Article 32 of the Uniform Code of Military Justice
- coalition briefing
- Criminal Investigation Division

Web Resources

- **Department of Defense Detainee Investigations** (contains links to several official documents, including many of the investigative reports and briefings, related to the abuse scandal) www.defenselink.mil/news/detainee_investigations.html

- **Taguba Report** www.globalsecurity.org/intell/library/reports/2004/800-mp-bde.htm

- **Uniform Code of Military Justice** www.au.af.mil/au/awc/awcgate/ucmj.htm

- **CBS 60 Minutes II "Abuse of Iraqi POWs by GIs Probed"** www.cbsnews.com/stories/2004/04/27/60II/main614063.shtml

- **The New Yorker "Torture at Abu Ghraib"** by Seymour M. Hersh www.newyorker.com/printables/fact/040510fa_fact

- **Geneva Conventions** (Office of the United Nations High Commissioner of Human Rights) www.unhchr.ch/html/menu3/b/91.htm

Abu Ghraib: Part 2

Damage Control: The U.S. Government's Response

In Part 1 of this case study, you were introduced to the initial public announcements and some of the findings of a secret investigation of the detainee abuse scandal at Abu Ghraib. In Part 2, the author examines in some detail the responses of the U.S. military, the White House, and the Department of Defense during the first week after CBS's *60 Minutes II* story was released.

This case study does not include all the official responses; what follows are representative examples from the official "chain of command" that is inherent to military operations. Included are comments and actions of the Joint Coalition in Iraq to the Department of Defense and ultimately the chief of the Armed Forces, President Bush. Not included in this analysis are comments from congressional leaders, the 2004 Democratic presidential candidate John Kerry, and nonmilitary experts.

APRIL 30, 2004—PRESIDENT GEORGE BUSH (WHITE HOUSE)

Two days after the *60 Minutes II* broadcast, President George W. Bush and Canadian Prime Minister Paul Martin held a "press availability" event in the White House Rose Garden. A reporter asked President Bush for his reaction to the photos of U.S. soldiers abusing Iraqi prisoners:[69]

Yes, I shared a deep disgust that those prisoners were treated the way they were treated. Their treatment does not reflect the nature of the American people. That's not the way we do things in America. And so I—I didn't like it one bit.

But I also want to remind people that those few people who did that do not reflect the nature of the men and women we've sent overseas. That's not the way the people are, that's not their character, that are serving our nation in the cause of freedom. And there will be an investigation. I think—they'll be taken care of.

APRIL 30, 2004—WHITE HOUSE SPOKESPERSON (WHITE HOUSE)

Later that afternoon at a White House press briefing, White House spokesperson Scott McClellan reiterated Bush's disgust when he saw the photos and repeated that the incidents did not reflect the "great work of the vast majority—the 99 percent of our men and women in uniform who are committed to upholding the values that America holds dear."[70] He said that the president did not know about the Department of Defense request to CBS to delay airing its story. He also noted that the military was "pursuing criminal charges. They are looking at additional criminal charges. And we need to let that process work."[71]

APRIL 30, 2004—JOINT COALITION MEDIA BRIEFING (IRAQ)

At the same time in Iraq, General Kimmitt was answering more questions from reporters at his April 30 briefing:[72]

Question: Quinn O'Toole (sp) with NPR. Arabic television stations began broadcasting pictures of prisoners and detainees that were abused at Abu Ghraib today. What are you planning to do, and what can you do to counter those images that are now being seen by large portions of the Iraqi people?

General Kimmitt: That's a very good question. I talked with the Arab press two nights ago, before the 60 Minutes show was broadcast because I wanted the Arab press to understand and possibly communicate to their fellow Iraqis a couple of key points. Number one, we are absolutely appalled by what

we saw. There is no excuse for what you see in those photos. And I'm not going to stand up here and try to apologize for what those soldiers did. As I've said before, those soldiers wear the same uniform as 150,000 other soldiers that are operating proudly and properly here in Iraq. And those soldiers let us down; they simply let us down. They have all—that you saw in those pictures—are facing criminal charges. That process is moving forward.

But very simply what I would say to the people of Iraq if asked that question is this is a very small minority of the hundreds and hundreds of guards that we have operating in Abu Ghraib prison. It's a very small minority of the soldiers that walk up and down your streets every day trying to provide safety and security for the people of Iraq. We've had thousands—we've had tens of thousands of security internees at Abu Ghraib, and we believe that this involves less than 20.

Am I going to apologize for those soldiers? Hell, no. They did wrong. It would appear to us that if, in fact, the pictures are what they appear to be, they will face a court of law, a criminal court of law, and they will have to face a judge and a jury for their actions.

But please don't for a moment think that that's the entire U.S. Army or the U.S. military, because it's not. And if you think those soldiers that are walking up and down the street approve of what they saw, condone what they saw or excuse what they saw, I can tell you that I've got 150,000 other American soldiers who feel as appalled and disappointed as I do at the actions of those few.

Question (through interpreter): I have two questions. You spoke about the inappropriate conduct among American soldiers. What kind of assurance do we have that these conditions won't be repeated? And are you going to allow the humanitarian associations to come and organizations to visit them? . . .

General Kimmitt: As to your first question, I think that that's a very good question; how can we guarantee that these types of activities will not happen again in the future? We are taking, as a coalition, as an army, very aggressive steps to ensure that the risk of this happening again is absolutely minimized. We have brought a two-star general in whose previous job was running the detention facility at Guantanamo Bay; probably the military expert in the world today on conducting appropriate detainee operations. He's on the ground now. He's already making a significant difference.

The new units that are coming in to conduct the detention operations have all had significant additional training to ensure that any excuse of, "well, I wasn't properly trained," is no longer an excuse.

We're conducting another investigation—two more investigations, as a matter of fact: an administrative investigation as to the conduct of the leadership, who should have known, who should have been able to ensure that their soldiers were doing the right thing—and would appear that that wasn't in fact happening. So not only are we going—are conducting a criminal investigation on those who actually participated in the criminal acts, we are also taking a hard look at the chain of command of the organizations that should have known what was happening inside of their unit. And third, we're also taking a hard look at the interrogation procedures and the interrogation policies that are being used out there as well.

Are we opening this up to humanitarian organizations? The International Committee of the Red Cross does frequent visits with our detention personnel for the purpose of answering that question. And I would also tell you—how else can we provide some public oversight? I would expect that in the next couple of weeks, we will in fact organize, within some restrictions—such as no taking of pictures—not only the recent visit of the interim Governing Council out to Abu Ghraib, but we are entertaining the notion of making a press visit out there as well. So you can yourself judge how we're doing out there.

APRIL 30, 2004—U.S. DEPARTMENT OF STATE

The U.S. Department of State spokesperson Richard Boucher said this in his daily briefing to a reporter's question:[73]

Question: About the photos. Obviously, you know, the President has expressed his disgust and I'm sure there's a lot of discussion discussed in Washington. But what are you doing to help Arab governments see that this is, you know, the exception that breaks the rule? And how is it affecting your public diplomacy?

Mr. Boucher: I think we've been quite up front on this. And not only the President addressed it today, I think the military has gone out and addressed this very forthrightly and said, "We take these charges very, very seriously, so seriously, in fact, that we're proceeding with court martial. We have court martial proceedings against the people in question. These practices don't reflect the professionalism of the U.S. military or the actions or policies of the Coalition Authority. They are as abhorrent to us as they are to others and if we can prove the charges, people will be prosecuted."

So it's, I think, we've been open and up front that we don't allow countenance in any way, abuse of prisoners that are *in U.S. hands, and if we find out about it, it's a crime that deserves prosecution.*

Now our military's been very, very clear on that. They have also been clear that it's a very small number of people that were involved. In fact, it's relatively small, compared to the whole number of prisoners involved. We've released hundreds and hundreds of prisoners. We're very sorry this happened to these people and we'll do everything in our power to make sure it doesn't happen again.

MAY 3, 2004—DEPARTMENT OF DEFENSE SPOKESPERSON (PENTAGON)

At the Pentagon, officials provided a media availability with Lawrence Di Rita, principal deputy assistant secretary of defense, public affairs (Department of Defense spokesperson) on May 3, 2004.

Questions centered on when certain events occurred, identities of those charged or reassigned, the role of private contractors, other ongoing investigations, and when Secretary of Defense Donald Rumsfeld knew about the abuse. Di Rita told reporters Rumsfeld still had not been briefed on the detailed findings of the Taguba report; he thought the first time Rumsfeld saw the abuse photos was "when they appeared on television."[74] Di Rita, however, said that Rumsfeld knew there was a criminal investigation underway "when it was first reported in the chain of command."[75]

MAY 4, 2004—Joint Coalition's Deputy Commanding General of Detention Operations (Iraq)

A media availability provided by Maj. Gen. Geoffrey Miller, the recently appointed deputy commanding general of detention operations, answered reporter questions about authorized interrogation practices in Iraqi detention centers.

Miller was the former commanding general of Joint Task Force Guantanamo, responsible for detention and interrogation operations at Camp Delta at Guantanamo Bay, a facility in Cuba holding hundreds of prisoners captured during the "Global War on Terrorism," primarily in Afghanistan and Iraq.

Miller and a team of detention and interrogation specialists had visited Abu Ghraib and other detention facilities in August and September 2003, prior to the documented October and November 2003 detainee abuses, to assess the detention and interrogation process and recommend ways so that "they worked in parallel towards success."[76] That included "passive reporting" based on MP interaction with the detainee.

Miller denied a reporter's claim attributed to Brig. Gen. Janis Karpinski of the Army Reserve, commander of the 800th MP Brigade (and later relieved of her command and demoted in rank), that Miller was brought over to "Gitmo-ize" their practices.[77] Miller said:[78]

I'll be frank with you. Every recommendation that we made was in the bounds of what was authorized by the theater and was within standard practices. We're enormously proud of what we had done at Guantanamo, to be able to set that kind of environment where we were focused on gaining the maximum amount of intelligence. But we detained the people in a humane manner, in accordance with the 3rd and 4th Geneva Conventions.

Miller said his team saw no evidence of abuse during a two-week visit. He went into detail about acceptable interrogation techniques, saying interrogators followed the Geneva Convention detainee guidelines. He noted that current interrogation techniques in the Iraqi theater of operations for detainees did not allow threats to detainees, but "aggressive" conversations were acceptable; unacceptable practices included physical contact between detainees, stress positions, sleep deprivation (unless approved at the general officer level), hooding, and stripping detainees of their clothing.[79]

Defense Department Operational Update Briefing with Secretary Rumsfeld

Secretary of Defense Rumsfeld and General Peter Pace, vice chairman of the Joint Chiefs of Staff, met with reporters and read a statement:[80]

The vast majority of the men and women in uniform serve our country with honor, and they uphold the values of our country as they battle enemies that show little compassion or respect for innocent human life. That's one of the many reasons why it's so troubling to find instances in which the trust we are establishing has been damaged.

The images that we've seen that include U.S. forces are deeply disturbing, both because of the fundamental unacceptability of what they depicted and because the actions by U.S. military personnel in those photos do not in any way represent the values of our country or the armed forces. As President Bush has stated, their treatment does not reflect the nature of the American people.

Have no doubt that we will take these charges and allegations most seriously. . . . We're taking and will continue to take whatever steps are necessary to hold accountable those who may have violated the code of military conduct and betrayed the trust placed in them by the American people. . . .

Rumsfeld then described six separate investigations into the abuse at Abu Ghraib. General Pace explained the often lengthy process by which investigative reports such as the Taguba probe worked their way up the chain of command.

When Rumsfeld was asked if the abuse scandal had "damaged U.S. attempts to

establish trust in the country" and was a "major setback for U.S. efforts in Iraq," he replied, it was "an exception." When asked about reports that Rumsfeld had not seen the Taguba report until recent days, Rumsfeld defended the methodic chain of command process that investigative reports took:[81]

I guess the way to put it is that the department has been aware of it since it was first noticed, and up the chain of command we're told that there were investigations into alleged abuses as long ago as last January 16th. It takes time for reports to be finished—correction— to be gathered. This is a very comprehensive report. . . .

He later admitted that he had "seen the executive summary" and read the conclusions of the Taguba report.[82] While he was aware of the photographs, he did not actually see the photos until they were broadcast on CBS because the DoD didn't have copies.

In response to criticism about Congress being "kept in the dark" about the abuse and investigations, Rumsfeld said:[83]

Well, we informed the world on January 16th that these investigations were under way. It seems to me that that is a perfectly proper thing to do. The investigations were announced. The world knew it. It was briefed to the press and the world.

When asked if the Taguba report indicated a rare exception that U.S. soldiers used torture, Rumsfeld said: "My impression is that what has been charged thus far is abuse, which I believe technically is different from torture."[84]

Reporter: In all of this debate in recent days, there hasn't been any apology for these actions or alleged actions of American troops. Wouldn't that help in this sort of war of ideas?[85]

Rumsfeld: . . . I haven't been focused on the war of ideas, to be honest with you, since this issue—with respect to this issue. It is important in that context, to be sure. We have to deal with this issue from a standpoint of the Uniform Code of Military Justice. We have to deal with it from the standpoint of how we're organized and trained and led. And that has been my focus. There may be things that we can do that would be helpful in helping the world understand that this is an exceptional situation; it is not a pattern or a practice. And any suggestion that it is I think would be incorrect.

Special Defense Department Briefing with the Vice Chief of Staff of the Army and Provost Marshal General

General George Casey, vice chief of staff of the Army, and Maj. Gen. Donald Ryder, provost marshal general, met with reporters at the Pentagon. Following a brief statement that included "we in the Army are extremely disappointed that anyone would engage in the mistreatment and humiliation of detainees or take such pictures,"[86] he also said it represented "a complete breakdown in discipline."

Most questions posed by reporters focused on the identities and status of the soldiers involved in the scandal (which were not provided) and what steps had been taken to correct the problems. Ryder described a visit to Abu Ghraib in October 2003 as part of an overall assessment of the Iraqi penal system. He noted that during his visit he noticed "there was a tension between military police and the interrogators" but did not clarify the comment during follow-up questions.[87]

MAY 5, 2004—President Bush with Alhurra and Al Arabiya Television Stations

President Bush conducted interviews with two Arabic television stations to respond to the detainee abuse. An Arabic reporter

asked why Iraqis should consider Americans different from Saddam Hussein's regime after the torture of Iraqi prisoners.[88]

President Bush: First, people in Iraq must understand that I view those practices as abhorrent. They must also understand that what took place in that prison does not represent America that I know. The America I know is a compassionate country that believes in freedom. The America I know cares about every individual. The America I know has sent troops into Iraq to promote freedom—good, honorable citizens that are helping the Iraqis every day.

It's also important for the people of Iraq to know that in a democracy, everything is not perfect, that mistakes are made. But in a democracy, as well, those mistakes will be investigated and people will be brought to justice. We're an open society. We're a society that is willing to investigate, fully investigate in this case, what took place in that prison.

That stands in stark contrast to life under Saddam Hussein. His trained torturers were never brought to justice under his regime. There were no investigations about mistreatment of people. There will be investigations. People will be brought to justice.

Bush also said he first saw the abuse photos when they were aired on CBS, but he reminded the audience that his government's investigations began in January 2004. He discussed the ongoing investigations and expressed confidence in Rumsfeld and in the commanders in Iraq.[89]

In the second interview with Al Arabiya television, Bush repeated the detainee abuse was "abhorrent" and didn't represent America. He promised "to find the truth . . . and justice will be served."[90] When asked how he thought the abuse would affect Middle East perceptions of America, Bush answered:[91]

> Terrible. I think people in the Middle East who want to dislike America will use this as an excuse to remind people about their dislike. I think the average citizen will say, this isn't a country that I've been told about. We're a great country because we're a free country, and we do not tolerate these kind of abuses.
>
> The people of the Middle East must be assured that we will investigate fully, that we will find out the truth. They will know the truth, just like the American citizens will know the truth, and justice will be served.
>
> Secondly, it's very important for the people of the Middle East to realize that the troops we have overseas are decent, honorable citizens who care about freedom and peace; that are working daily in Iraq to improve the lives of the Iraqi citizens, and these actions of a few people do not reflect the nature of the men and women who serve our country. . . .

ABC's *Good Morning America* with Secretary Rumsfeld

Rumsfeld was interviewed by many news organizations including two network morning shows. On ABC's *Good Morning America*, Diane Sawyer's first question to Rumsfeld was why he did not offer an apology to the Iraqis the day before; she asked him if he wanted to apologize during their interview.[92]

Rumsfeld said: "Oh my goodness. Anyone, any American who sees the photographs that we've seen has to feel apologetic to the Iraqi people who were abused and recognize that that is something that is unacceptable and certainly un-American."[93] Later in the interview, Rumsfeld

said, "There is certainly no excuse for anyone in the armed forces to behave they way these photographs indicated some individuals behaved."[94]

NBC *Today* with Secretary Rumsfeld

When NBC's Matt Lauer asked Rumsfeld: "Who is ultimately responsible for that unsupervised and dangerous setting?" Rumsfeld replied: "Well, clearly, it's the United States Army and the Central Command that have the responsibility for the management of the prisons in that part of the world."[95]

When asked if he would issue a formal apology to the Iraqi people for the abuses, Rumsfeld said: "Well, anyone who sees the photographs does, in fact, apologize to the people who were abused. That is wrong. It shouldn't have happened. It's un-American. It's unacceptable. And we all know that. And that apology is there to any individual who was abused."[96]

CBS *Early Show* with General Peter Pace

On the CBS morning program *The Early Show*, Hannah Storm interviewed General Peter Pace, vice chairman of the Joint Chiefs. Her first question was why Taguba's report, completed in March, was not forwarded to the Joint Chiefs of Staff chairman Richard Myers or the president. Pace explained the deliberate nature of "reporting up the chain of command" that all investigative reports take in the Army.[97] He said that "everybody" was informed orally about the investigation, including General Myers.

When asked why Congress was not informed sooner, he said General Kimmitt provided public announcements in joint coalition briefings dating back to January 16, 2004, and confirmed that congressional leaders were notified of the Taguba investigation's results the prior week. He also explained that the deliberateness of the investigation protected people's rights to fair judicial treatment.[98]

White House Press Briefing with Scott McClellan

The White House press corps questioned McClellan during a 40-minute briefing. Topics included exactly when President Bush was informed of the precise nature of the abuse allegations and why the president did not give a personal apology when Arabic television stations interviewed him earlier that day.

McClellan said the president learned about the allegations of prisoner abuse in a "general sense" from Rumsfeld at an unidentified time before the CBS report aired.[99] He clarified that the president "learned more about the precise nature just within the recent days." No specific times were given as to when Rumsfeld initially informed the president of the abuses or when the president found out about the Abu Ghraib photos.

In response to why the president did not specifically apologize on Arabic television that morning, McClellan said:[100]

Well, we've already said that we are deeply sorry for what occurred, and we're deeply sorry to the families and what they must be feeling and going through, as well. The President is sorry for what occurred and the pain that it has caused. It does not represent what America stands for. America stands for much better than what happened.

Coalition Provisional Authority Briefing with General Mark Kimmitt

General Kimmitt answered more questions about the treatment of detainees at Abu Ghraib, particularly for reporters who had taken the first media tour of the facility conducted by General Miller's public affairs officers.

He also apologized on behalf of the Army for the detainee abuse:[101]

It was reprehensible and it was unacceptable. And it is more than just words, that we have to take

those words into action and ensure that never happens again. And we will make a full-faith effort to ensure that never happens again.

Maj. Gen. Geoffrey Miller at Abu Ghraib

During a press tour of the Abu Ghraib detention facility, Commander of U.S.-run prisons in Iraq Maj. Gen. Geoffrey Miller also apologized for the abuse incidents:[102]

I would like to apologize for our nation and for our military for the small number of soldiers who committed illegal or unauthorized acts here at Abu Ghraib.

These are violations not only of our national policy but of how we conduct ourselves as members of the international community.

It has brought a cloud over all the efforts of all of our soldiers and we will work our hardest to re-establish the trust that Iraqis feel for the coalition and the confidence people in America have in their military.

Questions for Discussion

Due to the complexity of this case and limited space in the text, you may find it necessary to access full transcripts of various comments and briefings to answer questions below. References to these transcripts are listed at the end of the case.

1. What was the overall public relations response strategy of the Department of Defense and military to Abu Ghraib? What would you do differently?

2. What are the channels available for sending messages to the public in this case?

3. What was the most effective channel of communication used? Why?

4. Why did it take more than three months for the CBS story with detainee abuse photos to break following the initial investigation announcement?

5. What were the key messages delivered in the aftermath of the CBS report on detainee abuse? What was the most effective message?

6. Who was the most credible spokesperson for the government's response?

7. How did President Bush take his message to the Iraqi people?

8. Why did President Bush stop short of a full apology to the Iraqi people?

9. Examine the responses of government officials. Who did apologize for the detainee abuse? Who do you think was most credible and effective in presenting the U.S. position? Explain your reasons.

10. Why was the matter of an official apology important?

11. Reporters asked many questions about who knew what and when, particularly as it related to Secretary of Defense Donald Rumsfeld and President Bush. Why was this important?

12. This case study examines the first seven days of the crisis (starting the day of the CBS report). What would be your public relations strategy for the second week?

Do some Research

1. Research Iraq, its news media, and its culture. What public relations strategy would you recommend to rebuild the U.S. reputation among Iraqis?

2. Examine the full transcript of White House spokesperson Scott McClellan's press briefing on May 5, 2005. Do you think McClellan did a good job of emphasizing the president's role in this crisis?

Terminology

- public affairs officer
- daily briefings
- background briefing
- detainee
- prisoner
- abuse (government's definition)
- torture (government's definition)

- Article 32 investigation
- chain of command
- military police
- military intelligence
- interrogation

Web Resources

- **Department of Defense Detainee Investigations** (contains links to several official documents, including many of the investigative reports and briefings, related to the abuse scandal) www.defenselink.mil/news/detainee_investigations.html
- **Taguba Report** www.globalsecurity.org/intell/library/reports/2004/800-mp-bde.htm
- **Uniform Code of Military Justice:** www.au.af.mil/au/awc/awcgate/ucmj.htm
- **Schlesinger Report** (Final Report of the Independent Panel to Review DoD Detention Operations) www.defenselink.mil/news/detainee_investigations.html
- **Army Inspector General Detainee Operations Inspections report** www.au.af.mil/au/awc/awcgate/army/ig_detainee_ops.pdf
- **CBS 60 Minutes II "Abuse of Iraqi POWs by GIs Probed"** www.cbsnews.com/stories/2004/04/27/60II/main614063.shtml
- **The New Yorker "Torture at Abu Ghraib" by Seymour M. Hersh** www.newyorker.com/printables/fact/040510fa_fact
- **Geneva Conventions** (Office of the United Nations High Commissioner of Human Rights) www.unhchr.ch/html/menu3/b/91.htm
- **Jones/Fay Report** (Investigation of Intelligence Activities at Abu Ghraib) www.globalsecurity.org/intell/library/reports/2004/intell-abu-ghraib_ar15-6.pdf
- **International Committee of the Red Cross** www.icrc.org
- **Report of the International Committee of the Red Cross on the Treatment**

by the Coalition Forces of Prisoners of War and Other Protected Persons by the Geneva Conventions in Iraq during Arrest, Internment and Interrogation, February 2004 www.cbsnews.com/htdocs/pdf/redcrossabuse.pdf
- International Committee of the Red Cross, Protecting Prisoners and Detainees in Wartime: Iraq: ICRC Explains Position over Detention Report and

Treatment of Prisoners www.icrc.org/Web/Eng/siteeng0.nsf/htmlall/detention
- Center for Media and Democracy, SourceWatch www.sourcewatch.org/index.php?title=Abu_Ghraib
- Army Inspector General Detainee Operations Inspections Report www.au.af.mil/au/awc/awcgate/army/ig_detainee_ops.pdf

Abu Ghraib: Part 3
On-the-Ground Response

Part 3 of the case study introduces you to the public affairs organization in the Iraqi war theater and some of the steps the public affairs officers responsible for the Abu Ghraib facility took after the initial news accounts were broadcast or published.

Similar to civilian public relations practice, the U.S. military's public affairs officers are charged with telling the military's story in order to build support for the Iraqi campaign at home and among Iraqis. The public affairs efforts also provided information to coalition troops and support staff stationed in Iraq and beyond.

In the Iraqi war theater, the public affairs operations at the time of the Abu Ghraib scandal were handled by three entities: Office of Strategic Communications (STRATCOM), the Coalition Press Information Center (CPIC) and the military divisions of the Multinational Force (MNF). There were approximately 200 public affairs officers who worked in the areas of media relations and command information (news for soldiers) in Iraq in 2005, said Lt. Col. Barry Johnson, the public affairs officer for Maj. Gen. Geoffrey Miller.

Office of Strategic Communications, located in the protected "Green Zone" in the U.S. embassy, was responsible for coordinating the strategic communication efforts of the entire Iraqi war theater. That included working with the six regional headquarters to devise strategies for issues, such as Abu Ghraib, that had long-term implications for the war effort, Johnson said.

STRATCOM coordinated public affairs activities as well as information operations (IO), a separate communication effort from the public affairs that seeks to influence or change the perceptions and behavior of its audience.[103] The staff worked closely with the U.S. embassy in developing public diplomacy messages and helping the Iraqi government groom its messages to build support for the multinational force.

Combined Press Information Center (CPIC), also located in the Green Zone in central Baghdad, handled the day-to-day media relations tactical operations. Opened 24 hours a day, it was the site where coalition briefings were held for reporters and where reporters could go to obtain specific answers to their questions or request interviews with military officials.[104] These briefings typically covered the day's troop activities, including military operations and deaths. The CPIC produced daily news releases on combat operations as well as a variety of good news stories about the MNF. It published the MNF's newsletters, such as *Scimitar*, and operated the Armed Forces Network, providing radio programming for MNF troops. Its operations were authorized by STRATCOM, Johnson said.

Multinational Divisions, engaged in on-the-ground missions, were commanded by generals with public affairs officers. They advised the commanding general in communication strategies and tactics to address various public relations and communication issues, Johnson said.

In the case study involving the Abu Ghraib detainee scandal, there was no public affairs officer working with Brig. Gen. Janis Karpinski, commander of the 800th Military Police Brigade, which was made up of eight battalions with 1,700 National Guard and Army Reservists.[105] The 800th MP Brigade provided security for the Iraqi penal system and detainee operations throughout Iraq. This included Abu Ghraib and other detention facilities and prisons.

Public affairs activities for her command were addressed by the Combined Joint Task Force, later called the Multinational Force, said Johnson. Until the prisoner abuse story broke in late April 2004, information about the 800th Military MP Brigade was filed with STRATCOM and the CPIC and was disseminated mostly from coalition briefings.

Once the story broke, the new commander of Iraqi detainee operations, Maj. Gen. Geoffrey Miller, authorized a media relations program including news conferences, media opportunities, and media tours of Abu Ghraib. The first media tour was held May 5, 2004, and allowed reporters their first look at the detention center, including the two blocks of cells where the

detainee abuse occurred and the tent area where most detainees were housed.

The message strategy was to remind reporters that an investigation was launched immediately when the abuse was reported, the investigation followed procedures, that those responsible were being held accountable, and that corrective action had been taken to prevent further abuse, said Johnson.

Media tours were considered the best way to show the world that detainees were being treated according to Geneva Conventions. Reporters could see the medical facilities and talk to soldiers. No interviews were allowed with detainees, which the coalition determined would be a violation of the Geneva Conventions. Three media tours were conducted in May 2004 and then were discontinued because of the mob scenes that ensued when detainees saw media cameras while driving through the tent cities.

Instead, Johnson began taking individual or small groups of journalists into the facility. His approach was "be up front." If a question could not be answered, due to the ongoing investigations or other reasons, he explained why. His job was to focus on what had been accomplished since the scandal and how things were improving for detainees.

Most media requests came from Western journalists; Iraqi journalists who reported the story were less interested, Johnson said. He said Iraqi journalists often followed the Western journalists' story coverage, but most Iraqis interviewed for comment basically shrugged and said those at Abu Ghraib were "there for a reason," said Johnson.

"It [Abu Ghraib] was not seen every day [in the news]. It was not the predominant topic; they were fighting for the survival of their country." Opposition leaders and insurgents used the scandal to fuel their agendas, Johnson said.

To maintain a consistent message about detainee operations, centralizing media relations was a goal for Johnson. He requested that the Press Information Center and STRATCOM refer all questions to him. It allowed Johnson to build relationships with the media and become more strategic than reactive in communicating the military's mission.

Hundreds of reporters were on the story, and not every journalist was treated equally, Johnson said. He had his favorites who, he felt, were reporting fairly and had the audience reach to influence public opinion the most. He built relationships by offering better access to people and the facility and by offering new stories ideas.

Johnson also monitored media coverage daily. If he read a story that he did not feel was reflective of what was going on, he would contact the journalist and invite him or her to come to Abu Ghraib to "really show you what's happening."

Instead of seeing Abu Ghraib from the military's viewpoint, Johnson paid attention to what journalists saw and said, and any vocalized perceptions. Each time he took in a television crew or print journalist into Abu Ghraib, he noticed what they photographed and what they asked as potential clues into what might need improvement.

Iraqi communication channels included television, radio, and newspapers. Many Iraqis at the time had access to satellite television, and news programs were popular sources of information about the war. Radio also was an important way to reach average Iraqis. Newspapers played a less important role due to high illiteracy rates among commoners, but remained important among key influencers in the country. The rumor mill also was a major source of information for Iraqis. To discover the word on the street, the military conducted weekly focus groups with Iraqi citizens to discover their perceptions about issues and what ones were important, said Johnson. Based on this research, the military developed strategic messages to address the issues or erroneous information delivered by coalition and Iraqi government officials.

In the immediate aftermath of Abu Ghraib (and before the emergence of widespread sectarian violence later), other factors included working with the tribal and religious leaders. The military ground forces' civil affairs units and commanders met often to find out people's concerns (such as sewer improvements) and how they could be addressed. Soldiers also tried to reach out to Iraqis in positive ways including handing out donated supplies of food, shoes, clothing and toys.

EPILOGUE

By June 2006, 11 low-ranking soldiers had been convicted in connection with abuse activity at Abu Ghraib. According to a report by Salon.com, "[T]hree soldiers and one officer received nonjudicial punishments, and four soldiers and eight officers received official reprimands." According to a public affairs officer quoted in the story, "a number of officers were suspended or relieved of their duties." This included Brig. Gen. Janis Karpinski, commander of the 800th Military Police Brigade, who was relieved of her command, demoted, and reprimanded.[106] Col. Thomas M. Pappas, commander of the 205th Military Intelligence Brigade, was also relieved of his command and reprimanded.[107] The former head of the interrogation center at Abu Ghraib, Lt. Col. Steven L. Jordan, was charged in 2006 with violations of the Uniform Code of Military Justice.

Questions for Discussion

1. What was the public relations strategy for public affairs officers at Abu Ghraib?

2. Media tours were used in the aftermath of the Abu Ghraib scandal. What was their strategic purpose? Why were they discontinued?

3. What are the most effective communication channels in Iraq?

4. What key messages did the public affairs officers give to reporters visiting Abu Ghraib?

5. How did the military deal with the rumor mill?

Do some Research

1. Research why tribal and religious leaders were important to the coalition's public relations campaign. How would you use them for strategic communication purposes?

2. Examine the type of information released by the Multinational Force in Iraq. How would you characterize the information? Who is the primary audience, and what is the information's purpose?

Web Resources

- **Multinational Force, Iraq** http://www .mnf-iraq.com/
- **U.S. Strategic Command** www.stratcom .mil/
- **Coalition Provisional Authority** http:// www.cpa-iraq.org/
- **Azzaman: Iraqi newspaper** http://www. azzaman.com/english/

Chapter Twelve

International Public Relations

Economic globalization and the resulting increase in global communication are connecting the world as never before and providing growing opportunities for public relations.

The United States has a rich diversity of human resources and public relations expertise to actively participate in developing multinational public relations programs. This is often accomplished when public relations firms partner with other practitioners "born into the culture."[1]

To be successful, practitioners need to be aware of different value systems (what people value or place importance on) and a particular nation's cultural identity. Culture refers to how people live their lives or to simply the way things are done; it includes shared experiences and activities, such as language, religion, dress, food, and the environment, as well as the common history and government that bind a country or region together into a distinct social system.

Well-known American brands and popular culture, from McDonald's to *Desperate Housewives,* are present in many nations around the world. Concerned about the dominance of U.S. culture and values, many nations are attempting to maintain their distinct, native cultures by enacting policies and regulations aimed at dampening American influence abroad. France, for example, has sought measures to ensure that French films are shown in French theaters.

Beyond protection of countries' heritage and history are the stark realities facing many countries just trying to provide basic necessities for their populations. *The Human Development Report 2005* noted "extreme inequalities" exist around the globe.[2] Nearly 40 percent of the world's populations live on less than $2 a day. The richest 10 percent of the population in high-income countries account for 54 percent of the global income.[3] According to the *Human Development Report 2005,* 10.7 million children every year don't live past their fifth birthday.[4]

Sensitivity to and appreciation for cultural differences are necessary to build trusting relationships. The Rotary International Student Exchange program reminds its participating students that just because something is different does not mean it's bad. Public relations practitioners responsible for developing a cooperative partnership in another country should make every effort to learn that country's culture and language.

Communicating poorly in one language is bad enough, but doing so in a second language can send unintended and, at times, humorous messages. Fraser Seitel's book *The Practice of Public Relations* gives some examples:[5]

* A food company named its giant burrito a *Burrada,* which means "big mistake" in colloquial Spanish.
* Estee Lauder's proposed Country Mist got a name change because *mist* is German slang for "manure."
* When Chevrolet introduced its Nova model, it didn't take off among Spanish-speaking customers, since *nova* in Spanish means "does not go."

All translated messages, including brand names, should be reviewed by native speakers and tested within the target market before they are implemented.

Beyond language and meaning, practitioners should understand the demographics and technological infrastructure of the country. Some populations, for example, are highly educated with accompanying high literacy rates while others are not. Some countries are industrialized, with access to sophisticated communication technology. South Korea, for example, is considered one of the most "wired" populations on earth. All of these factors and population characteristics will affect communication strategies.

Researcher Maureen Taylor described eight societal factors that influence the practice of international public relations: the level of media development and professionalism; the level of economic development; political ideology; societal tolerance for activism; the strength of labor unions; the level of development of the legal system; state-to-state relations; and the relationship between government and business.[6]

In the book *Toward the Common Good: Perspectives in International Public Relations,* several themes emerge in the study of public relations abroad: "the interplay of democratic movements and emerging free-market economies; press freedom; the empowerment of public opinion; and the conflict of an aroused, mediated citizenry with authoritarian regimes and entrenched special interests."[7]

The book also noted:[8]

A convergence of three factors contributed to the emergence of public relations as a profession: a growth in the global acceptance of democratic principles, growing global social interdependence, and the emergence of direct instantaneous communication abilities. These factors have now empowered public opinion to a degree that public relations performance is no longer a choice on the part of the organization.

Two freedoms U.S. citizens are used to—freedom of expression and freedom of assembly—are not enjoyed universally. According to Freedom House's Freedom of the Press 2005 report of 194 countries and territories examined, 75 (39 percent) were rated free, while 50 (26 percent) were rated partly free and 69 (35 percent) were rated not free.[9]

Limitations on freedom of expression can adversely affect an organization's ability to communicate freely, particularly with the news media. Related to freedom of expression are the integrity and credibility of the country's news media. The "cash for editorial" practice is a growing concern. According to the International Public Relations Association's Campaign for Media Transparency survey of public relations professions, cash payment for story placement is common in eastern and southern Europe, and in Central and South America.[10] Even Internet sites, which Americans assume are unregulated and unstoppable on the Internet, can be shut down. China, for example, has frequently clamped down on or blocked Web sites not authorized by the government.

Limits on freedom of assembly can also present challenges. Since public relations is responsible for building relationships, simply gathering people together in some countries for meetings, events, or demonstrations could be monitored or stopped. This eliminates an effective face-to-face communication tool.

Other practical considerations include the effect of female practitioners in a paternalistic society, where men make virtually all important life decisions. Also, the experience and educational level of the partner practitioner as well as the way public relations is practiced in a particular country can make a difference. Authors of *This Is PR: The Realities of Public Relations* note that "in only a few countries is public relations practiced at the strategic level where the PR person has the power and authority to affect policy."[11]

Web Resources

- **Human Development Report** (with statistics by country) hdr.undp.org/
- **United Nation, UN Collections Worldwide** (has a number of downloadable publications and statistical information about countries) www.un.org/Depts/dhl/
- **Library of Congress, Global Gateway: World Cultures and Resources** (provides links by country that were selected by area specialists and other library staff) international.loc.gov/intldl/intldlhome.html.

Containing the Deadly Marburg Virus

Taking a Culturally Based Communication Approach

Burial customs are an important social tradition for many indigenous Angolans. The funeral rites include spending significant time with the body and often performing a ceremonial body washing and kissing it goodbye.[12] The deceased are handled with loving care and respect because, according to traditional beliefs, a neglected spirit might "turn vengeful."[13]

These cultural considerations were ignored initially in the rush to contain a deadly outbreak of Marburg identified in Uige, Angola, in March 2005.

Marburg hemorrhagic fever is a highly fatal disease caused by a virus from the same family as Ebola. Fatality rates have been as high as 80 percent with no vaccine or curative treatment available.[14] While incidents are rare, outbreaks of the disease

WHO/CNRS/Alain Epelboin.

In outbreaks of viral hemorrhagic fevers, including Marburg, unprotected exposure to dead bodies is a significant cause of further spread. Safe burial is essential to controlling the outbreak. Prior to the burial, the team talks to the family and the community leader to give information on Marburg. Traditional burial practices must be modified in ways that allow families to mourn in accordance with their beliefs yet minimize the risk of exposure to the body and disease.

in Africa received widespread media attention due to its horrific hemorrhagic symptoms and fears of global spread.

Like Ebola, Marburg is transmitted through direct contact with a victim involving exposure to blood, saliva, or other bodily fluids. According to the Centers for Disease Control, the virus had been known to survive for several days on contaminated surfaces.[15] Symptoms include fever, chills, and headache and become increasingly severe. Of the initial 124 cases reported between October 1, 2004, and March 29, 2005, 117 were fatal.[16]

International agencies working with Angola's ministry of health included the World Health Organization (WHO), Centers for Disease Control (CDC), and Médecins Sans Frontières (MSF), a medical charity. Outbreak control efforts included providing technical assistance for the medical care of victims, improving infection control in hospitals, improving surveillance and contact tracing, and educating local residents about the disease and its modes of transmission.[17]

According to one news account, when foreign health workers showed up in Uige's outlying villages, they did not offer a friendly handshake or condolences to distraught families, nor did they allow families to perform traditional burial customs.[18] Dressed from head to toe in white protective clothing—a color associated with witchcraft[19]—the alien-looking health workers were focused on containing the disease quickly. While well meaning, the health workers did not take the time to understand villagers' concerns, frustrations, and traditions. They did not tap into the existing social structure of traditional healers and village leaders.

Fear, distrust, and grief soon turned to anger. Villagers threw rocks at mobile contact unit vehicles sent in search of suspected Marburg cases or hidden bodies.[20]

To build trust with villagers, better communication efforts were implemented and procedures were altered. WHO added two medical anthropologists to its social mobilization teams to develop positive relationships. Health workers began to work with community leaders, healers, and midwives

to convince Angolans of the importance of providing information on suspected Marburg cases and deaths. Educational pamphlets were printed in Portuguese, the official Angolan language, as well as in French, Lingalla, and Kikongo. Five television spots were produced in Portuguese, and five radio spots were translated into eight of the country's most widely spoken indigenous languages.[21]

To reduce fears, health workers arrived at homes in street clothes first and then, in view of the family, put on personal protection garments. They took the time to talk to families and formally recognized their loss or expressed concern for a sick family member.

Burial customs were modified to allow families to carry out burial rites safely. For example, bodies were placed in open body bags for viewing, and ceremonial washings were replaced with sprinkling the body with a mixture of water and bleach.[22] The family was present when the body was removed from the home and family could accompany the body to the burial site.

The *New York Times* quoted Dr. Pierre Formenty, a virologist assisting in the Angolan disease containment efforts: "We are fighting the battle of the disease. But first we have to win the battle of the heart, and the battle of the funeral."[23]

When Marburg claimed the life of a well-known Uige musician, the singer's band renamed itself the "Trio against Marburg" and wrote the "Song against Marburg."[24] The song advised listeners what to do when they suspected a Marburg case.

Most deaths in Uige, the outbreak's epicenter, occurred in children under the age of five; as the outbreak grew, more adults were affected. When a local teacher died from Marburg, this provided an opportunity to step up educational efforts within the schools.[25]

Complicating the response efforts to the Marburg outbreak was minimal infrastructure, a result of a devastating 27-year civil war that ensued after Angola's independence from Portugal in 1976. At the time of the outbreak, life expectancy was 36 years, and half the population was illiterate. Seventy percent lived below the poverty line, with 80 percent of the population involved in subsistence farming.[26]

The country's medical system lacked basic necessities, including equipment and trained staff. The Uige hospital was identified as the source of most early Marburg cases during the outbreak.[27] Many Uige residents were afraid to take their loved ones to the hospital because initial lack of protective clothing for health care workers had helped spread the disease.[28]

According to the CDC guidelines for infection control of hemorrhagic fevers, such as Marburg, the following steps are recommended to mobilize community resources and conduct community education:[29]

- Create a mobilization committee.
- Identify key community resources.
- Meet with community leaders and assess the current situation.
- Describe the target population.
- Describe problems contributing to transmission risk.
- Identify barriers to carrying out recommended changes or actions.
- Develop specific messages.
- Select activities for communicating messages.
- Assign tasks and carry out activities.
- Evaluate activities.
- Obtain community feedback.
- Meet regularly with mobilization committee.

According to the guidelines, health care workers should initially assess the community's resources, such as local governments, religious groups, businesses, schools, and service organizations. Workers would then gather and record information about each group's expertise, leaders, and available resources.

The next step was the identification of community leaders and educating them on the disease. In Angola, this included building relationships with traditional healers.[30] The social mobilization committee would communicate the outbreak status to community leaders, and they would be educated in the symptoms of the disease, how it is spread, personal precautions to prevent spread of the disease, the importance of notifying health care workers of suspected cases, proper decontamination methods, and so forth.

By July 2005, after 329 deaths, the outbreak had been mostly contained.[31] While the World Health Organization relied on traditional methods, such as case finding, contact tracing and isolation, and high-quality care for infected people, WHO also learned it took effective communication and cultural awareness to truly accomplish its mission.

Questions for Discussion

1. What were the cultural or geographic problems posed by the Marburg outbreak in Angola?

2. What steps were taken to regain the trust of Angolans during this crisis?

3. What were the complicating factors from a political and historical perspective?

4. Rapid response to this crisis after confirmation of the Marburg outbreak led to deployment of sophisticated diagnostic field teams in the affected towns and villages. Why did this response backfire?

5. How would you reduce fear and rumors within the population?

6. What would be your key messages and communication channels based on demographic, economic, and other social conditions of Angola?

7. How would you use the Trio against Marburg to further communication goals?

Do Some Research

1. Explain the role of the Centers for Disease Control and the United Nation's World Health Organization in medical emergencies worldwide.

2. Examine the guidelines from the Centers for Disease Control's *Infection*

Control Manual for mobilizing community resources and conducting community education at www.cdc.gov/ncidod/dvrd/spb/mnpages/dispages/marburg.htm. How would you improve this strategy for Angola?

Terminology

- Marburg disease
- Ebola disease
- hemorrhagic fever
- mobilization committee

- community surveillance
- medical anthropologist

Web Resources

- **Centers for Disease Control** www.cdc.gov
- **World Health Organization's Marburg information** www.who.int/csr/don/archive/disease/marburg_virus_disease/en/
- **Central Intelligence Agency,** *World Factbook* www.cia.gov/cia/publications/factbook

Shark Fin Soup
Hong Kong Disneyland Seeks Cultural and Environmental Balance

Despite careful planning, the grand opening of the first magic kingdom in China—Hong Kong Disneyland—was overshadowed by weeks of unfavorable international news coverage involving complaints over its cost, its noisy and polluting fireworks, the mistreatment of laborers and stray dogs, and its shark fin cuisine.

The 310-acre amusement park was a joint venture between the Hong Kong government and Disney. Hong Kong owns 57 percent of the project after a $2.9 billion investment.[32] The government expected the western-styled resort to become a family vacation destination to complement the city's already vibrant financial hub. The project also created jobs—18,000 for the local economy, including 4,000 construction workers and 5,000 Disney employees, which would eventually grow to 36,000 new jobs with an economic value of $19 billion over a 40-year period.[33] A whopping 5.6 million visitors were expected its first year of operation.[34]

Located 30 minutes from downtown Hong Kong on the island of Lan Tau, the resort took seven years to build from its initial announcement. Hong Kong, formerly a British colony until 1997, is a modern commercial city of 7 million people. Because Hong Kong is a special administrative region of China, its successful ventures are often considered preludes to future expansion to the much larger market on mainland China.[35]

Hong Kong Disneyland, with the Lan Tau mountains behind it and Hong Kong's dramatic skyline in front of it, was faithfully adapted from the original American Disneyland but on a smaller scale. Visitors can experience Tomorrowland, Adventureland, and Fantasyland, just like the 50-year-old versions half a world away.[36]

Several Chinese touches were included to ensure its Asian guests felt comfortable while still getting an authentic Disney experience.

HONG KONG DISNEYLAND
Design

Disney made changes to the new resort's design after consulting a feng shui master who recommended rotating the orientation of the entire park by a several degrees and placing three large boulders in certain locations to ensure harmony with spiritual forces.[37]

Two new features designed especially for Hong Kong were Fantasy Gardens and a musical extravaganza called the *Golden Mickeys at Disney's Storybook Theater*.[38] Fantasy Gardens' lush and fanciful gardens provided visitors "picture perfect" opportunities for autographs and photos with their favorite Disney characters.

The *Golden Mickeys at Disney's Storybook Theater* honored many Disney films with plenty of glitz and glamour reminiscent of a red-carpet Hollywood awards show.[39]

Opening Ceremonies

Hong Kong Disney opened September 12, 2005, with children singing in English, Cantonese, and Putonghua (standard Mandarin); Chinese acrobats; and a performance of the traditional Chinese lion dance in front of the pink Sleeping Beauty's Castle.[40] The ribbon-cutting ceremony included the chief executive officer and president of Walt Disney; Zeng Quinghong, vice president of the People's Republic of China; and the chief executive of Hong Kong. The day before the grand opening, the resort invited special guests and the media to a preview event that featured numerous well-known singers and entertainers from Hong Kong.

Asian-Friendly Language and Food

In another nod to cultural sensitivity, rides and shows were trilingual, using Cantonese, Mandarin, and English.[41] Employees' prescribed banter, delivered to customers during rides, was carefully checked by linguists to ensure accurate translation.

A food and beverage team carefully tested Western, Chinese, and Asian items to provide a diverse menu to satisfy all taste buds. Popular dishes from the Jiangnan region in northwest Asia and Guangdong province in mainland China were included on menus.[42] Different styles of cooking, such as steamed dishes (dim sum), stir fries, noodles, curry dishes, and barbeque dishes such as Hong Kong char siew pork were featured.

Community Relations

Hong Kong Disneyland follows the long Disney tradition of taking an active role in the local community. Eight days before the grand opening, its first Charity Day was held to benefit the city's largest charity organization, the Community Chest.[43] Hong Kong Disneyland and its volunteers hosted storytelling sessions at public libraries during the summer and participated in charity walks and hospital visits. It sponsored the annual Jiminy Cricket's "Environmentality Challenge" that encourages young students to "think green" and the Disney's Imagination Day that challenges students to apply their creative energies.

ACTIVISTS GRAB HEADLINES

Despite careful planning, Hong Kong Disneyland attracted negative publicity before and after its grand opening on September 12, 2005.

Shark Fin Soup

Months before its opening, Hong Kong Disneyland encountered the wrath of environmentalists worldwide when Disney unveiled its Fairy Tale Wedding packages. Couples could choose from a Western-style celebration or an elegant Chinese-banquet style reception.[44] The menu included shark fin soup, a cultural mainstay of most Chinese banquets and upscale restaurants. According to the *New York Times*, "Without shark fin, a Chinese banquet does not look like one at all," said Chiu Ching-cheung, chairman of the Shark Fin Trade Merchants' Association.[45]

Shark fin, a delicacy in middle- and upper-class Asian diets, has been under scrutiny by environmentalists around the world who claim overfishing has led to sharp declines in the world's largest shark species. Environmentalists also oppose the practice of shark "finning," in which fins are chopped off and the rest of the shark is thrown back into the ocean and dies.[46] Environmentalists said fishermen were not interested in shark meat because of its "rough texture and poor taste." Shark fin merchants in Hong Kong said the "finning" practice seldom occurs and that shark meat is eaten in poor countries.[47] Shark fin fans believe the delicacy offers medicinal or aphrodisiac qualities; a bowl of shark fin soup can cost up to $200, making sharks a highly lucrative business.[48]

Protests came from groups such as the Sea Shepherd Conservation Society and the World Wildlife Fund, and Hong Kong environmentalists.

At first, the park responded to the controversy by offering to give guests leaflets describing the ecological harm of shark finning in hopes of dissuading shark fin soup orders.[49] It also said it would buy from only "reliable and responsible suppliers," and it would offer non-shark fin soup options for banquets. After a month of protests, Disney President Robert Iger announced the park was removing shark fin soup from its wedding menu.[50]

Air and Noise Pollution

Another controversy emerged when environmentalists protested the traditional nightly fireworks show because of increased air and noise pollution, although the fireworks display is smaller than the U.S. display. Hong Kong already suffers from smog pollution created by factories elsewhere in China and the use of coal in Hong Kong.[51] Environmentalists requested Disney use new pyrotechnics technology that uses compressed air to lift fireworks, significantly reducing noise and ground-level smoke from black powder.[52] Since the fireworks' pollution levels were within regulatory limitations, Hong Kong Disneyland did not implement the new technology.

Labor Issues

News media reports carried charges by labor activists that Disney forced its park staff to work 11- and 13-hour days, provided inadequate breaks, and rewrote daily work schedules without notice.[53] Student groups, who investigated factories on China's mainland that produced products for the park, found labor abuses. They accused Disney of underpaying its workers for a 10- to 12-hour day and a six-day week.[54]

Wild Dogs

Animal rights activists protested the killing of about 45 dogs that were part of a wild dog pack roaming the hills surrounding the park. According to news accounts, the wild dogs, which are common on the island, threatened workers and visitors. While government workers tried to find homes for the dogs, sick ones were killed to protect the safety of workers and visitors.[55]

Overcrowding

Some visitors complained that the park was too small, with only 21 attractions, and was overcrowded. This was especially true when the park encountered an unexpected snafu for the Lunar New Year holiday, the biggest holiday of the year. The park was swamped with visitors trying to use a dual system of "flexible" tickets, which allowed one visit within a six-month period, and "date-specific" tickets, which are issued for special events or holidays.[56] Many mainland tourists with eager children were turned away at the gate.

Bill Ernest, executive vice president and managing director of the park, apologized: "We regret that anyone may have been inconvenienced . . . No one is more disappointed than we are. As a father, I understand how frustrating it is to disappoint your children . . . But our first priority is to protect our children."[57] The *South China Morning Post* noted in its story that the theme park giant needed a better understanding of Chinese culture.

Open Scenario Challenge

A major amusement park company is considering a proposal to build a park resort just outside of Mumbai (Bombay), India. As a communication specialist for the company, you are asked to research the culture and customs of India. Your public relations boss would like to know about the culture, including language, religion, political structure, and other considerations for communicating and developing a public relations and community relations program there for the launch of Mumbai's amusement park. He also wants to know if there are any major holidays or festivals in the Mumbai area that should be avoided for a launch date. What types of alliances should the organization consider in India?

Questions for Discussion

1. What is culture?
2. Why is an understanding of culture important in public relations and communication?
3. What actions did Disney take to ensure that Hong Kong Disney would cater to Asian culture?
4. What were the specific cultural problems presented in this case study?
5. Why did environmental activists target Hong Kong Disney for proposing to serve shark fin soup when other restaurants and banquet halls offered the same dish?
6. Disney did not issue any corporate news releases in response to problems outlined in this case study. Hong Kong Disney managers did respond to media requests and were quoted in news media stories. What do you think about this strategy?

Do Some Research

Research the culture and customs of another country, such as Mexico or Afghanistan. What should a U.S. organization keep in mind when planning to conduct business in that country? Make a list of recommendations for a U.S. business client. What are the opportunities and challenges presented by the country's culture?

Web Resources

* **Animals Asia Foundation** www.animalsasia.org/
* **Sea Shepherd Conservation Society** www.seashepherd.org/
* **Hong Kong Disneyland** www.hongkongdisneyland.com
* **The Disney blog** http://thedisney blog.typepad.com/tdb/hong_kong _disneyland/
* **Disney's corporate Web site** corporate.disney.go.com/index.html
* **Laughing Place, a Disney fan site** www.laughingplace.com/news-coverage26.asp

Don't Do Evil

China's Censorship Policies Put Unwanted Spotlight on U.S. Internet Search Companies

Google's corporate mantra "Don't Do Evil" rang a bit hollow when news reports surfaced that it, along with other U.S. technology companies, had voluntarily agreed to follow China's censorship policies for Internet searches in 2006.

Chinese who typed in the words *democracy, Falun Gong,* or *Tiananmen massacre* on any of the Chinese search engines were likely to get very different results from those produced by Internet searches in democratic countries. The Chinese search engines routinely blocked many sites considered critical of the government and, in some cases, automatically directed users to progovernment sites.

For example, a search of China's Google's images for Tiananmen Square, site of the 1989 Chinese antigovernment protests that allegedly left hundreds dead and thousands detained, showed a different picture literally. A U.S. Google.com image search immediately brought up the iconic photo of the lone man stopping a column of tanks and Tiananmen Square filled with thousands of Chinese protestors.[58] A search of the Chinese-based Google.cn provided two pages of happy tourist photos.[59]

Americans wondered how Internet search companies Google, Yahoo!, and MSN and hardware provider Cisco Systems could reconcile doing business in China when doing business meant curtailing freedom of expression and handing over Internet records that jailed Chinese "cyberdissidents."

Reporters without Borders, an international media watchdog group, cited specific examples in congressional testimony of U.S. companies collaborating with Web censors in China:[60]

- Since 2002, Yahoo! has agreed to censor the results obtained by the Chinese version of its search engine in accordance with a blacklist provided by the Chinese government. Yahoo! helped the Chinese police identify and then sentence to jail at least one journalist and one cyberdissident who criticized human rights abuses in China. Yahoo!'s Chinese division e-mail servers are located inside China.

- Microsoft censors the Chinese version of its MSN Spaces blog tool. Search strings such as "democracy" or "human rights in China" are automatically rejected by the system. Microsoft also closed down a Chinese journalist's blog when pressured by the Beijing government. This blog was hosted on servers located in the United States.

- All news and information sources censored in China have been withdrawn by Google from the Chinese version of its news search engine, Google News. Google also launched a China-based Google.cn, which is censored in accordance with Chinese law.

- Cisco Systems has marketed equipment specifically designed to make it easier for the Chinese police to carry out surveillance of electronic communications. Cisco is also suspected of giving Chinese engineers training in how to use its products to censor the Internet.

Reporters without Borders called China "the world's largest prison for journalists and cyberdissidents" with 81 behind bars.[61] According to the organization's World Press Freedom Index, China ranked 159th out of 167 countries.[62]

In 2006, China's legislature considered a law that could fine news agencies thousands of dollars for unauthorized reporting of "emergencies" such as riots or natural disasters.[63]

With more than 110 million Web users and 400 million daily search queries at the time, China had the second largest Internet user population after the United States.[64] While its Web users represented only 8 percent of its total population, China's continued economic growth was fueling dramatic increases in China's Internet population.[65]

U.S. Representative Chris Smith said at a February 15, 2006, congressional hearing that he would propose legislation limiting what American Internet companies could do in other countries if those actions curtailed freedom of speech or endangered an individual's freedom.[66] Smith had strong criticism for the companies:[67]

Women and men are going to the gulag and being tortured as a direct result of information handed over to Chinese officials. When Yahoo was asked to explain its actions,

Yahoo said that it must adhere to local laws in all countries where it operates. But my response to that is: if the secret police a half century ago asked where Anne Frank was hiding, would the correct answer be to hand over the information in order to comply with local laws? These are not victimless crimes. We must stand with the oppressed, not the oppressors . . .

I believe that two of the two most essential pillars that prop up totalitarian regimes are the secret police and propaganda. Yet for the sake of market share and profits, leading U.S. companies like Google, Yahoo, Cisco and Microsoft have compromised both the integrity of their product and their duties as responsible corporate citizens. They have aided and abetted the Chinese regime to prop up both of these pillars, propagating the message of the dictatorship unabated and supporting the secret police in a myriad of ways, including surveillance and invasion of privacy, in order to effectuate the massive crackdown on its citizens.

In response to Shi Tao, the imprisoned Chinese journalist, Yahoo! senior vice president and general counsel Michael Callahan said:[68]

At the time the demand was made for information in this case, Yahoo! China was legally obligated to comply with the requirements of Chinese law enforcement. When we had operational control of Yahoo! China, we took steps to make clear our Beijing operation would honor such instructions only if they came through authorized law enforcement officers and only if the demand for information met

rigorous standards establishing the legal validity of the demand.

When we receive a demand from law enforcement authorized under the law of the country in which we operate, we must comply. This is a real example of why this issue is bigger than any one company and any one industry. All companies must respond in the same way. When a foreign telecommunications company operating in the United States receives an order from U.S. law enforcement, it must comply. Failure to comply in China could have subjected Yahoo! China and its employees to criminal charges, including imprisonment. Ultimately, U.S. companies in China face a choice: comply with Chinese law, or leave.

Google's vice president of Global Communication and Public Affairs Elliot Schrage explained how Google arrived at its difficult decision to enter China with a self-censored product:[69]

Understandably, many are puzzled or upset by our decision. But our decision was based on a judgment that Google.cn will make a meaningful—though imperfect—contribution to the overall expansion of access to information in China . . .

Google's problem was that its U.S.-based Chinese-language version of Google.com was "slow and unreliable." "According to our measurements, Google.com appears to be unreachable around 10% of the time," said Schrage in his testimony. The cause was "extensive filtering performed by China's licensed Internet Service Providers," he said. These problems meant that Chinese Internet users were bypassing Google for Chinese-based

Internet companies, such as China's popular search engine Baidu.[70]

Google could only resolve its access and speed problems by locating its servers on Chinese soil, which meant its services would be subject to "regulatory requirements to filter and remove links to content that is considered illegal in China."[71]

Google based its decision on its "business commitment to satisfy the interest of users," Schrage explained, and by its "conviction that expanding access to information to anyone who wants it will make our world a better more informed and freer place." However, for China, a third factor had to be considered: "Be responsive to local conditions."[72]

Schrage said some new elements were added to Google.cn to soften the impact of its decision to self-censor "a handful of politically sensitive subjects":[73]

> **Disclosure to users:** [Google] will give notification to Chinese users whenever search results have been removed.
>
> **Protection of user privacy:** [Google] will not maintain on Chinese soil any services, like email, that involve personal or confidential data. This means [Google] will not, for example, host Gmail or Blogger, [Google's] email and blogging tools in China.
>
> **Continued availability of Google .com:** [Google] will not terminate the availability of our unfiltered Chinese-language Google.com service. [While Google does not self-censor this off-China site, the Chinese government filters user queries—slowing down the service or making it unreliable.]

Schrage's testimony continued:[74]

> Our hope is that our mix of measures, though far from our ideal, would accomplish more for Chinese citizens' access to information than the alternative. We don't pretend

that this is the single "right" answer to the dilemma faced by information companies in China, but rather a reasonable approach that seems likely to bring our users greater access to more information than any other search engine in China. And by serving our users better, we hope it will be good for our business, too, over the long run.

> To be clear, these are not easy, black and white issues. As our co-founder Sergey Brin has said, we understand and respect the perspective of people who disagree with our decision; indeed, we recognize that the opposing point of view is a reasonable one to hold. Nonetheless, in a situation where there are only imperfect options, we think we have made a reasonable choice.

Google and other technology companies that testified also called on the U.S. government for help. Google recommended that the Internet industry "define common principles to guide the practices of technology firms in countries that restrict access to information."[75] Google and others called for the U.S. government to begin the political and diplomatic debate to consider treating "censorship as a barrier to trade."[76]

An Amnesty International's Business Human Rights Program representative who spoke to lawmakers said in a news media interview that companies can work together to promote change within authoritarian governments. The U.S. apparel and footwear industry dealt with labor rights violations in their supply chains by creating unified standards and monitoring factories where the goods were produced.[77]

On the same day Congress was holding its hearing on the issue, the U.S. Department of State announced that it would form a global Internet freedom task force to study foreign policy implications of the Internet and make recommendations to the secretary of state.[78]

Open Scenario Challenge

You are Google's global communications and public affairs director. The day after the congressional hearing, you are dismayed but not surprised that news coverage focused on U.S. technology companies' reluctant but still cooperative participation in China's censorship policies. Very little of the root causes to the problem or Google's actions to minimize the effects of the Chinese government's authoritarian policies have been fully explained in the news media.

You are asked to develop key messages that could be placed in advocacy advertisements and other publications to explain Google's efforts to hold true to its corporate mantra "Don't Do Evil."

Questions for Discussion

1. Why should a company like Google be concerned about its reputation?

2. Why were U.S. Internet technology companies asked to testify to the U.S. House of Representatives Subcommittee on Africa, Global Human Rights, and International Operations?

3. Are there any ethical issues involved in this case? If so, how could future ethical issues be averted?

4. Why were human rights groups and journalism groups upset?

5. Why was the U.S. House of Representatives investigating this situation?

6. Why was Yahoo! involved in this debate?

7. What is Google's unofficial motto? Why was Google receiving negative publicity regarding its business in China?

8. What did Google do in China to minimize the potential censorship problems?

9. Examine the testimony of Google and Yahoo! Who, in your opinion, did a better job of protecting his company's reputation?

10. How can coalition or alliance building help U.S. Internet companies in the future?

Web Resources

- **U.S. House of Representatives, hearing transcripts of the Subcommittee on Asia and the Pacific, and the Subcommittee on Africa, Global Human Rights, and International Operations** wwwc.house.gov/international_relations/afhear.htm

- **Google, testimony of Google before the Subcommittee on Asia and the Pacific, and the Subcommittee on Africa, Global Human Rights, and International Operations on February 15, 2006** googleblog.blogspot.com/2006/02/testimony-internet-in-china.html

- **Amnesty International Business and Human Rights Program** www.amnestyusa.org/business/index.do

- **Reporters without Borders** (contains information about Internet filtering and censorship, Including news releases and a report entitled "Internet under Surveillance 2004") www.rsf.org/

- **Google** (corporate information about its culture and philosophy, as well as news releases and other background material) www.google.com/corporate/history.html

- **U.S. Department of State** (contains information about economic, business and agricultural affairs, and democracy and global affairs efforts) www.state.gov/

Corn Aids Europe's Green Revolution

NatureWorks LLC's Biodegradable Plastic Products Fit Eco Trend

Corn is more than just feedstock. Many things that can be made from petroleum can also be made from corn, or more accurately, corn sugar (dextrose). Raw corn kernels can be fermented and turned into sugary syrup, then into clear pellets that can be spun into silky fabric or formed into a variety of plastic containers or parts.

Corn is the most abundantly grown source of natural sugar in the world, and it's relatively cheap compared to rising oil prices. The United States grows 42 percent of the world's corn supply.[79]

One U.S. company is using its commitment to sustainability and environmentally friendly production practices to create products that leave "smaller, greener footprints" on the environment.

NatureWorks LLC, headquartered in Minnetonka, Minnesota, is an independent business unit owned by Cargill, a leading agricultural processor. The business is dedicated to meeting the world's needs today without compromising the earth's ability to meet the needs of tomorrow.

The corn-derived polymer PLA (polylactic acid) offers customers in Europe, Asia, and North America a meaningful way to help achieve compliance with the Kyoto Protocol for reduction of greenhouse gases. This international treaty agreement pledged 163 countries to stabilize greenhouse emissions that many scientists believe contribute to global climate change.

"Since 2000, when NatureWorks PLA was introduced, the European market has been an early leader in adopting renewable-resource-based products," said Dennis McGrew, president and CEO of Nature-Works LLC. "Heightened environmental awareness in European countries, including Italy, France, Germany, Belgium, and the U.K., has been key for bringing nature-based plastics into the mainstream."

The process involves fermentation, distillation, and polymerization of dextrose, a simple plant sugar made from field maize (corn). NatureWorks essentially harvests the carbon stored in the sugars to make polylactic acid (PLA), a polymer with similar characteristics to traditional thermoplastics.

NatureWorks PLA looks and feels like traditional plastic packaging—it is strong and durable to protect food and retain freshness, and crystal clear to allow consumers to see the food inside.

In addition to the appeal of its annually renewable feedstock, NatureWorks PLA offered many other environmentally preferred benefits. It was the world's first greenhouse-gas-neutral polymer (based on the purchase of renewable energy certificates by NatureWorks LLC). In addition, from cradle to resin, its production used 68 percent less fossil fuel resources than traditional plastics.

Even without the energy certificates, NatureWorks PLA polymers represented a 30 to 50 percent reduction in fossil fuel use and a 30 to 55 percent reduction in greenhouse gas emissions versus petroleum-based polymers.

Products made from NatureWorks PLA could be disposed of in several ways. The material was compatible with existing recycling systems, could be composted, and incinerated cleanly.

From a marketing communication standpoint, NatureWorks PLA was an interesting sell. "Consumers are intrigued by the notion of packaging from corn and want to see, touch and try the new containers," said Steve Halsey, vice president of Gibbs and Soell Public Relations in Chicago. "The challenge is getting retailers, brands, and supply chains to switch out their existing plastic packaging for the newer material."

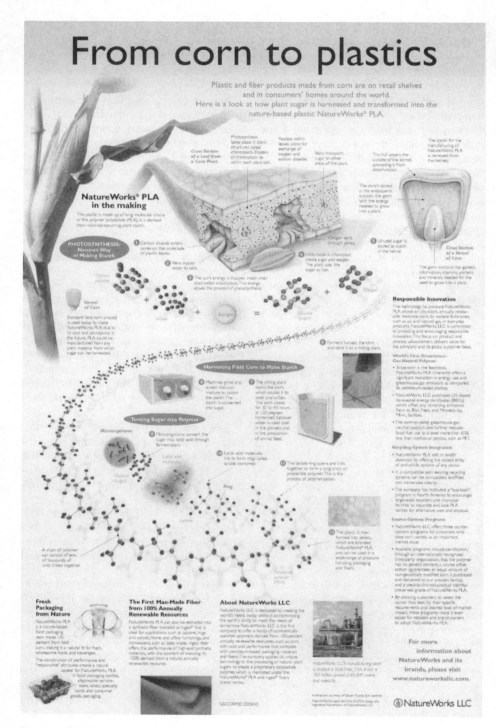

Courtesy of NatureWorks LLC

Gibbs and Soell is a leading independent public relations firm serving Fortune 500 clients and a range of other industry-leading companies. The firm has been working with NatureWorks LLC since 1997, using its consumer, industrial, and agricultural communications expertise to help create global awareness for the company and technology.

RESEARCH

Bio-based products were finding success in the marketplace because corn and soybean costs had been relatively stable over the long term, oil was selling at record prices, and consumers were looking for energy alternatives.

Still, bio-based products face challenges. A majority of existing processes, products, and systems were based on petroleum. In addition, consumers generally do not equate everyday products with petroleum dependence, and do not want to sacrifice convenience. "Consumers are fickle and tend to pull toward what they know and trust," said Halsey. There were also some misperceptions about bio-based products to overcome:

- Cost prohibitive
- Poor performance
- A niche product
- Requires heavy subsidies
- For environmentalists, not mainstream consumers

But research conducted in 2003 and 2004 showed some consumer movement toward change. In Western Europe, 59 percent of consumers in Germany, France, Italy, and the United Kingdom ranked the concept of fresh foods in natural packaging as "very desirable." Of respondents, 72 percent were also willing to pay an additional 10 Euro cents more per food item for this bio-based option.

Even less environmentally conscious Americans were showing a willingness to go green. The survey indicated 41 percent found the concept of nature-based packaging for fresh foods "very desirable." The respondents were also willing to pay an additional 5 cents per packaged food item.

STRATEGY

To take advantage of European interest in environmentally friendly products, NatureWorks and Gibbs and Soell developed a marketing communication plan that emphasized message framing, said Halsey. Some of the framing strategies included: "It works just like . . ."; "It has similar performance to . . ."; "It features improved . . ."; and "You'll benefit from . . ."

The communication strategy also included product facts and proof. "Just saying you're better because your product or technology is bio-based is not good enough . . . you must prove it," said Halsey. Retailers and brand owners want a sure thing. NatureWorks LLC needed to tell potential retail business customers that there was a viable market for bio-based plastics; that it was relevant for their format, product mix, and customers; and that it would work for them.

Education was another major component of the communication strategy. "You can't assume that everyone shares your vision," Halsey said. "Change is hard and risky." Therefore, vision and reality must be communicated in unison. At the end of the day, "I may embrace a vision, but I can buy a reality. That is why having a product on store shelves is so critical." Successful marketing of bio-based products requires a product with competitive pricing and proof that it fits the retailer's and customer's needs. Halsey said educational efforts have focused on keeping messages relevant, simple, and intuitive, as well as having fun with it.

Backgrounders, such as its "The Tool Life Cycle Assessment," explain in layperson's terms how NatureWorks LLC is environmentally friendly and meets International Standards ISO 14040–14043. This certification is widely recognized and understood by Europeans, who are generally considered more concerned with environmental issues than U.S. consumers.

BELGIUM'S TOAST TO NATUREWORKS PLA

The NatureWorks PLA push into Europe and Asia was successful because consumers were eager for environmentally friendly packaging options. One Belgium brewery decided to serve its brew in compostable cups.

Alken-Maes, the second-largest brewery in Belgium, decided to position itself as a leader in its innovative use of compostable cups, which reduced the amount of waste generated at large music festivals. It provided more than 1.5 million servings of beer at the high-traffic festivals during the launch of this new initiative.

Working closely with the client, Gibbs and Soell developed a media relations and promotions plan. It included the creation of signage and support material (backgrounders, key messages, talking points, etc.) needed to promote and educate customers about the new environmentally friendly cups. Trade media support included media alerts, news releases, feature pitching, interviews with representatives from Nature-Works and Alken-Maes, a news conference for top-tier trade publications, and a post-event news release. In preparation for the launch, Alken-Maes also supplied each of its employees with a NatureWorks cup and a copy of a news release.

Open Scenario Challenge

NatureWorks LLC wants to be known as the global leader and as the more responsible and desired alternative to traditional petroleum-based resins. However, some skeptics question whether NatureWorks PLA has the performance and the staying power to thrive. To help drive industry adoption, NatureWorks LLC wants to continue demonstrating the viability of Nature-Works PLA to attract customers and government funding and increase the market visibility of its products.

Develop a campaign to communicate to targeted global media about the innovative technology's marketplace success and potential. Campaign elements should include: message development and training, award submissions, and proactive editorial outreach.

Questions for Discussion

1. What are some key considerations when introducing a new technology?
2. What are the marketing communication challenges for bio-based products?
3. What are the benefits of bio-based products?
4. Why are Europe and Asia considered prime markets for NatureWorks PLA products?
5. How is the Life Cycle Assessment used to promote products such as Nature-Works PLA?
6. What are some of the marketing-communication techniques used to promote business-to-business awareness for products such as NatureWorks PLA?

Terminology

- award submissions
- backgrounders
- bio-based products
- ISO
- Kyoto Protocol
- message development and training
- proactive editorial outreach
- Renewable Energy Certificates
- "smaller, greener footprints"

Web Resources

- **NatureWorks LLC** www.cargill.com/about/organization/dow.htm
- **Cargill** www.cargill.com/
- **International Organization for Standardization** www.iso.ch/iso/en/ISOOnline.frontpage
- **U.S. Grains Council** www.grains.org/page.ww?section=Barley%2C+Corn+%26+Sorghum&name=Corn

Chapter Thirteen

Financial Relations

Public relations professionals are known for their ability as communicators—not always for their business acumen. Often, professionals bemoan the lack of basic business knowledge exhibited by public relations graduates.

If public relations' goal is to ensure the survivability of an organization, shouldn't the practitioner understand how the organization's bottom line works? After all, if the practitioner doesn't know how the organization makes money, he or she will be unable to effectively communicate it to the public. It only takes one blank look in a room full of senior management to sideline the public relations practitioner who can't explain the basics of a company balance sheet.

Public relations students should take business classes, including economics and accounting, as part of their educational program. Students can also pick up business knowledge on their own by paying attention to business-related news publications and shows. The business section of a local newspaper is a good place to begin. Start monitoring your favorite shopping destinations or entertainment outlets. Check out their annual reports online. Little by little, the world of business will begin to make sense.

Not only does a general knowledge of an organization's business model and strategy help a practitioner do his or her job better with credibility among management, but it can eventually lead to opportunities to specialize in investor relations.

This specialized area of public relations deals with publicly held companies. According to the National Investor Relations Institute:[1]

> Investor relations is defined as a strategic management responsibility that integrates finance, communication, marketing and securities law compliance to enable the most effective two-way communication between a company and the financial community and other constituencies, which ultimately contributes to a company's securities achieving fair valuation.

Publics that investor relations managers communicate with include financial analysts and current and prospective investors: institutional, individual, and employee investors. Another important public that investor relations professionals focus on is the financial news industry. This includes financial writers and their publications such as *Wall Street Journal, Forbes, Barron's, Business Week, Fortune,* and the *Kiplinger Letter,* along with financial columnists, and cable and broadcast television and radio shows with a financial emphasis.[2] In addition, the investor relations officer provides feedback and competitive intelligence to senior management.

A QUICK BASIC BUSINESS PRIMER

This section provides a very basic overview of some business terms and concepts to start, but further reading and discussion are helpful.

The first lesson of business is that businesses exist to make money. The goal of financial relations is to build positive relationships with all key stakeholders who affect the business's ability to survive and make money.

Every business needs money (i.e., capital) to operate. Businesses can be either privately or publicly owned. Private companies are often run by the company's founders, management, or a group of private investors. Private businesses use profits, bonds, or bank loans to provide the necessary money to expand or undertake new activities.

A publicly held company has sold a portion of itself to the public by selling stock (a piece of the company) or by issuing debt (usually in the form of corporate bonds), which means that its shareholders (owners of stock) and/or debt holders (owners of the bonds) have a claim on the company's assets and profits. The money raised from public offerings allows companies to expand, modernize, conduct research, or engage in other activities to expand the business. Publicly held companies have thousands, if not millions, of owners, thanks to the popularity of average Americans' investing in stocks and bonds for retirement savings.

As long as investors are confident that the company is on the right track and either provides a share of its profit earnings (a dividend) or has good indications of future profits, investors are likely keep their money in the company. Management must share its business strategy plan with its investors so that they can determine if the strategy is likely to move the company in the right direction. Financial analysts examine these business strategies and other company indicators (earnings, debt, and competitors, etc.) to comment positively or negatively about a company's performance and future prospects. With positive future prospects and accompanying high investor confidence, the company's stock value rises. This is because there are a limited number of shares available, and if demand outstrips supply, the price for a share of stock rises. In this situation, future stock purchases by investors in the company will cost more, but it's usually worth more too, because of positive future profit predictions. If an investor eventually sells his or her stake in the company, the profit should be higher than the initial investment.

All kinds of factors and events, anticipated or not, can combine to create either positive or negative business conditions. Some of these factors include earnings or sales growth, new product releases, leadership changes, and legislation.[3] Rising gas prices that increase the cost of transporting goods or powerful hurricanes that destroy a company's facilities can have negative impacts on a business's ability to make a profit. Either could lead shareholders to pull their money out of the company and invest it somewhere else or prevent potential investors from buying shares. This loss of monetary investment reduces the overall value of the company, reduces its access to money, and often leads companies to find ways to reduce its costs, such as closing plants and laying off workers.

INVESTOR RELATIONS' ROLE

Investor confidence in a company is key to a publicly held business's success. It should be inspired by the company's financial performance, leadership, and future prospects truthfully communicated through various information tactics directed to investors and the financial media.[4] Along with senior management, investor relations professionals are responsible for getting the message out about the company's well-being. The key to investor relations is disclosure of material information needed for informed decision making and dissemination of that information to those who need it.

To protect investors from companies involved in misconduct, the federal government's U.S. Securities and Exchange Commission (SEC) "seeks to detect problems in the securities markets, prevent and deter violations of federal securities laws, and alert investors to possible wrongdoing."[5] The agency fosters informed investment decision making by "reviewing disclosures of companies and mutual funds to ensure that clear, complete, and accurate information is available to investors."[6] For example, *regulation fair disclosure* (commonly called Reg FD) is a Securities and Exchange Commission rule that attempts to prevent selective disclosure of information; in the past, individual investors may not have been privy to the same information provided to bigger institutional investors. Today, conference calls and informational meetings conducted by the company are open to the general public.[7] The right to equal access to this nonpublic "market-moving information"[8] was required by SEC's Regulation Fair Disclosure in 2000.

Another regulation, the Sarbanes-Oxley Act (SOX) of 2002, was created to protect investors from fraudulent accounting activities. Today, publicly traded companies must follow stricter auditor regulations and disclosure in their financial statements.[9] The Public Company Accounting Oversight Board (PCAOB) oversees the enforcement of this regulation.

If investors cannot get timely, reliable, and truthful information about a company's operations or other factors that may affect its operations, then investors will not risk their money. The most well-known type of disclosure problem is called *insider trading.* This involves a person having important knowledge, known as *material information*—such as advance information about a company sale, merger, product innovation, or launch—that other investors don't have and then using that information to make money by buying or selling stock. Material information is defined as any event or information considered important enough to influence a decision to buy or sell a publicly listed security and/or to influence a company's stock price.

According to the National Investor Relations Institute (NIRI):[10]

> Anyone in the spokesperson role must be completely
> familiar with the company's record of disclosure in order to
> guard against unauthorized disclosures of material, nonpublic
> information . . . under Reg FD, to detect inadvertent

disclosure of material, nonpublic information or to avoid potentially intentional disclosure of such information, the IRO should accompany senior officials in meetings with analysts or investors. If there should be an inadvertent disclosure of such information, the company must issue a news release within 24 hours of when the official became aware of such disclosure or before the next trading day, whichever is later.

Credibility comes not only from knowledge of the company and provision of accurate, complete and timely information, but also from a demonstrated willingness to correct or update changes in information on a timely basis. Failure to do so may cause long-term or irreparable damage to the company's management and the spokesperson's credibility.

NIRI suggests that investor relations officers (IRO) tread a narrow path that requires them to "balance public interests with those of their company and place those interests above their own." An IRO should possess the following qualities: personal integrity, professionalism, competence, and objectivity. He or she must also understand conditions for conflicts of interest and how to appropriately represent the company, especially when addressing matters related to future company performance.

IROs develop materials or directly interact with analysts and investors to accurately portray a business's value. The IRO constantly monitors investor communication and the competitive environment to respond to questions about trends, or other important developments in and outside the company that might have an effect on the business's value. This information is communicated back to management to develop effective communication strategies as part of the overall business strategy.

An investor relations counseling firm can provide any of the following strategic counseling and tactical activities to help organizations achieve their objectives:[11]

- Analysts and investor meetings
- Communication counsel for program and policy development and implementation
- Crisis communication
- Disclosure issues relating to financial reporting and policy development
- Financial communication tactics
- IR spokesperson training
- Media relations
- Message development

- Positioning strategies
- Research
- Overall strategy development

To ensure that companies are telling all investors what is going on in a timely manner, the SEC requires publicly held companies to adhere to numerous reporting rules. It requires publicly held companies with assets of $10 million or more and 500 shareholders to file three types of reports throughout the calendar or fiscal year: Form 10K, Form 10Q, and Form 8K. Any SEC-required company filings can be accessed from SEC's Web site (www.sec.gov) using the EDGAR database. The following descriptions are from the SEC Web site:[12]

REQUIRED FORMS

Form 10K (Annual Filings)

The annual report on Form 10K provides a comprehensive overview of the company's business and financial condition and includes audited financial statements. Although similarly named, the annual report on Form 10K is distinct from the "annual report to shareholders," which a company must send to its shareholders when it holds an annual meeting to elect directors.

Form 10Q (Quarterly Filings)

Form 10Q includes unaudited financial statements and provides a continuing view of the company's financial position during the year. The report must be filed for each of the first three quarters of the company's fiscal year.

Form 8K (Current Filings)

Public companies must report material corporate events on a more current basis. Form 8K is the "current report" companies must file with the SEC to announce major events that shareholders should know about.

Other Documents

Beyond these important reports, the investor relations officer should be familiar with other documents including:

- Registration statements for newly offered securities
- Proxy materials sent to shareholders before an annual meeting
- Annual reports sent to shareholders
- Documents concerning tender offers (an offer to buy a large number of shares of a corporation, usually at a premium above the current market price)

- Filings related to mergers and acquisitions
- NYSE and NASDAQ also have requirements for companies listed on their exchanges

The successful investor relations officer should develop and work to improve several skill areas, including a thorough knowledge of business concepts, communication, and relationship building and an ability to research and analyze financial information. Also the investor relations officer should share information with management and help incorporate it into the organization's business strategy.

NIRI recommends the following information dissemination guidelines:[13]

Technology: Companies are encouraged to use multiple technologies to reach the widest audience possible, including the individual investor. These technologies include: major wire services, conference calls, broadcast fax and fax-on-demand services, e-mail, video conferences, Web sites, and electronic EDGAR filings. The broadly disseminated news release is considered essential to the communication program.

Internet: While the Internet is widely used, companies must use more traditional sources of dissemination for those who request it. Companies should monitor Internet sites that discuss a company's performance but are not allowed to participate or respond in chat rooms as it could be considered a form of selective disclosure. Monitoring the Internet does help companies create communication strategies.

Conference Calls: Following news releases to the wire services, fully accessible webcast conference calls are the most widely used means for disseminating corporate information to the investment community. Conference calls are often used as a forum in which the company disseminates detailed information, expanding on information contained in the news release that has been issued prior to the call.

Regulation FD considers a fully accessible, nonexclusionary webcast or telephonic conference call as a means for real-time, full and fair disclosure.

One-on-one Meetings: Face-to-face meetings, such as one-on-one meetings with analysts and investors, help build goodwill and make a company more approachable in the eyes of the investment community. Companies should note that, as in all other types of meetings, there is the possibility that information may be selectively disclosed. Companies should conscientiously avoid discussing material, nonpublic information in one-on-one meetings. If there is an unintentional disclosure of such information, the IRO can issue a news release containing that information within 24 hours.

CHALLENGES IN INVESTOR RELATIONS

Investor relations is a demanding and important job. It requires high ethical standards, particularly in providing truthful information to all who require it even when pressured by others in the organization. The job also requires the ability to react quickly and appropriately in times of crisis; this includes reacting to rumors, actual poor performance reports, tender offers, or proxy fights.

A *tender offer* is an offer to buy a large number of shares of a corporation, usually at a premium above the current market price. Investor relations officers can help management strategize how best to communicate with shareholders, investors, and analysts to encourage confidence in the current leadership and company's direction.

A *proxy fight* happens when shareholders ask other shareholders, unable to attend an annual meeting, to cast their "absentee vote" for the issue advocated by the requesting shareholders. This often happens when shareholders are unhappy with management and want to vote down certain management proposals or change the organization's leadership by voting in new board directors. As with tender offers, a proxy fight requires the investor relations officer to help management communicate effectively with shareholders, investors, and analysts so that the current leadership maintains control of the company.

Web Resources

- **National Investor Relations Institute** www.niri.org/
- **National Investor Relations Institute Standards of Practice for Investor Relations, third edition, January 2004** www.niri.org/
- **U.S. Securities and Exchange Commission** www.sec.gov/
- **U.S. Securities and Exchange Commission; Filings and Forms (EDGAR)** www.sec.gov/edgar.shtml
- **New York Stock Exchange** www.nyse.com/
- **NASDAQ: http** www.nasdaq.com/
- **Public Company Accounting Oversight Board (PCAOB)** www.pcaobus.org/
- **Public Relations Society of America: Financial Communications Section** www.prsa.org/_Networking/
- **Investopedia** www.investopedia.com/

From Humble Beginnings
The World-Class Story of Teva Pharmaceutical Industries, Ltd.

By Donna N. Stein, APR, Fellow PRSA, of Donna Stein and Partners

Teva Pharmaceutical Industries (NASDAQ: TEVA) is a global pharmaceutical company specializing in the development, production, and marketing of generic and proprietary-branded pharmaceuticals as well as active pharmaceutical ingredients. Teva is among the top 20 pharmaceutical companies and among the largest generic pharmaceutical companies in the world. Headquartered in Jerusalem, Israel, Teva has operations in Israel, North America, Europe, Mexico, and South and Latin America.[14]

In 1991 an investor relations firm in New York City was hired to create and implement a comprehensive "best practices" investor relations and financial media relations program to raise awareness and visibility for the company and its American depository receipts (ADRs) in the U.S. financial markets. ADRs are negotiable certificates issued by a U.S. bank representing a specific number of shares of a foreign stock traded on a U.S. stock exchange. ADRs make it easier for Americans to invest in foreign companies due to the widespread availability of dollar-denominated price information, lower transaction costs, and timely dividend dissemination.[15]

During the 1990s many Israeli-based companies looked to the United States for sources of capital to help them grow their businesses, and Teva was no different. When the account team first conducted its initial due diligence of the company in preparation for developing an investor relations plan, the team discovered that Teva was going to be a tough sell to members of the U.S. investment community for four primary reasons: (1) Teva was based in Israel, a politically unstable country; (2) as a foreign-based company, Teva was considered a high-risk investment because the company did not have to adhere to U.S. Financial Accounting Standards Board (FASB) accounting and U.S. SEC reporting standards; (3) generic pharmaceuticals were considered inferior to branded drugs; and (4) Teva was a "small cap," NASDAQ-traded stock, with approximately $200 million in annual revenues. Small cap stocks did not appeal to many institutional investors because of the limited "public float" of the company's shares available for purchase.

The investor relations team had to develop a multifaceted investor relations program that would address all these issues, which involved marketing the Teva investment story to a number of key constituents, including "sell-side" equity research analysts covering the generic pharmaceutical industry in addition to analysts covering Israeli-based stocks; high-quality "buy-side" institutional investors; and members of the U.S. business and financial press.

In addition, the investor relations team had to dispel the perceptions that Israeli stocks were "bad" news and that generic drugs were inferior methods of treatment. There were two other important image problems the company wanted to eliminate as well: the fear and trepidation of Teva's foreign financial reporting and a seven-hour time difference between Teva and the New York financial markets that made Teva's management seem inaccessible during the normal business day to U.S. investors.

To Teva management's credit, it fully understood and agreed with the consultant's situation analysis and readily agreed with the recommendation to start reporting its financial performance each quarter and annually under U.S. standards and generally accepted accounting principles (GAAP).

In addition, the company started hosting quarterly conference calls for analysts and investors with toll-free international access numbers. Once the conference call was concluded, senior management would board a plane for the United States to spend the next week on a "road show" meeting with existing and potential buy- and sell-side investors in New York, Boston, and other key U.S. markets.

The company would host group breakfast and luncheon meetings with elaborate slide and, in later years, PowerPoint presentations, as well as one-on-one meetings with analysts and key investors.

As Teva became more widely covered by research analysts, the company was invited to appear at brokerage-sponsored pharmaceutical and health care industry investment conferences. The investor relations consultants also initiated a proactive media relations effort to educate business and financial reporters about the value proposition of generic drugs and to provide an opportunity for Teva management to explain the company's growth strategy, key disease markets, emerging branded drug development efforts, and plans for international expansion.

As the company expanded through internal growth and by the acquisition of smaller drug companies, the next step was to schedule "investor days" at various company operations, once every two years, which included facility tours of manufacturing and research operations, and presentations by members of Teva's senior management team. These field trips included visiting operating facilities in North America, Israel, and Europe.

During the past two decades Teva had grown from $200 million in annual revenues to more than $5.3 billion in sales for 2005, from a small cap security to a large cap stock with more than a $32.3 billion market capitalization.[16]

Over two-thirds of the company's ADRs in the United States were owned by institutional investors and more than 4 million ADRs trade on an average day. Teva was the most actively traded stock on the Tel-Aviv Stock Exchange and its ADRs were among the most widely held Israeli issues on the NASDAQ exchange. Teva was ranked 15 on the NASDAQ 100 index. It had become one of the world's most respected public companies, one of the

highest-quality generic pharmaceutical providers, and an emerging researcher and developer of branded drugs. One example of that success was Teva's drug Copaxone, which represented one-third of the market for multiple sclerosis medications in 2005.

Questions for Discussion

1. What were the problems facing Teva?
2. What were the elements of the investor relations consulting firm's strategy for solving its problems?
3. Why are small cap companies unappealing to institutional investors?
4. Why did the consulting firm recommend that Teva begin reporting its financial performance each quarter and annually under U.S. standards and GAAP?
5. What is a conference call, and what is its purpose in financial and investor relations?
6. What face-to-face activities were initiated with key publics and why?

Do Some Research

Go to Teva's Web site at www.tevapharm.com. Find the Web site's investor relations section and locate the latest Webcast conference call explaining Teva's quarterly performance. What was your impression of the Webcast? What do you think were the goals of the conference call? Conduct some research about conference calls and best practices for this communication tactic. Is Teva following best practices for conference calls? Why or why not? Did Teva also issue a news release that provided supplementary or complementary information about the conference call?

Terminology

- ADRs
- buy-side
- conference calls
- due diligence
- FASB
- GAAP

- NASDAQ
- road show
- SEC
- Sell-side equity research analysts
- SWOT

Web Resources

- **Teva Pharmaceutical Industries** www.tevapharm.com
- **MarketVolume.com** (volume-based technical analysis of broad market indexes) www.marketvolume.com
- **Investopedia.com** (resource site with a dictionary of financial terms and other materials) www.investopedia.com
- **New York Stock Exchange** www.nyse.com
- **WordIQ.com** (provides definitions for financial terms) www.wordiq.com
- **Public Relations Society of America** (contains special professional interest sections, including one on financial communication) www.prsa.org
- **National Investor Relations Institute** www.niri.org.

Wal-Mart

Can It Repair Its Corporate Reputation in the Eyes of All Its Constituents?

By Donna N. Stein, APR, PRSA Fellow, of Donna Stein and Partners

Wal-Mart Stores, Inc. (NYSE: WMT) headquartered in Bentonville, Arkansas, is the world's largest retailer, employing 1.6 billion associates worldwide, with more than 1.2 million U.S. employees. The company has been publicly traded since 1970, and in 2005 generated more than $256 billion in revenue, with approximately 5,000 stores and wholesale clubs across 15 countries.[17]

For years, Sam Walton's beloved Wal-Mart has been "a lightning rod for activists and critics of big business who have questioned such things as the company's employee relations, benefits, policies and supplier relations."[18] The company has been accused "of paying poverty-level wages, providing inadequate health-care coverage to employees, hiring illegal immigrants, destroying communities, driving jobs overseas . . . Wal-Mart has become one of the great polarizing issues that divides American politics."[19]

It doesn't seem like any one of the company's constituencies has been untouched by one or more of the company's actions, which have become more than just public relations issues. Indeed, CEO Lee Scott formed a rapid response team that operates in a "war room," monitoring polls and conducting periodic surveys of "thought leaders" regarding Wal-Mart's reputation.

Scott assumed the position of the company's "chief reputation officer" and in early 2006 was stumping the "Wal-Mart is good" story to anyone and everyone who would listen to it. He maintained that a positive result of Wal-Mart's growth was job creation. That was, in part, a response to critics' claim that more U.S. jobs were lost every time Wal-Mart put the squeeze on U.S. suppliers to cut costs to reduce prices, requiring them to outsource or manufacture products overseas.

With employees, vendors and suppliers, activists, and critics all fighting for their just due from the giant retailer, how was the investment community faring? Investor confidence was shaken in 2005 when a scandal broke involving a top Wal-Mart executive who was accused of taking money, gift cards, and merchandise for personal use. He pleaded guilty to the charges on January 31, 2006.[20] Lawsuits are rarely viewed as good things. They cost money and take time away from running the business, and with Wal-Mart's rash of lawsuits, including discrimination suits filed by female employees, and a slowing organizational growth rate in 2005, analysts and investors had cause for concern. In a September 2005 issue of the *Wall Street Journal,* the company reported that it was going to start shaking up its retail mix, especially in apparel, to fight increased competition from Target Stores. Stories like "Looking Upscale, Wal-Mart Begins a Big Makeover" sent Wal-Mart's stock price to a new 52-week low.[21]

Wal-Mart's corporate reputation—which makes investors buy stocks, sustains employee morale, supports vendor and supplier relationships, and attracts customers to stores—was in shambles in 2005 and early 2006. Not even the generous assistance given to victims of Hurricane Katrina had helped improve the company's corporate reputation or report card scores for corporate social responsibility.

The company announced in March 2006 that it had retained an executive search firm to hire a director of global ethics who would work closely with the CEO and other senior managers to ensure that ethics were first and foremost in every department within the company.

Open Scenario Challenge

As Wal-Mart's investor relations officer, you are well aware of the many issues that have harmed the company's reputation. You and your staff must present a plan to company management on ways to rebuild its reputation with key publics.

First, determine the key issues that investors are most concerned with. Once identified, what would be your first course of action to address them?

Of immediate concern: the Wal-Mart annual meeting of shareholders in two months. What themes and main messages would you advise CEO Lee Scott to focus on in his formal presentation?

One major competitor is Target Stores. It is emerging as a strong competitor not only at the retail level but also for investment dollars on Wall Street. How would you gather intelligence regarding its investor relations efforts so that you can develop a communications program and strategy to put Wal-Mart in a more favorable light?

Questions for Discussion

1. Why does a company's reputation matter?

2. Why does Wal-Mart attract a large amount of negative publicity?

3. What has been the role of Wal-Mart's chief executive officer? Has he done a good job of protecting Wal-Mart's reputation?

4. What is the purpose of a rapid response strategy?

5. Why don't Wal-Mart's positive community actions and messages contained on its Web site gain wider acceptance?

6. Why has Wal-Mart decided to hire a global ethics officer?

Do Some Research

1. Research the duties of Wal-Mart's global ethics director. What does the job entail? What have been some of the actions of this position recently? How does this position help bolster the company's reputation? Does this position have anything to do with corporate social responsibility? If so, how?

2. Examine one of Wal-Mart's activist's groups Web sites, such as Wal-Mart

Watch or Wake Up Wal-Mart. What are the issues that the group has with Wal-Mart? Examine Wal-Mart's foundation Web site, called Wal-Mart Good Works. Does this counteract some of the issues raised by activist groups? If so, how?

Terminology

- rapid response team
- global ethics director

Web Resources

- **Wal-Mart** www.walmartstores.com/GlobalWMStoresWeb/navigate.do?catg=316
- **Wal-Mart Good Works** www.walmart foundation.org/wmstore/goodworks/scripts/index.jsp
- **Wal-Mart Watch** walmartwatch.com/
- **Wake Up Wal-Mart** www.wakeup walmart.com/

No Longer Boxed In
An Opportunity to Tell Iron Mountain's Dynamic Growth Story

By Donna N. Stein, APR, PRSA Fellow, of Donna Stein and Partners

Iron Mountain Incorporated (NYSE: IRM) is the world's trusted partner for outsourced records and information management services. Once known only as the "storage facilitator for boxed records," Iron Mountain is now one of the leading players in digital archiving services.[22]

Iron Mountain, based in Boston, Massachusetts, celebrated its 10th year as a public company traded on the New York Stock Exchange in 2006. It also marked chief executive officer Richard Reese's 25th year with Iron Mountain. The company began more than 50 years ago as a mushroom farm in the foothills north of New York City. It was transformed during the Cold War, becoming an underground "mine" to preserve and store boxes of documents in the event of a nuclear holocaust for companies located in and around New York. Throughout its history Iron Mountain has always had one primary focus: to provide superior value to its customers by protecting and managing their information as if it were its own, delivering reliable and responsive service, and providing real-world solutions.

Today, Iron Mountain provides a wide variety of information management products and services to more than 200,000 customer accounts around the globe. The company still stores and retrieves boxes of paper documents but also offers many other services: record management and program development and implementation based on best practices and expertise to help customers meet specific regulations, including SEC rules, Sarbanes-Oxley, and safe harbor; digital archiving for secure, legally compliant, cost-effective, and long-term record storage, such as SEC compliant e-mails; secure shredding and record destruction; and customized services for regulated industries, such as health care and financial services.

The company enjoys a wide following on Wall Street; Iron Mountain was covered favorably by 10 sell-side research analysts and has more than two-thirds of its stock held by buy-side institutional investors.[23] The company has had an active investor relations program headed by a director of investor relations and an active public relations effort headed by a director of corporate communications. To commemorate its 10th anniversary as a public company, Iron Mountain, working closely with its representative at the New York Stock Exchange, had arranged for Reese and other company executives to ring the closing bell on a Friday afternoon. This event was televised by CNBC and announced throughout the day by various financial media outlets that mention each day's bell ringers.

During the planning for this event, the company expressed the desire to use the 10th anniversary as a public company, Reese's 25th anniversary with the company, and Iron Mountain's rich history to raise visibility for the company with Wall Street and the business press.

Open Scenario Challenge

You are part of the investor relations staff for Iron Mountain, and a strategy meeting will take place to answer the following questions to take advantage of the national attention surrounding its 10th anniversary.

Here are some of the questions you have been thinking about:

1. For the bell-ringing ceremony, who should be on the platform with the company's CEO?
2. Who should be notified of the bell ringing at the NYSE? External audiences? Internal audiences? What type of reaction do you think people would have?
3. What public relations and corporate communications initiatives could be carried out to maximize the bell-ringing ceremony?
4. Iron Mountain wants to explore other investor relations activities in conjunction with being in New York to ring the closing bell. The company's top managers will be there, so how can you leverage this event for more positive coverage?

Do Some Research

Examine local public companies that have celebrated a major milestone year. How did the company take advantage of the event? Were awareness-building opportunities missed?

Terminology

- bell-ringing ceremony
- buy-side institutional investors
- New York Stock Exchange
- safe harbor
- Sarbanes-Oxley
- sell-side research analysts

Web Resources

- **Iron Mountain** www.ironmountain .com/index.asp
- **New York Stock Exchange** http://www .nyse.com/

Burger King Holdings' Initial Public Offering

Designing an Investor Relations Program to Whet Wall Street's Appetite for the Company's Stock

By Donna N. Stein, APR, PRSA Fellow, of Donna Stein and Partners

Burger King Holdings, the parent company of Burger King, in 2006 was the world's second-largest hamburger chain, behind McDonald's Corporation. Approximately 90 percent of the company's more than 11,100 restaurants in 65 countries and U.S. territories are owned by independent franchisees, many of which are family-owned businesses operating for decades. In addition to the popular Whopper sandwich, the company offers a wide variety of chicken sandwiches, salads, and breakfast items.

HIGHLIGHTS OF BURGER KING HOLDINGS' HISTORY:[24]

- 1954: James McLamore and David Edgerton open their first Burger King restaurant in Miami, Florida.
- 1957: The company debuts its famous Whopper sandwich.
- 1963: The company opens its first international franchise in Puerto Rico.
- 1967: The two founders sell the chain to food maker Pillsbury.
- 1988: Grand Metropolitan PLC, a British spirits and food maker, buys Pillsbury.
- 1997: Grand Metropolitan buys Guinness PLC and forms food and drink maker Diageo PLC.
- 2002: Private equity firms Texas Pacific Group, Bain Capital, and Goldman Sachs Group's Goldman Sachs Capital Partners buy Burger King for $1.5 billion from Diageo PLC.

Burger King Holdings priced its initial public offering (IPO) of 19 percent of the company, representing 25 million company shares, at $17 per share at the market close on May 17, 2006. The following day, the company's shares began trading on the New York Stock Exchange (NYSE) under the ticker symbol "BKC."

The company realized net proceeds from the IPO of approximately $393 million, of which $350 million was used to repay debt. In addition, the company's underwriters for the stock offering were authorized to sell an additional 3,750,000 shares of stock held by three selling stockholders, "the green shoe" (an over-allotment option to sell investors more shares than originally planned) if there was investor demand. After the IPO, the

three majority shareholders of Burger King Holdings—the investment firms of Texas Pacific Group, Bain Capital, and Goldman Sachs—each owned 25 percent, or a total of 75 percent, of the company's outstanding shares.[25]

Burger King Holdings reported revenues for the fiscal year ending June 30, 2005, of $1.9 billion.[26] In a press release issued prior to its IPO, the company said that it reported increased "comparable store sales" for the past eight consecutive quarters. For the third quarter of fiscal 2006, the company reported a 4.9 percent increase in comparable store sales over the third quarter of fiscal 2005; for the prior two years, the company reported a 14.5 percent systemwide increase in comparable store sales.[27]

The company had 17 publicly traded competitors in its peer group including: McDonald's Corporation, Chipotle Mexican Grill, Tim Horton's, Wendy's International, and Yum! Brands.[28]

Open Scenario Challenge

As Burger King Holdings' new investor relations officer (IRO), you have a long list of things to do in preparation for the launch of the company's investor relations program on June 22, 2006, which marks the 25th trading day of the company's stock and the end of the postoffering "quiet period."

You, with the support and assistance from your CEO, CFO, underwriters, and outside legal counsel, have already conducted an internal education program for Burger King Holdings' corporate staff about what it means to work for a public company, including a crash course in regulation fair disclosure, Sarbanes-Oxley, material disclosure, insider trading, and the role of company spokespersons with regard to inquiries from the investment community, shareholders, and the news media.

You've also already updated your news release distribution procedure to take into consideration SEC rules and regulations,

NYSE requirements, and the appropriate reporters at business and financial news outlets.

In developing your first year investor relations program, what are some of the basic goals you need to identify?

What resources will you need in this information-gathering process?

Questions for Discussion

1. What are the key objectives and goals for your investor relations plan? How did you determine these? Whom did you involve in this process?

2. Who are the company's key audiences? Internal? External?

3. How do you go about determining how Burger King Holdings wishes to be positioned in the investment community? What are the company's key messages? How will the company distinguish itself from other publicly traded restaurant stocks?

4. What communications vehicles will be used to communicate and conduct a proactive outreach to existing shareholders and members of the investment community?

5. What will be some of the communications tools employed to get the Burger King Holdings story out?

6. How would you go about developing a 12-month investor relations calendar? What events and activities would be included?

Terminology
- initial public offering (IPO)
- underwriters
- green shoe
- comparable sales
- private equity firms
- prospectus
- selling stockholders
- the market
- quiet period
- regulation fair disclosure
- SOX
- material disclosure
- insider trading
- company spokesperson

Web Resources
- **Burger King** www.burgerking.com
- **Hoovers** www.hoovers.com

Chapter **Fourteen**

Internships and Early Career

Public relations is a challenging field for established professionals, and the competition for an entry-level position necessary to launch a career is especially keen.[1] To improve your chances of getting the job you want after graduation, most programs encourage or require internships.[2]

Internships provide public relations students with real-world experience under the supervision of a public relations professional. While leaving the comfort zone of the college classroom can challenge or even intimidate some students, it's well worth the effort. Students are given entry-level tasks, including writing news releases, developing Web site content, and assisting with developing newsletters and brochures. Beyond writing tasks, students may be asked to take photographs of events or staff, research information for a campaign, and help plan special events.

Most students who worked hard in classes do well with an internship's assigned tasks. More often, students encounter problems with the social aspects of the internship. For example, students may feel uncomfortable in a new setting. Even star students may suddenly feel shy and unsure of themselves. They show up for work expecting complete, hands-on guidance; the employer, on the other hand, may not be prepared to offer full-time internship supervision.

Here are a few suggestions for avoiding some common internship and first-job problems:

INTERNSHIP TIPS

Clearly Understand the Expectations of Your Internship

You should know how your performance will be evaluated and what types of writing are required. For example, does your teacher expect five news releases, involvement in a special event, and some research? How often will you be evaluated? Ask for a printed copy of the academic expectations, including portfolio pieces. Also, ask your supervisor what his or her expectations are and how you can be successful.

Introduce Yourself

When you are assigned an internship, contact the supervisor to introduce yourself either in person or by telephone. Avoid using e-mail until your supervisor is aware of your e-mail address because it may be discarded as spam. If e-mail is your only choice, clearly communicate in the subject line the purpose of the e-mail. Keep all communication, especially e-mail, formal. That includes using correct grammar and spelling. Provide a copy of your résumé that describes work history and your public relations activities, such as classes, clubs, and projects. (Make sure someone you trust proofreads it before you submit it.)

First Impressions Are Important

Arrive early on your first day and be punctual thereafter. Show enthusiasm and appreciation for this opportunity whether or not the organization was your first choice for an internship; most supervisors are volunteering their time to help you. A positive attitude goes a long way toward establishing a good working relationship quickly with your supervisor. Show respect by dressing appropriately. If you don't know the dress requirements, ask. It is always better to be slightly overdressed; for example, no one will find fault with a male intern who mistakenly wears a tie on a casual Friday.

How to Establish a Trusting Relationship

One of the hardest tasks of an internship is to gain acceptance and trust quickly among your office coworkers. Remember, you are only in the office a few hours each week and will be gone at the end of the semester or summer. Unfortunately, for some office workers, there is little incentive on their part to know you—unless you make a special effort. Without interfering in people's own work tasks, get to know coworkers quickly; learn their names and show interest in what they do. Volunteer to help an organization with a special event outside the hours of the internship; your enthusiasm will make an impression. Trust, unlike likeability, takes time. Don't expect to be handed major tasks the first weeks of your internship.

Since your supervisor does not know your skills and knowledge level, the early assignments will gauge your abilities. Do each assigned task thoroughly and professionally. Show enthusiasm for learning and doing. After you have completed several assignments successfully, your supervisor will trust you with more challenging work.

Take the Initiative

In large and busy organizations, even the best intentions of a supervisor sometimes go awry. Remember: You are there as a favor, although many organizations rely on interns for help. If you feel ignored or forgotten, find your supervisor and ask for work. If the supervisor is not available, find the next person in charge or the supervisor's secretary. Don't just sit and wait to be told what to do! Get to know your organization by doing research and paying close attention to what goes on around you. Learn the names of as many people in your office as you can; take notes. If you know the organization well, you can identify potential work projects. For example, you might be able to suggest writing staff profiles for future newsletters or the Web site. You can also offer to research an upcoming event. If you don't know how to do certain tasks, ask your supervisor or college professor for help. You also can reread your textbooks and do your own research.

Ask for and Learn from Criticism

No one likes to be criticized, but it is important that you demand constructive criticism often from your supervisor. Sometimes supervisors are worried that a student will be upset by criticism and so avoid it. Or after criticizing a student's first assignment and receiving a negative reaction, a supervisor may think it's not worth the effort. In such cases, students are confused (and rightly so) when their final evaluation is poor. Some students may think all is well because a supervisor is always smiling and seems pleased with their work when, in reality, the supervisor didn't communicate his or her concerns. Assume that you have a lot to learn. If you are not receiving constructive feedback, tell your supervisor that you want it. Always agree to redo a project if it doesn't meet expectations.

And, remember, no one is perfect. Everyone makes mistakes, professionals as well as interns. What's important is that you learn from your mistakes and maintain a positive attitude.

Don't Engage in Gossip or Other Unprofessional Activities

Often office employees look forward to having a young, enthusiastic college student on board. However, don't participate in office gossip or politics, even when office workers want to include you. Stay focused on your work, and keep your discussions limited to professional topics. Sometimes this can be difficult, especially when others in the office are not doing their work. Long coffee breaks, surfing on the Internet, playing computer games, instant messaging your friends, and engaging in gossip are all unprofessional activities—even when your coworkers are engaged in it. While supervisors may seem unaware of what's going on in the office, they usually are not. Some low-performing employees may actually be targeted for dismissal, but supervisors have to build documentation first. It's best to stay focused on your own work activities.

When to Speak Up

Student interns are in a subordinate role to a supervisor and must accept reasonable work-related requests, even when they differ from how things were taught in class. For example, some offices will have their own local writing style instead of using the Associated Press style guide. Some supervisors may not know how to do adequate research for a campaign. Others may not follow journalism's inverted pyramid formula. Every office and every supervisor is different. It is acceptable to suggest different ways of doing things, but if your supervisor is resistant, follow the established protocol.

If, however, your supervisor or office colleague asks you to do something that you are uncomfortable doing, give it very careful consideration. Ask yourself: Is it ethical? If you feel it's wrong, there's a very good chance it is wrong. Never lie or cover up the truth in your work assignments. If you are unsure of yourself, seek the advice of your teacher or other trusted adult.

Supervisors and office workers should never give unwanted attention to an intern as well, including inappropriate touching or asking personal questions that you'd rather not answer. Sometimes, students feel guilty that they are somehow to blame for unwanted attention, and they are afraid to report such behavior for fear it will affect their internship. Regardless, it is best to report it. Whenever you are in an uncomfortable situation, get away and contact your teacher or some other trusted adult quickly.

Remember to Thank Your Supervisor and Stay in Touch

At the end of your internship, write a thank-you letter to your supervisor expressing your appreciation for the time and effort your supervisor took to make your internship a success. Maintain the relationship after you leave or graduate. Your supervisor can serve as a résumé reference, write letters of support for you, and alert you to future job opportunities that he or she is aware of. Periodic contact could be in the form of an e-mail or a holiday card.

FIRST JOB TIPS

While many internship tips apply to your first job, there are a few additional ones to add.

Don't Make Changes Immediately

When you start your job, find out what your predecessor did, and don't rush to change anything until you are certain that it needs to be changed. Get to know who employees are, and don't jump to conclusions too quickly. Do more listening and less talking. No one likes a know-it-all even when the person is talented and experienced.

Understand Your Organization and Its People Thoroughly

Don't stay cooped up in your office all day. Get out and learn about your organization. Learn how your products are made and services are delivered. Read important documents such as annual reports to understand how your organization got to where it is today.

Be Positive When Suggesting Changes

Generally, people do not like change. Instead of announcing new ideas, frame them as enhancements rather than criticisms, and seek feedback from those whose support you'll need. Check with other managers first to learn the most acceptable strategy for getting your new ideas implemented successfully.

Create Alliances with Key People

Get to know the influential people in your organization, and develop a relationship with them. These people can help you further your vision and ideas.

Keep Learning

Never stop learning: Join a professional organization such as the Public Relations Society of America, which offers annual professional development opportunities nationally and locally. Remember, you are worth the investment. Read professional publications and the latest research about your field. In public relations, you will need to know more than what is happening in your field. Read *a lot*. Stay tuned to current events—and new trends and fads wherever you go.

Get a Mentor

All new practitioners can benefit from a professional mentor. Get to know your senior leadership, and find someone from outside your department who will take you under his or her wing. Don't forget to forge relationships with senior practitioners in other companies who will meet with you for lunch or talk over the phone when you have a problem or new challenge.

Track Your Accomplishments

Show a return on investment by tracking your accomplishments. Be able to document quantitatively how things have improved under your leadership and then communicate that to your boss.

The following case studies are based on real scenarios or composites of several incidents that have been modified to protect the identities of the participants.

Hey! Remember Me?

Getting the Most Out of an Internship Experience

"Just a minute," the receptionist silently mouthed to the young lady standing before her desk as she listened to the caller. The receptionist frantically scribbled a message, hung up, and immediately made another call to someone informing this person that some guy named Somers was "*not* happy . . . he wanted a meeting *pronto* to discuss their options."

Sonya Butler was excited by the conversation, but she pretended to ignore what was obviously a crisis situation unfolding over the phone.

So this was where the action was! It sounded exciting and important . . . and a little scary. Butler was starting her first day at the XYZ corporate headquarters in her

hometown. XYZ, a diversified conglomerate that included several major department stores across the country, occupied 10 floors of a 22-floor downtown building.

Butler had just completed her junior year as a public relations major at State University. Her three years at State University had been busy. She was vice president of her Public Relations Student Society of America chapter, had worked in the sports information office as a writer, and, when needed, as team statistician for women's lacrosse. Butler had also written stories for the college's student newspaper.

She had been determined to get an internship during the summer. During spring break, while talking to a neighbor, she learned that the company he worked for had a public relations department. She got more information and sent a letter and résumé requesting an internship. A few weeks later, she was called in for an interview—and a month later she was offered the position that paid $2 above the hourly minimum wage.

Everything seemed great in the interview except that this public relations department had never had an intern before. That was OK with Butler, who always considered herself ready for a challenge. At the interview, she handed Richard Bennett, director of corporate communication for XYZ, the internship requirements provided by her professor to get credit for the experience. Bennett glanced at the information but didn't really read it. He put it on top of a fairly large stack of papers, one of many stacks on his desk. Butler assumed Bennett would read it later. She left the interview looking forward to starting her internship in June.

Sitting in the receptionist's waiting area, Butler waited patiently. It was June 1—the first day of the internship. After 20 minutes, she got up and let the receptionist know that she was the intern for the public relations office. "The what?" came the reply from the harried worker. Repeating who she was, she asked if Mr. Bennett was available. "He's expecting me," Butler said.

"OK," said the receptionist. "Let me call him." The receptionist relayed the information to someone on the other end. There was an extended conversation in hushed tones that Butler couldn't make out. Finally, "Someone will be down in a few minutes for you."

Another 15 minutes passed. Butler's initial first-day excitement jitters were giving way to nervous trepidation. What's going on? she thought. Did I get the day wrong? Maybe I should have called last week to confirm everything. I haven't heard any-

thing since that interview six weeks ago. A woman entered the room and introduced herself.

"Hello. I'm Marsha Springfield, Mr. Bennett's secretary. I understand you're here to work as an intern. I wasn't aware of this, and Mr. Bennett is on vacation this week. Why don't you come up to our office, and I'll try to reach Mr. Bennett to see if we can sort this out."

Butler could hardly believe her ears. Embarrassed, she got up and silently followed Springfield to the elevator. Springfield chatted with her about the weather and what college Butler attended. Springfield's pleasant conversation made the situation a little less stressful. Once they arrived at the office, Springfield called Springfield's cell phone. Bennett must have answered because Springfield immediately began to explain the situation. Butler, still embarrassed, silently listened. Mostly, Springfield's end of the conversation consisted of: "Okay," "right," and other remarks that made no sense. Then she said, "I'll see you when you get back. Good-bye."

Bennett wouldn't be back for two weeks. He had totally forgotten that Butler was starting June 1, and he had just left that weekend for a family vacation out of state. Springfield put the best face on the situation and said Mr. Bennett had been extremely busy right before he left for vacation and had simply forgotten Butler's start date.

"Mr. Bennett has asked me to have you start working for me until he returns," said Springfield. "He thinks it will be a good thing anyway to start off slowly and get accustomed to how the office works. I have a lot of work, and I think you will find most of it interesting."

Butler was disappointed with how things had started, but she was resolved to continue. After all, it seemed like an innocent mistake, and Springfield was nice enough.

Springfield said she would have to work at a nearby conference table for the time being (without a computer or telephone) until office space could be created for her. Next, Springfield took her to the human resources department to fill out some paperwork. When Butler returned, Springfield had her first assignment: putting together a bulk mailing of the employee newsletter with a copy of the new corporate ethics code to all 1,200 employees. Stuffing envelopes was tedious, but, all things considered, she was just starting what she hoped would be a great learning experience. Things would get better.

Things did not get much better. For the next two weeks, Butler's internship was mostly clerical: assembling mailings and press kits, updating media lists, and clipping about 20 newspapers daily. Butler did the work without complaint and actually enjoyed working with Springfield, who always had great stories to tell.

When Bennett did return from his vacation, he apologized for Butler's awkward start and asked how things had been going. Butler began telling Bennett what she had accomplished, but the phone rang and he had to excuse himself. One phone call followed another. It was pretty obvious that he was swamped with postvacation makeup work. It seemed futile to discuss her future duties until his schedule slowed down a bit.

After all, things were not so bad. Springfield had created a comfortable work station with a laptop computer networked to a printer. She had been asked to proofread several text projects that had come in from freelancers, and she had her daily news clippings to assemble—plus any other office work that Springfield needed her to do. Butler knew she was a big help to Springfield (who had mentioned it several times), but she began to feel uneasy about fulfilling her internship requirements. In a few days she would be entering her fourth week at the site, and she didn't have one portfolio piece to show for all her efforts. Butler was worried about getting credit for her experience.

After several weeks in the office, she became aware of some potential projects that might be portfolio worthy: The annual stockholder's meeting was just three months away, some new employees were hired, a new employee benefits program could be promoted, and the company had been approached by an area nonprofit organization to help sponsor a fundraising event.

She decided that if things did not change soon, she would talk directly to Bennett and remind him of her internship criteria. She needed some writing samples and wanted to work on planning a special event. When Friday came with no change in her routine, she asked Springfield for a meeting with Bennett the following week.

"Can I tell him what this is about?" asked Springfield.

"I want to update him on my internship since I'm about halfway done," said Butler.

Open Scenario Challenge
The Meeting with Bennett

Butler had given a lot of thought to how this situation had developed. She knew that she was shy by nature, a little intimidated by her surroundings, but she was also a very hard worker and had talent and skills to offer! Was it her fault that she was stuck doing clerical work? Should she have been more assertive from the very beginning of her internship? Wouldn't that sound whiny or impertinent?

Should she have asked Bennett to give her specific public relations tasks? It seemed inappropriate for her to tell the director of public relations what she should be doing; wasn't he supposed to know what she was doing? However, this was the first time the department had used an intern, Butler recalled.

The meeting with Bennett was set for Tuesday morning. Butler dreaded the encounter because she didn't want to come across as ungrateful or overly demanding. After all, she was just a college student. But she knew it had to be done if she wanted to rescue the internship and get credit.

She wanted to make sure this was a positive meeting with Bennett, so she carefully thought out her strategy over the weekend, did some office research Monday, and rehearsed her talking points Monday night. When she entered Bennett's office Tuesday, Bennett was just getting off the telephone. "Hey Sonya! How are things going?"

Discussion Questions

1. What do you think was the cause of this internship situation? Could it have been avoided? How?

2. What would be your meeting strategy if you were Sonya Butler?

3. What would be your exact words to Bennett? What tone and attitude are appropriate in such situations?

4. To what degree do you think that Butler's situation is due to her personality or the fact that this was a new experience for XYZ?

5. What could have been done before the internship started to ensure a better experience?

6. Would you have called your internship teacher?

7. Should Butler leave if she cannot resolve the situation?

Role-Playing Activity

Role-play the meeting between Butler and Bennett. Discuss how to maintain respect for Bennett while making Butler's concerns known. Also discuss the difference between assertive and aggressive behavior. This is a good opportunity for students to talk about their previous experiences in internships or regular employment.

Close Encounter of the Unwanted Kind
Friendship, Fraternizing, or Harassment?

While crossing paths in a hallway, student Samantha Bradford asked when Professor Mary Doolittle held office hours; Doolittle expected it was just routine questions about the student's new internship. "No problem; stop by my office anytime during office hours," she told Bradford.

Doolittle was a public relations professor at the college and handled local student internship placements. Bradford, a junior, had completed a summer internship at the city zoo the previous summer. She received good marks for her work, especially because she had strong computer skills, including Web design. Bradford's knowledge came from working at the campus computer help desk and her own initiative to learn. With her combination of knowledge, technical ability, and public relations skills, Bradford was easy to place at an internship site.

She was assigned to work with a small nonprofit organization involved in poverty issues. The director of communications was a public relations alumnus who had supervised many student interns over the years, including some whose skill levels were less than stellar. In all cases, he saw his role as a professional mentor and students had positive experiences. Bradford would be working on news releases and the community newsletter, including desktop publishing work. To start off, however, she was assigned to work temporarily with another staff member on some special projects that involved visiting area businesses.

A couple of days after the hallway encounter, Doolittle saw Bradford again while standing in line at the campus café. Bradford repeated the request to meet. Doolittle, coffee in hand, had time then and suggested they talk at a nearby seating area.

"What's up?" asked Doolittle. "How's the internship going?"

"Well," said Bradford, searching for a way to begin. "I'm not really sure how to say this, but I'm pretty sure I have a problem at my internship."

"What kind of problem?" asked Doolittle. Students were encouraged to solve their problems first, but Doolittle was available if they needed guidance on how to handle things. Usually, student internship problems involved personality clashes or unchallenging work. Those were to be expected early in an internship until the organization figured out how best to use a student's skills.

"Well, I've been working with this staff member, and he's always asking me to 'hang out' with him after work," said Bradford. "He's really nice, and he's been helping me out a lot at work. But he's married, and he's got a little baby at home. That's made me a little uncomfortable because I think he should be home, don't you?"

Doolittle agreed. "Samantha, you need to firmly but nicely say no—and mean it when you say it."

"Yeah. I have, but he keeps asking me to hang out with him and his friends after work. They're really nice, but I'm not sure."

Sensing there was more to the situation than this, Doolittle asked: "Has he made you uncomfortable in other ways?"

"Well . . . yeah. He called me the other morning to ask why I wasn't there. It wasn't my day to work, and I told him so. Then he told me his friend had a Jacuzzi, and he'd love to see me in a swimming suit. I said no, but he kept on asking. I thought it was a little bit weird. I don't know what to do; I don't want to cause him any problems at work . . . I really like working there."

Doolittle listened carefully as Bradford debated with herself if there really was a problem or if she was just reading more into the situation than it warranted. Bradford's fellow worker, after all, she said, was just being overly pleasant and trying to include her in activities.

Open Scenario Challenge
Deciding What to Do
Bradford asked Doolittle what she thought and what she should do.

Questions for Discussion
1. Is it OK to develop friendships at an internship site? Why is fraternizing sometimes discouraged?
2. Why were the young man's attempts to include Bradford bothering her? What was her dilemma?
3. What is sexual harassment? Was this an example?
4. What were Bradford's options?
5. Should the organization's supervisor be involved? If so, how?
6. How could this problem be avoided?

Wanted: Media Relations Coordinator at State University

Part 1

Matt Silver, professor of public relations at State University, was asked to help evaluate applicants for a new college staff position: coordinator of media relations. It was the first search committee he had been asked to serve on since his arrival at State University a year ago. Campus hiring procedures required the formation of a five-member committee, comprised of faculty and staff, to read applicants' résumés and evaluate their qualifications. Committee members' evaluations would be used by the committee chair to determine which applicants would be invited to visit the campus for an interview.

A fat manila envelope was delivered to Silver's campus mailbox. It contained 35 résumés and cover letters in response to State University's newspaper ad:

COORDINATOR OF MEDIA RELATIONS

> Coordinator of Media Relations: *Duties include generating news releases and pitches and handling reporters' inquiries as well as other administrative tasks. Bachelor's degree in public relations, journalism, communication, or related field required. One year of experience in similar position preferred. Send cover letter, résumé with references to State University, Human Resources, College Town, USA. AA/EOE*

A note was attached to the top résumé: "Please also consider new grads as the pay is entry level. Rate each applicant on a scale of 1 (best) to 4 (worst)." Included in the envelope was an evaluation form to help with the initial weeding process; the form listed a number of criteria:

- Undergraduate or master's degree in one of the desired communication disciplines
- Current position in media relations or related communication field, and years at current position
- Previous relevant experience in media relations or related field
- If a recent grad, relevant internship experience
- Overall quality of writing in cover letter and résumé
- Personal Web pages such as MySpace or FaceBook or blogs on the Internet were also fair game for evaluating issues of professionalism and writing skills
- Residence—local or state
- Alumnus of State College

Silver began to read the letters and résumés. He noticed most of the applicants expressed enthusiasm for the job. Most of the cover letters were fairly well written. Poorly written letters were immediately given a "4" rating. For this job, there could be no room for misspellings or grammatical errors in the media relations position. "After all," Silver rightly reasoned, "the writing, grammar, and overall presentation in a résumé and cover letter should be the best the applicant can do."

While nearly every cover letter discussed the applicant's writing ability, Silver was struck by the applicants' failure, in their cover letters, to address how they would develop successful media relationships. He believed that would be a critical factor for the position's success. Silver also looked for indications of a strong work ethic and persistence. Good media relations, he felt, take effort; it would not be enough for the new media relations person just to send out news releases. Competition for airtime and print space in the local papers was fierce.

Silver rated the applications and sent them back to the chair of the search committee, State University's director of public relations.

In addition to excellent writing skills, experience, and educational background, he knew there were some intangibles that couldn't be measured by looking at a résumé and cover letter: teamwork, personality, problem-solving skills, and drive. Also, which applicants could speak well enough to communicate complicated ideas in only a few words? Verbal communication skills could be a key factor in this position. Silver tried to imagine how applicants would hold up during a two-minute phone conversation with busy editors, but he knew these traits would have to be sized up during face-to-face interviews.

Questions for Discussion

1. What does a media relations coordinator really do? How would you find out more about this position, beyond the description in the newspaper ad?

2. Why did some recent college graduates apply? What do you think when you see an entry-level job posting that requests one year or more of experience?

3. Write a cover letter that addresses specifically the knowledge and skills necessary for the media relations coordinator position. How would you demonstrate the intangible skills?

4. Why did Professor Silver consider oral skills a high priority?

5. What are some common mistakes of résumés? How would you customize a résumé for this particular job opening?

The Interview for Media Relations Coordinator at State University
Part 2

A few days later, Professor Silver received an e-mail from State University's public relations director, Sarah Dobre. "Based on the committee's recommendations, we have three final candidates that we want to interview," the e-mail read. "Can you meet August 2 for interviews?" Silver was available. Committee members were also asked to meet one hour before the interviews began, to discuss interview guidelines and applicant questions. Silver asked Dobre, who was chairing the committee, for a complete job description to review.

Other members of the five-member committee were Maureen Waters, State University's publications director; Joe Warchesny, Web content editor; and Tamera Smith, parent-alumni relations director. Dobre detailed how the new position would fit into the office configuration. Waters' position had included media relations with her publications writing duties, but her responsibilities had grown significantly in recent years, leaving little time for media relations work. With the addition of the new position, Waters would be able to focus her efforts on publication writing for various alumni, employee, and department publications as well as strategic planning.

The media relations person would handle media inquiries; develop news releases; and pitch story ideas to local, state, and national media outlets. The successful candidate would also need to be resourceful and constantly mine the faculty, staff, and students for story ideas.

State University had many well-respected and popular majors, but two were unique and held promise for large numbers of student recruits; one was an environmental science major in brownfield remediation, the other a cutting-edge program in bioengineering. Both had received good local media coverage but—so far—no statewide or national media interest. Faculty research initiatives and student activities had largely gone unreported. Basically, there were plenty of potential stories but no time to bring them to the attention of the news media.

The committee was interested in finding a candidate who was intelligent, articulate, and succinct in speech, enthusiastic, energetic; had strong interpersonal skills; understood the mind of a reporter; and had solid news writing skills. Personal interviews, the committee felt, would shed light on many of these intangibles.

Each committee member had standard questions to ask of each applicant to ensure fair, consistent comparisons:

- What do you know about State University?
- Why are you interested in this position?
- Tell us about your work and/or internship experience as it relates to media relations.
- How familiar are you with the local media? If you don't know the news media, how would you go about establishing relationships? How would you establish ties with the national media?
- In your opinion, what makes an effective pitch?

- What are the most common media relations mistakes?
- How would you pitch the construction of our new dorm as a potential news story, since it is not particularly newsworthy?
- How would you handle media relations in the event of a sexual assault involving a student?
- How would you cultivate faculty relationships? What types of news could be generated from the faculty?
- Under what circumstances would you use a news conference to generate publicity? What are the pros and cons of this tactic?
- Would you consider offering certain media outlets an exclusive? What are the pros and cons of this tactic?
- State University's Web site needs an online newsroom. What information and Web features could we offer?
- What do you consider to be your strengths and weaknesses?
- Where do you see yourself in five years?
- What questions do you have for us?

An hour was set aside for each interview, with an additional 15 minutes for committee members to discuss privately the candidate's performance.

CANDIDATE 1

Marian Wells, 24, received an undergraduate degree in English from a well-respected small liberal arts college two years ago with a 3.62 GPA. Since graduation she has worked as a copy editor for a weekly trade association newspaper for nearly two years and, for the past eight months, has worked as a bureau reporter for the local newspaper. Her public relations experience included an internship at a small chamber of commerce while in college.

For the interview, she dressed in neat khaki slacks and a button-down shirt. She appeared nervous, giggling some, and using hand gestures to make key points. She was intelligent, articulate, and pleasant in demeanor.

She knew of State University mostly from its local reputation, which she said was good. She mentioned she had made a college visit to State University when she was a prospective student but received a large academic scholarship from another school and went there instead.

Most of her answers on pitching story ideas to the news media focused on the potential story's unique elements. The new dorm question, she said, could be handled by stressing what's new or different about this project compared to other dorms at local colleges. Wells said if she got the job, she would also focus on presenting the "student perspective" in stories, and she thought faculty could be better promoted as "experts" within news stories.

She was not familiar with online news rooms but said she used organizational Web sites frequently for story research. Describing her strengths, she was a "good writer" and "approachable." Her self-described weakness was being her "own harshest critic," which often turned out to be a strength as she was never completely satisfied with her work and always strove to improve. Her portfolio was neatly organized and included samples of her copy editing and reporting work at the trade association newspaper along with more recent newspaper clips.

CANDIDATE 2

Kathy Miller, 27, was an alumna of the journalism program at State University. After graduating, she worked for five years as a reporter at a small newspaper in a neighboring town. She knew some, but not all, of the committee members.

Miller dressed in a professional black pants suit. As the interview progressed, committee members became aware of an unfortunate grooming issue: a tiny patch of lipstick on her front tooth. In addition,

dry mouth caused her to make a slight smacking sound as she spoke (while a bottle of water and glass went unused in front of her). Both the lipstick and dry mouth distracted committee members, but after the interview was over, each committee member recounted his or her own embarrassing job interview story. Still, attention to details—including minor personal grooming—was important since the successful candidate would have to cultivate relationships with the news media and faculty.

In her favor, Miller was an experienced journalist who was not afraid of hard work. She recounted how she sometimes wrote four or five stories a day and how she made sure she "got the story" even if it meant calling numerous contacts and doing research. She said her "strong work ethic" had resulted in several "scoops" for her newspaper. Miller also knew the reporter's mind and had specific ideas about how to approach a reporter when making a pitch. She recalled from her own experience how some public relations people didn't understand how to make their story ideas newsworthy and didn't respect a journalist's deadline. "When I need information now," she said, "I didn't mean tomorrow. I mean no later than 20 minutes." She went on to describe other experiences she had as a reporter as they related to various questions. Some were negative experiences she had dealing with people in a controversy, including one who was a prominent alumnus of State University.

When asked to respond to the new dorm question, she focused on the larger issue of growing school enrollments. "If I was the reporter, I'd like to know why the school has grown so much in recent years or if there was anything new in the building technology. There might be a good story hook there."

As an alumna, she was familiar with the academic programs and referred to them by name as she discussed her hypothetical plans as a media relations coordinator. When asked what her strengths were, she replied, "I work hard and have good writing skills." When asked about her weaknesses, she said she had no public relations experience. She brought along samples of her news clips, which were organized on loose leaf pages in a folder. Some of the samples included photos she had taken that were good quality.

CANDIDATE 3

The final candidate was Josh Crewsley, 24. He was a public relations graduate of State University and was employed as a public relations assistant for the local United Way. He was dressed in a conservative navy blue suit, crisp new white shirt, and tie.

As a student at State University, he had served as president of the Public Relations Student Society of America chapter and had two successful public relations internships, one in State University's public relations office.

Crewsley's work at the American Heart Association for the past two years included a significant amount of experience in computer publication design and layout. He had many examples of publication projects in his portfolio. He said that it was a busy office environment and that he had learned a great deal. When asked about his media relations experience, he noted with a hint of disappointment that while he did write news releases and interact with the news media, it was not to the degree that he wanted. "My efforts have been focused on publication design, although, I'd like to do more writing." When asked where he wanted to be in five years, he said, "working in public relations and doing media relations and writing."

When asked how he would make a new dorm newsworthy, he, too, focused on growing student enrollments. He also said he would see if any of the construction crew members had children attending the college. "That connection," he said, "would make an interesting human interest feature." He also had some ideas about State University's Web site and an online newsroom.

Just like Miller, most of the committee members knew Crewsley. In fact, Waters recalled after the interview was over how strong his writing had been and how well he took direction as a student intern. Silver, however, was not impressed with the news release samples in Crewsley's portfolio. While grammatically accurate, there was no news hook in any of the leads. Some started off with the date of the event as the lead, which Silver thought was unimaginative. Still, the portfolio was well organized and professional looking.

And Crewsley had a creative idea for the new dorm media pitch. But, overall, his was a pretty low-key interview. While he was articulate and thoughtful, he did not really show much enthusiasm for his work. He was nice but quiet. Small talk was not something that came naturally to him.

Questions for Discussion

1. How would you prepare for this interview?

2. How would you answer the questions?

3. What do you think is more important, a background in news/journalism or public relations?

4. How important are the intangibles such as presentation, articulate and succinct speech, enthusiasm, energy, strong interpersonal skills, and knowing the mind of a reporter?

5. Whom would you pick for this job and why?

Do Some Research

1. Invite your campus media relations coordinator to class, and ask him or her what skills and attributes are necessary for success.

2. Invite a news editor to your class, and ask him or her about the common mistakes organizations make when seeking media coverage.

Web Resources

- **Salary Expert** www.salaryexpert.com/
- **Career Magazine with career and interviewing tools** www.careermag.com/
- **Career Bank with career and interviewing tools** www.careerbank.com/
- **Career Builder with career and interviewing tools** www.careerbuilder.com
- **Hot Jobs with career tools** hotjobs .yahoo.com/

Should I Take This Job?

Melissa Jones sat outside the director's office of Middletown's Arts Council. This was her first real job interview, and she was glad to have it. She was graduating from college in three weeks, and this interview might be her only chance to secure a public relations job before graduation.

For the past year, the economic slowdown had prevented several of last year's public relations graduates from finding jobs in the field. In discussing the bleak job outlook last fall, Jones's teacher had reminded seniors to begin the job search early: Start networking with family and friends to develop job contacts, volunteer in public relations offices, create a résumé and portfolio, and research the market. Jones did all that and it had worked. Her aunt had seen a job advertised in her home newspaper and e-mailed her the classified ad. Jones did some quick research on her college's library databases about the organization; she then customized her cover letter and résumé to reflect the ad's job duties and convey an understanding of the organization.

Arriving 15 minutes early for the interview, Jones had an opportunity for last-minute preparation as she sat in a waiting area just down the hall from the director's office. She remembered what one alumnus television news director had told a group of students asking for interview advice: "When you interview with me, I'm thinking that how you present yourself during the job interview is the best you'll ever be. So if you come in with slightly scuffed shoes and you don't know anything about my organization, I'm thinking this is the best you have to offer and it isn't good enough. Remember, I'm trying to find reasons not to hire you from the final candidate pool." The shoe remark had stayed with Jones; the night before the interview she bought a new pair of black shoes to ensure a serious, professional first impression.

As she sat, Jones's mind began to wander. She was still in shock thinking how quickly senior year had passed. Soon she would be facing her first hefty college loan repayments, a car payment, and rent, not to mention the hopeful expectations of her parents who had financed nearly half of her college education.

Time to focus, she reminded herself as she mentally prepared for her interview. She looked over research notes she had put together using a newspaper database. Her aunt had picked up brochures and an annual report from the organization, so she could familiarize herself with its mission and services. She had also asked friends and family what they knew about the Arts Council. This was helpful because she learned the organization had several special fundraising and educational events throughout the year. The Arts Council had a major presence in the community and relied on its high profile to garner support for its activities.

Finally, John Fitzgerald, Arts Council director, entered the waiting room and welcomed Jones with a firm handshake, which Jones returned. The interview took place in Fitzgerald's office and lasted 45 minutes. During the interview, Fitzgerald described the job position in detail.

As director of public relations, the successful candidate would be a one-person office with access to a volunteer staff. The Arts Council promoted a network of arts groups throughout a three-county region. Its mission was to keep the arts alive and well by applying for private grants; securing local, state, and national funding; and by hosting and supporting numerous art events supported by the Arts Council. The public relations director's job would support all these activities with involvement in grant writing, member relations, government relations, and special events. The successful candidate's responsibilities would include producing a quarterly newsletter, handling all the media relations for the Arts Council's special events, including photography, and expanding and maintaining the organization's outdated, limited Web site.

Jones had several questions prepared for the interview and many more once the job was described. It all sounded exciting. Jones was a creative person and enjoyed the prospect of working with an arts organization; she also liked the idea of being in charge of her own program. She had worked for the past year at her college's public relations department and felt she had gained valuable experience in planning and implementing a wide variety of public relations activities. She also had Web and photography experience and made sure to mention these abilities in the interview.

As the interview was coming to a close, Fitzgerald said, "I'm letting you know right now that you are a strong candidate; I've interviewed three candidates, and I have one more to interview tomorrow. So far you are the strongest candidate." He also mentioned the position, which was salaried, paid $28,000 with health and dental coverage. While thrilled to be a finalist for the job, Jones was mildly disappointed in the salary but did not show it. She knew this was a small nonprofit organization. Instead, she thanked Fitzgerald for his time and asked when he would be making his final decision. He told her early next week, once references were checked.

Questions for Discussion

1. What job-hunting strategies did Jones use?

2. What other strategies can you use to find a job?

3. What did Jones do to prepare for the interview?

4. If you were Jones, what questions would you have ready for your first interview?

5. What kinds of questions are appropriate to ask once a job has been offered?

6. Beyond salary, how else can Jones assess the job offer?

7. What should Jones do after the interview?

Establishing a New Public Relations Program

Nelson Perry was the new public relations director at ComXSoft Corporation, in North Carolina. The company developed computer software products for handheld devices such as PalmPilot and Blackberry. Recently, ComXSoft had launched its own handheld computer device tailored for the college student market. Its funky colors, low cost, and rugged but sleek construction made it a best seller.

ComXSoft, a privately held company, employed 900 people, including software developers, assemblers, and sales staff. As a new company that had grown quickly since its creation five years ago, it had begun to formalize some of its management operations.

Perry, who graduated from college five years ago with a degree in public relations and a minor in business, had worked at a small advertising and public relations agency as an account executive before accepting the job at ComXSoft. He was self-motivated, articulate, a strong writer, and a creative public relations practitioner.

Perry was impressed by the hiring interviews at ComXSoft. Everyone during the interview process, from company CEO Kenneth Purdon on down, had positive answers to Perry's questions: This was a company with a future, and a vigorous research and development program that promised years of innovative products; public relations' role would be important to the company's future success.

It was clear to Perry that Purdon was an intelligent and articulate person who seemed knowledgeable about every aspect of the company's operations. Perry's immediate task, Purdon told him, would be to organize public relations and product marketing functions in the company through the creation of a public relations department. Perry would be free to review existing practices and recommend changes.

Not only did the company's financial prospects look healthy, but Perry also felt comfortable with the people. The company had created a relaxed but energized environment for its employees. The dress code was business casual, and employees seemed genuinely happy to be there. Perry also noticed there were many other young people.

ComXSoft encouraged employees to contribute their ideas for improvements in whatever they found lacking: from restroom cleanliness to ideas for increased productivity, job efficiency, or new products. Anyone could be awarded a bonus for a suggestion or solution that moved the company forward, whether the employee was a line worker or a software engineer. Success was a total team effort.

Perry was hired to develop a public relations department from scratch. Currently, product publicity and media relations were handled by separate advertising agencies, each known for its particular expertise, and employee communication was loosely managed by an administrative assistant from the human resources department. The company's Web site was maintained by the information technology department but only contained product and ordering information; it had few photos and the text was mostly technical descriptions of products. As the company grew, the need for a more coordinated and strategic communication program became apparent.

As a new position in a new department, Perry's first task was to revise and expand the public relations director's job description based on the classified advertisement and discussions with Purdon and the human resources director. As a Public Relations Society of America member, Perry also gathered sample job descriptions from similar-sized technology companies by contacting members.

As Perry was revising the position description, Purdon stopped by for a chat. Purdon admitted that he was no expert in public relations or marketing, but he had attended a well-respected management seminar program over the summer and learned that his company needed a strategic communication program. During the course of their conversation, he also threw out some other terms such as corporate reputation, employee relations, corporate social responsibility, and return on investment. Purdon did most of the talking, and Perry listened carefully, asking no questions.

Later, Perry thought about the meeting with Purdon. Clearly, this was going to be a big job—maybe an even bigger job than was revealed during the interview process. Perry decided the first priority was to get better acquainted with ComXSoft.

Questions for Discussion

1. Why is getting acquainted with the company a good, first action for a new public relations director?

2. How could Perry get better acquainted with the company?

3. How would you go about establishing a new strategic communications program, especially where none has existed before?

4. What types of research could Perry use to plan strategy?

5. When you started a new job, what did you do to feel comfortable in your new job?

6. Should Perry have asked Purdon more questions before taking the job? Should Perry have asked questions during the office conversation?

Do Some Research

1. Research how you would select and hire a public relations firm to handle a special project that your office cannot handle on its own. The Council of Public Relations Firms (www.prfirms .org/) has a guide entitled "Standards for Conducting a Public Relations Firm Search: Principles and Practices" that can serve as a good information source.

2. If you need to contract with an outside public relations firm, how do you write a *request for proposal* (RFP)? Ask a public relations firm to share a copy of an RFP. Examine it and decide how you would respond to a similar request.

Web Resources

- **The Council of Public Relations Firms** http://www.prfirms.org/

- **Public Relations Society of America** http://www.prsa.org/

Notes

CHAPTER 1

[1] Dennis L. Wilcox and Glen T. Cameron (2006). *Public Relations Strategies and Tactics*, Boston, MA: Allyn and Bacon, p. 24.

[2] *Making a Case: The Birth of an HBS Case Study*, Harvard Business School's Enterprise newsletter, Harvard Business School, Harvard University, http://www.hbs.edu/corporate/enterprise/case.html.

[3] David M. Dozier with Larissa A. Grunig and James E. Grunig (1995). *Manager's Guide to Excellence in Public Relations and Communication Management*, Mahwah, NJ: Lawrence Erlbaum Associates, p. 64.

[4] Ibid.

[5] Ronald D. Smith (2005). *Strategic Planning for Public Relations*, Mahwah, NJ: Lawrence Erlbaum Associates, p. 42.

[6] James Grunig and Todd Hunt (1984). *Managing Public Relations*, New York, NY: Holt, Rinehart and Winston.

[7] C. I. Hovland, I. L. Janis, and H. H. Kelley (1953). *Communication and Persuasion*. New Haven, CT: Yale University Press.

[8] Elihu Katz and Paul Lazarsfeld (1955). *Personal Influence: The Part Played by People in the Flow of Communications*. New York: Free Press.

[9] Leon Festinger (1957). *A Theory of Cognitive Dissonance*. Stanford, CA: Standford University Press.

[10] Leon Festinger (1962). "Cognitive Dissonance," *Scientific American* 207:93.

[11] Dennis Wilcox (2005). *Public Relations Writing and Media Tactics*, Boston, MA: Allyn and Bacon, p. 42.

[12] Elihu Katz, Jay Blumler, and Michael Gurevitch (1974). "Utilization of Mass Communication by the Individual," in J. G. Blumler and E. Katz, eds., *The Uses of Mass Communication: Current Perspectives on Gratification Research*, Beverly Hills, CA: Sage.

[13] Abraham Maslow (1970). *Motivation and Personality*, 2nd ed., New York: Harper & Row.

[14] Bernard Cohen (1963). *The Press and Foreign Policy*. Princeton, NJ: Princeton University Press.

[15] Elihu Katz and Paul Lazarsfeld (1955). *Personal Influence: The Part Played by People in the Flow of Communications*, New York: Free Press.

[16] Everett Rogers (1962). *Diffusion of Innovations*, New York: Free Press.

[17] Larissa A. Grunig, James E. Grunig, and David M. Dozier (2002). *Excellence in Public Relations and Communication Management in Three Countries*, Mahwah, NJ: Erlbaum.

[18] James E. Grunig and Todd Hunt (1984). *Managing Public Relations*, New York: Holt, Rinehart & Winston.

CHAPTER 2

[1] James Grunig and Todd Hunt (1984), *Managing Public Relations*. New York: Holt, Rinehart & Winston.

[2] Ronald D. Smith (2005). *Strategic Planning for Public Relations*, Mahwah, NJ: Lawrence Erlbaum Associates, p. 54.

[3] Ibid., p. 72.

CHAPTER 3

[1] Ronald D. Smith (2005). *Strategic Planning for Public Relations*, Mahwah, NJ: Lawrence Erlbaum Associates, p. 83.

[2] Ibid., p. 101.

[3] Ibid., pp. 157–209.

CHAPTER 4

[1] Dan Lattimore, Otis Baskin, Suzette Heiman, Elizabeth Toth, and James VanLeuven (2004). *Public Relations: The Profession and the Practice,* p. 79.

[2] "PRSA Member Code of Ethics," Public Relations Society of America, accessed from prsa.org/_About/ethics/preamble.asp?ident=eth3.

[3] Kathy R. Fitzpatrick, "Ethical Decision-Making Guide Helps Resolve Ethical Dilemmas," Public Relations Society of America, PRSA Code of Ethics, Ethics Resources, accessed May 30, 2006, from prsa.org/_About/ethics/index.asp?ident=eth1.

[4] Patrick McGreevy, "Chalk One Up to Advisory Panels; Council Scales Back DWP Rate Request in the Face of Wide Opposition from Community Boards," *Los Angeles Times,* May 12, 2004, Metro Desk, Part B, p. 1.

[5] "LADWP: A Century of Service, Our Service and History," Los Angeles Department of Water and Power, www.ladwp.com/ladwp/cms/ladwp000508.jsp.

[6] Ibid.

[7] "Chick Audit Finds $4.2 Million in Unsubstantiated, Unsupported and Questionable PR Bills: City Controller Demands the Money Back," news release, Los Angeles City Controller Office, accessed Nov. 16, 2004, from http://www.lacity.org/ctr.

[8] Patrick McGreevy, "City to Audit DWP's Contract with PR Firm; Billings for Unspecified Services; Prompt Scrutiny; Some Council Members Ask About the Necessity of Using an Outside Firm at All," *Los Angeles Times*, April 2, 2004, Metro Desk, Part B, Pg. 3.

[9] Ibid.

[10] Beth Barrett and James Nash, "Comptroller Questions DWP's P.R. Contract," *Daily News of Los Angeles,* April 2, 2004, p. N-5.

[11] "Fleishman-Hillard January 2003 Public Affairs Counsel and Communications Strategy: Project Code: 450131–000," billing statement accessed from the Los Angeles Office of City Controller, http://www.lacity.org/ctr/, Nov. 15, 2004, and also reported in Steve Lopez, Points West; "There's a Reason For Sky-High DWP Bills," Metro Desk, *Los Angeles Times,* July 23, 2004, Part B, Pg. 1, accessed September 2, 2004.

[12] Patrick McGreevy, "City to Audit DWP's Contract with PR Firm; Billings for Unspecified Services Prompt Scrutiny; Some Council Members Ask About the Necessity of Using an Outside Firm at All."

[13] Ibid.

[14] James Nash, "Council Opens Faucets, Hikes Water Rate 11%," *Daily News of Los Angeles,* p. N1.

[15] Patrick McGreevy, "City to Audit DWP's Contract with PR Firm; Billings for Unspecified Services Prompt Scrutiny; Some Council Members Ask About the Necessity of Using an Outside Firm at All," *Los Angeles Times,* April 2, 2004, Metro Desk, Part B, Pg. 3.

[16] "DWP," City News Service, Inc., July 15, 2004, accessed from Lexis-Nexis.

[17] Ted Rohrlich, Ralph Frammolino and Patrick McGreevy, "PR Exec Placed on Paid Leave; Fleishman-Hillard, Accused of Falsely Billing the DWP, Removes the Former Head of Its L.A. Office. Los Angeles Sues the Company," *Los Angeles Times,* July 17, Metro Desk, Part B, Pg. 1.

[18] "F-H Reels from Contract Controversy," Jack O'Dwyer's Newsletter, July 21, 2004, Pg. 2.

[19] "Important Message," Fleishman-Hillard, internal e-mail message from John Graham, July 15, 2004.

[20] "Public Relations Firm Fleishman-Hillard Accused of Defrauding L.A. Department of Water and Power," Los Angeles Office of City Attorney, news release. July 16, 2004, http://www.cityofla.org/atty.

[21] "Important Message," Fleishman-Hillard internal e-mail message from John Graham, July 16, 2004.

[22] Ted Rohrlich, Ralph Frammolino and Patrick McGreevy, "PR Exec Placed on Paid Leave; Fleishman-Hillard, Accused of Falsely Billing the DWP, Removes the Former Head of its L.A. Office; Los Angeles Sues the Company," *Los Angeles Times,* July 17, 2004, Metro Desk, Part B, p.1.

[23] Allyce Bess, "Fleishman Won't Renew LA Contracts/Public Relations Firm is Under Scrutiny for Work with Agencies," *St. Louis Post-Dispatch,* April 21, 2004, Business, Pg. C1.

[24] "Statement by Richard Kline, Regional President, Fleishman-Hillard, and General Manager, Los Angeles," public statement, April 20, 2004.

[25] David Streitfeld, "PR Firm in Billing Probe Failed to Take Own Advice," *Los Angeles Times*, July 26, 2004," accessed from Latimes.com, http://www/latimes.com/la-fi-fleishman26jul26,1,4146977.story.

[26] "July 29 Ltr.," internal document, letter to colleagues by John Graham, Fleishman-Hillard, July 29, 2004.

[27] Ibid.

[28] "Important Message," Fleishman-Hillard, internal e-mail message "E-mail to FH Staff Worldwide" from John Graham, August 5, 2004.

[29] Professional Standards Advisory PS-2 (July 2004), Public Relations Society of America, http://www.prsa.org/News/leaders/beps071904.asp.

[30] "Chick Audit Finds $4.2 Million in Unsubstantiated, Unsupported and Questionable PR Bills: City Controller Demands the Money Back," news release, Los Angeles City Controller Office, November 16, 2004, http://www.lacity.org/ctr/.

[31] "City Attorney Rocky Delgadillo Recovers Nearly $6 Million from Fleishman-Hillard: Settlement Reached in DWP Overbilling Case," news release, Los Angeles Office of City Attorney, April 19, 2005.

[32] "Los Angeles City Attorney and Fleishman-Hillard Agree to Settle All City Civil Claims," news release, Fleishman-Hillard, April 19, 2005.

[33] Ibid.

[34] James Nash, "Council Opens Faucets: Hikes Water Rate 11%," *Daily News of Los Angeles,* May 12, 2004, p. N1.

[35] James Nash, "Acting DWP Chief Demoted over Scandal: Martinez to Replace Salas as Interim General Manager," *Daily News of Los Angeles,* July 21, 2004, p. N3.

[36] Anita Chabria, "LA Mayor's Decision Puts Several Agencies' Contracts into Question," *PR Week,* May 3, 2004, p. 1.

[37] David Streitfeld, "PR Firm in Billing Probe Failed to Take Own Advice."

[38] Patrick McGreevy, "City Refuses to Pay DWP Consultant's Billing for $74,000," *Los Angeles Times,* August 31, 2004, Metro Desk, Part B, p. 3.

[39] Beth Barrett, "PR Execs Guilty on All Counts; Dowie: Stodder May Draw Long Terms in DWP Fraud," *Daily News of Los Angeles,* May 17, 2006, p. N1.

[40] Laura Mecoy Bee, "Villaraigosa Wins L.A. Mayor's Race: He Will Be the First Latino to Lead the City Since 1872," *Sacramento Bee,* May 18, 2005, p. 1A.

[41] "Mayor Villaraigosa Names Appointees to the Board of Water and Power Commissioners," news release, news release, Office of the Mayor, August 15, 2005, accessed March 5, 2006 from www.lacity.org/mayor/myree/mayormyree246633218_08152005.pdf.

[42] Julia Hood, "Analysis: Fleishman's LA Office—Fleishman's LA controversy raises questions for all firms," *PR Week,* August 2, 2004, p. 9.

[43] Robert Pear, "U.S. Videos, for TV News, Come Under Scrutiny," *New York Times,* March 15, 2004, Section A, p. 1.

[44] Robert Pear, "Congress Investigating TV Segments on Medicare," *New York Times,* March 16, 2004, p. 3.

[45] Vicki Kemper, "Mock News on Medicare Called Illegal: The General Accounting Office says Viewers of the Segments Played by 40 TV stations Weren't Told they Were Produced for a Government Agency," *Los Angeles Times,* May 20, 2004, Part A, p. 16.

[46] Government Accountability Office, "Video News Releases: Unattributed Prepackaged News Stories Violate Publicity or Propaganda Prohibition," statement of Susan A. Poling, managing associate general counsel, Office of General Counsel, May 12, 2005.

[47] Robert Pear, "U.S. Videos, for TV News, Come Under Scrutiny."

[48] Paul Griffo, "Spotlight On Video News Releases: Karen Ryan, PR Professional," *Public Relations Tactics,* Public Relations Society of America, www.prsa.org/_Publications/magazines/0604spot1.asp.

[49] Greg Hazley, "Ethics Questioned: VNR Pros Sound Off," *O'Dwyer's PR Services Report,* April 2004.

[50] Robert Pear, "Ruling Says White House's Medicare Videos Were Illegal," *New York Times,* May 20, 2004, Section A, p. 24.

[51] Vicki Kemper, "Mock News on Medicare Called Illegal."

[52] Greg Hazley, "Ethics Questioned, VNR Pros Sound Off," p. 1.

[53] Robert Pear, "U.S. Videos, for TV News, Come under Scrutiny," *New York Times,* March 15, 2004, Section A, p. 1.

[54] "HHS Unveils New Medicare Education Campaign," news release, February 3, 2004, accessed September 5, 2004 from www.hhs.gov/news/press/2004pres/20040203a.html.

[55] Jan Uebelherr, "Media Video News Release Raises Media Hackles," *Milwaukee Journal Sentinel,* March 19, 2004, p. 8B.

[56] Greg Hazley, "Ethics Questioned, VNR Pros Sound Off."

[57] Ibid.

[58] Ibid.

[59] Ibid.

[60] Judith Turner Phair, President and CEO, Public Relations Society of America, testimony, U.S. Senate Committee on Commerce, Science and Transportation, May 12, 2005, accessed March 5, 2006, from commerce.senate.gov/hearings/testimony.cfm?id=1497&7it_id=4265.

[61] Jerry Walker, "Ethics Questioned, VNR Pros Sound Off."

[62] U.S. Government Accountability Office, "Video News Releases: Unattributed Prepackaged News Stories Violate Publicity or Propaganda Prohibition."

[63] U.S. Government Accountability Office, "Department of Health and Human Services, Centers for Medicare & Medicaid Services—Video News Releases," decision, file B-302710, May 19, 2004, p. 15.

[64] U.S. Government Accountability Office. "Video News Releases: Unattributed Prepackaged News Stories Violate Publicity or Propaganda Prohibition," May 12, 2005, pp. 5–6.

[65] Ibid.

[66] Ibid.

[67] U.S. General Accountability Office, "Media Contracts: Activities and Financial Obligations of Seven Federal Departments, January 2006, accessed from http://www.democrats.reform.house.gov/Documents/20060213110539–14835.pdf.

[68] "Memorandum Opinion for the General Counsel Department of Health and Human Services: Expenditure of Appropriated Funds for Informational Video News Releases," U.S. Department of Justice, July 30, 2004.

[69] Federal Communication Commission Public Notice, "Commission Reminds Broadcast Licensees, Cable Operators and Others of Requirements Applicable to Video News Releases and Seeks Comment on the Use of Video News Releases by Broadcast Licensees and Cable Operators," April 13, 2005.

[70] U.S. House of Representatives Committee on Government Reform—Minority Staff Special Investigations Division, "Federal Public Relations Spending," January 2005, accessed May 30, 2006, from www.house.gov/georgemiller/pr_report_final.pdf.

[71] Doug Clark, "Williams Trips over Ethical Mistake," editorial, *News & Record* (Greensboro, NC), January 12, 2005, p. A9.

[72] Ibid.

[73] Armstrong Williams.com, Television, The Right Side, Web site, accessed May 31, 2006, from www.armstrongwilliams.com.

[74] Armstrong Williams.com, Armstrong Williams Biography, Web site, accessed September 14, 2006 from www.armstrongwilliams.com.

[75] Armstrong Williams Web site, The Graham Williams Group, accessed May 31, 2006, from www. armstrongwilliams.com.

[76] Greg Toppo, "White House Paid Commentator to Promote Law," *USA Today,* January 7, 2005, p. 1A.

[77] Dave Astor, "Armstrong Williams's Column Axed by TMS," *Editor & Publisher,* January 7, 2005.

[78] Ibid.

[79] U.S. Government Accountability Office, "Department of Education—Contract to Obtain Services of Armstrong Williams," p. 2.

[80] "Statement of Work for Task Order No. 9," The Graham Williams Group/Ketchum Contract for the Minority Outreach for the Department of Education's No Child Left Behind Minority Outreach Campaign.

[81] Ibid.

[82] Ibid.

[83] Ibid.

[84] America's Black Forum, About America's Black Forum, Web site, accessed from www. americasblackforum.com/about.

[85] "CREW Files FOIAs to Uncover Government Agency Dealings with PR Firms," news release, Citizens for Responsibility and Ethics in Washington, January 11, 2005, www.citizensforethics.org.

[86] U.S. Government Accountability Office, Department of Education—Contract to Obtain Services of Armstrong Williams, September 30, 2005, p. 7.

[87] "The Right Side with Armstrong Williams," letter to readers, January 9, 2005, www.armstrongwilliams. com.

[88] Rod Paige, "Statement of Secretary Paige," news release, Department of Education, January 13, 2005, accessed from www.ed.gov/news/pressreleases/2005.

[89] George Miller, "Representative Miller's Response to Secretary Paige Statement on Propaganda: The Secretary and President Bush Cannot Even Bring Themselves to Admit They Were Wrong," news release, January 13, 2005, accessed from edworkforce.house.gove/democrats/releases/rel11305.html.

[90] Ray Kotcher, "Williams Scandal Is a 'Transformational Event' in PR," *PR Week,* January 17, 2005, p. 8.

[91] Ibid.

[92] Erica Iacono, "Ketchum Pins Liability for DoE Disclosure on Williams," *PR Week,* January 17, 2005, p. 1.

[93] "Williams Episode Sparks Debate on Disclosure Ethics," *PR Week,* January 17, 2005, p. 1.

[94] Julia Hood, "Ketchum Must Accept Share of Responsibility Regarding the Armstrong Williams Imbroglio," *PR Week,* January 17, 2005, p. 8.

[95] Ray Kotcher, CEO of Ketchum, statement to the news media, Ketchum, January 19, 2005.

[96] "Interview with Ray Kotcher: Kotcher Discusses Impact of DoE Episode on Ketchum," *PR Week,* April 4, 2005, p. 7.

[97] Ibid.

[98] "Review of Formation Issues Regarding the Department of Education's Fiscal Year 2003 Contract with Ketchum, Inc., for Media Relations Services" (ED-OIG/A10-F0007), U.S. Department of Education Office of Inspector General, April 2005, accessed May 31, 2006, from www.ed.gov/about/offices/list/ oig/aireports/a19f0007.doc.

[99] Ibid.

[100] Ibid.

[101] Ibid.

[102] Ibid.

[103] Ibid.

[104] U.S. Government Accountability Office, "Department of Education—Contract to Obtain Services of Armstrong Williams," pp. 14–15.

[105] Jason Marshall, "Soldier Proud of Work in Iraq," *Mountain View Telegraph,* New Mexico, Guest View letter to the editor, September 11, 2003, accessed March 5, 2006, from www.mvtelegraph.com/opinion/83932mtnview09-11-03.htm.

[106] Adam C. Connell, "GIs Have Made Things Better in Iraq," September 14, 2003, *Boston Globe,* Letters, p. D12, accessed September 11, 2004, from Lexis-Nexis.

[107] John Brennan, "Letter Raises Ruckus," *Mountain View Telegraph,* New Mexico, October 16, 2003, accessed from Lexis-Nexis, p. A1.

[108] Barbara Slavin, "Global Realities Force Bush to Rethink Strategy," *USA Today*, September 23, 2003, p. 8A.

[109] Ledyard King, "Newspapers Print Same Letter Signed by Different Soldiers," Gannett News Service, *USA Today,* October 13, 2003, p. 7A.

[110] Charles Reinken, "Duty to Our Readers Dictates Not Using Cookie-Cutter Letters: Any Letter Coming to the *World-Herald's* Editorial Page that Looks Suspicious—A Little Too Pat, Too Good to be True—Is Run Through a Number of Search Engines," editorial, *The Omaha World-Herald Company,* November 9, 2003, p. 15b.

[111] Ledyard King, "Officer Was the One behind 500 Letters," Gannett News Service, *USA Today*, October 15, 2003, p. 14A.

[112] Ibid.

[113] Charles Reinken, "Duty to Our Readers Dictates Not Using Cookie-Cutter Letters," p. 15b.

[114] Julia Hood, "The Use of Contrived Soldiers' Letters Isn't a Solid PR Plan to Combat Anti-war Sentiment in the U.S.," editorial, *PR Week,* October 20, 2003, p. 8.

[116] John Brennan, "Letter Raises Ruckus," *Mountain View Telegraph.*

[117] De Kock Communications, "'Don't Throw Away Gains in UK Wine Market,' Urges Leading Wine Marketer," Wine of South Africa, accessed May 31, 2006, from www.wine.co.za/News/News.aspx?NEWSID=8250&Source=News.

[118] Wines of South Africa, Web site, Worldwide Statistics, accessed May 31, 2006, from www.wosa.co.za/SA/statistics.htm.

[119] Ibid.

[120] "WIETA Code: What is Contained in the WIETA Code?" Wine Industry Ethical Trade Association, Web site, accessed September 15, 2006, from http://www.wieta.org.za/code.htmlhttp://www.wieta.org.za/code.html

[121] "WIETA News," Wine Industry Ethical Trade Association, Web site, accessed June 1, 2006, from http://www.wieta.org.za/news.html#WIETA_Training_&_Materials_Development_Programme.

[123] "WIETA Members," Wine Industry Ethical Trade Association, Web site, accessed June 1, 2006, from www.wieta.org.za/members.html.

[124] "Questions & Answers," Wine Industry Ethical Trade Association, Web site, accessed February 26, 2005, from www.wieta.org.za/q&a.html.

CHAPTER 5

[1] Dennis L. Wilcox (2005). *Public Relations Writing and Media Techniques,* Boston: Pearson Education, pp. 94–101.

[2] BurrellesLuce Media Contacts Directory, BurrellesLuce, Web site, accessed from http://www.burrellesluce.com/MediaContacts/default.php.

[3] "2000 Global Color Popularity," DuPont Automotive, brochure, accessed from http://www.performancecoatings.dupont.com/dpc/en/us/html/color/dpc/Colorpop.pdf.

[4] Brett Clanton, "DuPont Lays Off 50 in Troy," *Detroit News,* May 3, 2005, accessed December 20, 2005 from www.detnews.com/2005/autosinsider/0505/06/C06–169356.htm.

[5] "Car Buyers' 'Appetite for Color' Eats into Silver's Long Reign: 2005 DuPont Automotive Color Popularity Report Finds Technology Drives Broader Palette," DuPont Automotive, news release, accessed December 22, 2005 from www2.dupont.com/Automotive/en_US/news_events/article20051123.html.

[6] Sarah Marshall, "Texas' Family Violence Shelters: Not Just Emergency Care, but Providing Life Changing Opportunities," Texas Council on Family Violence, *The River,* summer 2004, pp. 1, 4, 5, accessed December 29, 2004, from www.tcfv.org/pr/newsletter.html.

[7] "National Statistics on Abuse," based on Bureau of Justice Statistics Crime Data Brief, Intimate Partner Violence, 1993–2001, February 2003, accessed December 30, 2004 from www.makethecall.org.

[8] "Texas Council on Family Violence Announces Statewide Domestic Violence Public Awareness Campaign 'Break the Silence. Make the Call.' " Texas Council on Family Violence, news release, October 6, 2002, accessed December 29, 2004 from www.vollmerpr.com/clients/default. asp?which=releases&clientid=200&releaseid=2123.

[9] "Abuse in Texas: 2003 in Texas at a Glance," Texas Council on Family Violence, accessed December 29, 2004 from www.tcfv.org/abuse_in_texas.htm; and "National Statistics on Abuse."

[10] "Prevalence, Perceptions and Awareness of Domestic Violence in Texas," executive summary, a quantitative study conducted for the Texas Council on Family Violence by Saurage Research, February 11, 2003.

[11] "Statewide Survey Indicates Domestic Violence Is Nearing Epidemic Proportions," Texas Council on Family Violence news release, February 11, 2003, accessed December 29, 2004, from www.vollmerpr. com/clients/default.asp?which=release&clientid-200&releaseid=2122.

[12] "Hispanic Texans and Domestic Violence: A Statewide Study," executive summary, June 17, 2003, a study conducted for Texas Council on Family Violence by Saurage Research, accessed June 1, 2006, from www.tcfv.org/pdf/PAC_Hisp_Exec_Summary_final.pdf.

[13] "Building Partnerships to Break the Silence: A Case Study in Social Marketing," 2004 Public Relations Society of America International Conference, October 25, 2004, p. 17.

[14] "Friends and Family Campaign," Resource Download Center, The National Domestic Violence Hotline, accessed June 1, 2006, from www.ndvh.org/press/resource_center.html.

[15] Ibid.

[16] "Texas Council on Family Violence Announces Statewide Domestic Violence Public Awareness Campaign 'Break the Silence. Make the Call.' "

[17] "Building Partnerships to Break the Silence: A Case Study in Social Marketing," 2004 Public Relations Society of America International Conference, October 25, 2004, pp. 29–31.

[18] Ibid., p. 30.

[19] Ibid., p. 32.

[20] "Best Hospitals: Pediatrics," *U.S. News and World Report* online, accessed January 22, 2005, from www. usnews.com/usnews/health/best-hospitals/rankings/specreppedi.htm.

[21] Avery Comarow, "Methodology behind the Rankings," Best Hospitals 2004, *U.S. News and World Report* online, accessed January 22, 2005, from www.usnews.com/usnews/health/best-hospitals/ methodology.htm.

[22] "2005's 10 Best Children's Hospitals," *Child* magazine online, accessed January 22, 2005, from www. child.com/kids/health_nutrition/top_hospitals05.jsp?page=2.

[23] Greg Gatlin, "Harvard Is Hot in Reputation, PR Study Says," *Boston Herald,* October 20, 2004, accessed from Lexis-Nexis, p. 37; and "Non-profit Organizations Dominate Upper Ranks of 2004 Massachusetts Corporate Reputation Survey: Children's Hospital Boston Ranks as Highest Medical Institution," news release, Children's Hospital Boston, October 22, 2004, accessed January 4, 2005 from www.childrenshospital.org.

[24] Jerome Groopman, "The Pediatric Gap," *The New Yorker,* January 10, 2005, p. 32.

[25] "New Data Validate Low Glycemic Diet."

[26] J. M. Hirsch, "Diet: Doctors Say Kids Should Skip Juice—Even the Natural Kind—and Stick with Water, Milk," Associated Press, February 10, 2005, accessed from Lexis-Nexis.

[27] "World Vision Profile," World Vision, backgrounder, January 2005.

[28] "World Vision's Media Relations Function," World Vision, backgrounder, January 2005.

[29] Ibid.

[30] Ibid.

[31] "World Vision Profile," World Vision, backgrounder.

[32] "World Vision Sets $50 Million Goal for South Asia Disaster: Humanitarian Leader Will Travel to Region on Monday: Relief Supplies Being Airlifted," press release, World Vision, December 31, 2004.

[33] "World Vision Mounts Massive Response: Death Toll Exceeds 10,000 in Asia," news release, World Vision, December 28, 2004.

[34] "World Vision Launches Response to Tsunami Devastation: In India, 'Wall of Water So Strong Cars Were Thrown Like Toys,'" World Vision, news release, December 27, 2004.

[35] "World Vision Staff Head to Asia for Earthquake/Tsunami Response: Federal Way-Based Agency Will Send Communications Team to India," World Vision, news release, December 27, 2004.

[36] "Relief Officials Fear Diseases from Rotting Corpses: Bodies of People, Livestock Litter Asia's shorelines: Mass Graves Replace Traditional Funeral Pyres," World Vision, news release, December 27, 2004.

[37] "From 'Do-gooders' to Better-Organized Relief Professionals: Aid Agencies Have Greatly Improved Coordination over Two Decades," World Vision, news release, December 28, 2004.

[38] "Notes from the Disaster Zone: Survivors Ask, 'Why Us?' They Wish They Had Been Swept Away," World Vision, news release, December 28, 2004.

[39] "Top 10 Myths of Disaster Relief: Aid Groups Address Public Stereotypes about Overseas Disasters," World Vision, news release, December 29, 2004.

[40] "Global Relief Efforts 'Just Scratching the Surface': World Vision Emergency Communication Manager Available for Interview," World Vision, news release, December 29, 2004.

[41] "World Vision Experts to Conduct Chicago Press Briefing: World Vision Reports more than $8 Million from U.S. Donors: World Vision Worldwide Has Raised between $15–20 Million," World Vision, news release, December 30, 2004.

[42] "World Vision Sets $50 Million Goal for South Asia Disaster," World Vision.

[43] "World Vision Relief Supplies Leaving Denver for Tsunami Zone: Press Availability Planned for Friday, December 31," World Vision, news release, December 31, 2004.

[44] "Donors Should Insist on Responsible Use of Relief Funds: Generous Response to Tsunami Disaster Presents Opportunities for Aid Agencies;" World Vision, news release, December 31, 2004.

[45] "Media Alert: Play Golf and Help Tsunami Victims: The Tsunami Disaster Affected Millions of Lives—Upcoming Fundraising Golf Tournaments to Benefit the Tsunami Survivors," World Vision, media alert, December 31, 2004.

[46] "America's Generosity 'Unprecedented and Overwhelming': Businesses, Church, Individuals Respond to Tsunami Tragedy," World Vision, January 3, 2005, "World Vision Implements Programs to Keep Children Safe from Sexual Exploitation in the Wake of the Tsunami: Relief Organization Sets Up Child-Friendly Safe Centers to Protect Children in Hardest Hit Countries," January 7, 2005, and "Bush Urges Aid Agencies to Protect Tsunami-Affected Children: World Vision and Other Aid Agencies Meet with President about Response," World Vision, news releases, January 10, 2005.

[47] "Northwest Aid Agencies Fly Relief to Tsunami Victims," January 12, 2005, and "From Billings to Banda Aceh: World Vision Sends Helicopters to Tsunami Zone: Cargo Choppers Will Help Relief Workers Bring Needed Supplies to Inaccessible Areas," World Vision, news release, January 19, 2005.

[48] "Tsunami Response Media Team Operational Analysis," internal document World Vision.

[49] "World Vision Media Coverage of the South Asia Tsunami: A Combined Report of the Offices of Marketing Communication and Media Relations," World Vision, internal document.

[50] Ibid.

[51] Ibid.

[52] "Five Pillars of Response," World Vision, internal document.

[53] "Kodak's '4Cs' Define a Great Picture: Launch of Kodak High Definition Film," campaign plan and Public Relations Society of America silver anvil entry materials, provided by Eastman Kodak. This case study was based on these materials and on interviews with Charles Smith, Kodak's director of communications and vice president of Film and Photofinishing Systems Group.

CHAPTER 6

[1] "Myths in Crisis Management," Institute for Crisis Management, accessed June 29, 2006, from www.crisisexperts.com/myths.htm.

[2] Andrea Gerlin, "How Jury Gave $2.9 Million for Coffee Spill: McDonald's Callousness Was Real Issue," *Pittsburgh Post-Gazette*, September 4, 1994, p. B2, accessed from Lexis-Nexis.

[3] David Field, "Intel Works to Repair New Pentium Chip Flaw and Keep Image Intact," *USA Today*, May 12, 1997, p. 2B, accessed from Lexis-Nexis.

[4] Eric Lipton, "U.S. Report Faults Nation's Preparedness for Disaster," June 17, 2006, p. 10, accessed from Lexis-Nexis.

[5] Timothy Coombs, "Designing Post-Crisis Messages: Lessons for Crisis Response Strategies," *Review of Business,* Fall 2000, p. 37.

[6] Ronald D. Smith (2005), *Strategic Planning for Public Relations,* 2nd ed., Mahwah, NJ: Lawrence Erlbaum, pp. 100–114.

[7] Dennis Wilcox, Glen T. Cameron, Philip H. Ault, and Warren K. Agee (2003). *Public Relations Strategies and Tactics,* Boston: Allyn and Bacon, p. 183.

[8] Jeremy Laurance, "Analysis Smallpox Vaccine: Bioterrorists Present a Dilemma for Doctors," *The Independent* (London), October 10, 2002, p. 19.

[9] Ibid.

[10] "What You Should Know about a Smallpox Outbreak," U.S. Department of Health and Human Services, Center for Disease Control and Prevention, accessed June 3, 2006, from www.bt.cdc.gov/agent/smallpox/basics/outbreak.asp.

[11] Ibid.

[12] Jeff Nesmith, "Millions Still Have Smallpox Resistance," *Atlanta Journal-Constitution,* August 18, 2003, p1A.

[13] Sarah Bosely and Julian Borger, "U.S. Scientists Push for Go-Ahead to Genetically Modify Smallpox Virus," *Guardian* (London), May 16, 2005, p. 3.

[14] U.S. Department of Health and Human Services, Centers for Disease Control and Prevention, "Guide E Smallpox Preparation and Response Activities: Communication Plan and Activities," version 3, accessed June 3, 2006, from www.bt.cdc.gov/agent/smallpox/response-plan/files/guide-e.pdf.

[15] Ibid.

[16] Peter M. Sandman and Jody Lanard, "Dilemmas in Emergency Communication Policy," accessed June 16, 2005, from www.psandman.com/articles/dilemmas.pdf; and "Fear of Fear: The Role of Fear in Preparedness and Why It Terrifies Officials," accessed June 16, 2005, from www.psandman.com/col/fear.htm.

[17] "Guide E Smallpox Preparation and Response Activities," U.S. Department of Health and Human Services.

[18] Ibid.

[19] "Public Health Information Network (PHIN), accessed June 16, 2005, from www.cdc.gov/phin/index.html.

[20] "Guide E Smallpox Preparation and Response Activities," U.S. Department of Health and Human Services.

[21] Ibid.

[22] Ibid.

[23] Ibid.

[24] Donald G. McNeil Jr., "KFC Supplier Accused of Animal Cruelty," *New York Times*, July 20, 2004, Business Section, p. 2.

[25] "Pilgrim's Pride," videotape, People for the Ethical Treatment of Animals, July 20, 2004.

[26] Mika Brzezinski, "PETA Releases Videotape of Cruelty to Chickens by Some Workers at a Slaughterhouse That Provides Food to KFC," *CBS Evening News,* July 20, 2004.

[27] Ned Potter, "A Closer Look: Animal Cruelty," *World News Tonight,* ABC, July 20, 2004.

[28] Anderson Cooper, *Anderson Cooper 360 Degrees,* CNN transcript 072000CN.V98, July 20, 2004.

[29] Donald G. McNeil Jr., "KFC Supplier Accused of Animal Cruelty."

[30] "KFC Cruelty: Cruelty in the KFC Slaughterhouse," People for the Ethical Treatment of Animals, accessed October 16, 2004, from www.peta.org/feat/moorefield.

[31] Ibid.

[32] O. B. Goolsby, "Statement from O. B. Goolsby to All Pilgrim's Pride Employees," Pilgrim's Pride, statement, accessed October 16, 2004, from www.pilgrimspride.com/consumers/president.asp.

[33] Donald G. McNeil Jr., "KFC Supplier Accused of Animal Cruelty."

[34] O. B. Goolsby, "Response to Allegations Regarding Animal Welfare Practices in Moorefield, West Virginia," Pilgrim's Pride, news release, July 20, 2004, accessed October 16, 2004, from www. pilgrimspride.com/consumers/statement.asp.

[35] Ibid.

[36] "Statement by Pilgrim's Pride: Pilgrim's Pride Terminates 11 Employees Based on Moorefield, West Virginia, Investigation," July 21, 2004, accessed October 16, 2004, from www.pilgrimspride.com/consumers/statement2.asp.

[37] Ibid.

[38] "Pilgrim's Pride Statement," Pilgrim's Pride, August 3, 2004.

[39] "KFC Response Statement to Pilgrim's Pride Incident," KFC, statement, July 20, 2004, accessed October 16, 2004, from www.kfc.com/about/pr/072004.htm.

[40] Ibid.

[41] Ibid.

[42] Gregg Dedrick, "Press Conference Comments by KFC President Gregg Dedrick," KFC, statement, July 21, 2004, accessed October 16, 2004, from www.kfc.com/about/pr/072104.htm.

[43] Ibid.

[44] Ibid.

[45] Vicki Smith, "USDA Sends Compliance Officers to W. Virginia Chicken Plant," Associated Press, July 24, 2004, accessed from Lexis-Nexis on October 17, 2004.

[46] Vicki Smith, "Feds Still Reviewing Chicken Cruelty Case," Associated Press, August 11, 2004, accessed from Lexis-Nexis on October 17, 2004.

[47] Vicki Smith, "Chicken Cruelty Scandal Won't Stop Poultry Festival," Associated Press, July 27, 2004, accessed from Lexis-Nexis on October 17, 2004.

[48] Vicki Smith, "Jury Won't Indict Chicken Plant Workers," Associated Press, June 8, 2005, accessed September 29, 2006 from Lexis-Nexis.

[49] Wyatt Buchanan, "Mission District Cyclist Blew Whistle on Flawed Lock," *San Francisco Chronicle,* September 19, 2004, Bay Area, p. B1, accessed from Lexis-Nexis.

[50] Ibid.

[51] Chris Brennan, aka Unaesthetic, "Your Brand New Bicycle U-Lock Is Not Safe," Bike Forums, September 12, 2004, accessed December 28, 2004, from www.bikeforums.net/showthread.php?t=67493&highlight=benjamin+running.

[52] Bike Forums, Post #128, by "unaesthetic," September 13, 2004, 8:45 p.m., accessed from www.BikeForums.net

[53] Benjamin Running, "Take This Quiz," September 14, 2004, blog, accessed June 4, 2006, from thirdrate.com/page/9/.

[54] Benjamin Running, "So. This Kryptonite Lock Deal," blog, September 15, 2004, accessed June 4, 2006, from thirdrate.com/page/9/.

[55] "About Kryptonite: Round 1," Kryptonite, Web site, accessed from www.kryptonitelock.com/inetisscripts/abtinetis.exe/templateform@public?tn=about_story.tem.

[56] "About Kryptonite: Round 2," Kryptonite, Web site, accessed from www.kryptonitelock.com/inetisscripts/abtinetis.exe/templateform@public?tn=about_story.tem.

[58] "The Pen is Mightier than the . . . U-Lock," BikeBiz.com, September 16, 2004, accessed January 17, 2005 from www.bikebiz.co.uk/daily-news/article.php?id=4637.

[59] Ibid.

[60] Ross Kerber, "Cyclists: Bike Locks Easy Prey for Thieves: Kryptonite Promises More Secure Product," *Boston Globe,* September 16, 2004, p. E1.

[61] Ibid.

[62] Lydia Polgreen, "The Pen Is Mightier than the Lock: A Ballpoint Trick Infuriates Bicyclists," *New York Times,* September 17, 2004, Section B, p. 1, accessed from Lexis-Nexis.

[63] "Kryptonite Issues Statement on Tubular Cylinder Lock Consumer Concerns," news release, Kryptonite, September 16, 2004, accessed March 29, 2005, from Lexis-Nexis.

[64] Lydia Polgreen, "The Pen Is Mightier than the Lock."

[65] Jay Lindsay, "Kryptonite Faces Bike Lock-Picking Fiasco," Associated Press Online, September 17, 2004, accessed from Lexis-Nexis.

[66] Kryptonite, "Kryptonite Offering Free Upgrade Worldwide for Consumers' High End Tubular Cylinder Locks," news release, September 17, 2004, accessed March 29, 2005, accessed from Lexis-Nexis.

[67] *PR News,* "Q&A: Kryptonite's Close Call," March 16, 2005, accessed from Lexis-Nexis.

[68] Ibid.

[69] Ibid.

[70] Vermont Teddy Bear Company Web site, accessed January 22, 2005, from shop.store.yahoo.com/vtbear/crazyforyou.html.

[71] Jerry Goessel, letter to Vermont Teddy Bear Company president, January 10, 2005, provided by NAMI Vermont.

[72] "Statement from The Vermont Teddy Bear Company," January 12, 2005, provided by the Vermont Teddy Bear Company.

[73] Jerry Goessel, Anne Donahue, Ken Libertoff, and David Fassler, letter to Vermont Teddy Bear Company president, January 13, 2005, provided by NAMI Vermont.

[74] Jerry Goessel, e-mail communication to author, January 27, 2005.

[75] Ibid.

[76] "The Vermont Teddy Bear Company Statement," January 13, 2005, provided by the Vermont Teddy Bear Company.

[77] Jerry Goessel, letter to Vermont Teddy Bear Company president, January 17, 2005, provided by NAMI Vermont.

[78] "The Vermont Teddy Bear Company Announces Meeting with NAMI; The Company and NAMI Officials to Talk about Controversial 'Crazy for You' Bear," news release, January 20, 2005, accessed May 24, 2005, from ir.vtbearcompany.com/index.php?id=181.

[79] "Vermont Teddy Bear Sells Out of 'Crazy for You' Bear and Stands by Its Promise Not to Make More," news release, February 3, 2005, accessed from ir.vtbearcompany.com/index.php?id=182.

[80] David Gram, "Teddy Bear CEO Resigns from Hospital Board," Associated Press, February 9, 2005.

[81] Justice Oliver Wendell Holmes said that "the most stringent protection of free speech would not protect a man in falsely shouting fire in a theatre and causing a panic," *Schenck v. United States,* March 3, 1919.

[82] Joan Hinde Stewart, "Letter to Hamilton Community: President Discusses Kirkland Project/Ward Churchill Event," February 9, 2005, accessed February 12, 2005, at www.hamilton.edu/news/more_news/display.cfm?ID=9011; and Jorge L. Hernandez, "Professor Holds Firm Despite Pressure over Speaker: Rabinowitz Stresses Free Idea Exchange," *Observer-Dispatch* (Utica, NY), February 2, 2005, p. 1B.

[83] "Panel Discussion 'Limits of Dissent' Thursday, February 3: Kirkland Project Presents Panel and Q&A," news release, Hamilton College, February 1, 2005, accessed from www.hamilton.edu/news/more_news/display.cfm?ID=9019 on February 1, 2005.

[84] "Hamilton Facts 2005–2006," Hamilton College, accessed from www.hamilton.edu/college/institutional_research/extdashboard0506.htm.

[85] Cecilia Le, "Ex-Radical Declines Position," *Observer-Dispatch* (Utica, NY), December 9, 2004, accessed from Lexis-Nexis.

[86] Roger Kimball, "Meet the Newest Member of the Faculty," commentary, Taste, *Weekend Wall Street Journal,* December 3, 2004, p. W. 15, accessed from Lexis-Nexis.

[87] "Susan Rosenberg Withdraws: Memoir Writing Seminar Cancelled," news release, December 8, 2004, Hamilton College, accessed February 1, 2005 from www.hamilton.edu/news/more_news/display.cfm?ID=8827.

[88] Scott Smallwood, "Inside a Free-Speech Firestorm: How a Professor's 3-Year-Old Essay Sparked a National Controversy," *Chronicle of Higher Education,* February 18, 2005, pp. 10–11.

[89] Ward Churchill, "Some People Push Back: On the Justice of Roosting Chickens," accessed June 5, 2006, from www.darknightpress.org/index/php?i=print&article=9.

[90] Ibid.

[91] Ibid.

[92] Scott Smallwood, "Inside a Free-Speech Firestorm."

[93] Jorge L. Hernandez, "Professor Holds Firm Despite Pressure over Speaker."

[94] Ibid.

[95] Michelle York, "Remark on 9/11 Sparks Storm at College," *New York Times,* January 31, 2004, p. B3.

[96] Ian Mandel, "Controversial Speaker to Visit Hill," *Spectator* (Clinton, NY), January 21, 2005, accessed February 12, 2005, from spec.hamilton.edu/sports.cfm?action=display&news=476.

[97] Alaina Potrikus, "Controversy Festers on Hamilton Campus Again," *Post Standard* (Syracuse, NY), January 26, 2005.

[98] "The Anti-American Academy," blog, Little Green Footballs, accessed June 5, 2006, from littlegreenfootballs.com/weblog/?entry=14482&only.

[99] "'Limits of Dissent' to Be Discussed by Three-Member Panel: Topics Range from Pragmatic Pacifism to Criminalizing Dissent," news release, Hamilton College, January 26, 2005.

[100] "College Issues Statement Concerning Churchill Visit, Kirkland Project Speaker to Appear February 3," news release, Hamilton College, January 26, 2005, accessed from www.hamilton.edu/news/more_news/display.cfm?ID=8991.

[101] "Talking Points Memo and Top Story," *The O'Reilly Factor,* Fox News Network, accessed from Lexis-Nexis, January 28, 2005.

[102] Ibid.

[103] "I have a Son . . ." post 174, Hamilton College, accessed February 12, 2005, from www.hamilton.edu/news/wardchurchill/comments.html?startrow=161.

[104] "I Am a Student Looking . . ." post 53, Hamilton College, accessed February 12, 2005, from www.hamilton.edu/news/wardchurchill/comments.html?startrow=161.

[105] "Your College Is Actually . . ." post 45, Hamilton College, accessed February 12, 2005, from www.hamilton.edu/news/wardchurchill/comments.html?startrow=161.

[106] "President Stewart Sends Message to Hamilton Community: Memo Updates Campus on Kirkland Project Panel," Hamilton College, January 30, 2005, accessed February 12, 2005, from www.hamilton.edu/news/more_news/display.cfm?ID=9011.

[107] Ward Churchill, University of Colorado at Boulder, press release, January 31, 2005, accessed February 3, 2005, from www.colorado.edu/news.

[108] Bill O'Reilly, "Impact: Professor Says 9/11 Victims Deserved Fate," *The O'Reilly Factor,* FOX News Network accessed from Lexis-Nexis, January 31, 2005.

[109] "Panel Discussion 'Limits of Dissent' Thursday, February 3: Kirkland Project Presents Panel and Q&A," news release, Hamilton College, February 1, 2005.

[110] Joan Hinde Stewart, "Letter to the Hamilton Community: President Discusses Kirkland Project/Ward Churchill," letter, Hamilton College.

[111] Ibid.

[112] Ibid.

[113] "Kirkland Project Cancelled: Public Safety Cited," news release, Hamilton College, February 1, 2005, accessed February 1, 2005 from www.hamilton,edu/news/more_news/display.cfm?ID=9020.

[114] Joan Hinde Stewart, "Letter to the Hamilton Community: President Discusses Kirkland Project/Ward Churchill."

[115] "Hamilton Facts 2005–2006," fact sheet, Hamilton College, accessed from http://www.hamilton.edu/college/institutional_research/extdashboard0506.htm.

[116] "Contributions to Hamilton College Campaign Top $100 Million," news release, Hamilton College, accessed from www.hamilton.edu/news/more_news/display.cfm?ID=10191.

[117] "Hamilton College Ranks #15 in *U.S. News* 2006 Ranking," news release, Hamilton College, Aug. 22, 2005, accessed from http://www.hamilton.edu/magazine/news200509.cfm?ID=9721.

[118] "Report of the Investigative Committee of the Standing Committee on Research Misconduct at the University of Colorado at Boulder concerning Allegations of Academic Misconduct against Professor Ward Churchill," University of Colorado, Boulder, May 16, 2006, accessed from www.colorado.edu/news/reports/churchill/.

[119] Jennifer Brown, "Churchill Issues Stinging Rebuttal: CU Panel Scolded for 'Fallacies,' " *Denver Post,* May 25, 2006, p. A1, accessed from Lexis-Nexis.

CHAPTER 7

[1] Timothy O'Connor, "The Need for Change, Challenges and Opportunities in the Fresh Potato Market," U.S. Potato Board, January 2002, www.uspotatoes.com/research.htm.

[2] Ibid.

[3] "About the United States Potato Board," accessed June 11, 2006 from www.uspotatoes.com/about_nppb.htm.

[4] "Consumer Confusion Inspires New Healthy Potato Campaign," news release, February 13, 2004, accessed September 12, 2004 from www.healthypotato.com/media_pr_080504_1.asp.

[5] Ibid.

[6] Mary Duenwald, "Don't Play a Numbers Game, Experts Say, Just Eat Your Vegetables," *New York Times*, September 14, 2004, accessed from Lexis-Nexis.

[7] "U.S. Potato Board Leadership Strengthens Nutrition Campaign with Additional Funding," news release, U.S. Potato Board, August 19, 2004, accessed June 11, 2006, from www.uspotatoes.com/downloads/PDF/More_Funding_for_nutrition.pdf.

[8] "Aggressive Potato Nutrition Campaign Primed to Go: US Potato Board Voted to Allocate Monies from Reserves to Fund New Initiative," news release, U.S. Potato Board, January 9, 2004, www.uspotatoes.com.

[9] Ibid.

[10] "Fall Ad Buy to Increase Reach and Frequency of the Healthy Potato Ad," news release, U.S. Potato Board, August 23, 2004, accessed June 11, 2006 from www.uspotatoes.com/downloads/PDF/Fall_ad_buy.pdf.

[11] "The Healthy Potato: Relaunching America's Favorite Vegetable in the Era of Atkins," Fleishman-Hillard, contest entry for U.S. Potato Board.

[12] "The Long and Short of It: USPB Nutrition Campaign Launch Impressive," news release, U.S. Potato Board, March 2004, accessed June 11, 2006 from www.uspotatoes.com/downloads/PDF/Marchcampaigncoverageupdate.pdf.

[13] "'www.healthy.potato.com' Designed to Spotlight Potato Nutrition On-line," news release, U.S. Potato Board, October 7, 2004, accessed June 11, 2006 from www.uspotatoes.com/downloads/PDF/healthypotato.com.pdf.

[14] "Carbohydrate Basics," U.S. Potato Board, accessed June 11, 2006, from www.healthypotato.com/downloads/CarbohydrateBasics.pdf.

[15] Ibid.

[16] "The Healthy Potato," U.S. Potato Board, accessed June 11, 2006, from www.healthypotato.com/nutrition/consumers.asp.

[17] "Potato and Satiety Request for Proposal," nutrition section of Healthy Potato Web site, U.S. Potato Board, accessed September 12, 2004, from www.healthypotato.com/nutrition.asp.

[18] "Educating the General Population: Notes for the Presenter," health educators section of Healthy Potato Web site, U.S. Potato Board, accessed September 12, 2004, from www.healthypotato.com/health.asp.

[19] "Carbohydrate Confusion Q&A," health educators section of Healthy Potato Web site, U.S. Potato Board, accessed September 12, 2004, from www.healthypotato.com/carbo.asp.

[20] "Recipes," recipes section of Healthy Potato Web site, U.S. Potato Board, accessed September 12, 2004, from www.healthypotato.com/featured_recipe.asp.

[21] "National Academy of Sciences Recommends More Potassium, Potato #1 Source," August 2, 2004, news release, accessed June 11, 2006, from www.uspotatoes.com/downloads/PDF/POTASSIUM.pdf.

[22] "Weight Watchers Partnership to Tell 'The Truth About Carbs,'" news release, U.S. Potato Board, January 5, 2004, accessed June 11, 2006, from www.uspotatoes.com/downloads/PDF/WeightWatchersPartnership.pdf.

[23] Fleishman-Hillard, "The Healthy Potato: Relaunching America's Favorite Vegetable in the Era of Atkins."

[24] "It's All About Strategy," news release, from the Administrative Committee Summering Meeting, LaConner, Washington, August 11–12, 25, 2004, U.S. Potato Board, accessed June 11, 2006, from www.uspotatoes.com/downloads/PDF/summer_meeting.pdf.

[25] "National Academy of Sciences Recommends More Potassium, Potato #1 Source."

[26] "About RVIA: RVIA Review," Recreation Vehicle Industry Association, accessed June 13, 2006, from www.rvia.org/about/Functions.htm.

[27] "For the Media," Recreation Vehicle Industry Association, accessed June 13, 2006, from www.rvia.org/media/.

[28] "Budget-Minded Consumers Find RV Vacations Cut Costs, Not Comforts," news release, undated, accessed June 13, 2006, from www.rv.com/resources/budget.htm, and "RV Vacations Are Least Expensive, Study Says," Recreation Vehicle Industry Association, undated, accessed June 13, 2006, from www.rvia.org/media/newsreleases/breakingnews/p0533.htm.

[29] "As Temperatures Fall, RV Travel Stays Hot," news release, Recreation Vehicle Industry Association, October 24, 2004, provided by RVIA.

[30] "RVers Have Big Summer Travel Plans Despite High Fuel Prices: Survey Finds Continuing Trend of More RV Mini Vacations, Closer to Home," news release, Recreation Vehicle Industry Association, June 14, 2005, accessed June 13, 2006 from www.rvia.org/media/newsreleases/breakingnews/p0530.htm.

[31] "Strong RV Shipments Expected in 2005," *RV Roadsigns*, Recreation Vehicle Industry Association, Winter 2004.

[32] "Population Trends," *RV Roadsigns*, Recreation Vehicle Industry Association, Winter 2004.

[33] "RV Shipments Up 20% at Mid-Year Point: On Pace to Break Quarter-Century Record," news release, Recreation Vehicle Industry Association, August 16, 2004, accessed from Lexis-Nexis.

[34] Ibid.

[35] "Early Summer Blitz Kick Off Summer Media Coverage," *RVIA Today*, Recreation Vehicle Industry Association, July 2004, p. 14, and pitch letters provided by RVIA.

[36] "High Tech Features, Cool Gadgets Boost Appeal of Today's RVs," updated news release, Recreation Vehicle Industry Association, accessed January 3, 2005, from www.rvia.org.media/newsreleases/breakingnews/pgrv0140.htm.

[37] "Public Relations and Advertising Department," report to RVIA Board of Directors, Recreation Vehicle Industry Association, August 30, 2004, p. 3.

[38] "RV Historian David Woodworth," Recreation Vehicle Industry Association, accessed January 3, 2005, from www.rvia.org/media/quotable.htm.

[39] "Brad and Amy Herzog," Recreation Vehicle Industry Association, accessed January 3, 2005, from www.rvia.org/media/quotable.htm.

[40] "Media Talking Points: Impact of Rising Fuel Prices on RV Travel and Market Growth," fax, Recreation Vehicle Industry Association, April 12, 2004.

[41] "Vacation Cost Comparison," 1999 study, PKF Consulting, accessed June 13, 2006, from rvia.hbp.com/itemdisplay.cfm?pid=16; and RVIA, "RVers Planning to Take More Mini-Vacations This Summer," *RVIA Today,* May–June 2004, p. 10.

[42] "Media Talking Points," Recreation Vehicle Industry Association.

[43] "Public Relations and Advertising Department," report to RVIA Board of Directors," Recreation Vehicle Industry Association, p. 8.

[44] "Public Relations Presentation: RVIA Annual Membership Meeting: All Summer Long, We Sang Our Song," Recreation Vehicle Industry Association, September 28, 2004, p. 2.

[45] "Public Relations and Advertising Department: PR 'Halo Effect' Shines On," report to RVIA Board of Directors, Recreation Vehicle Industry Association, May 17, 2004, p. 5.

[46] "Public Relations Presentation: RVIA Annual Membership Meeting: All Summer Long," Recreation Vehicle Industry Association, p. 5.

[47] "Public Relations and Advertising Department: PR 'Halo Effect' Shines On," Recreation Vehicle Industry Association, p. 5.

[48] "Public Relations Presentation: RVIA Annual Membership Meeting: All Summer Long," Recreation Vehicle Industry Association, p. 5.

[49] Ibid., p. 6.

[50] "Things to Do: NASCAR Events," Recreation Vehicle Industry Association, www.rvia.org/consumers/recreationvehicles/enjoying/Thingstodo.htm.

[51] "How to Host a Football Tailgating Party—RV Style: Recipes Galore for a 'Kitchen on Wheels' at GoRVings.com, news release, Recreation Vehicle Industry Association, undated, accessed January 3, 2005, from www.rvia.org/media/newsreleases/breakingnews/p0333.htm.

[52] "Public Relations and Advertising Department: RVIA Climbs on the Election Coverage Bandwagon," report to RVIA Board of Directors, Recreation Vehicle Industry Association, August 30, 2004, pp. 1–2.

[53] "Public Relations Presentation: RVIA Annual Membership Meeting: All Summer Long," Recreation Vehicle Industry Association, p. 6.

[54] Pitch letter, Recreation Vehicle Industry Association, May 2004.

[55] "Public Relations and Advertising Department: RVIA Climbs on the Election Coverage Bandwagon," Recreation Vehicle Industry Association, pp. 2–3.

[56] Ibid. p. 6.

[57] "Big Thinking behind Launch of the New Kansas Brand Image," news release, Kansas Department of Commerce, January 7, 2005, accessed January 27, 2005, from www.thinkkansas.com/newsroom/release_01.html.

[58] Ibid.

[59] "Creating a Dynamic Sustainable Brand Image for Our State: Kansas;" PowerPoint slide "Objectives of Kansas Branding," Kansas Department of Commerce, January 7, 2005.

[60] Ibid.

[61] "Brand Image Explanations," Kansas Department of Commerce, January 7, 2005, accessed January 27, 2005, from www.thinkkansas.com/newsroom/release_01.html.

[62] Ibid.

[63] "Creating a Dynamic Sustainable Brand Image for Our State: Kansas;" PowerPoint slide "Research," Kansas Department of Commerce, January 7, 2005, accessed June 15, 2006, from www.thinkkansas.org/newsroom/index.html.

[64] Ibid.

[65] Ibid.

[66] Ibid.

[67] "Kansas Travel and Tourism: 2004 Consumer Research Overview," Callahan Creek, June 13, 2006, from kdoch.state.ks.us/KDOCHdocs/TT/2004_Tourism_Research.pdf.

[68] Ibid.

[69] "An Important Investment for Kansas," Kansas Department of Commerce.

[70] "Creating a Dynamic Sustainable Brand Image for Our State: Kansas," PowerPoint slide "Positioning Statement," Kansas Department of Commerce, January 7, 2005, accessed June 15, 2006, from www.thinkkansas.org/newsroom/index.html.

[71] Ibid.

[72] "Brand Image Explanations—Why Is the State Spending Money to Promote the Image within Kansas?" Kansas Department of Commerce, January 7, 2005, accessed January 27, 2005, from www.thinkkansas.com/newsroom/release_01.html.

[73] "An Important Investment for Kansas," Kansas Department of Commerce.

[74] "Brand Image Explanations: What Are the Goals of the Brand Image Campaign?" Kansas Department of Commerce, January 7, 2005, accessed January 27, 2005, from www.thinkkansas.com/newsroom/release_01.html.

[75] "Brand Image Explanations: What Will You Be Promoting and Who Is the Audience?" Kansas Department of Commerce.

[76] Travel-related magazines, provided to the author, Kansas Department of Commerce.

[77] "An Important Investment for Kansas," Kansas Department of Commerce.

[78] Kansas Legislature, House Wildlife, Parks and Tourism Committee minutes, March 3, 2004, accessed June 15, 2006, from kdoch.state.ks.us/KDOCHdocs/TT/House_Testimony_3_2_2005.pdf.

[79] "Impact of Travel on State Economies, 2004 Edition," Washington, DC, Travel Industry Association of America, July 2004.

[80] "Euro Sport Casual, Fashion Athletics and Short Boots to Be Hot Fall Footwear Trends Says Style Expert/TV Talk Show Host Star Jones," news release, Payless ShoeSource, September 12, 2002, accessed June 15, 2006, from www.prnewswire.com/cgi-bin/stories.pl?ACCT=104&STORY=/www/story/09-12-2002/0001798338&EDATE=.

[81] "Getting it Right," 2003 annual report, Payless ShoeSource.

[82] "About Our Company," Payless ShoeSource, accessed February 3, 2005, from www.payless.com/en-US/Corporate/Company/About.htm.

[83] "Payless Corporate Strategy," Payless ShoeSource, accessed February 3, 2005, from www.payless.com/NR/exeres/A51C13FC-6578-42D7-9C14-E8F3D083E160.htm.

[84] Ibid.

[85] Ibid.

[86] "Payless ShoeSource and Its Customers Raise more than Half Million Dollars for Breast Cancer Awareness," news release, Payless ShoeSource, accessed June 15, 2006, from www.prnewswire.com/cgi-bin/stories.pl?ACCT=104&STORY=/www/story/01-31-2005/0002939252&EDATE=.

[87] "Scholastic Goes Back to Press for a Third Printing of 800,000 Copies of *Harry Potter and the Order of the Phoenix* after Record-Breaking First Day Sales of 5 Million," news release, Scholastic, June 24, 2003, accessed December 12, 2004, from www.scholastic.com/aboutscholastic/news/press_062403.htm.

[88] "Scholastic Sells 11 Million Copies of *Harry Potter and the Order of the Phoenix* in Twelve Weeks," news release, Scholastic, September 23, 2003, accessed from www.scholastic.com/aboutscholastic/news/press_092303b.htm.

[89] "Scholastic Announces Multi-Million Dollar Marketing Campaign for *Harry Potter and the Order of the Phoenix*," news release, Scholastic, May 19, 2003.

[90] "J. K. Rowling's *Harry Potter and the Order of the Phoenix* to Be Published June 21, 2003 in the United States, Britain, Canada and Australia," news release, Scholastic, January 15, 2003.

[91] "Scholastic Announces Multi-Million Dollar Marketing Campaign," Scholastic.

[92] "Scholastic Announces Harry Potter Contest for American Kids," news release, Scholastic, May 2, 2003.

[93] "Scholastic Announces Multi-Million Dollar Marketing Campaign," Scholastic.

[94] Ibid.

[95] Ibid.

[96] "Scholastic Delivers U.S. First and Only Signed Copy by J. K. Rowling of *Harry Potter and the Order of the Phoenix* from Scotland," news release, Scholastic, June 21, 2003.

[97] "An Unexpected Christmas Present Arrives: J. K. Rowling's *Harry Potter and the Half-Blood Prince* to Be Published on July 16, 2005, in the United States, Britain, Canada and Australia," news release, Scholastic, December 21, 2004.

[98] Ibid.

[99] "Why Harry Potter Rules: The Shy Sorceress," *Time* magazine, June 23, 2003, p. 67.

[100] "Hardee's Introduces New Monster Thickburger: The New 2/3 Lb. Thickburger Takes Decadence to a New Level," news release, Hardee's, November 15, 2004, accessed December 31, 2004, and CKE Restaurants, press releases, 2004 archives at phx.corporate-ir.net/phoenix.zhtml?c=117249&p=irol-news2004.

[101] Ibid.

[102] "Nutritional Calculator," Hardee's, accessed June 16, 2006 from www.hardees.com/nutrition/.

[103] "Hardee's Introduces New Monster Thickburger," Hardee's.

CHAPTER 8

[1] "NAICS 71 and 72: Leisure and Hospitality," U.S. Department of Labor, Bureau of Labor Statistics, accessed June 29, 2006, from www.bls.gov/iag/leisurehosp.htm.

[2] "Did You Know? Travel Facts," Travel Industry Association of America, accessed June 29, 2006, from www.tia.org/index.html.

[3] Chris Nuttall, "Video Games $18 bn Impact on U.S. Economy," *Financial Times*, May 10, 2006, accessed from Lexis-Nexis.

[4] "Sport Industry Trends," Plunkett Research, Ltd., accessed July 3, 2006, from www.plunkettresearch.com/Industries/Sports/SportsTrends/tabid/274/Default.aspx.

[5] Dennis Wilcox and Glen Cameron (2006). *Public Relations Strategies and Tactics*, 8th ed., pp. 593–594.

[6] Jason Manheim, "Regis Philbin, Winner of the 2005 PR.com 'Best Celebrity Nickname' Award," PR.com, accessed June 29, 2006, from www.pr.com/article/1020.

[7] Wilcox and Cameron (2006). *Public Relations Strategies and Tactics*, p. 592.

[8] Guy Trebay, "Being Bad: The Career Move," *New York Times*, April 20, 2006, p. 1G.

[9] Allison Enright, "You Don't Say," *Marketing News*, June 15, 2006, accessed from Lexis-Nexis.

[10] Wilcox, and Cameron (2006). *Public Relations Tactics and Strategies*, pp. 603–604.

[11] "The Federal Response to Hurricane Katrina: Lessons Learned," White House, February 2006, accessed May 19, 2006, from www.whitehouse.gov/reports/katrina-lessons-learned/.

[12] Michael O'Keefe, "The Terror Dome: Sports Palaces Play Role in American Tragedy," *Daily News*, September 4, 2005, p. 96, accessed June 27, 2006, from Lexis-Nexis.

[13] Mike McDaniel, "Katrina Aftermath: Television Plays a Role in Hurricane Recovery," *Houston Chronicle*, September 10, 2005, p. 10, accessed from Lexis-Nexis.

[14] "Oprah on Location: Inside the Katrina Catastrophe," *Oprah Winfrey Show*, from www2.oprah.com. accessed May 19, 2006.

[15] Ibid.

[16] Ibid.

[17] Tara Young, "The Stars Are Out at the Astrodome: Celebrities Visit with Evacuees at Sports Complex," *Times-Picayune*, September 6, 2005.

[18] "Oprah Goes Inside Hurricane Katrina Devastation: On the Ground with the People," news release, Oprah.com, September 5, 2005, accessed May 18, 2006, from www.oprah.com/about/press/releases/200509/press_releases_20050905.jhtml.

[19] "America's Second Harvest," news release, Oprah.com, no date, accessed May 19, 2006, from www.orpah.com/uyl/volunteer/community/vol_community_food_01.jhtml.

[20] "Oprah Announces 'Oprah's Katrina Homes' Online Initiative and Everyone can Join the Crusade to Rebuild Lives!" news release, Oprah.com, September 19, 2005, accessed May 19, 2006, from www.oprah.com/about/press/releases/200509/press_releases_20050919.jhtml.

[21] "Oprah on Location: Operation Katrina Homes Move-In Day Special: Families Move into New Homes on Angel Lane," *Oprah Winfrey Show,* February 22, 2006, accessed from Lexis-Nexis.

[22] "Oprah's Angel Network: Oprah Katrina Homes," slide number 3, Oprah.com, accessed May 19, 2006, from www2.oprah.com/uyl/Katrina/Katrina_284_103.jhtml.

[23] "Oprah on Location: Operation Katrina Homes Move-In Day Special," *Oprah Winfrey Show.*

[24] "The Oprah Winfrey Show: True American Heroes/Oprah's Favorite Things," slide 1, Oprah.com, accessed May 25, 2006, from www2.oprah.com/tows/slide/200511/20051121/slide_20051121_284_101.jhtml.

[25] Tanisha A. Sykes, "Oprah Winfrey: America's Ultimate Brand," *Black Enterprise,* July 2005, p. 28, accessed from Lexis-Nexis.

[26] "Oprah Announces 'Oprah's Katrina Homes' Online Initiative," Oprah.com.

[27] "Oprah Key Stats," *Variety,* November 21–27, 2005, p. B1, accessed from Lexis-Nexis.

[28] Ibid.

[29] Morgan Campbell, "Bryant Shows It's Possible to Rebound," *Toronto Star,* March 4, 2006, p. D3, accessed from Lexis-Nexis.

[30] "The Man Who Kept Oprah Awake at Night: A Million Little Pieces: James Frey Discusses His Drug Addition and Recovery," *Oprah Winfrey Show,* October 26, 2005, accessed May 16, 2006, from Lexis-Nexis.

[31] "The Man Who Conned Oprah," The Smoking Gun, January 8, 2006, accessed May 26, 2006, from www.thesmokinggun.com/jamesfrey/0104061jamesfrey1.html, p. 2.

[32] Hillel Italie, "Oprah Dismisses Claims about Frey Memoir," Associated Press Online, January 12, 2006, accessed from Lexis-Nexis on May 16, 2006.

[33] "Interview with James Frey," *CNN Larry King Live,* January 11, 2006 (released January 14, 2006), accessed from Lexis-Nexis on May 16, 2006.

[34] "Ichiro Suzuki Artifacts Added to Hall of Fame Collection: Eclipses One of Baseball's Oldest Records, Held by Hall of Fame First Baseman George Sisler," National Baseball Hall of Fame and Museum, accessed from www.baseballhalloffame.org/history/2004/040928.htm.

[35] Jeff Idelson, "Texas at Seattle, October 1–3, 2004, Witness to History: Ichiro Breaks Single-Season Hit Mark," National Baseball Hall of Fame and Museum, accessed June 17, 2006, from www. baseballhalloffame.org/hisotry/2004/041105.htm.

[36] Ibid.

[37] Steve Moore Victim Impact Statement, CTV.ca, accessed June 17, 2006, from www.ctv.ca/servlet/ ArticleNews/story/CTVNews/1103806928681_237.

[38] Ibid.

[39] "Canucks' Bertuzzi Apologetic," Sports Network, March 11, 2004, accessed from Lexis-Nexis; and "Bertuzzi's Suspension Fires Debate about Fighting," video clip, Associated Press, March 13, 2004, www.msnbc.msn.com/id/4483528/.

[40] "Bertuzzi Suspended 12 Games Plus All of 2004 Playoff Games," news release, Canucks.com, March 11, 2004, accessed June 17, 2006, from www.canucks.com/news/pressreleases.asp?sectionID=31&id=392.

[41] "Canucks Players, Staff Close Ranks," London Free Press (Ontario, Canada), March 12, 2004, p. D2.

[42] Ibid.

[43] Ibid.

[44] Ibid.

[45] Rick Sadowski, "A Positive Approach: Taking One Day at a Time, Moore Set on Regaining Full Health," *Rocky Mountain News* (Denver, CO), March 30, 2004, accessed June 17, 2006, from Lexis-Nexis.

[46] Ibid.

[47] Ibid.

[48] Ibid.

[49] "Canucks Statement Regarding Steve Moore Press Conference," news release, Canucks.com, March 29, 2004, accessed June 17, 2006, from www.canucks.com/news/pressreleases.asp?sectionID=31&id=398. Canucks Statement Regarding Steve Moore Press Conference.

[50] "Bertuzzi Pleads Guilty to On-Ice Assault," Associated Press State & Local Wire, December 22, 2004, accessed January 29, 2005, from Lexis-Nexis.

[51] Ethan Baron, "'I Don't Think of Myself as a Criminal': Plea Deal Allows Bert to Avoid Criminal Record, and Play in U.S.," *Vancouver Province* (British Columbia), December 23, 2004, p. 8A.

[52] "Bertuzzi Pleads Guilty to On-Ice Assault," Associated Press State & Local Wire.

[53] Jeff Lee, "Bertuzzi Takes Deal for Hit That Changed Life Forever," *Ottawa Citizen,* December 23, 2004, p. A1, accessed from Lexis-Nexis.

[54] Gary Bettman, "Decision Regarding Supplementary Discipline for Todd Bertuzzi," National Hockey League, accessed June 17, 2006 from www.canucks.com/images/news/bertuzzi.pdf.

[55] "Maurice Cheeks Chronology," Associated Press State & Local Wire, March 2, 2005, accessed from Lexis-Nexis.

[56] Michael Steinberger, "Trail Blazed from Love to Loathing," *Financial Times* (London, UK), March 23, 2004, p. 18, accessed from Lexis-Nexis.

[57] Jim Beseda, Gail Kinsey Hill, and Jeff Manning, "Restyled Blazers Lack Luxury of Good Will, Good Economy," *Sunday Oregonian,* February 29, 2004, accessed from Lexis-Nexis.

[58] Brian Meehan, "Wells' Words Just the Latest Affront to Fans," *Oregonian,* December 20, 2001, accessed from Lexis-Nexis.

[59] Michael Steinberger, "Trail Blazed from Love to Loathing," p. 18.

[60] "Patterson Placed on Inactive List, After Confrontation with Coach," Associated Press State & Local Wire, March 21, 2005, accessed from Lexis-Nexis.

[61] Michael Steinberger, "Trail Blazed from Love to Loathing," p. 18.

[62] Ryan White, "Allen Lays Down the Law," *Sunday Oregonian,* April 6, 2003, accessed from Lexis-Nexis.

[63] "Woods' Dog Abuse Case Settled," February 7, 2006, NBA Notes, p. S17, *Toronto Sun,* accessed from Lexis-Nexis.

[64] Jason Quick, "He's Still Dr. Bonzi . . . and Mr. Wells," *Oregonian,* March 3, 2004, accessed from Lexis-Nexis.

[65] "Paul Allen Addresses Fans," Web site, Trail Blazers, April 5, 2003, accessed January 26, 2006, from www.nba.com/blazers/news/Paul_Allen_Addresses_Fans-71876-41.html.

[66] Jason Quick, "Blazers' Code of Conduct: Can It Make a Difference?" *Sunday Oregonian,* November 9, 2003, accessed from Lexis-Nexis.

[67] "Trail Blazers Pledge to Fans," Web site, Blazers.com, accessed January 28, 2006, from www.nba.com/blazers/features/Blazers_Pledge_to_Fans-81965-41.html.

[68] Beseda, Hill, and Manning, "Restyled Blazers Lack Luxury of Good Will," p. A10.

[69] Mike Tokito, "Small Rose Garden Crowd Sets an Attendance Low for Blazers," *Oregonian,* November 10, 2005, accessed from Lexis-Nexis.

[70] Jason Quick, "The Trail Blazers: A Look Back: Blazers 2004–2005 Timeline," *Oregonian,* April 21, 2005, accessed form Lexis-Nexis.

[71] Ibid.

[72] Andrew Gordon, "Beleaguered NBA Trailblazers Name Sasse Comms VP," *PR Week,* October 31, 2005, p. 5, accessed from Nexis-Lexis.

[73] Rachel Bachman, "Blazers Court Fans Whose Buzz Fell to Blahs," *Oregonian,* November 6, 2005, p. A1, accessed from Lexis-Nexis.

[74] Ibid.

[75] *Official 2005/2006 Guidebook & Map,* brochure, Destination Salem, accessed from www.salem.org/visitors.asp, and www.salem.org/pdf/visitorsguide.pdf, February 4, 2006.

[76] Ibid.

[77] Kathleen Burge, "Witch City Brews a New Image," *Boston Globe,* September 30, 2004, accessed from Lexis-Nexis.

[78] Jesse Noyes, "Fright Night Scares Up $$$," *Boston Herald,* October 27, 2005, accessed from Lexis-Nexis.

[79] "The Witching Hour: About the Symposium," accessed February 4, 2006, from www.witchinghour.org/about/index.html.

[80] Emily Sweeney, "State Seeks Local Ideas on Tourism," *Boston Globe,* November 6, 2005, accessed from Lexis-Nexis.com.

[81] Jay Lindsay, "Bewitching Salem Banks on Evil Past," *Sunday Mail* (SA), February 8, 2004, accessed from Lexis-Nexis.

[82] "National Trust Names Salem, Massachusetts, One of America's Dozen Distinctive Destinations: Annual List Promotes Heritage Tourism," Destination Salem, March 2, 2005, accessed June 18, 2006, from www.salem.org/media030205.asp.

[83] *Official 2005/2006 Guidebook & Map,* Destination Salem.

[84] "The Cruise Industry 2005 Economic Summary," International Council of Cruise Lines, accessed October 8, 2006, from http://www.cruising.org/press/research/Ecoimpact/2005%20Econ%20Impact%20Summary.pdf.

[85] Ibid.

[86] Ibid.

[87] "Company Profile, Cunard: The Most Famous Ocean Liners in the World," Cunard, accessed February 2, 2006, from www.cunard.com/aboutCunard.

[88] "Queen Mary 2 Fact Sheet and Queen Mary 2 Fun Facts: QM2 Press Kit," Cunard, accessed February 2, 2006, from www.cunard.com/aboutCunard/QM2 PressReleases.

[89] "World's Largest Cruise Ship Returns to Port," CNN.com, January 18, 2006, accessed from Lexis-Nexis; and "Cunard World Cruises and Exotic Voyages 2007," Cunard, accessed June 18, 2006 from www.cunard.be/Cunard/promos/0701_World_%20cruises%2007_B.pdf.

[90] "Coast Guard Will Conduct an Investigation of Queen Mary 2 Incident," U.S. Federal News, based on a U.S. Department of Homeland Security's U.S. Coast Guard, 7th District, press release, accessed from Lexis-Nexis.

[91] Caroline Gammell, "Cunard Boss Defends Pay-Out to Angry Passengers," Press Association Newsfile, January 25, 2006, accessed from Lexis-Nexis.

[92] "Queen Mary 2 Passengers to Get Full Refund," Associated Press, January 27, 2006.

[93] Caroline Gammell, "Cunard Boss Defends Pay-Out to Angry Passengers."

[94] Ibid.

[95] "QM2 Passengers Make Mutiny Threat," BBC News, January 22, 2006, accessed February 7, 2006, from news.bbc.co.uk/1/hi/world/americas/4637240.stm.

[96] "Cunard Caves in Over Cruise Mutiny," CNN.com, January 27, 2006, accessed from Lexis-Nexis.

[97] "Compensation and Apology for Disrupted Cruise Travellers," Agence France Presse-English, January 27, 2006, accessed from Lexis-Nexis.

[98] Chris Fox, "From Someone on the Inside," Ashlee Simpson official Web site, October 26, 2004, accessed June 19, 2006, from www.ashleesimpsonmusic.com/news.aspx?dt=10-01-2004.

[99] Lisa de Moraes, "Ashlee Simpson and That Lip-Syncing Feeling," *Washington Post,* October 26, 2004, p. C01, accessed from Lexis-Nexis.

[100] Lisa de Moraes, "The Sync That Sank Ashlee: *60 Minutes* Has It Covered," *Washington Post,* October 29, 2004, p. C7, accessed from Lexis-Nexis.

[101] Lesley Stahl, "Live from New York: The History and Making of *Saturday Night Live,*" CBS *60 Minutes,* October 31, 2004, accessed from Lexis-Nexis.

[102] Margo Whitmire, "Simpson's 'Autobiography' Soars to No. 1," news release, *Billboard,* July 28, 2004, accessed June 19, 2006 from www.billboard.com/bbcom/news/article_display.jsp?vnu_content_id=1000588138.

[103] "Jessica Simpson Biography," VH1, accessed June 19, 2006, from www.vh1.com/artists/az/simpson_jessica/bio.jhtml.

[104] Vinay Menon, "Moments of Truth on Live TV," *Toronto Star,* October 30, 2004, p. J5, accessed from Lexis-Nexis.

[105] Katie Couric, "Ashlee Simpson Discusses Her Performance on *Saturday Night Live,"* NBC *Today,* October 26, 2004, accessed from Lexis-Nexis.

[106] Ibid.

[107] Chris Fox, "From Someone on the Inside," posting, Ashlee Simpson official Web site, October 26, 2004, accessed June 19, 2006, from www.ashleesimpsonmusic.com.

[108] Ashlee Simpson, "Hey Guys!" Ashlee Simpson official Web site, October 26, 2004, accessed June 19, 2006, from www.ashleesimpsonmusic.com/news.aspx?dt=10-01-2004.

[109] Margo Whitmire, "Simpson Strikes Back: Ashlee Scores 2nd No. 1," *Billboard* news release, October 26, 2005, accessed June 19, 2006, from www.billboard.com/bbcom/news/article_display.jsp?vnu_content_id=1001390218.

[110] Rebecca Louie, "Back Live: It's Ashlee Simpson! The Singer Has Found her Voice & Moxie Following Last Year's 'SNL' Fuss," *Daily News,* October 16, 2005, p. 18, accessed from Lexis-Nexis.

[111] Jeremy Laurence, "Prince Harry's Nazi Gaffe Draws Condemnation," Reuters, January 13, 2005, accessed from www.reuters.com.

[112] Peter Griffiths (Reuters), "Consensus on Prince Harry's Gaffe: He Knows Nothing," *Washington Post,* January 13, 2005, p. C5 accessed from Lexis-Nexis.

[113] Glenn Frankel, "Prince Harry's Nazi Blunder Burns Old Blighty," *Washington Post,* January 14, 2005, accessed from Lexis-Nexis.

[114] "No Visit for Harry: He's Sorry, but Auschwitz Is Out," Reuters, *Toronto Sun,* January 14, 2005, p. 63, accessed from Lexis-Nexis.

CHAPTER 9

[1] Dan Lattimore, Dan Baskin, Suzette Heiman, Elizabeth Toth, and James Van Leuven (2004). *Public Relations: The Profession and the Practice,* New York: McGraw-Hill, 2004, p. 235.

[2] David D'Alessandro with Michele Owens (2001). *Brand Warfare: 10 Rules for Building the Killer Brand,* McGraw-Hill, pp. 70–71.

[3] Lattimore et al. (2004). *Public Relations,* p. 243.

[4] Douglas Quenqua, "When Activists Attack," *PR Week,* June 11, 2001, p. 15, reprinted in Lattimore et al. (2004), *Public Relations,* pp. 245–46.

[5] Karen Matthews, "Nazi Images Exhibit Opens in NY Jewish Museum: Draws Protesters Shouting "Don't Go In!'" Associated Press, March 17, 2002, accessed from Lexis-Nexis.

[6] Norman L. Kleeblatt, ed., *Mirroring Evil: Nazi Imagery/Recent Art,* (2002). Museum exhibit catalog, New Brunswick, NJ: Rutgers University Press.

[7] Julie Salamon, "At 100, Still Asking 'Why Should It Be Easy?'" *New York Times,* January 21, 2004, p. E1.

[8] "Mirroring Evil: Nazi Imagery/Recent Art," exhibit wall text, The Jewish Museum, 2002.

[9] "The Jewish Museum to Present 'Mirroring Evil: Nazi Imagery/Recent Art,' a New Exhibition Accompanied by Programs and Catalogue," news release, The Jewish Museum, undated, accessed July 25, 2003, from www.jewishmuseum.org/home/content/about/press_release_archive/evil.html.

[10] Lisa Gubernick, "Coming Museum Show with Nazi Theme Stirs New York's Art World," *Wall Street Journal,* January 10, 2002, p. B1, accessed from ProQuest.

[11] "The Jewish Museum to Present 'Mirroring Evil.' " The Jewish Museum.

[12] Alan Cooperman, "Museum Seeks to Ease Anger over Holocaust Art," *Washington Post,* March 2, 2002, p. A6, accessed from Lexis-Nexis.

[13] Dan Bischoff, (Newhouse News Service), "Protests Rage over Display of Modern Holocaust Art," *Star-Ledger* (Newark, NJ), March 11, 2002, accessed from Lexis-Nexis.

[14] Ibid.

[15] Ibid.

[16] Robert J. Hurst, "Mirroring Evil," statement, The Jewish Museum, undated.

[17] "Statement for the Press from The Jewish Museum," The Jewish Museum, March 2002.

[18] "The Jewish Museum to Present 'Mirroring Evil,' " The Jewish Museum.

[19] Ibid.

[20] Ibid.

[21] Ibid.

[22] Ibid.

[23] *Night Train to Nashville: Music City Rhythm & Blues* 1945–1970, exhibition catalog, Country Music Hall of Fame and Museum, Nashville: Country Music Foundation Press, 2004, pp. 17, 22.

[24] Ibid., p. 31.

[25] Ibid., pp. 42–43.

[26] "The Country Music Hall of Fame and Museum's Exhibition Night Train to Nashville: Music City Rhythm & Blues, 1945–1970 to Roll in with Groundbreaking Suntrust Bank Sponsorship, Accompanying CD Release and Grand Opening Nights," news release, Country Music Hall of Fame and Museum, March 5, 2004, accessed January 15, 2005 from www.sitemason.com/newspub/iewTCM?id=15174.

[27] Calvin Gilbert, "Climbing Aboard Night Train to Nashville," CMT.com, March 26, 2004, accessed January 15, 2005, from www.cmt.com/artists/news/1485999/03262004/little_richard.jhtml.

[28] "Night Train to Nashville: Music City Rhythm & Blues 1945–1970 to Open at the Country Music Hall of Fame and Museum Next Spring," news release, Country Music Hall of Fame and Museum, June 16, 2003.

[29] Ibid.

[30] "Country Music Hall of Fame and Museum: Survey of Market, August 2002," Perdue Research Group.

[31] "The Night Train to Nashville: Music City Rhythm & Blues: 1945 to 1970 Exhibit, Recordings, Publications and Related Programming," internal document, Country Music Hall of Fame and Museum, 2003.

[32] "Country Music Hall of Fame and Museum Joins Forces with Lost Highway to Release Night Train to Nashville: Music City Rhythm & Blues, 1945–1970, Two CD Historical Compilation in Stores February 24, 2004," news release, Country Music Hall of Fame and Museum, 2004.

[33] "Country Music Hall of Fame and Museum Celebrates Opening Night of Night Train to Nashville with Tours, Family Program, Panel Discussion and Concert," news release, Country Music Hall of Fame and Museum, March 4, 2004.

[34] "Magazines: Country Music; General Music and Entertainment, and Miscellaneous National Magazines," internal document, Country Music Hall of Fame and Museum, 2003.

[35] Martha T. Moore, "Women Rail against College's Coed Plans," *USA Today,* December 13, 2004, p. 3A.

[36] "Trustees Announce Decision: Wells Will Begin Admitting Men in the Fall of 2005," news release, Wells College, October 2004, accessed January 6, 2005, from www.wells.edu/whatsnew/wn2a.htm.

[37] Ibid.

[38] Lisa Marsh Ryerson, "Wells College President's Annual Report 2002–2003," *Wells College Express,* p. 1, and Lisa Marsh Ryerson, "Reunion 2004 Alumnae Address," June 12, 2004, at Wells College, accessed June 27, 2005, from www.wells.edu/whatsnew/wnspech49.htm.

[39] Ryerson, "Wells College President's Annual Report 2002_2003," p. 2.

[40] Ryerson, "Reunion 2004 Alumnae Address."

[41] Ibid.

[42] Ibid.

[43] "President's Message: Strategic Planning to Increase," *Wells College Express,* Winter 2004.

[44] "Trustees Announce Decision: Wells Will Begin Admitting Men in Fall 2005," *Wells College.*

[45] Ibid.

[46] Wells for Women, www.wellsforwomen.org.

[47] David L. Shaw and John Stith, "Wells College Votes to Admit Men in '05: Some Students Occupy Building to Protest Change," *Post-Standard* (Syracuse, NY), October 3, 2004, p. A1, accessed from Lexis-Nexis.

[48] Ibid.

[49] Moore, "Women Rail against College's Coed Plans."

[50] "WCAA Board Message: WCAA Board Shares Outlook on Co-education Decision," Wells College Alumnae Association, October 8, 2004, accessed May 26, 2005, from www.wells.edu/lconnect/wcaa_coed.htm.

[51] Ibid.

[52] Ibid.

[53] Moore, "Women Rail against College's Coed Plans."

[54] David L. Shaw, "Ryerson Target of Poll at Wells: College Says Only 22 Percent of Students Backed 'No Confidence' Measure," *Post-Standard* (Syracuse, NY), November 4, 2004, p. B1.

[55] "Results of Email Survey Sent to 1,455 Wells College Alumnae: Overwhelming Lack of Support for Coeducation," Wells for Women, accessed May 23, 2005, from wwwgeocities.com/wellscollegepetition/survey.html?200523.

[56] David L. Shaw, "Wells College's First Coed Year—Vibrancy, Some Discontentment: Administrators Pleased, Men Felt Welcomed, Resentment Lingers in Upperclassmen," *Post-Standard* (Syracuse, NY), May 18, 2006, p. A1, accessed from Lexis-Nexis.

[57] David L. Shaw, "Dean: Coed Wells Is Well; Dean Reports Only 1 of 17 Who've Left Recently Blamed End of All-Women Campus," *Post-Standard* (Syracuse, NY), January 13, 2006, p. B1, accessed from Lexis-Nexis.

[58] David L. Shaw, "Wells Sees Jump in Applications: Number of Applicants Has more than Doubled Compared with the Same Time Last Year," *Post-Standard* (Syracuse, NY), January 17, 2006, p. B1.

[59] "The Origins of the National Baseball Hall of Fame and Museum," National Baseball Hall of Fame and Museum, accessed June 20, 2006, from www.baseballhalloffame.org/about/history.htm.

[60] Ibid.

[61] "Fantasy Camp 2006," National Baseball Hall of Fame and Museum, accessed June 20, 2006, from www.baseballhalloffame.org/fantasycamps/default.htm.

[62] "Join the Greatest Team Ever," membership brochure, National Baseball Hall of Fame and Museum, undated.

[63] "The Origins of the National Baseball Hall of Fame and Museum," National Baseball Hall of Fame and Museum, accessed June 20, 2006, from www.baseballhalloffame.org/about/history.htm.

[64] Ibid.

[65] Dana Wakiji, " 'Baseball as America' Debuts in Detroit," National Baseball Hall of Fame and Museum, accessed July 17, 2006, from www.baseballhalloffame.org/news/2006/060310.htm.

[66] John Hancock, fact sheet, accessed June 22, 2006, from www.manulife.com/corporate/corporate2.nsf/LookupFiles/DownloadableFileFactSheetJohnHancock/$File/JohnHancock.pdf.

[67] Ibid.

[68] Kenneth E. Clow and Donald Baack (2004). *Integrated Advertising, Promotion, and Marketing Communications,* Upper Saddle River, NJ: Pearson Prentice Hall, pp. 424–425.

[69] "Our Sponsorships-Olympic Games," John Hancock, accessed February 11, 2006, from www.johnhancock.com/about/community/sponsors/com_olympic.jsp.

[70] U.S. Olympic Team, Web site, www.usolympicteam.com/12956_12975.htm.

[71] "Our Sponsorships—'Fantasy Day' at Fenway Park," John Hancock, accessed February 11, 2006, from www.johnhancock.com/about/community/sponsors/com_olympic.jsp.

[72] Ibid.

[73] "Step Up to the Plate for the Jimmy Fund," news release, The Jimmy Fund, Dana Farber Cancer Institute, February 26, 2006, accessed October 20, 2006 from https://www.jimmyfund.org/abo/press/pressreleases/2006/step-up-to-the-plate-for-the-jimmy-fund.asp.

[74] Jim Welch, "Monster Day at Fenway: Writer Lives Lifelong Dream in Batter's Box," *USA Today,* August 29, 1994, p. 4C.

[75] John Hancock Champions on Ice, 2006 tour, John Hancock, accessed June 22, 2006, from www.championsonice.com/.

[76] Joe Concannon, "With Religious Fervor, Ndeti Drives toward New Heights," *Boston Globe,* April 7, 1996, p. 43, accessed from Lexis-Nexis.

[77] John Powers, "Untarnished Gold: D'Alessandro Finds Marathon Safer Bet than Olympics: '99 Boston Marathon," *Boston Globe,* April 15, 1991, p. C1, accessed from Lexis-Nexis.

[78] John Connolly, "109th Boston Marathon: Carrying the Torch; Hancock on Steady Course," *Boston Globe,* April 17, 2005, p. B7, accessed from Lexis-Nexis.

[79] Joe Concannon, "Sponsor Is Open-Minded: '98 Boston Marathon," *Boston Globe,* April 20, 1998, p. D11, accessed from Lexis-Nexis.

[80] 110th Annual Boston Marathon, John Hancock sponsorship, Web site, accessed June 22, 2006, from marathon.jhancock.com/marathon/sponsorship/index.html.

[81] Ibid.

[82] "Inspiring Future Marathoners," Boston Athletic Association, Web site, accessed June 22, 2006, from www.bostonmarathon.org/BostonMarathon/Sponsors.asp.

[83] Ibid.

[84] 110th Annual Boston Marathon, John Hancock sponsorship.

[85] Ibid.

[86] Ibid.

[87] Sasha Talcott, "Hancock Still Game? Insurer's Parent Considers Cuts in Sports Marketing," *Boston Globe,* April 15, 2005, p. D1.

[88] Ibid.

[89] Ibid.

[90] Ibid.

CHAPTER 10

[1] K. Sriramesh, James E. Grunig, and Jody Buffington (1992). "Corporate Culture and Public Relations," in *Excellence in Public Relations and Communication Management,* Mahwah, NJ: Lawrence Erlbaum, p. 591.

[2] Larissa A. Grunig, James E. Grunig, and David M. Dozier (2002). *Excellent Public Relations and Effective Organizations: A Study of Communication Management in Three Countries,* Mahwah, NJ: Lawrence Erlbaum, pp. 482–83.

[3] Ibid.

[4] Ibid., p. 482.

[5] "Survey: American Consumers' Definition of the Socially Responsible Company Runs Counter to Established Beliefs," news release, National Consumers League, May 31, 2006.

[6] Dan Lattimore, Otis Baskin, Suzette T. Heiman, Elizabeth L. Toth, and James K. Van Leuven (2004). *Public Relations: The Profession and the Practice,* p. 206.

[7] Scott Cutlip, Allen Center, and Glen Broom (2006). *Effective Public Relations,* Upper Saddle River, NJ: Pearson Prentice Hall, p. 223.

[8] Ibid.

[9] Ibid., pp. 234–36.

[10] "Sago Mine Accident Investigation Overview," U.S. Department of Labor, Mine Safety and Health Administration, accessed June 22, 2006, from www.msha.gov/sagomine/publichearings/publichearings.asp.

[11] Ibid.

[12] Ibid., slide 25.

[13] Ibid., slide 8.

[14] "Comparison of Year to Date and Total Fatalities for M/NM and Coal," U.S. Department of Labor, Mine Safety and Health Administration, accessed June 22, 2006, from www.msha.gov/stats/daily/d2006bar.pdf.

[15] Karen Grigsby Bates, "The Most Dangerous Jobs in America," National Public Radio, Day to Day show, January 5, 2006, accessed from Lexis-Nexis.

[16] "Testimony of Bruce Watzman, vice president of safety and health, National Mining Association, Committee on Appropriations, Subcommittee on Labor, Health and Human Services, Education and Related Agencies of the U.S. Senate, January 23, 2006, U.S. Senate Committee on Appropriations," accessed June 22, 2006, from appropriations.senate.gov/subcommittees/record.cfm?id=250653.

[17] "Hearing on the Sago Mine Disaster and Mine Safety," Senate Appropriations Committee, Labor, Health and Human Services, Education and Related Agencies Subcommittee, January 23, 2006, accessed from Lexis-Nexis.

[18] "Questions and Answers on the Sago Mine Accident," www.msha.gov/sagomine, U.S. Department of Labor Mine Safety and Health Administration, accessed January 16, 2006.

[19] Ibid.

[20] "U.S. Senator Arlen Specter (R-PA) Holds Hearing on the Sago Mine Disaster and Mine Safety, Testimony of Ray McKinney, administrator, U.S. Department of Labor, Mine Safety and Health Administration," Congressional Quarterly, Subcommittee on Labor, Health and Human Services, Education and Related Agencies of the U.S. Senate, January 23, 2006, accessed from Lexis-Nexis.

[21] Ibid.

[22] Jonathan Peterson and Stephanie Simon, "West Virginia Mine Tragedy: Cruel Hope Began with a Garbled Message '12 Alive,'" *Los Angeles Times,* January 5, 2006, p. 1A.

[23] Dave Gustafson, " 'We Deeply Regret': Families Should Have Been Told Sooner, Company Says," *Charleston Gazette,* January 5, 2005, www.wvgazette.com, accessed January 16, 2006.

[24] Dave Gustafson, "Only 1 Survives: Family Members Had Thought for 3 Hours That 12 Were Alive," *Charleston Gazette,* January 4, 2005, accessed January 16, 2006, from www.wvgazette.com.

[25] Dave Gustafson, " 'We Deeply Regret.' "

[26] Ibid.

[27] International Coal Group, "Sago Mine FAQs: Answers to Frequently Asked Questions," accessed January 16, 2006, from www.intlcoal.com.

[28] "International Coal Group Statement Regarding Miner Tragedy," news release, International Coal Group, accessed January 16, 2006, from www.intlcoal.com.

[29] "International Coal Group to Resume Operations at Sago Mine: Announces Initial Findings of Independent Accident Investigation," news release, International Coal Group, March 14, 2006, accessed from www.intlcoal.com/pages/news/2006/20060314sago.pdf.

[30] "Facts about Hallmark Cards, Inc.," Hallmark Cards, accessed June 23, 2006, from pressroom.hallmark.com/hmk_fact_sheet.html.

[31] Ibid.

[32] Ibid.

[33] Ibid.

[34] "The Facts about Greeting Cards," Greeting Card Association, accessed www.greetingcard.org/pdf/FactsAboutGreetingCardsFactSheet.pdf.

[35] Ibid.

[36] Ibid.

[37] "Hallmark Writers on Tour 2004," news release, Hallmark Cards, accessed January 26, 2005, from pressroom.hallmark.com/writers_on_tour_release.html.

[38] "Valentine Déjà Vu: Reflections from Linda in Texas," "All about Hallmark Writers on Tour," Hallmark Cards, accessed January 26, 2005, from www.hallmark.com.

[39] "2004: Minneapolis/St. Paul," "About Hallmark Writers on Tour," Hallmark Cards, accessed January 26, 2005, from www.hallmark.com.

[40] Ibid.

[41] Ibid.

[42] "Hallmark Writers on Tour: Meaningful Moments and Memories: A Case Study," Hallmark Cards and Fleishman-Hillard, October 24, 2004.

[43] Ibid.

[44] Ibid.

[45] Ibid.

[46] Ibid.

[47] Ibid.

[48] Ibid.

[49] Ibid.

[50] Ibid.

[51] "2003: Kansas City," "About Hallmark Writers on Tour," Hallmark Cards, accessed January 26, 2005, from www.hallmark.com/.

[52] "You've Got Someone Reading Your E-mail," *New York Times,* June 12, 2006, p. C5.

CHAPTER 11

[1] Dennis Wilcox and Glen Cameron (2006). *Public Relations: Strategies and Tactics,* Upper Saddle, NJ: Pearson, p. 481.

[2] Ibid., p. 483.

[3] Ibid., p. 488.

[4] Ibid., p. 488.

[5] Ibid., p. 495.

[6] Scott Cutlip, Allen Center, and Glen Broom (2006). *Effective Public Relations,* 9th ed., Upper Saddle, NJ: Pearson, p. 410.

[7] Wilcox and Cameron (2006). *Public Relations,* p. 496.

[8] Cutlip, Center, and Broom (2006). *Effective Public Relations,* p. 434.

[9] Pamela Keeton and Mark McCann, "Information Operations, STRATCOM, and Public Affairs," *Military Review*, November–December 2005, accessed June 29, 2006, from usacac.leavenworth.army.mil/CAC/milreview/.

[10] Jim Garamone, "BRAC 2005: Rumsfeld Recommends 5 to 11 Percent Cut in Infrastructure," American Forces press release, American Forces Information Service, May 12, 2005, accessed January 22, 2006, from www.defenselink.mil.

[11] Eric Schmitt, "Pentagon Seeks to Shut Dozens of Bases Across Nation," *New York Times,* May 14, 2005, p. 1A, accessed from Lexis-Nexis.

[12] Donna Miles, "BRAC 2005: Service Leaders Support DOD Recommendations," American Forces Press Service, American Forces Information Service, May 12, 2005, accessed from www.defenselink.mil.

[13] Elizabeth Cooper, "Relief, Resolve in Rome," *Observer-Dispatch* (Utica, NY), May 14, 2005, accessed from NewsBank.

[14] "DFAS Rome: Model Facility, Regional Economic Engine, National Asset," white paper, Mohawk Valley EDGE July 28, 2005, p. 10.

[15] 2000 and 1990 Census Data for Metropolitan Areas, American Fact Finder, U.S. Census Bureau, accessed June 27, 2006, from factfinder.census.gov/home/saff/main.html?_lang=en and Elizabeth Cooper, "Base-Closure Decision Coming Soon," *Observer-Dispatch* (Utica, NY.), May 8, 2005, accessed from www.infoweb.newsbank.com, accessed January 17, 2006 (the Oneida County population dropped from 250,836 in 1990 to 235, 469 in 2000).

[16] Jim Garamone, "BRAC 2005: Rumsfeld Recommends 5 to 11 Percent Cut in Infrastructure," American Forces Press Service, May 12, 2005, accessed January 22, 2006, www.defenselink.mil.

[17] "Jim Garamone, "BRAC 2005: Base Closure, Realignment Recommendations Follow Lengthy Process," American Forces Press Service, May 3, 2005, accessed January 22, 2006, www.defenselink.mil.

[18] Jim Garamone, "BRAC 2005: DOD Briefs Commissioners on Strategy Concerns," American Forces Press Service, May 5, 2005, www.defenselink.mil.

[19] Michael W. Wynne, "Base Closure and Realignment Selection Criteria," memorandum, January 4, 2005, accessed January 17, 2006, www.defenselink.mil/brac/.

[20] Sherwood Boehlert, "Military Value Highest Ever," guest column, *Observer-Dispatch* (Utica, NY), March 13, 2005, infoweb.newsband.com, accessed January 17, 2006.

[21] "Economic Impact Analysis: AFRL Rome Research Site and Defense Finance and Accounting Services (DFAS)," executive summary, p. 1, July 1, 2005.

[22] Ibid., p. 11.

[23] "DFAS Rome: Model Facility, Regional Economic Engine, National Asset," white paper, Mohawk Valley EDGE, July 19, 2005, p. 2.

[24] "Final Report to the President, BRAC Commission Report," appendix E, accessed March 4, 2006, from www.brac.gov/docs/final/AppendixE.pdf.

[25] Elizabeth Cooper, "Lab Investment: Will It Pay Off?" *Observer-Dispatch* (Utica, NY), May 8, 2005, accessed from NewsBank.

[26] Elizabeth Cooper, "Fight for Rome Lab Went Down to the Wire," *Observer-Dispatch* (Utica, NY), May 14, 2005, accessed from NewsBank, Inc.

[27] Elizabeth Cooper, "Lab Investment: Will It Pay Off?".

[28] "2005 Year and Review: Griffiss Business and Technology Park," slide 4, Griffiss Local Development Corporation, Dec. 22, 2005, griffiss.mvedge.org/documents/2005GriffissYIR.pdf, accessed June 27, 2006.

[29] *Department of Defense Base Closure and Realignment Report: Volume I, Part I of 2: Results and Process,* U.S. Department of Defense, May 2005, section 5, p. 37, and section 10, p. 22, accessed June 27, 2006, from www.defenselink.mil/brac/pdf/Vol_I_Part_1_DOD_BRAC.pdf.

[30] Elizabeth Cooper, "Base Closure Decision Coming Soon," *Observer-Dispatch* (Utica, NY), May 8, 2005, infoweb.newsbank.com.

[31] Elizabeth Cooper, "Big Gains for Griffiss," *Observer-Dispatch* (Utica, NY), August 26, 2005, accessed from NewsBank.

[32] Ibid.

[33] "Abu Ghurayb Prison," accessed May 17, 2005, from www.globalsecurity.org/intell/world/iraq/abu-ghurayb-prison.htm; and Peter Finn, "Shedding Light on a Symbol of Iraqi Terror; Ex-Prisoners Describe Horrors, Call for Justice," *Washington Post,* GlobalSecurity.org, October 6, 2003, accessed from Lexis-Nexis.

[34] Peter Finn, "Shedding Light on a Symbol of Iraqi Terror," p. A01.

[35] Jim Garamone, "War Begins: Coalition Aircraft Attack Iraqi Targets," American Forces Press Service, news release, March 19, 2003, accessed June 24, 2006, from www.defenselink.mil/news/Mar2003/n03192003_200303199.html.

[36] Kathleen T. Rhem, "President Bush Proclaims End to Major Combat Ops in Iraq," American Forces Press Service, news release, May 1, 2003, accessed June 24, 2006, from www.defenselink.mil/news/May2003/n05012003_200305018.html.

[37] Larry Kaplow, "Confusion over Amnesty Angers Iraqis," *Atlanta Journal-Constitution,* January 9, 2004, accessed from Lexis-Nexis.

[38] Ibid.

[39] "Article 15–6 Investigation of the 800th Military Police Brigade" (Taguba report), p. 8, National Public Radio, accessed June 24, 2006, from www.npr.org/iraq/2004/prison_abuse_report.pdf.

[40] Ibid.

[41] Ibid.

[42] Ibid.

[43] Ibid.

[44] Ibid.

[45] Ibid.

[46] "Senate Hearing on Iraq Prison Abuse," transcript, *Washington Post,* May 19, 2004, accessed June 25, 2006, from www.washingtonpost.com/ac2/wp-dyn/A39851-2004May19?language=printer.

[47] "Article 15–6 Investigation of the 800th Military Police Brigade," National Public Radio.

[48] Ibid.

[49] Kate Zernike, "Only a Few Spoke Up on Abuse as Many Soldiers Stayed Silent," *New York Times,* May 22, 2004, p. 1.

[50] "Detainee Treatment Investigation," news release, Headquarters United States Central Command, January 16, 2004, accessed from www.centcom.

[51] Coalition Provisional Authority Briefing, Baghdad, Iraq, March 20, 2004, at www.iraqcoalition.org/transcripts.

[52] Ibid.

[53] "Iraq: Military Police Charged with Abusing Prisoners," *Ottawa Citizen,* CanWest News Service, March 21, 2004, p. A11.

[54] "Coalition Provisional Authority Briefing," news transcript, U.S. Department of Defense, March 22, 2004, accessed June 14, 2005, from www.defenselink.mil/transcripts/2004/tr20040322-1302.html.

[55] *Report of the International Committee of the Red Cross (ICRC) on the Treatment by the Coalition Forces of Prisoners of War and Other Protected Persons by the Geneva Conventions in Iraq during Arrest, Internment and Interrogation,* International Committee of the Red Cross (ICRC), February 2004, accessed June 27, 2006, from GlobalSecurity.org, www.globalsecurity.org/military/library/report/2004/icrc_report_iraq_feb2004.htm.

[56] Ibid.

[57] Ibid.

[58] Ibid.

[59] Barbara Starr, "Soldiers Charged with Abusing Iraqi Prisoners," CNN.com, March 20, 2004, accessed June 13, 2005, from Lexis-Nexis.

[60] Carol Rosenberg, "Few Details in Iraq Abuse Case: U.S. Army Shields Soldiers Charged: 4 More GIs Killed," *Pittsburgh Post-Gazette,* March 22, 2004, p. A5, accessed June 13, 2005, from Lexis-Nexis.

[61] "Article 15-6 Investigation of the 800th Military Police Brigade," National Public Radio.

[62] Ibid.

[63] "Hearing of the House Armed Services Committee: Iraqi Prisoner Abuse," chaired by Representative Duncan Hunter, Federal News Service, May 7, 2004, accessed June 10, 2005, from Lexis-Nexis.

[64] Dan Rather, "Abuse of Iraqi POWs by GIs Probed," *CBS News, 60 Minutes II,* April 28, 2004, accessed June 11, 2005, from www.cbsnews.com/stories/2004/04/27/60II/printable614063.shtml.

[65] "Coalition Provisional Authority Briefing," news transcript, U.S. Department of Defense, April 28, 2004, accessed June 13, 2005, from www.defenselink.mil/transcripts/2004/tr20040428-1381.html.

[66] Ibid.

[67] Dan Rather, "Abuse of Iraqi POWs by GIs Probed."

[68] Seymour M. Hersh, "Torture at Abu Ghraib," *New Yorker,* May 10, 2004, accessed from www.newyorker.com/printables/fact/040510fa_fact.

[69] "President Bush Welcomes Canadian Prime Minister Martin to the White House: Remarks by President Bush and Prime Minister Martin of Canada in a Press Availability, The Rose Garden," White House, April 30, 2004, accessed June 13, 2005, from www.whitehouse.gov/news/releases/2004/04/20040430-2.html.

[70] "The White House Press Briefing by Scott McClellan," White House, April 30, 2004, accessed June 13, 2005, from www.whitehouse.gov/news/releases/2004/04/20040430-4.html.

[71] Ibid.

[72] "Coalition Provisional Authority Briefing," U.S. Department of Defense, April 30, 2004, at www.defenselinke.mil/transcripts/2004.

[73] "Richard Boucher, Daily Briefing," U.S. Department of State, April 30, 2004, accessed June 26, 2006, from www.state.gov/r/pa/prs/dpb/2004/32045.htm.

[74] "Media Availability with Principal Deputy Assistant Secretary of Defense Public Affairs Lawrence Di Rita," news transcript, U.S. Department of Defense, May 3, 2004, accessed June 13, 2005, at www. defenselink.mil/transcripts/2004.

[75] Ibid.

[76] "Detainee Operations Briefing," U.S. Department of Defense, May 4, 2004, accessed June 13, 2005, at defenselink.mil/transcripts/2004.

[77] Ibid.

[78] Ibid.

[79] Ibid.

[80] Ibid.

[81] Ibid.

[82] Ibid.

[83] Ibid.

[84] Ibid.

[85] Ibid.

[86] Ibid.

[87] Ibid.

[88] "President Bush Meets with Alhurra Television on Wednesday," White House, May 5, 2004, accessed June 13, 2005, from www.whitehouse.gov/news/releases/2004/05/20040505-3.html.

[89] Ibid.

[90] Ibid.

[91] "President Bush Meets with Al Arabiya Television on Wednesday," White House, May 5, 2004, accessed June 13, 2005, from www.whitehouse.gov/news/releases/2004/05/20040505-2.htm.

[92] "Secretary Rumsfeld on ABC's *Today Show [sic] with Diane Sawyer,*" news transcript, U.S. Department of Defense, May 5, 2004, accessed June 26, 2006, from www.defenselink.mil/transcripts/2004/ tr20040505-secdef0703.html.

[93] Ibid.

[94] Ibid.

[95] "Secretary Rumsfeld Interview with Matt Lauer, NBC *Today,*" news transcript, U.S. Department of Defense, May 5, 2004, accessed June 26, 2006, from www.defenselink.mil/transcripts/2004/ tr20040505-secdef1425.html.

[96] Ibid.

[97] "General Pace Interview with Hannah Storm, CBS *Early Show,*" news transcript, U.S. Department of Defense, May 5, 2004, accessed June 26, 2006, from www.defenselink.mil/transcripts/2004/ tr20040505-1427.html.

[98] Ibid.

[99] "Press Briefing by Scott McClellan," White House, May 5, 2004, at www.whitehouse.gov/news/ releases/2004/05/20040505-3.html.

[100] Ibid.

[101] "Coalition Provisional Authority Briefing," U.S. Department of Defense, May 5, 2004, accessed June 13, 2005, from defenselinek.mil/transcripts/2004/tr20040505-0702.html.

[102] Jim Krane, "Commander of Coalition Prisons Apologizes for Abuse of Iraqi Inmates," Associated Press, May 5, 2004, accessed June 27, 2006, from Lexis-Nexis.

[103] Pamela Keeton and Mark McCann, "Information Operations, STRATCOM, and Public Affairs," *Military Review,* November-December 2005, accessed June 27, 2006, from U.S. Combined Arms Center and Fort Leavenworth, usacac.army.mil/CAC/milreview/download/English/NovDec05/keeton.pdf.

[104] "Operation Iraqi Freedom," official site of Multi-National Force, Iraq, accessed June 27, 2006, from www.mnf-iraq.com/index.html.

[105] Global Security, "800th Military Police Brigade," accessed June 27, 2006, from www.globalsecurity. org/military/agency/army/800mp-bde.htm.

[106] "Abu Ghraib: Prosecutions and Convictions," Salon.com, March 14, 2006, accessed June 27, 2006, from Lexis-Nexis.

[107] "Abu Ghraib Intelligence Boss Relieved of Command," American Forces Press Service, May 13, 2005, accessed June 27, 2006, from U.S. Department of Defense, American Forces Information Service, www.defenselink.mil/news/May2005/20050513_1061.html.

CHAPTER 12

[1] Doug Newsom, Judy VanSlyke Turk, and Dean Kruckeberg (2004). *This Is PR: The Realities of Public Relations,* 8th ed., p. 352.

[2] *The Human Development Report 2005,* p. 5, Human Development Report, accessed July 3, 2006, from hdr.undp.org/reports/view_reports.cfm?type=1.

[3] Ibid., p. 4.

[4] Ibid., p. 3.

[5] Fraser P. Seitel (2004). *The Practice of Public Relations,* Upper Saddle, NJ: Pearson Prentice Hall, , p. 387.

[6] Maureen Taylor, "Internationalizing the Public Relations Curriculum," *Public Relations Review* 27(1), 2001, pp. 73–88.

[7] Donn James Tilson and Emmanuel C. Alozie (2004) *Toward the Common Good: Perspectives in International Public Relations,* Boston, MA: Pearson Education, p. 2.

[8] Ibid., p. 15.

[9] "Study Finds Decline in Global Press Freedom," news release, Freedom House, April 27, 2005. Accessed January 7, 2005, from freedomhouse.org.

[10] "Unethical Media Practices Revealed by IPRA Report: International Public Relations Association Survey Reveals Widespread Incidences of 'Cash for Editorial,' " news release, International Public Relations Association, June 14, 2002, accessed January 7, 2005, from www.ipra.org.

[11] Doug Newsom, Judy VanSlyke Turk, and Dean Kruckeberg (2007). This Is PR: *The Realities of Public Relations,* 9th ed., Belmont, CA: Thompson Wadsworth, p. 346.

[12] John Reed, "Agencies Learn to Put a Human Face on Suffering: Modern Solutions to Dealing with the Deadly Marburg Virus in Angola Have Had to Adapt to Ancient Traditions," *Financial Times* (London, UK), April 16, 2005, p. 8, accessed from Lexis-Nexis.

[13] Denise Grady, "Deadly Virus Alters Angola's Traditions: Usual Funeral Rites Clash with Safety," *New York Times,* April 19, 2005, p. A3, accessed from Lexis-Nexis.

[14] "Brief Report: Outbreak of Marburg Virus Hemorrhagic Fever: Angola, October 1, 2004-March 29, 2005," *Morbidity and Mortality Weekly Report,* April 1, 2005, pp. 308–309, U.S. Centers for Disease Control, accessed May 23, 2005, from www.cdc.gov/mmwr/preview/mmwrhtml/mm5412a5.htm.

[15] Ibid.

[16] Ibid.

[17] Ibid.

[18] John Reed, "Agencies Learn to Put a Human Face on Suffering," p. 8.

[19] Ibid.

[20] Ibid.

[21] "Angola 2005: Marburg Hemorrhagic Fever Outbreak Response; Flash Appeal," World Health Organization, accessed June 28, 2006, from www.who.int/hac/crises/ago/appeal/Flash_2005_Angola.pdf.

[22] M. A. J. McKenna, "CDC Beefs Up Team Treating Angolan Fever: Deadly Marburg Outbreak Worst on Record," *Atlanta Journal-Constitution,* April 15, 2005, p. 1C, accessed from Lexis-Nexis; and John Reed, "Agencies Learn to Put a Human Face on Suffering," p. 8.

[23] Denise Grady, "Deadly Virus Alters Angola's Traditions," p. A3.

[24] Jan Hennop and Florence Panoussian, "In Angola, Marburg Trio Musicians Sing against Killer Virus," Agence France Presse, April 12, 2005, accessed from Lexis-Nexis.

[25] Ibid.

[26] *World Factbook,* Central Intelligence Agency at www.cia.gov/cia/publications/factbook.

[27] "Angola 2005: Marburg Hemorrhagic Fever Outbreak Response," World Health Organization.

[28] Ibid.

[29] "Infection Control for Viral Hemorrhagic Fevers in the African Health Care Setting; Section 8: Mobilize Community Resources and Conduct Community Education," Centers for Disease Control, accessed from www.cdc.gov/ncidod.

[30] "Angolan Optimistic About Containing Marburg Virus Outbreak," States News Service, State Department, April 19, 2005, accessed from Lexis-Nexis.

[31] World Health Organization, "World Health Organization: WHO Year in Review 2005," slide 16, accessed June 28, 2006, from www.who.int/publications/publications/YEAR2005REVIEW-EN.pdf.

[32] Paul Wiseman, "Miscues Mar Opening of Hong Kong Disney," *Money,* November 10, 2005, p. 5B, accessed from Lexis-Nexis.

[33] "Facts and Figures for Hong Kong Disneyland," Hong Kong Disneyland, accessed February 12, 2006, from www.hongkongdisneyland.com/eng/discover/2004_fs.html.

[34] Ibid.

[35] Bill Savadove, "Shanghai Awaits Approval for Park," *South China Morning Post,* September 15, 2005, p. 3, accessed from Lexis-Nexis.

[36] Hong Kong Disneyland, Web site, accessed June 28, 2006, from park.hongkongdisneyland.com/hkdl/en_US/home/home?name=HomePage.

[37] Keith Bradsher, "Disney Is Tailoring New Park to Fit Hong Kong Sensitivities," *New York Times,* October 13, 2004, Section 2, p. 1, accessed from Lexis-Nexis.

[38] Robert Marquand, "Mickey Greets Hong Kong," *Christian Science Monitor,* September 12, 2005, p. 7, accessed from Lexis-Nexis.

[39] Hong Kong Disneyland, Web site.

[40] "Hong Kong Welcomes a New Era of Family Entertainment with Grand Opening of Hong Kong Disneyland Resort," PR Newswire, Hong Kong Disneyland, September 12, 2005, accessed from Lexis-Nexis.

[41] Marquand, "Mickey Greets Hong Kong."

[42] "Hong Kong Disneyland Showcases the Magic behind Its Food: Celebrates Move of Kitchen with Sneak Peek at Park Menu," news release, Hong Kong Disneyland, August 10, 2004, accessed February 14, 2006 from www.hongkongdisneyland.com/eng/discover/20040810.html.

[43] "Hong Kong Disneyland and Guests Raise HK$9.7 Million on Charity Day—Eight Days before the Grand Opening," news releases, Hong Kong Disneyland, September 4, 2005, accessed February 14, 2006 from www.hongkongdisneyland.com/eng/discover/20050904.html.

[44] "Hong Kong Disneyland Presents the Beauty and Majesty of Fairy Tale Weddings," news release, Hong Kong Disneyland, May 17, 2005, accessed February 14, 2006 from www.hongkongdisneyland.com/eng/discover/20050517.html.

[45] Juan Forero, "Hidden Cost of Shark Fin Soup: Its Source May Vanish," *New York Times,* January 5, 2006, Section A, p. 4, accessed from Lexis-Nexis.

[46] "The Brutal Business of Shark Finning," Sea Shepherd Conservation Society, accessed June 28, 2006, from www.seashepherd.org/longline/longline_shark_finning.html.

[47] Forero, "Hidden Cost of Shark Fin Soup: Its Source May Vanish."

[48] Ibid.

[49] Simon Perry, "Shark Fin at Disney will Come with a Sermon," *South China Morning Post,* June 10, 2005, p. 4, accessed from Lexis-Nexis.

[50] Helen Luk, "Hong Kong Disneyland Takes Shark Fin Soup off Its Menu," Associated Press Worldstream, June 25, 2005, accessed from Lexis-Nexis.

[51] Bradsher, "Disney Is Tailoring New Park to Fit Hong Kong Sensitivities."

[52] "Disney Debuts New Safer, Quieter and More Environmentally-Friendly Fireworks Technology: First Major Pyrotechnics Breakthrough in Decades," news release, Disney, June 28, 2004, accessed February 12, 2006, from corporate.disney.go.com/environmentality/press_releases/2004/2004_0628.html.

[53] Paul Wiseman, "Miscues Mar Opening of Hong Kong Disney," *USA Today,* November 10, 2005, p. 5B, accessed from Lexis-Nexis.

[54] Richard Spencer, "Shark's Fin Lands Disney in the Hong Kong Soup," *Daily Telegraph* (London, UK), September 1, 2005, p. 17, accessed from Lexis-Nexis.

[55] Don Lee and Kim Christensen, "Translating Anaheim for Asia: Developers of Hong Kong Disneyland, Which Is Modeled on the Original Park, Took Pains to Be Mindful of Cultural Sensitivities," *Los Angeles Times,* September 6, 2005, p. 1C, accessed from Lexis-Nexis.

[56] May Chan, "Disney Chief Choke on His Words, But Gets Out an Apology," South China Morning Press, February 5, 2006, p. 1, accessed from Lexis-Nexis.

[57] Ibid.

[58] Google.com, Tiananmen Square images, accessed June 28, 2006, from images.google.com/images?q=tiananmen+square&hl=en.

[59] Google.cn, Tiananmen Square images, accessed June 28, 2006, from images.google.cn/images?q=tiananmen+square&hl=zh-CN.

[60] Testimony of Lucie Morillon, Washington Representative, Reporters Without Borders, Briefing on "The Internet in China: A Tool for Freedom or Suppression?" Committee on International Relations, U.S. House of Representatives, pp. 3, 156–157, February 15, 2006, accessed June 28, 2006, from wwwc.house.gov/international_relations/109/26075.pdf.

[61] Ibid., p. 156.

[62] Ibid.

[63] Gillian Wong, "Report: Chinese Media Could Face Fines for Reporting on Emergencies," Associated Press, June 26, 2006, accessed from Lexis-Nexis.

[64] Testimony of Michael Callahan, Senior Vice President and General Counsel, Yahoo! Inc., Before the Subcommittees on Africa, Global Human Rights and International Operations, and Asia and the Pacific," U.S. House of Representatives, February 15, 2006, p. 58, accessed June 28, 2006, from wwwc.house.gov/international_relations/109/26075.pdf.

[65] Testimony of Google Inc., Before the Subcommittee on Asia and the Pacific, and the Subcommittee of Africa, Global Human Rights, and International Operations, Committee on International Relations, U.S. House of Representatives, February 15, 2005; Elliot Schrage, vice president, Global Communications and Public Affairs, Google, Inc., p. 71, accessed June 28, 2006 from wwwc.house.gov/international_relations/109/26075.pdf.

[66] "The Internet in China: A Tool for Freedom or Suppression?" Committee on International Relations, U.S. House of Representatives, comments by U.S. Representative Christopher H. Smith, subcommittee chairman, pp. 10, 156, February 15, 2006, accessed June 28, 2006, from wwwc.house.gov/international_relations/109/26075.pdf.

[67] Ibid.

[68] Testimony of Michael Callahan, p. 59.

[69] Testimony of Google Inc., p. 68.

[70] Ibid. p. 72.

[71] Ibid., pp. 72–73.

[72] Ibid., p. 69.

[73] Ibid., p. 69–70.

[74] Ibid., p. 70.

[75] Ibid., p. 76.

[76] Ibid.

[77] Laura Sydell, "Hearings to Review Human Rights in China," *All Things Considered,* National Public Radio, February 14, 2006, accessed from Lexis-Nexis.

[78] Josette S. Shiner and Paula Dobriansky, "Remarks on Global Internet Freedom," U.S. Department of State, accessed June 28, 2006, from www.state.gov/e/eb/rls/rm/2006/61182.htm.

[79] U.S. Grains Council, Web site, corn, accessed June 30, 2006, from www.grains.org/page.ww?section=Barley%2C+Corn+%26+Sorghum&name=Corn.

CHAPTER 13

[1] "Standards of Practice for Investor Relations," National Investor Relations Institute, accessed October 28, 2006, from http://www.niri.org/memberpdf/IRStandards.pdf, p.5.

[2] Dan Lattimore, Otis Baskin, Suzette Heiman, Elizabeth Toth, and James Van Leuven (2004). Public Relations: The Profession and the Practice, New York: McGraw-Hill, p. 289.

[3] "Stock Market Savvy: Investing for Your Future," New York Stock Exchange, accessed June 29, 2006, from www.nyse.com/about/education/1098034584990.html.

[4] Lattimore et al., Public Relations, p. 281.

[5] "U.S. Securities and Exchange Commission 2005 Performance and Accountability Report," Securities and Exchange Commission, accessed June 29, 2006, from www.sec.gov/about/secpar/secpar2005.pdf, p. 5.

[6] Ibid.

[7] Investopedia.com, accessed March 8, 2006, from www.investopedia.com/terms/s/sarbanesoxleyact.asp.

[8] Standards of Practice for Investor Relations," National Investor Relations Institute, accessed October 28, 2006, from http://www.niri.org/memberpdf/IRStandards.pdf, p. 5.

[9] Ibid.

[10] "Standards of Practice for Investor Relations," National Investor Relations Institute, p.10.

[11] Ibid., pp. 18–19.

[12] "Fast Answers-Key Topics," U.S. Securities and Exchange Commission, accessed June 29, 2006, from www.sec.gov/answers.shtml#f-entries.

[13] "Standards of Practice for Investor Relations," National Investor Relations Institute, pp. 30–33.

[14] Teva's, Web site, accessed March 8, 2006, from www.tevapharm.com/.

[15] InvestorWords.com, accessed March 8, 2006, from www.investorwords.com.

[16] Teva's.

[17] Wal-Mart Web site, accessed March 8, 2006, from www.walmartstores.com/GlobalWMStoresWeb/navigate.do?catg=316.

[18] Stephen Taub, "Wanted: Wal-Mart Global Ethics Czar," CFO.com, March 3, 2006, accessed from proquest.umi.com/pqdweb?did=997679141&sid=2&Fmt=3&clientId=47962&RQT=309&VName=PQD.

[19] Alan Murray, "Business: Can Wal-Mart Sustain a Softer Image?" Wall Street Journal, February 8, 2006, accessed from proquest.umi.com/pqdweb?did=983214771&sid=1&Fmt=3&clientId=47962&RQT=309&VName=PQD.

[20] Statement of Tom Coughlin, news release, PR Newswire, January 31, 2006, accessed from Lexis-Nexis.

[21] Ann Zimmerman and Kris Hudson, "Looking Upscale, Wal-Mart Begins a Big Makeover: As American Economy Shifts Retailer Redesigns Stores to Be Trendier," Wall Street Journal, September 17, 2005, accessed from proquest.umi.com/pqdweb?did=898321791&sid=1&Fmt=3&clientId=47962&RQT=309&VName=PQD.

[22] Iron Mountain, Web site, accessed March 8, 2006, from www.ironmountain.com/Index.asp.

[23] "Investor Relations," Iron Mountain, accessed March 8, 2006, from www.corporate-ir.net/ireye/ir_site.zhtml?ticker=IRM&script=500.

[24] Janet Adamy and Ian McDonald, "Can Burger King Serve Big IPO?" Wall Street Journal, May 11, 2006.

[25] "Burger King Holdings, Inc. Announces Pricing of Its Initial Public Offering," press release, Burger King Holdings, May 17, 2006, accessed from investor.bk.com/phoenix.zhtml?c=87140&p=irol-newsArticle&ID=858265&highlight=.

[26] Prospectus, Edgar filing, Burger King Holdings, Inc., accessed June 29, 2006, from sec.edgar-online.com/2006/02/16/0000950103-06-000353/Section6.asp.

[27] "Burger King Corporation Announces 8th Quarter of Positive Comparable Sales," news release, Burger King Holdings, April 6, 2006, accessed June 29, 2006, from investor.bk.com/phoenix.zhtml?c=87140&p=irol-newsArticle&ID=853048&highlight=.

[28] Hoovers, accessed June 29, 2006, from www.hoovers.com.

CHAPTER 14

[1] Bureau of Labor Statistics, "Advertising, Marketing, Promotions, Public Relations, and Sales Managers," August 4, 2006, accessed from http://www.bls.gov/oco/content/ocos020.stm.

[2] Ibid.

Index